Foundation Blender Compositing

Roger D. Wickes

friendsof

DESIGNER TO DESIGNER™

an Apress® company

Foundation Blender Compositing

Credits

To the future, embodied in my children, Rebecca and Alexander, and all the volunteer programmers, documenters, and web site hosts who enable and spread low-cost global communication that unites our thoughts, dreams, and aspirations.

CONTENTS AT A GLANCE

About the Author...xvii

About the Technical Reviewer xix

About the Cover Image Designer.............................xxi

Acknowledgments... xxiii

Introduction...xiv

Chapter 1 **BLENDER OVERVIEW** 1

Chapter 2 **BLENDER IN THE PIPELINE** 25

Chapter 3 **WELCOME TO BLENDER!** 53

Chapter 4 **FORMATS** 89

Chapter 5 **3D ELEMENTS** 111

Chapter 6 **CAMERA AND WORLD** 143

Chapter 7 **SHADING** 173

Chapter 8 **ANIMATED EFFECTS** 201

Chapter 9 **RENDERING** 247

Chapter 10 **NODE-BASED COMPOSITING** 273

Chapter 11 **MANIPULATING IMAGES** 313

Chapter 12 **ADVANCED NODES** 351

Chapter 13 **NONLINEAR VIDEO EDITOR** 391

Chapter 14 **SEQUENCER EFFECTS** 423

Index 451

CONTENTS

About the Author...xvii

About the Technical Reviewer xix

About the Cover Image Designer...........................xxi

Acknowledgments...xxiii

Introduction..xiv

Chapter 1 **BLENDER OVERVIEW** 1
What is Blender? 1
What is digital compositing? 3
    Special effects 4
    Compositing activities 5
        Reformatting images and video 6
        Adjusting images and video 7
        Animating elements 7
        Compositing elements 8
        Sequencing video 9
Is Blender for you? 10
How does Blender support creativity? 12
What can you produce using Blender? 13
Trends in digital compositing 14
    Music videos and movies 14
    User-generated content 15
    Convergence 15
Blender setup 16
    Blender requirements 16
    Generic vs. optimized versions 17
    Notes on installing Blender 17
    Blender is multilingual 18
    The Verse server 18
Compositing tools in Blender 19
Working with Blender 21
    Properties, actions, and tools 21
    Window types 23
Summary 23

Chapter 2 **BLENDER IN THE PIPELINE** **25**

An overview of the media pipeline 26
Open source products in the pipeline 28
Work products 32
Interoperability 35
Digital rights management 36
Blender compositing pipeline 38
When does compositing start? 40
When does compositing end? 42
Blender work products 43
Practical digital asset management 43
Links to assets 43
Project folder organization 45
Library folders 47
Content and digital asset management systems 48
Image sources 49
Disk space 50
Summary 50

Chapter 3 **WELCOME TO BLENDER!** **53**

Starting Blender 53
Getting information from the console window 54
Working in the interface window 55
Window panes 56
Mice and input devices 58
Introducing Blender's core window types 58
User preferences window 59
Setting view and control preferences 60
Saving your preferences 61
3D view window 61
Orientation and perspectives 62
View Properties panel 64
Transform Properties panel 64
Background Image panel 65
Render background buffer 68
File browser window 68
Buttons window 69
Getting organized 70
Reusable assets 70
Cloning assets 70
Appending and linking assets 72
Layers 73
Groups 76
Parenting 76
Scenes 77
Adding scenes 77
Linking scenes 78
Object visibility 78

Importing elements 80
    Importing from the current blend file 80
    Appending or linking from another blend file 80
        Importing from another application 81
        Importing images as elements 82
Your first composite in 30 minutes or less 83
Saving blend files 86
Summary 87

Chapter 4 **FORMATS** **89**

Asset file formats 90
Interchange file formats 91
Image file formats 93
    BMP and color channels support 93
    JPEG 93
    PNG and the alpha channel 96
    Targa and TIFF 99
    OpenEXR, the Z-buffer, and multilayer 99
        Z-depth pixel information 99
        Multilayer format 101
Video formats 101
    NTSC and PAL formats 101
    HD formats 103
    Frame sequences 103
    Codecs 106
Audio file formats 106
Container formats 107
Players 108
Summary 108

Chapter 5 **3D ELEMENTS** **111**

Working with objects 111
    Object modes 112
    Hotkey commands 112
    Adding objects 114
    Setting Edit Methods preferences 115
    Editing 3D objects 115
Working with images 116
    UV mapping 117
    Changing image shapes (morphing) 121
    Rotoscoping with shape keys 123
Layering elements in 3D space 123
Masking 125
    Setting up the 3D view and camera for masking 125
    Masking with Bezier curves 127
    Creating elements from masked images 131
    Masking with meshes 132
Using empty targets 134

ix

Working with text 137
    Setting text properties 137
    Getting text files into Blender 140
    Animating text 140
Summary 140

Chapter 6 **CAMERA AND WORLD** **143**

Blender cameras 143
    Camera properties 144
    Tracking the camera to an object 145
        Parenting the camera 145
        Using the Track To constraint 146
    Perspectives and vanishing points 147
        Matching vanishing points 148
        Using two-point perspective 151
        Using one-point perspective 153
        Using zero-point perspective (orthogonal) 153
    The rule of thirds 155
The Blender world 156
    World colors 156
    Exposure and dynamic range 157
    Mist and stars 159
    World textures 161
        Sphere maps 161
        Angular maps 164
A Big Buck Bunny world compositing example 166
    Examining the world textures 167
    Using matte paintings 170
Summary 171

Chapter 7 **SHADING** **173**

Shading categories 173
Materials 174
    Adding a material 174
    Defining a material 176
        Material colors 177
        Shader algorithms 178
    Shading a solid material 179
        Shadeless materials 179
        Only shadows materials 179
        Halo material 180
        Wire material 184
        OnlyCast material 184

Textures 184
   Adding a texture 185
   Mapping textures 186
      Orienting a texture 186
      Mapping to a material aspect 187
   Mixing textures 187
   Working with image textures 188
      Recoloring image elements 191
      Interpolating image texture 192
      Stretching an image 193
      Blending computer-generated elements into photos 195
   Working with procedural (computed) textures 196
      Using a Clouds texture 196
      Using a Blend texture 196
  Summary 198

Chapter 8 **ANIMATED EFFECTS** **201**

Object animation 204
   Navigating in time 204
   Moving an element into view 204
      Using the timeline window 208
      Using the Ipo (animation) window 209
      Making things change 210
      Animating an object 212
   Animating a layer 213
   Moving elements into range 215
      Camera clipping range 215
      World (mist) range 216
   Adding the finishing touches to element motion 218
Camera animation 219
   Flying the camera through a field of dreams 219
   Creating camera shake 219
   Following a path 220
Shader animation 222
   Animated textures 223
   Moving subtitles 226
Lighting animation 227
   Fake light 227
   Matching a Live-Action Plate 228
   Fairy light 230
   Lightning 230
   Glowing orbs 230
Animating masks 231
   Match moving and rotoscoping 231
   Animating shapes 232
Particle effects 233

Generating Particles 234
   Creating a new particle system 234
   Blender's Emitter particle system 235
   Colliders 238
   Force fields 238
   Blender's boids physics engine 239
   Combining particle effects 243
   Baking 244
Coordinating your animation 244
Summary 245

Chapter 9 **RENDERING** **247**

Rendering an image 248
   Start with the aspect ratio 248
   Determine the resolution 248
      Proxy rendering 250
      OpenGL rendering 250
      Border rendering 251
      Pipeline components 251
      Alpha channel rendering 251
   Test render 253
   Pleasantries for rendering 253
      Anti-aliasing 253
      Motion blur 254
      Edge rendering 255
      Information stamping 255
   Which image standard to use? 256
   A place for everything 257
   Multithreaded rendering 258
   Rendering curves 259
   Dealing with rendering issues 260
      The black render of darkness 260
      Broken links 261
      Overly bright or miscolored elements 261
      Render crashes 261
Rendering video 262
   Develop your storyboard 262
   Set frames per second 263
   Set the duration 263
   Trade off quality with time 264
      Step rendering 264
      Override shading 264
      Interlacing (fields rendering) 264
   Select sequence or container 265
   Choose your destination 266
   Complete the animation 266
   Render the video 267
   Package it 268
   Play back your animation 268

Of containers and codecs 268
    QuickTime container 269
    AVI container 269
    FFmpeg container 269
Render farms 270
Summary 271

Chapter 10 **NODE-BASED COMPOSITING** **273**
Working with the compositor 274
    Compositing screen layout 275
    The node editor 276
        Node editor header 276
        Node editor workspace 277
    Typical node controls 279
        Node header 280
        Sockets 281
        Threading 281
        Cyclic dependencies 281
        Node editor window's Node menu 282
Feed me (input nodes) 284
    Getting in the view 284
        Render Layer node 284
        Alpha Channel Socket 286
        Render passes 287
        Visualizing render passes 288
        Render Layers panel 289
    Image node 292
        Sequences and movies 293
        Working with different image resolutions 294
    Texture node 294
    Value node 295
    Time node for animation 296
        The curves widget 297
    RGB (color) node 297
Getting something out of it 298
    Composite node 298
    Viewer node 298
    Split Viewer node 299
    Using the UV/Image Editor window 299
    File Output node 300
The distort processing nodes 300
    Crop 300
    Displace 301
    Lens Distortion node 301
    Map UV 303
    Rotate 304
    Scale 304
    Translate 305
Shake, rattle, and roll 305

Format conversion 307
    One image to another 307
    One medium to another 308
    Cropping and letterboxing 309
    Upscaling and downscaling 310
Summary 310

Chapter 11 MANIPULATING IMAGES **313**

Color nodes 313
    Invert node 314
    Bright/Contrast node 315
    Gamma node 315
    RGB Curves node 316
    AlphaOver node 320
        Seeing ghosts 321
    Mix node 321
        Color math 323
        Hue, saturation, and value 323
        Dodge and burn 324
    Handy techniques 326
        Sepia 326
        Fades and transitions 326
        Adjusting for print: CMYK 327
    Z Combine node 328
        Full–screen sample anti-aliasing 329
    Tonemap node 329
Conversion nodes 330
    RGB to BW node 331
    Set Alpha node 331
    Math node 331
        Using Math to use watermarks 332
    Alpha Convert node 334
    ColorRamp node 334
    Separate/Combine channel nodes 334
    Pulling an object's mask using the ID Mask node 338
Matte nodes 340
    Luminance Key node 341
    Channel Key node 342
    Difference Key node 344
    Chroma Key node 346
    Deinterlacing with Blender 347
Summary 348

Chapter 12 **ADVANCED NODES** 351

Vector nodes 351
   Normalize node 352
   Normal node 353
      Changing apparent light direction 354
   Map Value node 356
Filter nodes 357
   Blur node 357
      Faking a focusing act 359
   Soften filter 360
   Sharpen filter 361
   Laplace filter 361
   Sobel filter 364
   Prewitt filter 365
   Kirsch filter 366
   Shadow filter 366
   Dilate/Erode node 367
      Glowing magic aura with Dilate 368
   Depth of field with the Defocus node 370
      Making or faking a Z-buffer 372
      Rack focus 375
   Directional Blur node 375
   Bilateral Blur node 377
   Motion blur via the Vector Blur node 377
   Glare node 380
Node groups 381
Posterizing and retro 382
Grease Pencil tool 383
Visualizing the win 385
Summary 388

Chapter 13 **NONLINEAR VIDEO EDITOR** 391

The VSE window display modes 392
   Sequence display mode 393
      What is a video strip? 394
      Do sequence 396
   Image preview display mode 396
   Luma waveform display mode 397
   Chroma vectorscope display mode 398
   Histogram display mode 399
An NLE screen layout 400

Scene sequencer buttons 402
    Sequencer Input panel 402
        Preprocessing strips using crop and translate 402
    Sequencer Filter panel 405
    Sequencer Proxy panel 405
        Making a proxy 406
    Sequencer Edit panel 408
Practical Examples 410
    Adjusting lift and gain 410
    Making a slide show 412
        Cross and fade transitions 413
        Cut splice transitions 416
    Image-format conversion 417
Summary 421

Chapter 14 **SEQUENCER EFFECTS** **423**

Loading combined audio/video 423
Editing strips 427
    Editing multiple takes 429
    Interleaving multiple cameras 430
Splice and transition effects 430
    Gamma cross-fade 432
    Wipe effect and other effects in general 433
    Juxtapose 434
Glow effect 435
Speed Control effect 436
Offset blending effect 437
Masking in the sequencer 438
Animating VSE effects 440
VSE plug-in effects 441
    Example plug-in: green screen 441
    Other plug-ins 442
Audio sequences 443
Mashups 446
Summary 447
Apress License Agreement (Single-User Products) 449
    Apress Software License Disclaimer of Warranty 449

Index 451

ABOUT THE AUTHOR

Roger Wickes has been involved with software for several decades, has had the privilege of seeing monumental revolutions come and go, and has somehow managed to capitalize on most of the convergences that have shaped computing, networking, and communications as we now know them. He started his career learning leadership at Admiral Farragut and the USCG Academy and fell in love with computerized simulation. His first commercial job was working for CSC at the Naval Underwater Systems Center on big secret things that go boom. He then learned how to run an entrepreneurial startup by joining Technology Applications and Development Company in Newport, Rhode Island. Tired of the snow, he joined EDS in Georgia where he really learned how to run a technology business, ultimately leading more than 120 professionals developing software on all the major platforms. Sensing the opportunity of the Web, he helped form Information Technology Group and filled all roles from CIO to CFO, enabling and leading the development of the first Internet-based payroll and staff exchange systems. He fell in love with visual imagery and Blender a decade ago and is a Blender Certified Instructor. Currently he is managing and developing graphical and business solutions for international companies and global initiatives. He enjoys scuba diving, skiing, travel, and helping others. His web site is http://wickes.webs.com.

ABOUT THE TECHNICAL REVIEWER

Roland Hess has been working with graphics and imaging software for more than 20 years. He saved his pocket change for an "advanced" graphics programming package for his home computer in the early 1980s and has been hooked ever since. As one of a handful of people involved with Blender who is both an active user of the software and a member of the development team, he brings a unique perspective to Blender instruction that helps bridge the difficult gap between technical knowledge and artistic endeavor.

ABOUT THE COVER IMAGE DESIGNER

Corné van Dooren designed the front cover image for this book. After taking a brief from friends of ED to create a new design for the Foundation series, he worked at combining technological and organic forms, with the results now appearing on this and other books' covers.

Corné spent his childhood drawing on everything at hand and then began exploring the infinite world of multimedia—and his journey of discovery hasn't stopped since. His mantra has always been "The only limit to multimedia is the imagination," a saying that keeps him moving forward constantly.

Corné works for many international clients, writes features for multimedia magazines, reviews and tests software, authors multimedia studies, and works on many other friends of ED books. You can see more of his work, as well as contact him, at his web site, http://www.cornevandooren.com.

ACKNOWLEDGMENTS

This book would not have been possible without Michelle Lowman's devotion and persistence in bringing an Apress Blender title to reality. My heartfelt thanks go to Beth Christmas for cracking the whip, to Roland Hess for tirelessly double-checking and correcting all my mistakes, and to Marilyn Smith for actually making it readable. Many thanks to the Blender Foundation for creating a global community and spirit of cooperation and contribution and to all the members who contribute to making Blender ever better for the millions of users. I wish to thank my client, Rob Collins, who supported me in the production of this book, and Robert J. Tiess, who has granted us insider access to one of his fantastic productions. Many thanks to DARPA for giving us the Internet, to the W3C for giving us all a way of communicating, and to Linus Torvalds for giving us a real operating system. Last but not least, thank you dear Donna, for holding down a real job while I play in my gimp-cavern.

INTRODUCTION

This book is for beginning professionals who are new to film and video production and for experienced professionals who are new to Blender. This book is intended to serve compositors and post-production professionals who want to use Blender in their pipelines, who just need to know the tools available in Blender, or who possibly need a few examples to get them started.

In writing this book, I sought to break down some of the barriers to using Blender as a real-world compositor. These barriers include a lack of accurate documentation, lack of widespread knowledge and experience in using Blender professionally, the complexity of Blender itself, and the issue of integrating Blender into the compositing workflow. Like the documentation of many open source projects, the freely available material for Blender education and training is mostly created by individuals working sporadically in an uncoordinated fashion. These online materials quickly become out-of-date since Blender is codified by more than 50 programmers. Because there isn't any commercial impetus, many authors create a tutorial to document a problem or challenge that they solved, but once solved, there is no motivation to keep it up-to-date or to extend it in any way. With disjointed individual tutorials, there is no formal review and editing process to ensure that the material presented is factually accurate. Thus, the user-generated online tutorials on Blender are frequently out-of-date and often not entirely accurate. Having written and contributed to much of the online user manual for Blender, I thought it was time to pull all of that disparate knowledge together and target it toward a specific need: compositing. However, this type of culmination is not possible without the backing of a large publisher, and Apress stepped up to the plate.

There are very few experienced users with an abundance of free time available to contribute reliable knowledge and experience tailored to Blender. A much wider audience would use Blender if it was well documented, if its features were fully explained, and if its utility within the workflow showed it to be a productive tool in compositing. To this end, I have documented the basic functionality of a broad spectrum of Blender functionality already in some online books and video tutorials at Lynda.com. However, people aren't connected to the Internet all the time, and the format and searchability of a book, coupled with the tactile element, make that format very attractive. We printed this book in full color at considerable expense to bring you the highest-quality experience possible. The DVD contains all the files and assets used in this book (and of course, a recent copy of Blender!). The DVD also includes gigabytes of mattes, models, and textures used in the first two open movies: *Elephants Dream* and *Big Buck Bunny*. The book takes you from start to finish, and I hope you enjoy reading it as much as I enjoyed writing it.

Happy Blendering!

Roger D. Wickes

Layout conventions

To keep this book as clear and easy to follow as possible, the following text conventions are used throughout.

Important words or concepts are normally highlighted on the first appearance in *italics*.

Filenames, directories, and paths are presented in `fixed-width` font.

Menu commands are written in the form Menu ➤ Submenu ➤ Submenu.

Where I want to draw your attention to something, I've highlighted it like this:

> *Ahem, don't say I didn't warn you.*

Chapter 1

BLENDER OVERVIEW

This chapter introduces Blender, the world's foremost open source software package for compositing and postproduction. You'll learn about the features that make Blender stand out in the compositing world, as well as get some background on digital compositing. Then you'll get started by setting up Blender and taking a look at its interface.

What is Blender?

Blender is a full-featured, integrated, 3D animation application that provides a complete workbench for creating and producing video content. For compositing, Blender has three main workbenches: 3D texturing, node-based compositing, and nonlinear video sequence editing. Each of these workbenches is integrated to work together in a seamless workflow. An example of this integration is shown in Figure 1-1, which illustrates the production of a video on interior design.

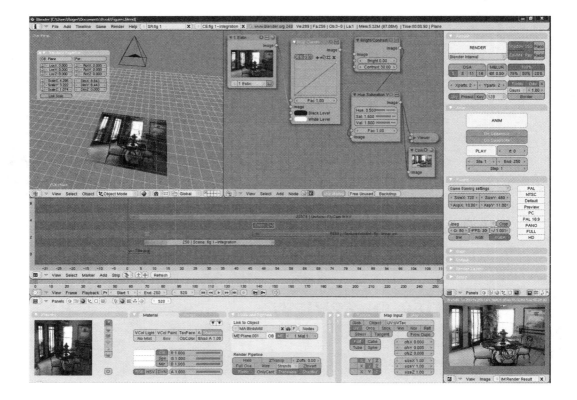

Figure 1-1. A Compositing desktop in Blender

In Figure 1-1, I have used Blender's 3D modeling tools to construct a virtual set that uses a virtual camera to "film" a plane, textured with an image. That original photo was taken with the camera tilted down, and so the room looked skewed. I used UV projection onto the model and adjusted the UV texture mapping to correct this perspective distortion. Using the compositor, I color-corrected that perspective-corrected image. I can now feed it into the sequencer, where it will be mixed with an audio track for final output to an AVI file for TV broadcast. After the rendering, I could rerender this same setup for webcast in Europe with two mouse clicks, or for the Web with another two mouse clicks.

All of your video work happens inside one package: Blender. Your work is faster, because you don't need to stop, switch to a different package, save, export, import, refresh, and resume work. This also means that you don't have to "context swap" when you switch between two applications, as you adjust to the different user interface (UI) and recall how to access that particular application's features. Since you work within only one application, and the UI is consistent across functional areas, you do not waste time context swapping.

Blender is extremely important in the compositing world because it has the following characteristics:

- **Functional**: In addition to a rich set of features, the software is stable and relatively bug-free.

- **Free**: You can download Blender for free. Any work you produce is free from any royalty or restrictions. You can install Blender on as many computers as you want, and even make an in-house render farm.

- **Multiplatform**: Blender runs on all the popular operating systems, including Microsoft Windows versions (from Windows 98 to Vista), Linux flavors (Ubuntu, Debian, and so on), Solaris, and Mac OS X versions (Leopard).

- **Open source**: You can get the source code for Blender, which is written in C, and tailor it to meet your needs. You can write your own extensions and functionality. You are not required (but are encouraged) to share those changes with the rest of the community, and thus can use Blender as a base for your own proprietary platform. If you discover any bugs, you can use in-house programming resources to quickly fix them, without waiting for the vendor's next quarterly release.

- **Documented**: The source, architecture, philosophy, and end-user features are documented, giving you the background information to intelligently decide where and how to customize Blender.

- **Nonproprietary**: The development team goes to great lengths to ensure that all the source code and all libraries used fall under the GNU Public License (version 2), and do not require you to pay any royalties or license any modules for a fee at any time. Any work products you produce using Blender are totally yours.

- **Supported**: Blender is supported by a global community of people and publishers who provide nearly 24/7 end-user support through forums, newspapers, e-magazines, and open projects.

- **Interoperable**: Blender operates with many other popular packages. You can easily import and export a wide variety of file formats.

- **Industrial-strength**: Blender supports the leading formats used in the industry, such as OpenEXR, as well as file sizes and video durations exceeding one hour.

- **Recognized**: Blender is globally recognized and used by professional houses as a tool within their pipeline.

Blender finds many users in the academic community, especially the European postgraduate arena. As these students have graduated and moved into professional fields, Blender has penetrated the professional market in film, video, web, architecture, design, and many other industries, with heavy adoption in Europe, South America, Southeast Asia, and Japan.

What is digital compositing?

Compositing is the most visually rewarding experience in computer graphics. Just as a painter starts with a canvas, some tools (paint, brushes, and so on), and most important, a vision, compositing sets visual imagery in motion from a base of many elements.

Digital compositing generally refers to activities that mostly happen during postproduction and includes anything done to an image or video after it has been recorded. In today's high-budget video projects, filled with computer-generated special effects, compositing activities have extended all the way forward in the life cycle of a film into preproduction, where some activities help filmmakers plan and visualize the rest of their project.

A long time ago, compositing was not digital and consisted of editing the film with razor blades and tape. Many physical techniques were developed to achieve artistic effects. These effects are what we see in old films, and are what we have largely come to expect and take for granted now. For example, the *cross-fade* is a smooth transition from one shot to another. This is in contrast to a *cut*, which is where the film was literally cut and taped together.

Special effects

While editing was done with cutters and by splicing film together, compositing itself didn't really exist. Special effects were generally done "in camera," meaning that they were captured with live photography, often using tricks like forced perspective and projected backgrounds. The closest thing to digital compositing would be split screens and matting, which would be used to join two different takes or locations into a single frame. One example is a scene in Alfred Hitchcock's *Vertigo,* where Jimmy Stewart climbs up a rickety staircase and envisions falling down the center column. At the Hitchcock museum, I saw the preserved set of the staircase scene, shown in Figure 1-2, and fell in love with the idea of special effects and using tricks to fake reality.

Figure 1-2. Vertigo staircase

In the 1940s version of *The Miracle Worker* (a movie about Helen Keller directed by Arthur Penn and starring Anne Bancroft and Patty Duke), I observed a cross-fade, but the fading shot rotated in a strange way that moved off camera. Curious, I set about to figure out how I would do that with real film. I found that in a documentary that used a similar effect, a clever director of photography projected one shot onto a screen, and another shot onto a glass plate using another projector. By filming the composite, moving the glass plate off to the side, turning the light off the glass projector, and filming the result, he got an image overlay and a panning motion of the first image. (I don't know if this is how the effect was done in *The Miracle Worker*.) In Blender, this effect is called a *translating cross-fade*.

With the advent of the digital age, your initial efforts should go into how to achieve those legacy physical effects when working with digital media, and work your way up a learning pyramid, as illustrated in Figure 1-3. In other words, using a computer, how can you re-create an effect done with (sometimes literally) smoke and mirrors? This area of learning is just about dealing with the complexities of working with digital media, such as digital image formats, since there is no physical media to manipulate.

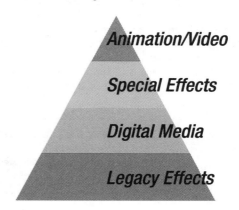

Figure 1-3. Learning pyramid

After you've mastered re-creating legacy effects, you're ready to try new effects. Producers and directors are always looking for a fresh approach, to add a bold, spectacular, and/or memorable look to their films.

Once you have designed an effect or look, which is usually the end result of some sort of a storyboard or concept, perhaps even a single-frame mock-up, the pinnacle is figuring out how to apply that effect in a convincing way over a range of frames. How do you animate the effect itself and the transition from a frame that doesn't have it to a frame that does?

When developing a new effect, or more often trying to figure out how someone much smarter than myself achieved some new effect, I find it easier to follow a progression of thought that starts with "how would I get to a middle frame, or get the final result?" and work backward to what I have to start with—the tools I have available. Then I can visualize how to get from point A to point B to achieve the transition. What you see (or what the producer wants) is often a combination of effects that either build on one another or are layered or mixed with one another. Sometimes you need to take almost an analytical approach to break down an overall effect into its constituent parts.

Compositing activities

Compositing and postproduction activities generally fall into one of the following major categories:

- Reformat images and video
- Adjust and correct images and video
- Assemble and animate elements
- Composite and process image elements
- Sequence video strips with audio

Let's take a closer look at each of these areas.

Reformatting images and video

Reformatting is where you have a 1024×768 resolution image saved in the PNG format, but want it resampled and compressed into a 640×480 resolution JPG format to save disk space and maybe in preparation for a webcast. Another example is when you have a film shot in 2.43:1 aspect ratio that needs to be remastered for US TV broadcast, which uses a 4:3 aspect ratio. As illustrated in Figure 1-4, you must either letterbox or crop the image. Letterboxing adds black bars above and below the image. The other choice is to simply lop off the left and right sides of the image, and show only the middle, since that is where most of the action occurs.

> Since the shape of the movie resembles a letter mailed in an envelope via the post office (if you are old enough to remember snail mail), and the shape of a TV resembles a box, the term letterbox was coined to describe the look that was accomplished to fit the width of the film on a TV screen.

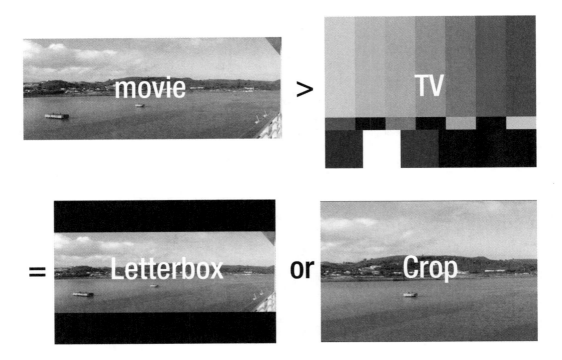

Figure 1-4. Example of reformatting for a different aspect ratio

Adjusting images and video

Another common task in postproduction is to adjust the image brightness, contrast, or tone to achieve a certain look. For example, you may want to adjust a shot that was filmed in bright white light (and is a little washed-out) to give it deeper hues, as shown in Figure 1-5. You could do this by changing the hue, saturation, and the color balance.

Figure 1-5. Example of adjusting an image

Animating elements

Video is motion, and even some still images convey motion through motion blur. Whether it is simply text titles moving over a TV commercial, a high-energy music video, or thousands of virtual birds swirling around a beach, movement of visual imagery captures the eye of the audience.

Blender has a full suite of animation tools that allow you to move elements around and change their color, shape, and visibility over time. You can manually animate and keyframe the location of objects in time, and Blender can even calculate the motion of an object, or hundreds of objects, for you based on rules that you set up. Figure 1-6 shows an example in which the movement and location of each fish within the school was automatically calculated by Blender.

Figure 1-6. Frame from an automatically-computed animation

Compositing elements

To me, a composite is like plywood; the end product is made up of layers of different elements, combined into one image. These elements may be entire photos, parts of photos, or from a computer-generated rendering.

In the example in Figure 1-7, in a shot from the open movie *Big Buck Bunny*, the main character is composited on top of an image of a tree trunk, while the backup actors are placed behind the tree. All of that is then layered on top of a background matte image of the sky and distant hills. When all of these elements are combined and layered together, a convincing, seamless image results.

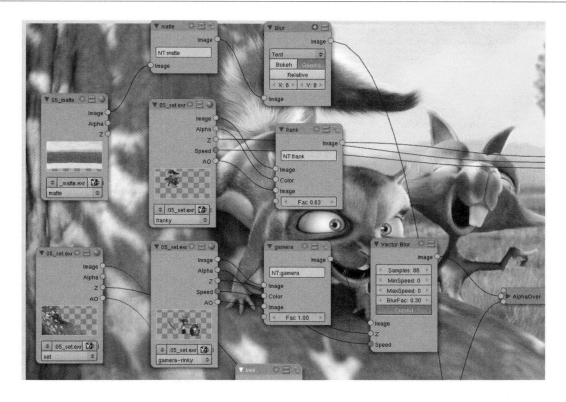

Figure 1-7. An example of a composite

Sequencing video

The final step is arranging the shots into a sequence of events that tells the story. Figure 1-8 shows four frames from the movie *Big Buck Bunny* that represent the first frame of each shot in the opening scene of the movie. The purpose of the first scene is to introduce the movie. These shots set the theme, look, and feel of the movie; let the viewer know that something is amiss (to start the rising tension); and anticipate the introduction of the main character.

Figure 1-8. An example of sequencing video from the *Big Buck Bunny* opening scene

This was not the only sequence that was envisioned for the opening scene. In practice, multiple versions of the sequence, or cuts, will be presented, discussed, and constructed before the final decision is made.

> *In film, several cuts may be produced by the editor: a general release cut of the film as rated by the Motion Picture Association of America (MPAA), an "uncensored" version, and a director's cut that may include extra footage. In rare cases, a movie may be remixed or remastered to be updated or to include additional footage. For these reasons, it is very important to preserve both the final version and the source material involved in any production. Even the "goofs" may find their way into a bloopers reel, sometimes decades later (footage from the original TV series* Star Trek, *with William Shatner and Leonard Nimoy, comes to mind).*

Is Blender for you?

Blender is useful at all stages of the production process and for a large variety of artistic endeavors. Blender is used by many talented people involved in the production process, including the following:

- **Storyboarder/sketch artist**: Works with the director to lay out action, camera angles, and shots. This job includes sketching and making clay models of main actors and props. Storyboards are used to create an animatic (a very rough approximation of the final animation), which can be accomplished using Blender. Line art is used as a reference image when modeling in Blender.

- **Modeler**: Makes a virtual reality of props, scenes, and characters. Specialties include character, prop, and landscapes/stage modelers. Blender modeling and sculpting tools are used to make virtual models of objects.

- **Director of photography, cameraman**: Sets up the camera and plans/executes its motion in the virtual computer-generated scene, and shoots the live action. This job involves matching Blender's camera to the real camera used to film the live-action plate, animating the camera movement, and setting camera properties. The director of photography sets render options and settings, reviews renders, and provides live-action plates and green-screen video.

- **Technical director**: Customizes and programs Blender and Python tools, integrates the work flow, and renders the output frames.

- **Texture painter**: Paints the set, the actors, and anything that moves. If it doesn't move, the texture painter paints it anyway, using Blender's shaders and vertex and texture painting tools.

- **Rigger**: Creates armatures and shapes, and makes things move using Blender's armatures.

- **Animator**: Uses the rigs to make the actors perform by creating actions and animations in Blender.

- **Special-purpose talent**: Uses Blender to add fluid, motion capture, and cloth into the computer-generated scene.
- **Lighting and color specialist**: Lights the stage and sets, adjusts colors to look good in the light, adds dust and dirt to the atmosphere, as well as smoke trails and mist to scenes.
- **Editor**: Takes all the raw footage from the director of photography and sequences it into an enjoyable movie using the Blender compositing and sequencing tools.

2D still image artists use Blender to arrange visual elements into a composite image. They can work with 2D vector graphics and/or photographic images to arrange and layer them for magazine covers, print media advertisements, product stands, menus, and all sorts of creative end products—even just art for art's sake.

2D movie artists use Blender to make cartoons and movies. While you can just work with 2D objects in Blender, Blender also has special shaders and edge features that make 3D objects appear 2D.

> *I regularly use Blender to produce Flash movies. Every year, Google sponsors Summer of Code, where a developer interns to make some enhancement to an open source project. Currently, there is a project to integrate the Freestyle renderer into Blender (see http://maximecurioni.com/freestyle/) for line-art renders. If successful, this project will greatly enhance Blender's capabilities for generating 2D content with a more traditional animation appearance, possibly creating a new look for animations.*

2D and 3D producers use Blender to create elements that are combined in Blender, and animated to make a TV commercial for broadcast, a commercial video for webcasting, or simply a video that is shown on TV or the Internet, such as the YouTube and Vimeo sites.

3D modelers use Blender to create virtual models of characters, sets, props, and entire virtual worlds. Artists use Blender to texture everything in this virtual world. Computer graphics lighting specialists can use Blender's lights and world settings to light a computer-generated scene, and use Blender's atmospherics and particles to add dust, haze, smoke, and other effects to the sky and scene.

Technical directors use Blender to make the final image components, and compositors use Blender to composite those elements into a frame. Film editors use Blender to sequence those shots into the finished move. Title houses can use Blender to add titles and credits. Publishers can use Blender to reformat a movie into any one of a variety of formats, for showing in digital theaters, broadcast over NTSC US TV in normal definition or high definition, broadcast over European TV, or viewed as a webcast.

Live-action film directors use Blender to previsualize the movie in two major aspects. First, the individual storyboard images (scanned versions of the hand-drawn sketches) can be sequenced and timed to present the sequence of shots and the whole movie. Second, rough sets can be constructed to previsualze in 3D, and turned into rough sketches and blueprints for set construction. Together with the film director, the director of photography can use Blender to plan camera angles and track location/layout for the trucks and dollies (rolling carts that move the camera).

Using the previsualization model, the set designer can use Blender to design the set prior to construction. As the dailies (the film shot on location, which is sent in daily at the end of the shooting day) are turned in, the editor can use Blender to select and postprocess the best takes, and to sequence camera footage into a shot, those shots into a scene, and those scenes into a movie.

The computer graphics artist can use Blender to add special effects and textured computer-generated objects to the film. Lighting specialists can use Blender to light the scene. The compositor can use Blender to add elements together to make the final image.

As you can see, Blender can be used by a wide variety of people in the film production process. And through the use of support tools like Verse (discussed in the "The Verse server" section later in this chapter), network sharing, and integrated digital asset management, the whole team can work together, synergistically and seamlessly, with improved efficiency.

How does Blender support creativity?

Creating art is an iterative and heuristic activity. After you create something initially, you edit your work. As you work through your editing cycles, your software can help you in several ways:

- As you experiment with different composite setups, you want a renderer that is very fast, even on your modest PC.
- You want to be able to reduce the quality of some settings and features (which chew up render time) and add them in gradually as you refine your work.
- When working in high-definition and large formats that can take a lot of memory, you want to be able to use thumbnails, called *proxy images*, to keep speed up and memory free.
- You want to save your work quickly and frequently, and you want to be able to back up your work so you can recover it if things go awry.

Blender supports all of these needs.

You may come up with several edits that tell the story or reveal things in a certain order. Blender allows you to splice film segments together any way you want, and can contain several versions (cuts) of a scene within the same file, thus allowing you to produce multiple versions.

Small file sizes and very fast intermediate saves are important in keeping the creative flow going. Larger models in other packages sometimes can take time—from 5 to 30 minutes—to load and save. In Blender, saving regularly takes only a few seconds. Because of this, you can have automatic backups run every 10 minutes in the background without interruption. When you need to back out of some changes or recover a file, you do not lose much work.

Blender includes a built-in text editor that you can use to document your work. Along with allowing you to name scenes, particularly useful for saving groups of work, you can also give each object a name. Additionally, you can set and name markers in the timeline. Having all these little "sticky notes" available really helps when you reopen old work.

In making a final software package, there is the concept of *late binding*, so that you delay making a locked-in commitment until as late in the process as possible (so that you can change your mind or let the user decide). For example, you can set your screen colors; those decisions are not bound up in the code. In a way, rendering (making the final image) is binding your concept to fixed images. Blender includes some features that allow for delaying binding for as late as possible, such as permitting you to retexture a computer-generated object in postproduction. As another example, you can render an image, but the actual saved image format is not locked in until you actually save the rendered image.

Compositing ends at mastering. After the video has been edited and mixed, and is in a final state, it is ready to be mastered. Mastering is the process of burning a master copy onto a DVD. With modern DVDs, that step involves authoring a main menu and linking video segments together so that the end viewer can explore the digital content packed onto the DVD. Therefore, the user directs the viewing experience, possibly choosing alternate endings. In a way then, we late-bind the actual movie.

What can you produce using Blender?

Blender is a complete modeling, animation, and rendering program that ultimately produces a still image, a single frame of an animation or a complete video. The video may be one brief shot or a series of shots in a mixed sequence. It could be a complete movie or TV commercial containing live action composited with computer-generated characters, elements, and special effects.

Blender reads and writes digital media in a wide variety of formats, including still images (BMP, SVG, JPG, TGA, PNG, and OpenEXR) and video (AVI, MOV, and MPEG) using a variety of compression/decompression algorithms (codecs), and readily converts any media among any of these formats. With the introduction and expanding presence of high-definition video, distributed by high-definition TV (HDTV) channels and movies, the clarity and superb realism of in-home entertainment is attaining new heights. You can create, edit, and composite in high-definition video using Blender.

Game developers have used Blender to create models for games, animation actions for game characters, and even entire games. Models have been developed of proteins, nanostructures, buildings, cars, planets, and solar systems. Blender has been used to visualize and previsualize an amazing array of real and imaginary objects and characters.

Since Blender covers such a broad spectrum, Blender exists in a tool space with many other products that offer similar functionality to some degree. This includes software such as Autodesk's 3ds Max and Maya, Adobe's After Effects, Apple's Shake and Final Cut Pro, eyeon Software's Fusion, Windows Movie Maker, Maxon's Cinema 4D, NewTek's LightWave, Side Effects Software's Houdini, and Avid Media Composer—to name a few. Blender has caught up with some of these packages in some areas of functionality, but because of its open source nature, development of new features is not geared toward keeping up with the Joneses, adding market share, or making the best X tool out there (pick your choice of word to substitute for the X).

The developers of Blender simply want to create tools that artists will find incredibly useful, and actively contribute code in the areas where they see a need and have some skill or understanding. Blender offers a complete suite of functionality across a broad spectrum of activities. While Blender may not be a better node-based compositor than Shake, it definitely has a better modeling feature set than Shake.

Many new users ask why Blender doesn't have feature X that is found in some other packages. The answer is that a developer has not gotten around to adding it yet. Developers add a feature when they think it is truly useful and fits into their interests and needs. Users can go to http://www.blenderstorm.org to submit ideas for new features. Users must always keep in mind that Blender is available only because of grants and volunteers.

Blender does not overtly compete against any other product; it simply *is*. If you like it, use it, extend it, contribute time and energy to make it better, and enjoy. If you cannot code, then write tutorials or develop detailed proposals to make it better, or buy great books like this to support future development. If you don't like it, and you can code, change it to suit your needs. Either way, you win.

Trends in digital compositing

Computer graphics tools that artificially generate images are growing in number, size, and complexity, driven by an industry need for "spectacular!" and "unbelievable!" special effects. As the costs for on-site shooting have skyrocketed, producers have exponentially demanded more image retouching, correction, and studio-shot green-screen integration. What started as a simple way to transition from shot to shot using razor blades and tape has progressed to being a major budget line involving dozens of digital artists and hundreds (thousands, even) of servers in a render farm.

Music videos and movies

Music videos have progressed from simply filming the band live in concert to dramatic 3- to 4-minute shorts, often featuring the singer as a lead actor, or completely computer-generated. A great example of this is a the video for a song by the Dublin band Kopek, titled "Stop." In this video, not only are the music and vocals engaging, but also the imagery (created with Blender) is stunning and representative of the song lyrics. And as icing on the cake, it also raises questions in the viewer's mind. This video has been released to the public on YouTube.

Sometimes it is easier and cheaper to shoot a film in green screen, and then construct the set digitally, rather than take the time and space (and planning) to construct a real set. An extreme example of this is *Sky Captain and the World of Tomorrow*, starring Angeline Jolie, where almost the entire film (except for the actors) was shot in front of a green screen, and then the set was constructed using 3D software. This movie is also a great story on one man creating his dream on his home PC—watch the extras if you ever rent it.

Postprocessing as an art form, to dramatically alter the entire look of the film, is also making its way to the big screen. The most dramatic example of this trend that comes to my mind is *Sin City*, starring Bruce Willis.

Completely computer-generated movies, once few and far between and within the exclusive domain of large houses, are being produced by smaller studios and individuals. Blender was used to previsualize *Spiderman*, and was used extensively in the feature film *Friday or Another Day* and the French film *Le Masque de la Mort Rouge* (*Mask of the Red Death*) for special effects. The award-winning short *Lighthouse* by ProMotion Studios was produced using Blender.

At the extreme end of this small-studio spectrum is the emerging open movie movement. People want to share their work with each other and with the world. Artists are always looking for ways to establish their brand and see their work grow. The world's first open movie project (Project Orange, conducted by the Blender Foundation) released all of the assets (the models, textures, animations, and shots) and the software (Blender!) used to produce, render, composite, and create those assets, including the entire film, to the public under the Creative Commons license. The movie that resulted, *Elephants Dream*, was the first high-definition movie released for broadcast in Europe. The goal of the project was to use Blender in a high-pressure professional production environment, in order to see how the software should be improved.

This open movie project was repeated again with the Blender Foundation's Project Peach, which resulted in both the film *Big Buck Bunny* and in massive improvements to the particle system that is used to create smoke, dust, and things like swarms of bees as special effects. The short film *Big Buck Bunny* was produced by a very talented team of a half dozen artists from around the world, and was funded by donations. Again, all of the assets—the characters, background mattes, textures, animations, scenes, and software (Blender and Python scripts) were released under the Creative Commons license to the public. Numerous sites host the content, which can be obtained for free.

User-generated content

User-generated content, or UGC, refers to media content produced by end users. Individuals and small teams now have the ability and infrastructure to connect, coordinate, generate, and publish high-quality images and video for a global audience. They do so sporadically, often without significant funding, planning, offices, or overhead.

UGC presents a freedom of expression and communication, a legacy, and a global understanding that transcend history and politics. In that sense, UGC represents a revolution in the world of publishing. By offering a free, full-featured product that an average person can use, Blender fully enables UGC.

Convergence

Convergence may be the most powerful term in technical business. Convergence describes the rare event when two seemingly unrelated technologies come together to form a new product or even an entirely new market.

The wired POTS (plain old telephone system) converged with the radio to form the wireless mobile phone market. DARPANet converged with POTS and with the pervasive home PC to create the Internet. The Internet converged with low-cost PC hardware and software (servers) to create the World Wide Web.

The Apple iPhone converges so many technologies it's almost insane: wireless phone, messaging (instant and e-mail), camera, photo album, recorded music, Internet access, global positioning, alarm clock, notepad, and day planner. Additionally, because the iPhone can be programmed, it brings gaming and other applications, such as streaming broadcast radio, together into a single device. The complete package was enabled by (and converges, if you will) advances in networking, chip design, battery design, and touchscreen design. Add on innovative ergonomic and elegant industrial design, and you have a wildly successful product.

Today, I see two major convergences occurring:

- Home video cameras (even cell phones can now take video) and webcams are converging with the Web, the availability of free/low-cost tools (like Blender), and a shift in public attitude toward self-promotion and a desire to communicate. The result is a situation where users, who were formerly subscribers and consumers, become publishers and content providers. This convergence is turning the music and video/entertainment industry upside down, and the truly successful media companies will figure out how to capitalize on it. Both my son and daughter have published dozens of high-quality videos, and my daughter even has her own youtube channel, Euchante.

- The merging of cellular phones, the Internet, home media recording and storage devices (such as TiVo and Windows Media Center), e-mail, and chat/messaging systems coupled with free, open-source web hosting software such as Linux, Apache, MySQL and PhP (called the LAMP suite), allow individuals to create personalized social spaces and media control. For example, you can (or will soon be able to) use your cell phone to command your home PC to record a media broadcast, and invite your friends over to watch it at some later date. A second example is to upload your own UGC video to a social networking site, where it is displayed on a screen in a virtual room (store, dance hall, or party room) that is under your control.

Blender setup

This Blender version used for this book is Blender 2.49, which is included on this book's companion DVD. Each Blender revision is backward-compatible with file formats of previous versions. When an old file is opened by a new version, Blender automatically converts the file to the new format when possible, so that you can use the new features while preserving most (if not all) of the original content.

Blender requirements

What kind of PC do you need to run Blender? The short answer is any type of PC will do. The longer answer is that Blender is developed by a team that believes that for software to be truly open, it must run under any major operating system.

When a new release is prepared, the source is compiled, and an installer package is created, at a minimum, for the following platforms:

- **Windows**: Windows 2000, Windows NT, and all Vista versions
- **Mac OS X**: Both PowerPC and Intel-based Macs
- **Linux**: Various distributions, such as Ubuntu, Red Hat, Debian, and so on
- **Solaris**: Solaris 2.8 on the Sparc workstation

Thus, Blender is not only open source, but also cross-platform. All of your work is saved in a blend file (a file with a .blend extension), which may link to other assets such as video footage. That blend file is also cross-platform. For example, you can work on a blend file on a Linux box, e-mail it to a friend running Blender on a Mac, and he can open it, work on it some more, and pass it back to you.

The Blender developers are almost fanatical about the size of the executable, and go to great pains to keep Blender's footprint as small as possible. Blender runs on machines with as little as 512MB of RAM. If you have more than 3GB of RAM, you need a 64-bit operating system, and should get an optimized version of Blender, as discussed in the next section.

Of course, the more memory and CPU cores you have, the better. To work productively in high-definition video, you need at least 2GB of RAM (although you can work with proxies and EXR tiles to get around many limitations, as described in Chapters 9 and 13). Otherwise, you will spend a lot of time waiting as your operating system thrashes about, swapping real memory out to virtual memory on disk.

Blender does not chew up a lot of disk space either (allowing you to chew it up with your high-definition images). This also means that Blender installs in a few minutes, not an hour. The files themselves are also very small, which means they are quick to save and back up.

Blender supports pen-sensitive tablets as well. Some painting options will have a p button to enable pen pressure sensitivity. Pen tablets are ideal for painting in Blender's image editor and for using the Grease Pencil feature to annotate comments and improvement suggestions.

Generic vs. optimized versions

I have included only the generic version of Blender for each platform on this book's companion DVD. There are other flavors of Blender available, optimized for your particular chip set on your particular machine. These flavors are often available from http://www.graphicall.org.

When you get to the GraphicAll.org site, you'll see two sections: Latest Blender builds and Optimized builds. Unless you are adventurous, scroll down to the Optimized builds section, and pick your operating system and chip set from the list. If you have a 64-bit machine, you should use the Large Address Aware (LAA) version. For example, if your PC has the AMD 64 chipset, you should get the SSE2 – LAA optimized flavor. These flavors run about 30% faster than the generic Blender version.

Notes on installing Blender

On Windows Vista platforms, Blender needs a Visual C library that is copyrighted and distributed by Microsoft, so I cannot include it on the DVD. You must download it from the Microsoft site if you need it. If you try to run Blender and get an error message like "The application failed to initialize properly," you need to install this package on your machine. Go to the Microsoft web site, search for Microsoft Visual C++ 2008 SPI Redistributable Package (x86), a.k.a MSVC, and download it.

For all flavors of Linux, you need glibc 2.36, which includes the FFmpeg libraries for containerizing video. The development team at Ubuntu likes to certify all its packages that you can obtain through apt-get or the application installer. Unfortunately, they seem to be perpetually trying to catch up. Therefore, you should use the Linux version that I have included on the companion DVD. It installs and runs fine on my Linux desktop.

I've also included the Mac OS X version of Blender, and you should be able to just run the executable after dragging it to your program folder.

Blender is multilingual

All Blender menus, panels, and messages can be in any one of many different languages shown in Figure 1-9. After you've installed Blender, you can change or choose a different language from the Languages tab of the user preferences window (see Chapter 3 for details on setting preferences through this window). On this tab, you can choose whether tooltips (handy little hints that pop up when you hover over a control), buttons (all the menus and things you can click in a panel), and toolbox (all the tools used) are in that language.

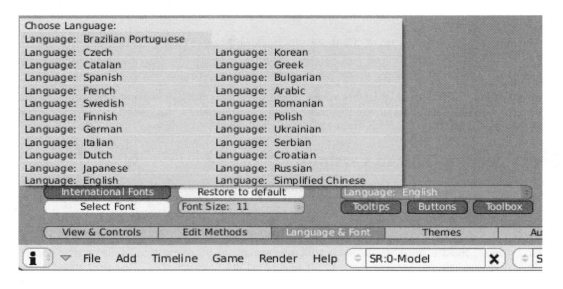

Figure 1-9. Setting the language for Blender

The Verse server

UGC is converging with the Internet to create what I will call TGC, short for team-generated content. For example, I worked on a project where the concept artist in Japan chatted with a director in New York, who sent her sketches to a modeler in Romania, who made a model, which was sent to me for rigging and animation in Atlanta, Georgia. These are globally distributed resources, each working in sequence. The next step is for those distributed resources to work in conjunction, simultaneously, seamlessly, and in continuous context with one another, often out of home offices. The project will be hosted at a virtual location, and instead of passing results "over the wall" to the next person. A team will work in a collaborative environment and synergistic results will emerge. A critical piece of TGC is a software tool to support this kind of globally distributed team.

Enter Verse. Verse is an open source application supported by the Uni-Verse team. The companion DVD includes version 6 of the Verse server for Windows (in an .exe file), Linux (in a tar.gz file), and Mac OS X (in a .dmg file) machines. Verse must be enabled in each application, and the companion DVD includes Versed versions of Blender. For more information about Verse and specific installation instructions, visit http://www.uni-verse.org.

The general architecture for Verse is that a Verse server runs somewhere in the Internet cloud, a Verse client opens a session with the server, and the client begins receiving memory updates. As you make changes to any object inside Blender, those changes are transmitted to all clients, who alter their working copies, and those changes are immediately available to every client. This all happens so fast that to users, it is almost looks like a ghost is working their keyboard and mouse.

> *While Verse may not be the ultimate solution, it is a very noteworthy step in the right direction, and I applaud the effort, as well as the working result. Another solution may be a globally accessible database, with each Blender instance reading and updating a shared, two-phase commit database.*

Compositing tools in Blender

Blender is a "Swiss-army knife" application that provides an integrated suite of functions that all work together. For example, in this one application, you can work dynamically with a colleague on the other side of the world to create a mask that hides a portion of the images in a video sequence, apply the mask and overlay to a fully rendered computer graphics object, animate the mask to match the movement in the video, smoke up and change the lighting of the composite, color-correct, splice that shot into a longer-running sequence, and output the whole video in to both a high-definition H.264 MOV file and a web-presented 640✕480 AVI file.

Within the domain of compositing in general, Blender provides facilities for the following activities:

- **Modeling**: Make a mask, used to extract an element.
- **Shading**: Texture a plane with a video so it can be used in a composite.
- **Lighting**: Alter the shading of an element.
- **Rendering**: Create images and video.
- **Simulation and gaming**: Add special effects, such as smoke and haze.
- **Compositing**: Assemble multiple elements together.
- **Sequencing**: Arrange video strips with audio.

Figure 1-10 shows the various tools in Blender and how they integrate.

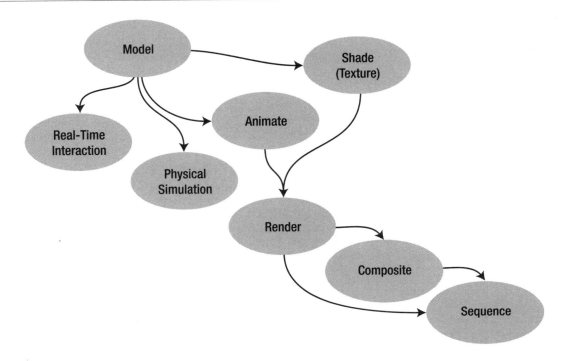

Figure 1-10. Blender compositing tool integration

For compositing, you can use Blender to model a mask that is the shape of some object in a video, animate it to match the live action movement in the video, adjust that portion of the image using the mask as a guide to add in visual effects, and composite a title overlay. It is simple to use Blender to generate titles and credits by converting text into 3D objects using any font or spacing, and then roll those credits into a video sequence on top of the original video.

Blender can composite any number of images together with any number of effects, using masks and greenscreen footage to postprocess raw footage into a final shot. Finally, Blender can sequence all of those shots and generated scenes into a final movie with a soundtrack.

For virtually any activity, you can extend the core functionality by writing scripts in the Python language. Blender even provides a text editor to allow you to enter text for programs as well as for inclusion as 3D objects, and these scripts can be run directly from Blender.

While Blender has many functional areas, this book focuses on the compositing tools. I will not, for example, go into the more advanced modeling and sculpting features, but will spend a lot of time discussing image format support, the compositor, and the sequencer. I will talk about the features you'll use to accomplish compositing with Blender, and then show you how to bring them all together. You'll also see some case studies of how Blender can be used for amateur and professional video production.

Working with Blender

In Blender, you are always working on digital objects. Figure 1-11 illustrates the relationship between an object and how you interact with it.

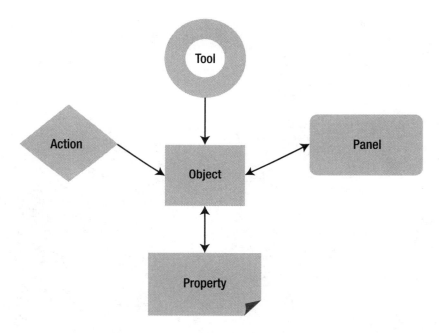

Figure 1-11. User access methods in Blender

An object is the digital data that represents something and is described to you through properties. It is important to remember that an image is just an array of pixels, and each pixel is just a color number. Two pixels can be added together and averaged according to some formula. You may see a blur effect, but to the computer, the effect is just numbers.

Properties, actions, and tools

You control and change objects in three ways: by setting properties, through an action, or by using a tool. For example, to change the location of an object, you can change the Loc properties directly in the properties panel, use the Grab action (press the G hotkey) to grab the object and move it where you want it to be, or use an object manipulator tool (widget) to move the object in 3D space.

Setting properties directly through a properties panel is like describing yourself. You would say you have a name, height, weight, and a gender. Your name is an arbitrary string of letters, like "Michelle Lowman." Your height is a number in some units, such as 1.8 meters. Your weight is a number in some units, such as 59 kilograms. Your gender might be a word: male or female. Those values for yourself would be shown in a panel. The same is true for objects in Blender.

Figure 1-12 shows two sample Blender panels. Each panel allows you to set and change the properties of a different object. The top panel shows you the properties for an object called Mask. The second panel allows you to control properties about the background image that is displayed in the view. In this example, I used an image as a guide in drawing my cowboy mask.

Figure 1-12. Setting object and background image properties

Another way you can control or modify objects in Blender is through some action. If you want to cut frames of roll up from a strip, click and drag the left handle of the strip. This action changes the offset. To thread a node in the compositor, click one socket and drag it to the other socket. When you release the mouse, Blender connects the output of one node to the input of the other, automatically performing any type conversion for you. Blender also supports mouse gestures, where you make a gesture, such as a swipe, and Blender interprets that to grab and move the selected object.

You can also modify objects in Blender through the use of a tool. For example, I use the transform tool all the time. When enabled, it gives you a multicolored tool around the selected object that lets you move, rotate, and scale the object by using the tool.

Window types

In your compositing work, you will be using several functional areas of Blender, each of which has its own window type:

- **3D view**: Construct masks and billboards (textured planes that always face the camera), to make masks change shape.
- **Materials**: Manage textures, and to make masks fade in and out.
- **Animation**: Move masks and billboards.
- **UV/image editor**: Map images to billboards, and perform some image distortion.
- **Node compositor**: Layer images and adjust colors and special effects.
- **Nonlinear editor**: Sequence and layer video strips.
- **Text editor**: Enter and import titles and credits.
- **Scenes**: Manage multiple subprojects.
- **Outliner**: Manage complexity.
- **User preferences**: Make Blender behave the way you want it to behave.
- **Buttons and controls**: Make renders.
- **Scripts**: Run customized solutions, such as exporters and importers.
- **Image browser**: Select textures, images, and video clips to use.
- **File browser**: Bring in textures, images, and video clips.

You'll explore the Blender UI in Chapter 3.

Summary

This chapter introduced Blender, a full-featured application that you can use to composite multiple image elements, and animate them to produce a video for TV and film. Because Blender is an established and relatively bug-free application with a lot of functionality for producing computer-generated video, it has a worldwide following.

Now that you have installed Blender on your PC, the next chapter talks about how to fit Blender into your organization and workflow, and how Blender interoperates with other commercial high-end products and digital assets.

Chapter 2

BLENDER IN THE PIPELINE

An oil pipeline transports a product from the drilling facility to the processing facility to storage tanks and, ultimately, to your gas tank or heater. The oil goes from a raw, unprocessed form to the finished product. Applying that metaphor to media creation, we have a pipeline of tools, standards, and interactions that delivers the media from its raw, conceptual stage, through development and production, into postproduction, and ultimately as a finished product for our loving audiences to enjoy.

Digital media content generally requires a huge up-front investment. Producers making this investment demand long-term archival preservation. The business manager recognizes the media as an important business asset that can provide revenue for years to come. The cost to produce such high-quality imagery demands care, reuse, and standardization. The effort required to produce the video stream within the time constraints requires a collaborative team working seamlessly through a streamlined workflow. All of these factors are driving the marketplace for knowledge on how to implement practical concepts that save money, reduce waste, and accelerate delivery. As you'll learn in this chapter, using Blender in the workflow presents the opportunity to achieve some of these objectives.

An overview of the media pipeline

In media production, *pipeline* refers to the tools that you use to accomplish a task. *Workflow* is the sequence (flow) of tasks and activities (work) that you perform. These tasks follow one another in a logical, efficient order that allows you to perform meaningful and productive work. In establishing a smooth workflow, we want to avoid waste, rework, blockages, holdups, and dependencies. In establishing a pipeline of tools, we want to have products that work well together in a seamless manner. *Seamless integration* means that tool B can pick up and use the files saved by tool A without losing anything or having to go through some complex conversion—they work so well together that you cannot see a seam where they are stitched together.

Figure 2-1 illustrates a fairly general idea of the network of tasks and activities that need to be performed to create any media, from 2D poster art and Flash video to 3D live-action film or computer-generated productions. This is a general process, and you should take some time to define a workflow (by tailoring this process) to reflect specific tasks and intermediate work products (described in the next section) that are needed for your specific kinds of projects. Each tailored process is called a *route*.

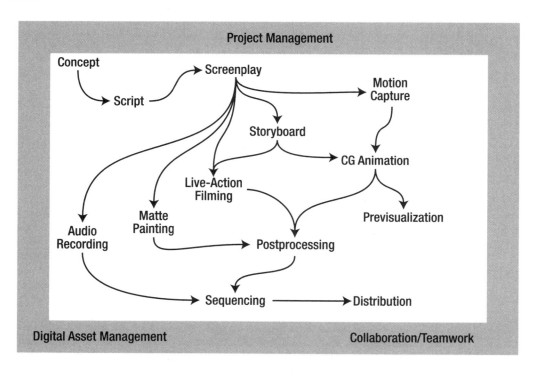

Figure 2-1. Generic media workflow

These tasks represent a kind of map of your country, and your goal is to find the best way to get from point A to point B. Just as with trip planning, you lay out a route, or sequence of waypoints, that you need to pass through in order to complete the journey. You want to pick the route that involves the shortest amount of time and costs the least amount of money, but also will get you there safely. With a media project, you want to get the project done in the shortest amount of time, for the least amount of money, but you don't want to take so many shortcuts that you risk the success of the project.

The general term for defining the workflow and routes is *methodology* (I usually just call it a "method to our madness"). You should take the time to define a methodology for your shop and workflow.

> *After you complete a project, think about the types of tasks you had to do. Consider what went well and what didn't go smoothly. Create a folder, and for each task, write down what should be done, as well as what should be avoided. Over time, you will build up a valuable intellectual property base of knowledge that will help your company excel. Instead of vague terms like "upload the tapes," you will have a detailed list of step-by-step procedures, along with critical settings to be used, to accomplish a task. Your coworkers can follow these routes, without having to ask questions. They can avoid repeating the same mistakes and needing to relearn what has already been proven.*

Here is a typical workflow route that a studio might follow in order to produce a finished webcast from footage that was originally filmed and captured to digital video (DV) tape:

1. Location shoot the footage and obtain the DV tapes.
2. Upload the tapes into an AVI format.
3. Input the AVI video and adjust for fields.
4. Resize (downscale) the image from 720×480i (DV) to 640×480-pixel resolution (Web).
5. Standardize the image (adjust color and contrast).
6. Save the video as a frame sequence.

   Milestone: **Raw video review**

7. Create titles and credits.
8. Composite the title and credits shot.
9. Watermark the video.

   Milestone: **Legal review**

10. Sequence the clips and overlay the audio track.
11. Save the video using H.264 compression into a QuickTime MOV file.
12. Upload the video to the video server and test the result.

    Milestone: **Focus group feedback**

13. Link in the video to existing web pages and add metatags.
14. Conduct a project review (retrospective)

    Milestone: **Project complete**

Workflow not only depends on what you need to accomplish, but also on which tools are available to you and your skill in using those tools. In the preceding workflow example, steps 3 through 11 can all be accomplished in Blender. You may need different routes, or even bypasses and work-arounds (detours), based on differences in your starting media and your target output. You'll need to be aware of what else your clients may request so you know what to save. They might ask for a webcast today and request a European broadcast next month. Blooper reels and "lost episodes" are good examples of footage that might have been tossed out but end up having value.

In addition, as you complete tasks of the project and have significant accomplishments, you pass a tollgate, or phase gate, where your results are accepted, and you can move on to the next phase. These are indicated as milestones in the preceding workflow list. For example, before using anyone's image in this book, I needed to obtain a property release. If I neglected to collect this form and have it on file, I could be sued, and that would just ruin my day. Also, we set up a process whereby what I wrote was reviewed by various people, and they helped point out errors and inconsistencies. This kind of quality control is built into any quality-assurance program. A quality-assurance program ensures that you have done the right things at the right times, so that you produce a high-quality product on a consistent basis.

Quality is generally defined as conformance to requirements. Media requirements generally include the following:

- Theme or vision of the content, expressed as an idea, storyline, plot and/or storyboard
- Duration of the video or commercial, or size of the printed output
- Cost to produce the content
- Time required/available to complete the project
- Expected benefit to the customer, in terms of either brand awareness or increased sales

> *Some of the earliest and simpler quality-assurance programs include Crosby's quality program, Deming's quality methods, and the Six Sigma (Lean Manufacturing) program. Ways to implement these programs on an enterprise level are well documented by the Capability Maturity Model Integrated (CMMI) framework, developed by Carnegie Mellon University's Software Engineering Institute (SEI); International Standards Organization (ISO) 9001, the quality management system standard; and the Information Technology Infrastructure Library (ITIL). While the latter applies to IT companies, many parallels can be drawn to media production, especially since media is so dependent on technology.*

Open source products in the pipeline

Software has progressed from custom-developed, to commercial off-the-shelf (COTS) licensed (boxed), to open source applications. It is now possible to perform video production using open source tools.

You generally want to reduce reliance on outside products and intellectual property that you do not control, as you will be locked into a licensing structure for as long as you use the product. All COTS products fall into this category. With COTS products, you do not have access or control over the source code for a core tool, so you cannot modify it or tailor it to your needs. If there is a bug, you are stuck with it until you pay for the next upgrade. An analogy is that if you were a race car driver, but didn't own the car you raced, one of your core success factors would be out of your control.

With commercial products, you don't have direct say in the direction or features that are incorporated into the product—the programmers don't work for you. Worse, since the product you have come to rely on may be purchased by a competitor, you lose your competitive edge. Even worse, the whole company that makes your core product may be purchased by a competitor, change the license, and charge you higher fees, which impacts your business.

So, at one end of the scale is a company that uses only licensed products, such as Autodesk's Maya and Apple Shake. At the other end of the spectrum are companies that have developed their own in-house applications for CG modeling and rendering. Pixar is a great example of a very successful company that develops and uses its own CG application suite. Not only does it retain control over the product, but it actually licenses part of its tool set (RenderMan) as a means to garner more revenue. Open source products fall somewhere in the middle.

As discussed in Chapter 1, open source tools contribute to the emerging UGC movement. As also discussed in Chapter 1, other converging technologies are the Internet and free video-hosting services (such as YouTube and Vimeo). So, with the cost of computing affordable to the average person, tools available to create media, knowledge available about how to create good media, and hosting services to distribute that content, we have a different sort of media pipeline. From a business perspective, UGC turns the publishing pyramid upside down. Consumers become content providers, and traditional broadcasters and publishers must figure out a way to incorporate UGC into their business model.

Figure 2-2 shows the video production workflow with the major open source tools used at each step in the process. Each of the tools noted in this figure is currently available for free, even dad's camera (but you may need to wash the car on the weekend). However, if you must buy a camera, you can find inexpensive digital video cameras that shoot good-quality video, and moderate-priced cameras that shoot high-resolution stills and video in high definition.

Each of the tools shown in Figure 2-2 provides a fairly complete solution for generating, publishing, and controlling UGC, as follows:

- Project planning and tracking: XPlanner (http://www.xplanner.org/)
- Idea tracking and linking: FreeMind (http://freemind.sourceforge.net)
- Tracking and managing media: Celtx (http://celtx.com/); free, but not open source
- General graphics drawing and image editing: GIMP (http://www.gimp.org/)
- Recording and editing sounds: Audacity (http://audacity.sourceforge.net/)
- Collaboration over the Internet: Verse (http://www.uni-verse.org)
- Digital asset management system: Fedora (http://fedora-commons.org/), DSpace (http://www.dspace.org/), or ResourceSpace (http://montala.net)

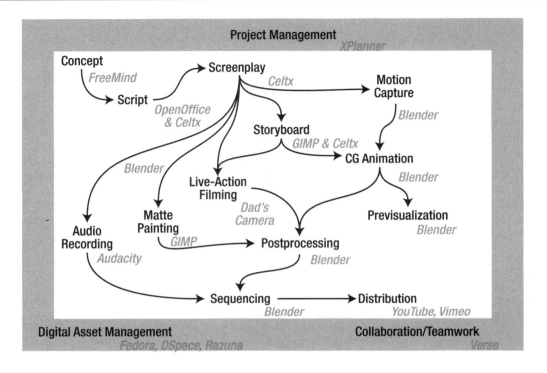

Figure 2-2. Open source pipeline

> *As an addition to or replacement for Verse, an effort being discussed, called dbBlender, will enable Blender to use an outside database management system, such as MySQL (http://www.sun.com/software/products/mysql/) to separate the data from the presentation layers within Blender. Thus, you could have many Blender sessions access the same database, enabling collaboration that way.*

While some products may not provide the same functionality as others, and do not have as rich a feature set as COTS products, the question is largely "Does the tool provide enough functionality to get the job done?" You must consider whether the job requires extra functionality that is worth the cost, or whether there is a work-around or way to use free tools to accomplish the same goal. The use of free tools and assets, combined with the ability for a team to get the source and customize it (thus creating valuable intellectual property) can have a dramatic effect on your total cost of ownership (TCO) numbers.

There are three ways to integrate open source tools (Blender, in this case) into your pipeline:

- **As is**: You use the software as is. With the as-Is model, you use Blender in the same way as everyone else, almost as if it were a COTS product. The advantage is that you can download the source code and compilation environment, and thus are protected if the company goes out of business. When I consulted with large companies in acquiring COTS, we always demanded that the source code, as well as the compilers and database management system, be placed in escrow in order to protect our interests. With open source, anyone can get the source and compilation environment (Subversion for Blender) and be able to build their own binaries.

- **Contributed**: You contribute something back, You devote a small portion of time to making enhancements in Blender. Your developer joins the team, participates in the weekly developer team meeting, subscribes to the coding standards in place, is adopted by a mentor, and starts helping out. His code is submitted to the main trunk of Blender through patches. These patches are reviewed and tested, and if accepted, become part of the main Blender trunk.

- **Branched**: You take the ball and run with it. You branch off on your own, making custom modifications to areas of Blender. When you are happy with the rewrite of that area, you submit that branch to the Blender Foundation where it is merged. You are then sharing those changes with the community. Your code base diverges from the main trunk (for those areas under development). The safety net for you is that should your developer ever break Blender badly, or leave you high and dry, you can always revert your code base back to trunk.

> *If you use open source products in your pipeline, please subscribe to the "Give a Little, Get a Lot" philosophy, and give a small percentage of the revenue you recognize from using those products back to the community from whence it came, preferably in the form of more and better code for the product. If you do not have a programmer on your staff, the Blender Foundation conducts Summer of Code and Summer of Documentation efforts, which always need sponsors to pay developers to add some neat features. If you want to sponsor someone and have a specific feature in mind, you can float your proposal to the Blender Foundation, and through the developer network, the chances of success are very high. You and the community will win by having a better product to use, and developers win by being paid to do what they love.*

Competing in the COTS space is very difficult, as is competing in any space in the digital realm. In the computer graphics application space, applications as a whole develop similar abilities to give photo-realistic results and there is a shrinking "higher ground" in the following areas:

- Ease of use/workflow
- Interoperability
- Rendering capability (notably photo-realism)
- Physical simulations:
  - Fluids
  - Particles (hair and dust)
  - Volumetrics (smoke, haze, clouds, and turbulence)
  - Cloth
  - Soft bodies (squishy things that aren't quite solid)

As you may have guessed, Blender has made recent improvements and has at least a preliminary implementation of each of these areas.

Work products

Along the way, as you complete each step in your workflow, you will develop and leave a trail of work products. If these have any lasting value, they become assets, used later on in your project or by some other project in the future. You might use assets produced by a previous project within your own company, or you may license assets produced by someone else.

> *For Blender, you can find great asset libraries at Blender.org. These include those in the Orange project for mechanical props, in the Peach project for outside (fields, flowers, and forest) and creatures, and in the Blender Model Repositories at http://www.katorlegaz.com/3d_models/ and http://www.blendermodels.org/models/.*

Figure 2-3 shows a flowchart of the tasks and work products that you, as a compositor, will deal with when working on producing a film or video.

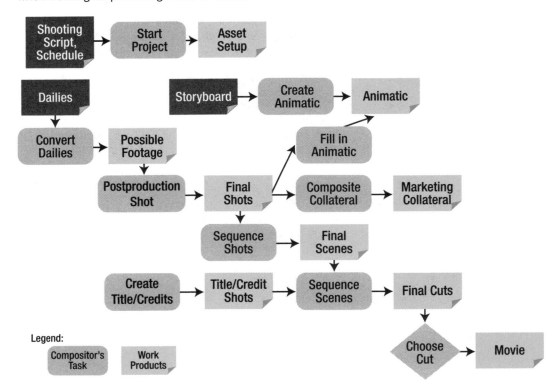

Figure 2-3. Compositor tasks and work products

In the workflow for compositing computer-generated and live-action movies, here's the general sequence of events:

1. Review the schedule, and set up your project folders and asset management.

2. Composite an animated storyboard.

3. Take in the dailies (raw DV footage, for example) from each camera perspective and save them as AVI or MOV files, each with their audio track (which may be from a separate audio recorder). Use your content management system or digital asset management system to keep track of what was shot: when it was shot, what it contains, who was in it, where it was shot, and so on.

4. Select the best takes, and strip them off into frame sequences and mated audio tracks.

5. Sequence the shot, possibly with variations, postprocessing each (such as with color correction), and saving the shot as an AVI file. Generally, you do not want to save with a codec or compression at this point, depending on the desired quality.

6. Save a proxy if you are working in high-definition. A *proxy* is a low-resolution video or image that stands in for the full-resolution production file in order to increase the working speed of your applications. More information about proxies is in Chapters 9 and 13.

7. Schedule and review with the director to select the best shot render, and get feedback on the postproduction effects.

8. After selecting the best shot, sequence the shots into a scene.

9. Create the title sequence and credits shots.

10. Sequence the shots into the movie.

> *Almost all stories are three-act plays—rising tension, climax, and conclusion—and those acts are broken down into scenes. Scenes are composed of shots. A shot is a brief segment, most often only a few seconds long, that conveys a thought or idea element of the story.*

In Blender, your work product is the `.blend` file, which contains the elements of your composition, and the assets used to render (stills or video). Video may be just the visual element without sound, or it may incorporate an audio track as well. The video that you produce can be an *animatic*, which is a video that shows the intent of the final product. Your work products can also be marketing collateral, such as a poster-sized image like the one shown in Figure 2-4.

Figure 2-4. *Big Buck Bunny* marketing collateral (poster)

Interoperability

Whatever tools you use in your pipeline, they must connect, like plumbing, and interoperate. They may interoperate either directly, by linking themselves together and being able to call one another, or indirectly, through a file exchange so that their work products can flow from one application to the next with a minimum of blockage (such as reformatting or lost information).

Figure 2-5 shows Blender in the pipeline where other products are used to perform tasks, even though Blender might be able to perform them as well or better. In this figure, the circles represent a major work process and the tool used to do that task. The connections indicate the formats of the work products that are passed between the applications. These formats are discussed in Chapter 4.

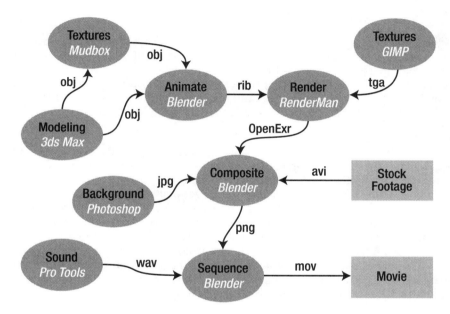

Figure 2-5. Possible pipeline (work product interoperability)

In the example in Figure 2-5, the computer-generated scene is developed using Autodesk 3ds Max, with high-resolution sculpting in Autodesk Mudbox. Blender is used for animation, compositing, and sequencing. In compositing, the rendering engine is of primary importance. In this example, RenderMan is the rendering engine. RenderMan is developed, licensed, and used internally by Pixar. This tool reads in the RenderMan Interface Bytestream (RIB) protocol file and produces any variety of output. In this case, the output is a series of OpenEXR files. Pixar maintains the specification for the RIB file (called the RenderMan Interface Specification) and the actual RenderMan software, which runs on Windows, Mac, and Linux machines. It takes in image textures painted using the open source GIMP package. Another firm likes Photoshop for the big backgrounds, and the musicians and sound engineers use the top-of-the-line Pro Tools. Blender creates the final movie in the QuickTime container.

This is purely a hypothetical example, designed to show that open source tools can be mixed and matched into a pipeline of closed source COTS tools that can vary widely in price.

The Blender internal renderer is also a very capable rendering engine, and was the rendering engine used to generate the *Elephants Dream* and *Big Buck Bunny* images. I discuss the Blender internal renderer in detail in Chapter 9. In addition, Blender can easily export information about the scene to be rendered in XML format for use by other external rendering engines, such as Indigo (http://www.indigorenderer.com) and natively interoperates with YafaRay (http://www.yafray.org).

For interoperability, Blender supports both images and video streams, which are largely treated in the same way. For example, a background image in the modeling view can be a still image, an image sequence, a video clip, or an internally generated test image.

Digital rights management

Here, I will touch briefly on the legal issues and copyright law, and ownership of a video, as they are important topics, and generally misunderstood (or not understood at all) when it comes to UGC. Some people think that all art should be free, and that would be good if no artist ever had to eat, pay rent, or buy clothes and computers. Some people think it is OK to steal from the rich, successful artists by using their art or music in their videos, without paying for it. Many times, you can simply avoid the issue, for example, by using royalty-free music (use Google to search for that term, and you'll get a long list).

A common question is, "Since Blender is free and available to anyone, does anything that you produce using Blender also have to be freely available?" The short answer is no. For example, suppose you rent a camera and take a picture of a brick. It's a really good-looking brick, and you license that image to a home design firm to use in marketing. You get money for that license (called a *royalty*). If you shot that image using a rented Nikon camera on Fuji film, the leasing company, Nikon, or Fuji cannot claim any ownership of the brick image. So, even though you do not own the camera, you own the work product that was produced using it. Of course, ownership is subject to the rental agreement that you signed, and Blender is licensed (akin to the camera being rented in this case) to you under the Creative Commons license. This license clearly states that you own the work products (images) produced by you using Blender. Now, if you produce a video using the QuickTime format, you do not own the rights to that format or to the encoding algorithms.

When working with digital assets and considering their various licenses, you need to be aware that, in many cases, a video or film work will have different licenses attached to its audio and video portions, each of which may even be owned or controlled by different legal entities. For example, the images and the audio to the open movie *Elephants Dream* are licensed differently. You can, for example, use the *Elephants Dream* assets to make and sell a movie of your own, for profit, because the software and the assets are licensed under the Creative Commons Attribution license, which you should read at http://creativecommons.org/licenses/by/2.5/. However, the audio files are distributed under the Creative Commons Attribution-Noncommercial-No-Derivative-Works license (http://creativecommons.org/licenses/by-nc-nd/2.5/), so you cannot use them in a movie that you plan to sell. The same advisory holds true for any models or assets that you download from the Internet. Even though you may *get* them for free, that does not necessarily mean you can *use* them for free for whatever purpose you desire.

When you use an image in your composition, you must ensure that you have the right to work with that image, since generally speaking, the right to own and use an image rests with the person who created that image. For example, suppose that you and a friend go out on a location shoot. You see a particularly neat building, and ask your friend to take a picture of it. The building is a corporate office and has the logo of a company on its side. Your friend snaps the picture and e-mails it to you. Do you own the image? The answer is probably no. Does your friend own the image? The answer is probably no. "What?" you ask, how can neither of us own the image? The answer is that the image is of someone else's property (the logo and the building), and thus, that property owner owns the rights to all representations of that image. Unless you get a release from the owner, you cannot use that image in your work. The logo is owned by the company that (probably) leases the building, and the building itself is probably owned by a commercial property management company.

In general, ownership of logos, names, and faces is a big deal, and you need to obtain a legal release from the owner or person prior to even taking the picture in the first place. Ownership of images of buildings is less of a big deal, since most buildings are fairly nondescript, and there generally is no damage to the building's reputation or business value as a result of you publishing the image of that building.

Where it may get tricky is if you publish a political activist/protest kind of video against, say, brick makers (OK, it will more likely be veal ranchers or whale fishermen, but you get the idea), and you shoot a video of someone holding a product (and showing the logo) while ranting about how bad these bricks are. The brick holder then throws the brick through the window of the CEO's car. (OK, maybe this example is a bit over the top, but you get the idea.) Obviously, no manufacturer wants its product to be shown in a bad way, especially being used to commit a crime. The counter-argument is the First Amendment right (if you live in the United States) or precedent of law in the country in which the video is shown. Some countries may ban your video from being shown there.

If you are pulling images from an archive or digital asset management system, you must take the time to read the license associated with that image, to ensure you are making *fair use* of that image as granted by the license.

Generally speaking, one or more legal entities can own the images that you use:

- You as an individual
- The person depicted in the image
- The company that controls the brand of the product shown in the image
- The company that created the logo of the product shown in the image
- The company you work for
- Your client, if your are working under contract
- Anyone who is assigned interest in the assets of any of the preceding parties

What those people do with that ownership is specified in the license that goes with that image. If you cannot locate a license, do *not* assume that you have permission.

> *Assets, like the Nike swoosh logo, are owned by someone and have value to them. So, before you use an image of someone else's asset, you must ensure that you have the right to use it in the way in which you intend. On an informal level, you never want a team member to say, "Hey, why did you use that clip of mine? I wasn't done with it!" There is really no good way to proceed with that conversation, except to begin with "I'm sorry . . ." and then back it out. Worse is getting a cease-and-desist letter from a lawyer, causing you to retract something you have already published. An ounce of prevention is worth a pound of cure.*

While some people won't object to you using their product's image in a video or composite, technically, you cannot do so without their written permission. When you request permission, you may find one of the following situations:

- The company responds to you and objects to how the image is being used.
- The company is in the process of selling or discontinuing the product or brand.
- The company wants to maintain strict control of how the brand is presented and distributed.
- The company wants to share in any potential future profits from your work.
- The company will not take on any potential liability.

The last one is the kicker, because it has implications that stretch into the future. An image can exist for a long time, and while it is in use, someone might get their dander up and sue the producer/owner for whatever reason. You might find yourself involved in a costly lawsuit years down the road, no matter how remote your image usage was from the use of the particular brand involved.

For these and other reasons, companies will probably be slow to respond to you in your request to use their asset unless you can show them how they will profit from it. My advice is to turn a liability into a revenue, and offer them free "product placement" to help them market their product. If they do respond, expect that they will want final authority over publication of the video.

If you end up not having the proper permissions to use an image, you can create a mask (as discussed in Chapters 3 and 5) to blur or block out sections of an image (using the compositor, as discussed in Chapter 12), so you can keep it in your video. This is how and why logos on hats and T-shirts are sometimes blurred on TV.

Blender compositing pipeline

Of course, since Blender can model, sculpt, animate, render, and postprocess, it provides a complete stand-alone, soup-to-nuts compositing package. Figure 2-6 shows the pipeline for digital compositing with only Blender.

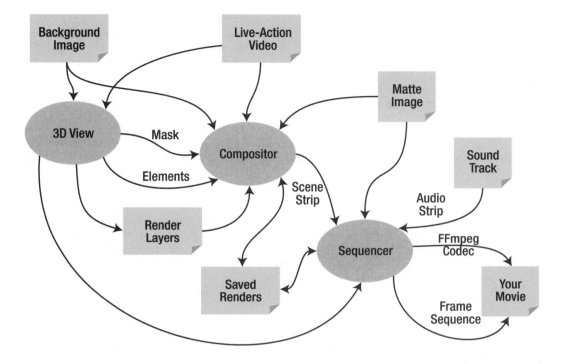

Figure 2-6. Compositing with Blender

With Blender, all video compositing is accomplished using one or more facilities:

- A 3D view, through scenes rendered by a virtual camera
- A compositor that alters images from files and/or the 3D view
- A sequencer that processes video segments from files, the compositor (if used), or the 3D view

Each of these facilities can interact as shown in Figure 2-6. They share common concepts and keyboard shortcuts, and run within the same window environment inside the Blender program instance. They are not separate, stand-alone programs that need to be run separately or concurrently.

Both the compositor and the sequencer can read in the scene render. If the compositor is used, then the sequencer reads in the composite output, instead of the raw scene. This allows on-the-fly post-processing; you can render your computer-generated scene, use the compositor to add gamma or color correction, and then pass that clip directly to the sequencer for movie output. Because a single .blend file can contain multiple scenes (as discussed in the "Blender work products" section later in this chapter), and the compositor and sequencer can load in multiple scenes in one pass, the possibilities for combining computer-generated scene renders, using previously saved renders, layering special effects, and so on to produce a composite are almost endless.

Scene renders can be saved to an image sequence or video file for subsequent processing. This technique is used when rendering is performed by a render farm. A *render farm* is a whole bunch of PCs that render either small portions of a single, very large image or individual frames of an animation. Sun, as well as other companies, maintains a large set of computers that are available for rent on a processor-by-processor basis. For the movie *Big Buck Bunny*, Sun Microcomputer graciously donated 50,000 CPU hours of some time on its grid. Users have access to this vast computing power to install, test, and run whatever software they need, buying more of the available power as their project requires it.

With Blender, you can render on your PC, buy time on the Sun grid or another commercial render farm, or use scripts like Farmerjoe to make your own render farm using any PCs you have on your network. You can even use the Big and Ugly Rendering Project (BURP) project. Tips for setting up and using a render farm are discussed in Chapter 9.

> *BURP is an attempt to use the Boinc protocol and network set up by Berkeley University for globally distributed rendering using all the spare time of PCs in the world. See http://boinc.berkeley.edu/ for more information about this open source project. I encourage you to sign up today and put all your PC's spare processing power to some good use, instead of just warming up your room.*

As you composite images, you can pass them off to the sequencer. If you wish to composite a sequenced shot, you can read that back in as a work in progress, reprocess that iteration, and pass it off again to the sequencer or write it back out to a file.

You do not need to render the completed image or the completed video all at once. Compositing is the act of arranging various image elements together into a final, complete image. Therefore, a scene is done when it is ready for rendering out to a certain frame set. The images and render layers still may need to be overlaid on top of backgrounds or stages to produce footage. The average footage length is a few seconds. Within that footage, certain things (like screen displays and special effects) still need to be composited over live-action shots. The main actors still need to be placed into their sets and background mattes included. Once that is finished, the main process of editing can begin.

When does compositing start?

Way back when, compositing was almost an afterthought, and postproduction started after all the shots "in the can" (an old phrase meaning that the exposed reels of film were in their tin containers) had been developed. In those days of physical film, postproduction tasks were handled by a lone editor in a windowless back room using his two-reel editing workbench.

Nowadays, digital compositing and postproduction tasks are essential in producing the product. Lately, for example in *Indiana Jones and the Kingdom of the Crystal Skull*, computer graphics tools have become integral to the process right from the start, helping to plan the camera moves and shots.

Generally, the overall workflow progresses from concept to creation. With regard to compositing and postproduction, planning starts when the production and film are envisioned. For computer-generated films, where live action is minimal or nonexistent, postproduction planning starts at the very beginning of the project. This planning is to estimate and allocate resources to handle the following:

- Number of computer-generated shots or shots needing compositing
- Level and degree to which those shots will need compositing, and possibly which custom shaders and postproduction software need to be developed
- Storage space required for the frames
- How much postprocessing will be needed (manpower)
- Demo/test renders to ensure that the desired look can be achieved

> See the CGSociety's behind-the-scenes article "The Day the Earth Stood Still: Creating Spheres and Particles" (http://features.cgsociety.org/story_custom.php?story_id=4841) for a peek at the complexity in developing special-effects software.

To determine the starting point for postproduction, you need to consider who is involved and the ultimate product. Here are some examples:

- **2D still**: The compositor should be involved right up-front, as elements to be extracted from photographs are identified, and the size of the print and needed resolution are being determined. Blender has been used to generate images for magazine print media, car wraps, and trade show banners. For extra large printing, there is a script called ReallyBigRender, which facilitates rending monstrous-sized images. If the art director starts describing a "fresh, innovative new style," accompanied by the requisite conjuring hand-wave motion, you are well advised to start collecting some comparable "is this the kind of thing you were envisioning?" samples to help turn all that activity into motion. (*Activity* is sometimes random and gets nowhere; *motion* is directed effort that accomplishes a goal.)

- **2D animation**: As a minimum, you get fully engaged in the project when alpha shots have been animated and are ready for rendering, or have been rendered out as image sequences in a suitable format, backgrounds have been painted, and the base art or picture has been painted. If a mixed-media kind of look (such as *South Park* or any of the Pokemon movies) is desired, then the 3D shadeless tooned characters should have been animated and shots rendered out to sequence files. While Flash is a very popular tool for this kind of media, Blender's toon shader can be used to achieve a cell-shading effect.

- **3D animation**: As with 2D animations, you are involved after the main elements have been modeled and shaded. Obviously, this is the mainstay of compositing, where everything must be rendered and composited, so you may even work with the director of photography to plan camera angles. You also work with the technical director to plan the rendering process, and begin collecting frames and render layers. *Jimmy Neutron* is a great (and entertaining) example of a high-volume 3D animation production.

- **Live action**: After the individual shots and alpha image sequences have been filmed and turned in daily (the dailies), you get involved in reviewing and cataloging the footage.

You may interact with the director after all the shots are in the can. The director may not be sure about the exact sequence of events in which to portray the movie, but have more than enough material to assemble a movie and tell a good story in the time allotted. A film editor may edit the video to produce one or more cuts (alternate sequences). Sometimes a movie is shot with alternate dialogue or alternate endings, so literally several variations of the movie can be arranged. Sometimes a goof is made, such as missing a key shot for the story line. In this case, different scenes may need to be arranged so that the audience doesn't notice, is distracted, or can fill in the gaps. By working early as or with the film editor, you can avoid wasting time compositing shots that end up on the cutting room floor.

When does compositing end?

You are finished compositing when you have learned something. What? "No," you say, "I'm finished after I've handed the master over to the duplication and distribution team, or uploaded it to Vimeo or YouTube, presented it to my client, or submitted it to an indie film festival." "Nay," say I.

OK, technically, yes, compositing ends when the video is completed. However, let's take a look at the big picture.

A movie is a set of images (video) and audio. The video is worked on digitally, and then distributed via film or DVD. That video is shown in theaters, in homes via DVD, or broadcast over the airwaves or Internet. For movies (shorts, indies, and feature films), compositing ends when the files have been sent over to the film production studio for developing into a real film, or sent to a cinema-hosting facility for electronic distribution to the theaters via TCP/IP wide-area networks.

> For the film Big Buck Bunny, the producer wanted a physical film. The digitally rendered electronic files were backed up to a high-capacity disk drive, and shipped to an imaging facility where a physical film was made for distribution to theaters. Many cinema chains now have digital projectors, and so physical film, for the mass market, is no longer an absolute requirement. Digital distribution can be secure and has huge cost and time advantages over physical film.

Consider that your work will go through review and approval cycles before any of your work products are final. Even up until the final showing, the director may choose to reshoot a scene or ask for rework on any particular shot. In those cases, you must be able to go back to the original footage (or audio) and recomposite the shot. You legal department may need to review the film for the inadvertent unauthorized capture of someone's logo or product. Additionally, you may need to make a final pass over the scene and make color corrections to give it a uniform presentation. In short, be prepared to rework and reopen your project, even after *you* think it is done.

Also consider the housekeeping involved after you have created your video. It is an asset, and you must catalog it. You also need to clean up your disk and project folder, removing unused assets and all the test renders you created.

Finally, a little retrospection is in order. Review your own skills and knowledge of the tools you used, and look for things you did well and things you should research and learn to do better. Stay abreast of changes in the industry and in the tools you use. A new version of Blender comes out a few times a year, so set aside some time to play with the new features, so that you can be aware of them, and possibly use them on your next project.

Next, review your team. Have a team meeting to talk about how all the different members, and their particular specialties, interacted. Review the estimates, and see where you lost time or wasted time because of rework, and modify your workflow route so that the next team (or your team) doesn't make the same mistakes.

In summary, learn from your project and consider the following tasks as part of compositing completion:

- Document your project (Blender saves text files inside the .blend file).
- Put away your work for future reference, moving local files to the server.
- Ensure you have readable backups made of all your files.
- Analyze your time card to determine your productivity (which helps make your next project's estimates that much more accurate).
- Examine your workflow and fill in/document added steps and lessons learned.
- Examine your pipeline to see how you could use your tools better next time.

Blender work products

The big work product you produce using Blender is the project file, called a *blend file*, because that's the file extension it is given. This one file can contain all the information about your project: the elements, the images, the motions, and the settings. Blender has the ability to hold information about multiple scenes and shots in a single blend file.

It is completely up to you, based on the size of the project, whether you keep one shot in one blend file or each shot as a scene in a separate blend file. For amateur use, you can even keep the whole movie in one blend file!

Another work product is the composited images themselves. When it comes to renders, Blender loves using the OpenEXR format, since it can save many render passes. Render layers and passes are discussed in Chapter 10.

Practical digital asset management

When you start out a new project, you will immediately be faced with the challenge of setting up a project space that is well organized. A project starts with a concept, and over time, progresses into a finished product (or is canceled, but we won't go there).

You will need to plan how you will set up both your project folder, for local assets specific to the project, and library folders, for assets you want to reuse from project to project. Also, the minute you download or copy something for your project, you will need to put it somewhere. This section contains some helpful hints as to how to set up a filing system that is compatible with Blender. That filing system is the way in which you manage your digital assets.

Links to assets

As I noted, Blender is able to pack all of the assets that are used in a project into its single blend file. Alternatively, it can simply contain a link to that file. The advantage to packing input textures into the blend file is that everything is all in one physical file, which makes it easy to e-mail and back up. Making a backup of one packed file ensures that you really do have everything you need to recover from a disk crash, and that you will not be missing one or two or more crucial images. The disadvantage is that the files can get huge!

In general, I recommend linking to assets from your blend file. When you link to an asset, such as a mask or image that is in another file, the blend file contains a link to that file. The link is either the full file specification or a relative path.

A full specification begins with the drive letter or resource name, and ends with the file extension. For example, the following link points to a QuickTime movie on a PC that is on the local network, named hydra:

> \\/hydra\public\shared\blender\lib\images\people\roger\2009\magic.mov

Note that the resource name begins with two backslashes (\\). In other cases, such as when the file is stored on your Windows PC, the link will begin with a drive letter.

The other way to link to an asset is to use a relative path specification, such as the following:

> //..\..\lib\images\people\rebe\baloonee.jpg

Note that this link begins with two forward slashes (//). These two slashes tell Blender to start in the directory where the .blend file is saved, and go from there. The two dots (..) are breadcrumbs, which mean to go up a directory. Figure 2-7 shows this relative path specification graphically. In this example, starting with spot501.blend, you need to go up two directory levels, and then over into the library, and then down to that image. The advantage to using relative paths is that you can move the whole c:\blender to another drive or folder, and your relative links will stay intact.

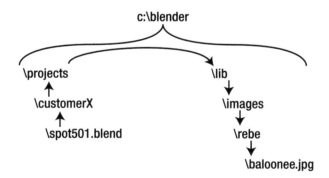

Figure 2-7. Relative paths trace through directory structure.

The File ➤ External Data submenu, shown in Figure 2-8, includes a number of options to convert and fix these links inside the blend file, as well as to help you locate an asset. For example, if baloonee.jpg in Figure 2-7 were moved into a subfolder under rebe, say \1998, you could choose the Find Missing Files option, and Blender would attempt to find the image and fix the link.

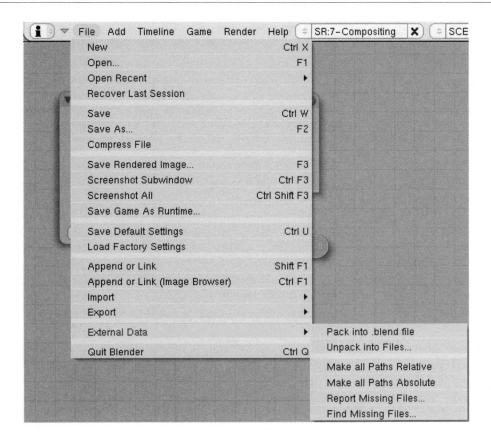

Figure 2-8. Options for fixing and converting broken paths

Project folder organization

As I mentioned, Blender is able to pack all the information and assets referenced in a project into a single blend file. Conversely, it is also able to unpack all those assets into separate files, creating an entire folder structure for your projects. To use this feature, create a new master folder for your next project and place the .blend file inside that folder. Then open the .blend file and unpack it by choosing File ➤ External Data ➤ Unpack into Files. Blender will automatically create all the subfolders needed for a medium-sized project.

You'll want to organize your project information in a fashion that supports the progress of the project and accommodates the specific project. Since each project is unique, I can give only some general recommendations of things that I have found helpful while using Blender on a daily basis.

On my hard drive, I have a /Blender/Work folder, and each new project gets its own folder under that. Under Windows, this might be off your C: drive or your documents folder. On Linux, it would be in your home folder.

As a compositor, you will find it helpful to have ready access to work products produced even during the early phases of the project to help guide you to a successful result. When naming folders, it is OK to abbreviate and use shorthand, as the folder structure can get quite deep. Otherwise, you could simply run out of room in file name boxes and such. And if you ever have to actually type in a folder name, you will thank the stars for shorthand folder names. Here are the names I use:

- Preprod: Preproduction material that is generated before principal filming begins.

- Script: The story, screenplay script, and shooting script. The compositor is mainly interested in the shooting script and project schedule.

- Sched: A schedule with dates and key milestones. Because of logistics, the filming may be in sequence or out of sequence according to the story line. This has a major impact on compositing and postproduction, because it tells you when you can expect the footage for each shot to start rolling in and what your expected workload will be.

- Story: The storyboard, which is the main artifact of preproduction. It is a series of images that depict the story, camera angle, and main motion.

- Audio: The audio track, from a preliminary reading that lays out a basic timeline for the story, usually narrated by the concept crew in front of the storyboard, to the final mixdown.

- Anim: Animatic, which is a *very* rough approximation of the movie, using the storyboard images and audio track. Storyboard images are eventually replaced with rough computer-generated sets or a representative daily.

- Art: Concept art of the story, characters, and scenes. Includes proof sheets of the characters. (A *proof sheet* is a bunch of thumbnails that depict the character's expressions and poses.)

- Ref: Reference material, such as the script and live-action footage (possibly of the concept crew narrating the storyboard or demonstrating concepts and motions, practice moves, and so on). Also includes any location shots and wardrobe test photo shoots.

- Xtra: Extras and special features planned, including interviews, alternate sound tracks, and DVD mastering goals. Especially with the newer formats like Blu-ray, a whole range of hyperlinked extras can be inserted, such as actor biographical information, location information, alternate scenes, and much more. Mastering is becoming a specialty all of its own, as the film becomes just a part of the whole entertainment experience.

- Prod: Production footage that goes into the final product. Figure 2-9 shows the Prod folder for the Peach DVD, so you can get an idea of their best practice for organizing work for distribution. Within each scene subfolder (scene 2 is selected), there is a blend file for each shot within that scene.

- Sales: Production material for printed posters, advertisements, trailers. Also includes a blog used to record the progress of the project and help sell it, to create the "buzz."

- Status: Status reports, time cards, issue lists, key e-mail messages, and other "administrivia."

Figure 2-9. Peach folder organization. Scene 2 has seven shots.

Library folders

You may have assets that you want to use in more than on project. These should go in your personal library, such as in Blender/Lib folder. Now you are faced with the challenge of how to organize and categorize all the different stuff that you might want to reuse some day, keeping in mind that you don't want to spend days searching for it. I have the following folders under my Lib folder:

- \images: Contains subfolders with names based on their source such as \NASA

- \materials: Contains blend files that have common/reusable shader settings, such as glass and smoke

- \object: Contains subfolders grouping types of objects, like buildings, trees, houses, machines, planets, and creatures

- \pose: For motion captures and animations of creatures

- \rigs: For armatures of reusable rigs such as Mancandy and the *Big Buck Bunny* creatures

- \textures: Contains special-purpose image files, organized into subfolders based on what the texture is commonly used for coloring: cars, cloth, hair, nature, roads, buildings, and so on

- \wav: Contains soundtracks (music folders based on genre like techno and jazz) and foley sound effects (gunshots, whizzes, racing engines, and so on)

You could set up your own library structure and use folder names that make sense to you, as I've done.

> *You can use the Blender Library script to create a library structure for you, and to contain all your reusable assets. To get and use this script, consult the BlenderArtists site, specifically the forum thread http://blenderartists.org/forum/showthread. php?t=65719. Download the script it into your scripts folder after you have installed Blender, and consult the thread and/or Blender user manual for more information about running a script.*

Content and digital asset management systems

A content management system (CMS) is a database and tracking system for assets. Similar to how you use a public library of books, you check in and check out assets, and can use the system to find the assets you need. A digital asset management (DAM) system goes one step further and tracks the asset throughout its life cycle, as it is created and modified, and provides (generally) much more flexible access, while at the same time guarding the digital rights of the asset's creators. CMS and DAM systems are almost always written using a database system that helps you, your team, your company, and the asset's creator track and use content appropriately and consistently.

The goal of any DAM is to provide access to stills, video, text, and audio, with an eye toward long-term storage and preservation. A DAM is a large repository of information controlled by and shared within a community. Items are submitted to the repository, and key properties about the collection are entered by the submitter, such as title, author, publisher, abstract, and license. As such, a DAM is a CMS on steroids. Using the DAM, an editor reviews the information, and when it's approved, the item is added to the collection and becomes available for use. Each community publishes a web site, which catalogs items in its collections. Users can search the collections to find what they want and check out items.

Hundreds of CMS and DAM systems are available, both open source and commercially licensed. One DAM system that runs cross-platform and is open source is DSpace (http://www.dspace.org), which was jointly developed by MIT Labs and HP Labs. It runs on Linux and Windows platforms. DSpace has a web front end, which makes it easy to use. DSpace is useful for public assets as well as an internal management system. For an example, check out the Smithsonian Institution Digital Repository, Communities and Collections, at http://si-pddr.si.edu/dspace/community-list. An example of an issue of Inside Smithsonian Research can be found at http://hdl.handle.net/10088/2804.

While DSpace/Fedora is the granddaddy of open source DAM, a relative newcomer called ResourceSpace is now available. ResourceSpace (http://www.montala.net/resourcespace.php) is a web-based, open source DAM system, with the ability to render previews of Blender files when they are added, making it a great solution for Blender asset management. ResourceSpace is based on PHP and MySQL, so a completely open source LAMP (Linux, Apache, MySQL, PHP) architecture DAM that supports Blender is now possible, and it's easily customized.

Image sources

Where do you get elements to use in conducting your postproduction work? Here are some sources:

- **Stock photos**: Many sites offer stock images, either for free or licensed. For example, the images on iStockphoto (http://www.iStockPhoto.com) come with an alpha channel format for easy layering, or a background that makes it very easy to extract your relevant element. Chapter 11 discusses how to use Blender to key on a color or range of colors in an image so that you can extract the element you want. Alternatively, Chapter 5 provides step-by-step instructions on how to make a mask, so that you can extract just the portion of the image you want.

- **Digital cameras**: High-quality digital cameras and webcams can be used to capture and get source images and video. Generally, you want to take the image at the highest possible resolution (size) with the least compression. You can always sample downward in both size and compression quality to suit the needs of your project, but that is mostly a one-way street. Still images are used as references, or you can extract elements that might be of use in your current composition or a future project. These elements should be saved as textures in your library. Many compositors grab their digital camera and take photos of, well, just about everything, to study how light plays in a scene or to get great skies, fences, buildings, ornaments, or anything that might add decoration to their scenes.

> *Remember to keep a release form in your bag for any people you might shoot (when their faces are recognizable). I had to obtain release forms and property releases for each of the images used in this book that I did not personally take or make. There are plenty of sample release forms available on the Internet. I cannot give you one for liability reasons.*

- **Scanned images**: It is possible to digitally scan your images from film or a paper photograph. Low-cost flatbed scanners are readily obtained that can scan at 2400 dpi. Since a 35mm image is 1 inch, this means you can scan images at 2K resolution for a few hundred dollars. However, quality and price go hand in hand. Many cheap flatbed scanned images may require significant blurring and filtering (touch-up) in order to be useful for high-quality or professional purposes.

- **Hand-painted**: Blender features a mini-paint program, which is useful for adding an alpha channel to an image and for minor touch-ups. For more professional results, a program like the Gnu Image Manipulation Program (GIMP) (which is open source) or Photoshop is much more useful.

- **Render layers and passes**: A *render layer* is part or all of the 3D view that is passed to the compositor. Several render layers can be combined (possibly with image elements) in the compositor to create a finished composite image. Each render layer contains one or more render passes. Blender gives you access to individual pieces of rendering information through these passes, which can be composited and worked with individually, and then recombined for maximum control of the final product. For example, a render pass might contain a specific portion of an image, such as the shadows cast by objects or the reflections.

Disk space

You don't have enough disk space. I could say a lot more about that, but it won't change the fact that you need more. Therefore, be prepared to compromise on compression. The amount of disk space has a secondary ramification as well, and that is backups. A third ramification is loading speed and network traffic. Plan ahead. You've been warned. Thankfully, the price of high-capacity internal hard drives has come down, and a half-terabyte drive can be purchased for a few hundred dollars (which is amazing to old-timers like me who remember being astounded just a short while ago when Microsoft announced the TerraServer).

While disk space can be an issue with normal-sized images, it is *nothing* compared to the disk space that high-definition (HD) and high-dynamic range (HDR) video consumes. Thankfully, there are flavors of high-definition formats that can save you space, but if you get into any decent-sized video project, especially DV, be prepared to buy more.

The *Big Buck Bunny* source files requires 2GB for all the blend files and textures, but the movie itself (the Open EXR files, including composite passes) requires 223GB of disk space.

Summary

This chapter discussed Blender in the pipeline. Work needs to be planned and organized, and you need a method to your madness. Without a method, all you have is madness! A methodology is a document that lays out a standard workflow for each kind of job that you take on. Routes tailor the workflow based on the particular needs of a particular kind of job. You can mix and match different tools, both open source and commercially licensed, so long as they can interoperate through some sort of file exchange using a common, well-defined and supported format. As you work, you produce work products that you need to keep organized, either by using a practical file folder structure or with a CMS or DAM system.

Chapter 3

WELCOME TO BLENDER!

Using Blender successfully involves the following:

- Understand the concepts and features available in Blender.
- Translate the task at hand into how to do it in Blender.
- Develop the muscle memory to use Blender to do what needs to done.
- Implement the Blender features in a creative way to create the images.

This chapter will get you started by introducing the Blender UI. You'll experiment with some of its main features, and even create your first composite.

Starting Blender

You can start Blender in two ways:

- Simply double-click the Blender icon on your desktop.
- Run Blender from a command line, either from a terminal window or inside a batch file (called *batch mode* or *headless mode*). You supply command-line parameters (well documented at http://wiki.blender.org/index.php/ Doc:Manual/Render/Command_Line_Options) to tell Blender what to do.

When you start Blender from your desktop, you'll see the Blender splash screen, which displays the version of Blender that you are using (and should make you smile, too). This image vanishes when you move your mouse or press any key.

> The splash graphic for Blender changes with every release. Among the user community, there's a contest to design each release's splash graphic, so put your thinking cap on!

After starting Blender, on Windows systems, you'll see the console window. For all platforms, the main window is called the interface window, which the UI runs under the control of the operating system. Let's get started by exploring these two windows.

Getting information from the console window

On a Windows PC, once you have moved the mouse, causing the splash screen to disappear, you should at least check the console window. This is a text box that displays system messages, as shown in Figure 3-1. Linux and Mac OS X users will need to start Blender from a command line to see this window. Mac OS X users can also launch the Mac OS X Console application to view messages for this window. Linux users can start Blender from a terminal window.

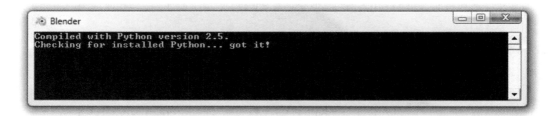

Figure 3-1. The console window gives warnings, feedback, and error meesages.

This is the window into the soul of Blender. When Blender has an issue, it will tell you in the console window. You cannot type into this window; it is only for Blender to talk to you.

When you first start Blender, the first line in the console window tells you how Blender was built. Normally, you want the build with Python, as you will be able to extend Blender using that scripting language. The second line tells you whether Blender was able to find your Python installation. If you have Python properly installed and have the PythonPath argument in your system variables, Blender can find it. If not, don't worry; Blender runs all functions and packaged scripts without it.

Python (http://www.python.org) is a very popular open source programming language. Python itself is free, and many editors, such as Eclipse (available free from http://www.eclipse.org) support plug-ins to use the Python syntax. For further information about getting and installing Python, consult http://wiki.blender.org/index.php/Doc:Manual/Introduction/Installing_Blender#Python.2C_the_Scripting_Language.

Working in the interface window

Blender is not a text-manipulation program, like OpenOffice.org Writer or Microsoft Word. Neither is it a graphics-manipulation program, like GIMP or Adobe Photoshop. Instead, it is an object-manipulation program that generates images. Depending on what you are doing with the objects, different kinds of windows allow you to do various kinds of tasks. Because of this behavior, Blender does not have what could be called a familiar UI. However, it does run inside a window—a Microsoft, Mac OS X, or Linux window.

While other applications use floating and overlapping windows, experience shows that you waste a lot of time just flipping and arranging them. Instead, Blender takes that big window, called the interface window, and divides it into window panes, as shown in Figure 3-2.

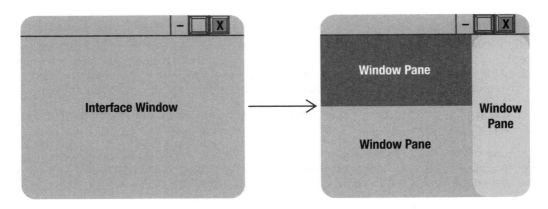

Figure 3-2. The interface window is divided into window panes.

As with any modern PC application, there are three controls in the interface window's header: minimize, maximize, and close. Closing the interface or console window quits Blender. Resizing the whole application window causes all the window panes to resize proportionally.

Each of these window pane arrangements is saved as a desktop or workbench, called a *screen layout* or simply a *screen*. The screen layout you use for your work will depend on the window panes and window types best suited for the task at hand. To pick a screen layout, select it from the user preferences header using the SR: selector, as shown in Figure 3-3. (The user preferences window is discussed in the next section.)

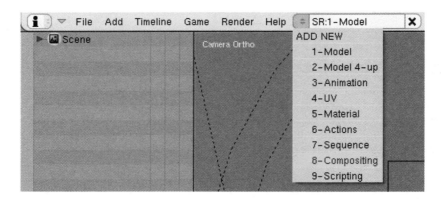

Figure 3-3. Selecting a screen layout

Window panes

Blender is very complex, in that it contains hundreds of functions and 16 different types of windows. But, it also contains some very simple and familiar types as well. One of these window types is a simple text editor, like Notepad, which allows you to make notes about your project. Another is an outliner, which is probably a familiar metaphor, in that it shows you an outline of what the scene contains.

Each operation or type of activity is done within a certain type of window, or window pane. You can have as many panes open as you wish within the Blender interface window.

Figure 3-4 shows a Blender window pane that contains a 3D view window. As indicated in this figure, a window pane has three components: the workspace in the middle, top and side borders, and a window header. The window header contains the following elements:

- Window type selector/icon (in Figure 3-4, a grid indicates this is a 3D view window type)
- Menu appropriate to that window type and mode
- Mode selector
- Tools unique to that window type and mode

The window in Figure 3-4 has its header at the bottom of the window pane. If you hover your mouse over a blank area of a window pane header and right-click, a pop-up menu allows you to change the header to be at the top of the pane, the bottom, or hidden (no header). If you hide a window pane header, you can restore it by hovering your mouse over the pane border, right-clicking, and selecting Add Header.

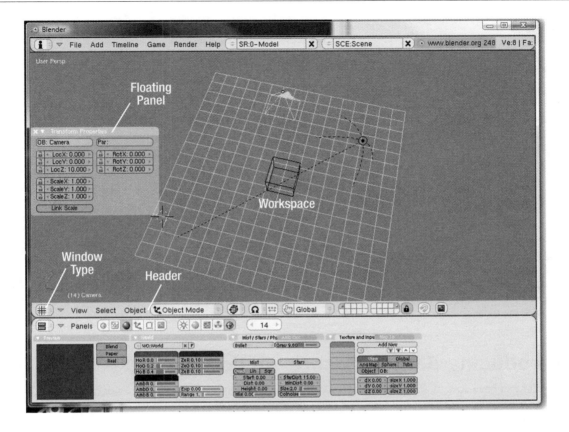

Figure 3-4. Components of a single window pane

If there are too many tools on a header to fit within the window width, you can collapse the menus by clicking the little collapse arrow to their left. You can also pan the header by dragging it left and right with your middle mouse button.

When working with a complicated scene, you may want to temporarily expand that window pane. Any window pane can be maximized to use up the full screen of the interface window by hovering your mouse cursor over that pane and pressing Ctrl+up arrow, Ctrl+down arrow, or Shift+spacebar. To restore a maximized pane, press any of those key combinations again.

To resize a pane, float your mouse cursor on the border, and, when your cursor changes to a double-headed arrow, click and drag to resize. For example, hover your mouse cursor over the line between the 3D view and an adjacent window pane, and your cursor will change to an up-down arrow. Click and drag your mouse up, and the 3D view workspace scales in that direction. If you have used the split-window feature of Microsoft Excel, this action will be familiar to you.

Right-clicking while your cursor is on the window pane border brings up a pop-up menu allowing you to split or merge the two windows, with one pane taking over the other pane (shown by a big arrow).

Move your mouse to indicate which window type should dominate and click. Play with this feature now, and then choose File ➤ New to reset the screen layout.

Mice and input devices

While Blender works well with tablets, such as those from Wacom, and supports pressure sensitivity, most of us mortals use a three-button scroll-wheel mouse. If you don't have one and are serious about using a graphical application, get one, or get a design controller (a 3D mouse) from Logitech. In this book, I assume that you have a three-button scroll-wheel mouse. This is a mouse with a left button, a right button, and a middle wheel that you can also click.

> *In this book, "click" refers to a left mouse button click. Right-click and clicking with the middle mouse button are noted specifically.*

Blender assumes that you know what you want to do when you do it, and every action has a specific outcome. In some applications, like Microsoft Word, you can just move the mouse around all day inside your desktop, and as long as you don't click anything, nothing really happens. This is not the case in Blender. Here, every action has a reaction. As you move your mouse cursor around inside the interface window, you'll notice the cursor changes every now and then, depending on what you are hovering over. Tooltips may pop up when you hover over a control.

Introducing Blender's core window types

After you have started and are working in Blender, you will be using different types of windows to do you work, and there are various arrangements (screen desktops) you can set up. For example, one of my favorite screens is shown in Figure 3-5.

The user preferences window pane is totally collapsed, and all that is showing of that window pane is a header. The second window pane has the 3D view window, which has a workspace (with a floating panel) and a header at the bottom. The window pane below it is a text editor, and its header is at the top of the pane. A screen layout philosophy is to keep frequently used options near the center of the display, to minimize mouse movement. Putting these headers adjacent like this keeps them toward the center of the display.

The outliner window pane is on the left, and a buttons window pane is on the right, and both of their headers are at the bottom of the window pane. The buttons window is nothing but panels, arranged vertically (four are expanded, and three are collapsed).

Any window pane within Blender can be set to show any of the 16 different window types. This section gets you started with the core window types, focusing on the features you'll use for compositing.

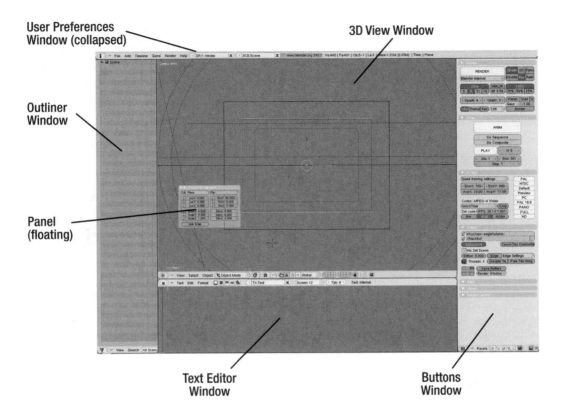

User Preferences
Window (collapsed)

3D View Window

Outliner
Window

Panel
(floating)

Text Editor
Window

Buttons
Window

Figure 3-5. Model screen layout

User preferences window

If you are used to working with another video-editing program, to some extent, you can configure
Blender to behave similarly. You customize Blender by making settings in the configuration panels in
the user preferences window.

At the top right of the interface window, you'll see an i icon, as shown in Figure 3-6. This is the user
preferences header. Move your mouse to the line between the i icon and the 3D view immediately
below it. It will change to an up-down arrow. Click and drag to pull down the user preferences window, like drawing down a window shade or projector screen, as shown in Figure 3-7.

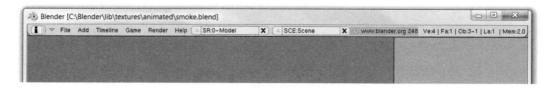

Figure 3-6. The top of the Blender interface window

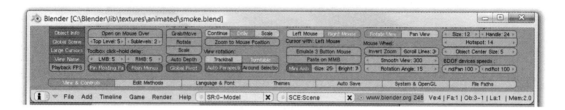

Figure 3-7. Dragging down the header to reveal the user preferences window

You can see seven tabs across the bottom of the screen: Views & Controls, Edit Methods, Language & Font, Themes, Auto Save, System & OpenGL, and File Paths. Each tab contains many settings related to its category. Here, we'll look at the View & Controls settings, which control how you interact with Blender.

Setting view and control preferences

On the View & Controls tab, you can change how the mouse behaves, adjust the window display, and modify other interface settings. If you are coming from another package, you might want to change the setups to match your muscle memory. If you are new to 3D and compositing tools, just leave the defaults as they are.

Eleven categories of views and controls are available. As you go through the following list, I encourage you to perform the actions to get comfortable with the user interface. If you mess up, you can always just reopen the file.

- **Display**: What kind of help and cursors are displayed in the window.
- **Menus**: Whether to open menus automatically on hover, and how long you need to hold down a button in 3D view to pop up the toolbox.
- **Toolbox click**: How long to hold down the mouse button before it's a "click."
- **Snap to grid**: When moving objects, whether they snap to displayed grid units (single or tenths).
- **View zoom**: Zoom by rolling the middle mouse wheel.
- **View rotation**: Rotate by clicking in the middle mouse wheel and moving the mouse.

- **Select with**: You normally select objects with the right mouse button, and use the left to position the 3D cursor. You can switch this, but the directions in this book and most resources use the default convention. Cursor with is a status message reminding you how to position the 3D cursor. Users of the antiquated two-button mouse can choose to emulate a two-button mouse by holding down the Alt key and the left mouse button. Mini-Axis shows and sets the size of your axis in the lower-left corner of the 3D view.

- **Middle mouse button**: When you click with the mouse wheel/middle button and move the mouse, normally the view rotates, whereas holding the Shift key while doing that will pan the view. You can reverse these actions by enabling Pan View.

- **Mouse wheel**: Rolling the mouse wheel up normally zooms in, but you can reverse that by enabling Invert Zoom. For Rotation Angle, using the even-numbered number keypad keys rotates the 3D view by the number of degrees set here.

- **3D transform widget**: On the 3D view header, there is a Maya-like widget to move an object or piece of an object (depending on the mode). If the widget is getting in your way, consider shrinking it using the settings here. You can also disable it by clicking the little pointing finger on the 3D view header.

- **6DOF**: Blender supports six degrees of freedom (6DOF) devices, like the 3D mouse from 3Dconnexion, as well as joysticks, game pads, and other input devices. You can set the device's sensitivity here.

Saving your preferences

When you make changes to your UI, save them by selecting File ➤ Save Default Settings or by pressing Ctrl+U (for User settings). This action writes out the current file and all its settings to a file called .B.blend in your Blender installation directory. But be careful! If your file has anything in it, like work in progress, it will become the new default whenever you choose File ➤ New. This is how Blender can start up with a camera and cube, for example.

> To save the .B.blend file, you must have write permissions to this folder. If you are not an administrator, Blender may not be able to save your customizations.

For compositing, I have changed my startup file from the generic one that comes with Blender to have my camera orthographic and pointing straight out onto a plane sized in the 4:3 aspect ratio. The material for the plane is initialized shadeless to map an image texture. I have also created several more screen layouts that are tailored to compositing. You can open this .B.blend file from the lib/scene folder on the accompanying DVD, and save it over the existing one in your installation directory (C:/ Program Files/Blender Foundation/Blender on my PC) simply by pressing Ctrl+U. The next time you start Blender or a new file, Blender uses that file (with the UI layouts) as the starting point.

3D view window

Blender has a rich history of being an awesome mesh editing tool in its own right, and it includes a ton of features to support heavy-duty modeling. In compositing, you won't be doing a lot of modeling (except for masks), so I won't detail those features here. However, many other compositing packages are essentially 2D, but Blender is a native 3D application, so working in 3D may be new to you. You do need to understand and be able to navigate in 3D space and Blender's axis system.

Orientation and perspectives

Within Blender, after you have loaded my B.blend and saved it as your default, choose the SR:2-Model 4-up screen layout, as shown in Figure 3-8. In this screen layout, you are peering into your 3D space through four perspectives, which are (going clockwise) top, camera, right side, and front. The name of the perspective is in the upper-left corner of the window. The axis orientation icon appears in the lower-left corner of the window, along with the name of the currently selected object.

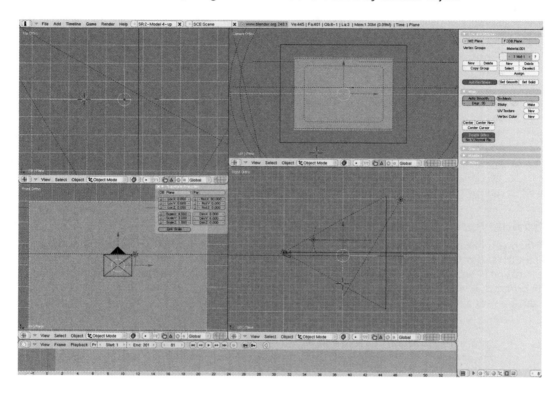

Figure 3-8. 4-up view. Each window pane's perspective is given in its upper left corner.

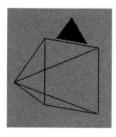

Figure 3-9. Virtual camera icon

Top view is really easy to visualize. Imagine you are a spy, like Tom Cruise in *Mission Impossible*, and you are suspended from the ceiling of a large ballroom, looking down on the room. That perspective is top view—from the top looking down. Camera view is equally easy to visualize. It's just like looking through the camera. The camera is in this 3D space and looks like Figure 3-9.

To visualize the front and right side view, imagine you are standing at the front doorway, looking into a big ballroom, or say you're shy, so you're standing against the right wall looking into the room. These views show those perspectives, again, all of the same space.

The plane should be selected. With your cursor in any of the 3D views, press G to grab it, and then move your mouse around. Observe how the plane moves, both in your view and in all the other views. Right-click to drop it back where it was, and repeat this in the other windows.

Now find the Transform Properties floating panel, and click the LocX, LocY, and LocZ controls to move the plane. As you can see, the location of the center of the plane is expressed as three coordinates. From front view, you would say that X is left/right, Y is toward/away from you, and Z is up/down. This is the native orientation of Blender, since many engineering students and simulations assume that Z is up/down. Other people like to work mostly in top view looking down, where X is left/right, Y is up/down, and Z is toward/away from you. It's your choice. What matters is that you will be layering and arranging things in a certain perspective, and the camera must be able to take a picture of it the way you want.

To change a perspective of a 3D view, use the number keypad for speed, as shown in Figure 3-10. You can press Ctrl with the number key for the view opposite to what is labeled in the figure; for example, press Ctrl+7 (on the number pad) to change to the bottom view (beneath looking up). You can also drag with the middle mouse button to rotate the view to get any perspective you wish, called a *user perspective*. In the lower-left corner of your 3D view is a colored axis orientation icon to help you see just which way is "up." Just remember RGB=XYZ—the red arrow indicates the X direction, green the Y direction, and blue the Z direction.

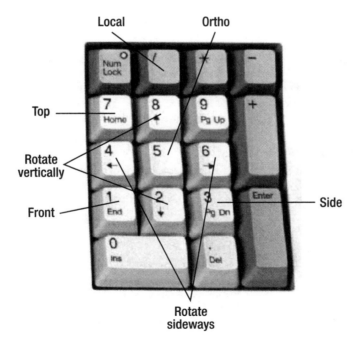

Figure 3-10. Keypad controls 3D view perspective. Press Ctrl with the key to get the opposite view.

View Properties panel

From the 3D view header, select View ➤ View Properties. A floating View Properties panel appears in the 3D view window, as shown in Figure 3-11.

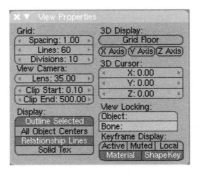

Figure 3-11. View Properties panel

This is a handy but often overlooked panel for positioning the 3D cursor exactly where you want it. I also use it to hide the grid and axis lines in 3D view, as they often clutter the display.

> To move any floating panel, simple click and hold on the header, move your mouse, and release the button to drop it in place—Blender's drag and drop. All panels have an X to put the panel away, and a little arrow to collapse the panel. Collapsing minimizes the panel from view, yet keeps it handy.

Transform Properties panel

The Transform Properties panel allows you to numerically control the selected object. For example, with the cube selected and your mouse cursor in the 3D view, press N to bring up the Transform Properties panel, which floats in the 3D view, as shown in Figure 3-12.

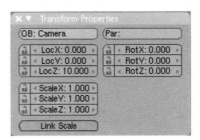

Figure 3-12. Transform Properties panel

Click the arrow on the right side of any field to increment the value in that field; click the arrow on the left side to decrement the value.

Click directly on the number in the LocX field; it will turn dark, and the number will have a red background. You can now enter any number you wish. When the whole number is highlighted, press 0 (zero) and Tab, and you should tab to the LocY field, again in edit mode. Press 0 and Tab repeatedly through the location and rotation fields. Enter 2 in the LocZ field. This puts the cube two units above your virtual desktop (if you prefer to think of your desktop at 0,0,0).

> *You can also choose* Object ➤ Clear/Apply ➤ Clear Location and/or Rotation *to reset the* Transform Properties *panel values to zero. The hotkey command for this is Alt+G.*

Background Image panel

When you are modeling or compositing over a live-action plate, it is very helpful to have a background image to use as a reference. For example, when I do compositing over live-action video, I use the video as a background image to a 3D View window in camera perspective, so that I can line up my computer-generated objects perfectly with the real-world video.

Each window pane that is a 3D view can have its own background image. This means you can have side, top, front, bottom, and so on perspective pictures of the object loaded, and use them to guide your modeling.

To load a background image, first look at the image and determine which perspective it is. If it is a front-on shot, go to your front ortho 3D view window pane and select View ➤ Background Image. This brings up a simple floating panel with one big blue button labeled Use Background Image. Click this button to enable the use of background images. Then click the Load button and navigate to the image, sequence, or video you want to use as the background image using the file browser (discussed shortly). Be sure to click Relative Paths in the header if you are using a library (discussed in Chapter 2). You can select a single image, a movie file, or the first image of a sequence. Then click Load Image. When the image is loaded, click the background of the window pane to activate and refresh the image display. Figure 3-13 shows a Background Image panel configured to show a video.

> *Once you use an image as a background, you can hide it by clicking the* Use Background Image *button again to disable the use of a background image.*

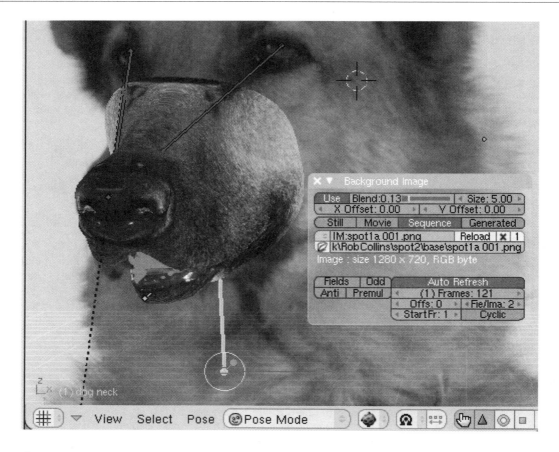

Figure 3-13. Background Image panel. Image courtesy Rob Collins Productions.

You choose to use any loaded image by using the yellow up-down arrow selector next to the IM field in the Background Image panel. To load an image sequence, locate the first Image, and then click Sequence in the panel. Additional sequence-related options will be displayed (as in Figure 3-13).

In total, the Background Image panel has a ton of options. Here's a quick rundown:

- Use: Display or hide the background image.
- Blend: The amount of which the 3D view background is blended in, having the effect of fading out the background image and thus making your computer-generated elements more visible.
- Size, X Offset, and Y Offset: Zoom and move the image off center, making it larger or smaller and enabling you to match up the image in computer-generated space with other reference images in other windows. Do not change this when compositing computer-generated objects with video. Change this only when you are modeling and need different-sized reference images to match up to one another (refer to a modeling book for more information).

- Still, Movie, Sequence, **or** Generated: This indicates the image type. With Still, a single still image, like a matte painting, is used, no matter which frame you are on in Blender. With Movie, any supported codec is used to show you the appropriate frame.

- IM: The name of the image. By default, it is taken from the file name, but you can change the name. For example, if the file name is DSC 0987.PNG, you might want to rename it to something a little more meaningful. This will not change the name of the actual file; it is only for your reference in Blender. As noted earlier, clicking the yellow up-down arrow to the left of IM allows you to switch between images that you have previously loaded anywhere in Blender (such as in the compositor).

- **File name**: This two-part field is a little file folder that changes a window to a file browser to allow you to pick a different image. The text area allows you to manually type in a file name. Note that you can use the full path, such as C:/Users/Work/MyImage.PNG, or a relative path, such as //.\shot01\0001.PNG to mean the images in a subfolder named shot01 under the folder where the blend file is saved. As explained in Chapter 2, use relative path specifications for images that are related to the project you are working on, and full specifications to point to common libraries of stock images.

- Image: This display line shows the size and internal channels available. The example in Figure 3-13 shows that I am working with an image that measures 1280×720 pixels, or 720p HD format.

- Fields **and** Odd: For interlaced video, enable Fields (Chapter 4 discusses interlaced video). When Fields is enabled on a sequence, every two images (from the movie file or image sequence) will be combined to give you a full-sized frame.

- Auto Refresh: When working with image sequences or movies, click Auto Refresh so that the proper image for that frame is displayed. Otherwise, the computer-generated object locations will not match up to the actual video frame that will be shown. You really need to do this! My voice of experience is shouting at you right now.

- Frames: Click to set the number of frames to use from the movie/sequence. The example in Figure 3-13 shows that I was working with a 4-second (121-frame) sequence. The current image being pulled from the sequence is shown in parentheses.

- Offs: While Frames defines the length of the strip, you may not want to start using the first frame of that strip. Your Blender frame 1 may start 2 seconds into the movie, for example, so you want to offset by 60 frames. Therefore, entering 60 in the Offs field will pull frame 61 as the first frame when you are on frame 1 in Blender, frame 62 from the movie as Blender frame 2, and so on.

- Fie/Img: When Fields is enabled, this defines how many physical frames from the movie or image should be interlaced to make one image. In the example in Figure 3-13, I was working with deinterlaced video, so 2 (the default) is the correct choice.

- StartFr : Sort of the inverse of Offset, this number is the frame number in Blender you want to start pulling images from the movie. So, if this were 30, the first image from the file would be shown while you were on Blender frames 1 to 30. *Then* the video would start playing as a background as you advanced Blender past that.

- Cyclic: Enable this to play the movie/sequence over after it has finished, as a video loop.

Render background buffer

When you do a simple composite over a still image, you don't need to get tied up using the sequencer or compositor. You can instead just tell Blender to use an image as the "sky" background, and the image generated is of whatever computer-generated objects you have in the camera and the background image you specify. A simple setting in the second line of the Output panel will cause Blender to use a still image as the background. When you use a still in the background of a shot like this, it is called a *matte*. Figure 3-14 shows an example of using the file spot1a 001.png located in a subfolder base under my blend file as the matte background.

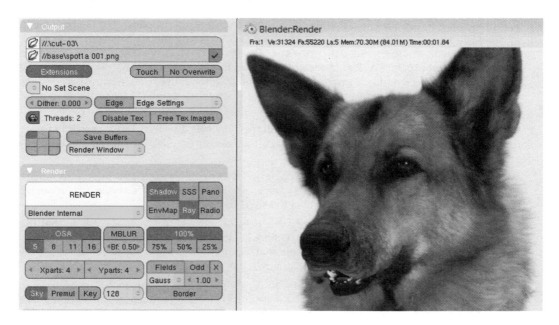

Figure 3-14. Output background buffer (Muzzle mesh by Philip Koreski)

Note that the check mark next to the file name in the Output panel must be enabled to use the image, and Sky must be selected in the Render panel for the image to be used. (The Render panel settings are discussed in Chapter 9.)

File browser window

The way you open a blend file or get assets into Blender is via the file browser and its close cousin, the asset browser, shown in Figure 3-15. For example, start a new Blender session and select File ➤ Open from the user preferences window header (at the top of your Interface window). One of your window panes will change to the file browser so you can locate the file.

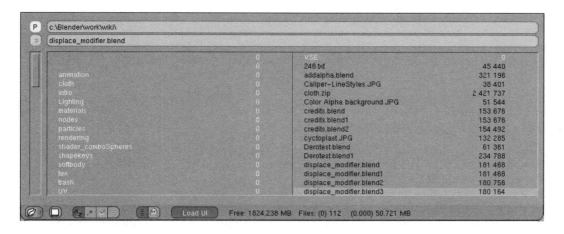

Figure 3-15. File browser window

The file browser window has many important components. Clicking the P takes you up a level to the parent directory. The yellow selector beneath the P pops up a list of most recently visited directories, and you can select one to jump there. The top line is the directory path. If you enter the name of a directory that doesn't exist here, Blender will ask, and then create that folder. The second line is the file name. In the working area of the window, a scrollbar on the left allows you to scroll through a long list. The body of the window lists breadcrumbs and then files. Clicking the .. breadcrumb goes up a directory level, and the . is there just as a placeholder. Each file type is recognized, and a color-coded square is shown in front of the file name. A yellow block beside a file name indicates that it is a blend file.

In the header, you can choose to make the window full-screen, and the next four buttons allow you to sort the file list by file name, extension, date/time, or size. The Pac-Man ghost icon in the header allows you to hide the breadcrumb files if you find them annoying.

Buttons window

The handy buttons window (right window pane in Figure 3-5) shows you the properties of an object or tool, and provides panels for changing them. There are so darn many properties for an object that they must be split across *contexts* (the first group of buttons) and the *subcontexts* (the next group of icons to the right), and then panels within that subcontext.

We won't work with the first two contexts, Game and Scriptlinks, in this book. The remaining four major contexts are generally related to workflow: Shading (discussed in Chapter 7), Object (discussed in Chapter 5), Editing (discussed in Chapter 5), and Rendering (discussed in Chapter 10).

A neat feature of Blender's buttons window panels is that all the text and controls inside them can be zoomed in or out. If you are using Blender on a high-resolution monitor and have great eyesight, you can make the panels very small. With your mouse cursor hovering in the buttons window, hold down the Ctrl key and drag with the middle mouse button up and down. Any panels, controls, and views zoom larger. For you folks who keep your right hand on the keyboard, you can hold the Ctrl key and then press the + or – keys on the number keypad.

This brings us to the major topic of getting and staying organized, and the complexity of dealing with potentially hundreds of objects floating around in 3D space. As you have seen, you can (and should!) name any object or class of thing, using a name that is meaningful to your project. Thankfully, Blender has many tools and facilities for helping you get and stay organized, and for associating objects with each other so that you can work on and select all logically related things simply, easily, and quickly.

Getting organized

A complex project may involve hundreds of computer-generated elements that need to be managed. Blender has quite a few facilities for helping you get and stay organized, so that you can focus on only the elements you want to work with:

- **Reusable assets**: You can define and reuse classes and objects.
- **Appending and linking**: Browse assets in blend files and append or link them to efficiently manage assets across many different files.
- **Layers**: Restrict viewing/rendering to only those elements of interest.
- **Groups**: Logically lump synergistic elements together to hide complexity.
- **Parenting**: Put child objects under control of a parent.
- **Scenes**: Major objects can be put into their own scene. Objects from one scene can be linked to another scene.
- **Object visibility**: Remove an object from the view and possibly the render pipeline, and filter object display through the outliner window.

Reusable assets

Blender is heavily object-oriented. Blender's reusable assets are classes and objects. An *object* is an instance of a *class*. My name is Roger, and despite accusations to the contrary by my kids, I am a human. My son's name is Alex, and I'm pretty sure he is human as well. Human is our class, but we are each different instances of that class. We both are reusable assets by my wife when the garage needs to be cleaned out.

Now let's see that in action in Blender.

Cloning assets

Start up Blender, and if you haven't done so already, please choose File ➤ Open from the user preferences window header. One of your windows will change to a file browser. Use it to find and open the \lib\scene\B.blend file from your DVD. Now press Ctrl+U to save this as your default. This blend file has common compositing layouts that I use quite frequently, which are used in the examples in this book.

In the main Model screen, you have a projection plane that you will be using to load image elements. Right-click the plane to select it. In the buttons window, on the Link and Materials panel of the Edit buttons (F9) context, note the two fields shown in Figure 3-16.

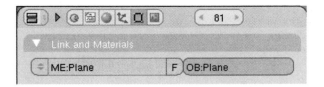

Figure 3-16. Links and Materials panel for a mesh object

This tells you that the selected object is a mesh (ME:) and its name is Plane. The object that is selected in 3D view is an object (OB:), which is also named Plane. In our analogy, that would be like naming your daughter Human. Change OB: Plane to OB: Becca (as I named my daughter). Now, with your cursor in 3D view, click next to the plane to put your 3D cursor there. You should be in object mode (the mode is shown in the 3D view header). Press the spacebar, and then select Add ➤ Mesh ➤ Monkey. A monkey mesh will be added at the location of your cursor, and you will be put in to edit mode. Press Tab to leave edit mode. Now that the monkey is selected, the Link and Materials panel should look like Figure 3-17.

> *You can also just click either mouse button, hold it still for a half second, and the tool-bar menu will pop up. This gesture is like poking someone to get their attention.*

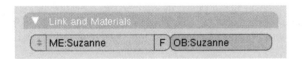

Figure 3-17. Link and Materials panel for a different mesh

You know that the selected object is still a mesh, since the field begins with ME:. Click the up-down selector on the left side of the ME: field. This pops up a list of meshes that have been used in this file, as shown in Figure 3-18. Select Plane from the list. Instantly, the Suzanne shape goes away and is replaced with a plane. Now, both the Becca and Suzanne objects share the same mesh. If you edit or change the plane mesh on one of the objects, you will see that it changes on both. Cloning assets in this way can save you a lot of time.

Figure 3-18. Cloning Suzanne to become a plane

If you examine the ME: *selection list again, you will see a little zero next to* Suzanne *in the drop-down list. This means the data block is currently unused and will be completely discarded if you close the file or quit Blender right now.*

You will also notice now a 2 in the ME: selector and an F to its right. The 2 means that there are two users of this data block, as a visual alert to you. If you make changes to this data block here, it will have an effect on the other one as well. If you want to make changes to this data block without affecting how it is used by the other object, you can click the user number. Doing so makes a new, separate single-user copy of the data block for the current object. This new copy is not linked to any other objects. If you want to be able to keep a data block with your file, it must be used by at least one object. If you don't have a use for it now, but want to keep it around anyway for later, you can click the F button to add a "F"ake user.

For practical use in compositing, you may use, for example, six mesh planes as screens to project photographic elements into your composite, say, of a tree. Rather than creating six separate meshes and texturing each of them with the image of the tree, simply make one and clone it five times. The hotkey to clone is Shift-D; the object is duplicated—move your mouse and click to drop it in place.

Appending and linking assets

Whenever you work with assets in Blender, you will use the file browser window (see Figure 3-15). If you are using the file browser to open a blend file, you may or may not want to use the user preferences that are saved in the asset file. If you only want to work on the assets inside and preserve your current UI settings, disable the Load UI button. This is useful if you are working with assets provided by someone else, and you would rather not deal with their personalized configuration of Blender.

The file browser window is also used to inspect and obtain assets from a blend file. With your mouse in any reasonably sized window, press Shift+F1 to activate the asset Append/Link function. As before, you use the file browser to find a blend file. When you click the blend file, you dive into the file to reveal the kinds of assets saved in that file. Figure 3-19 shows an example of the browser window delving into a blend file.

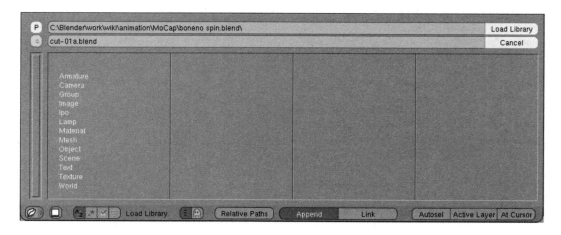

Figure 3-19. Asset browser window

Try navigating to the Peach/production/chars/rabbit.blend file on your DVD. If you want to reuse an object (OB:), such as the bunny mesh from the *Big Buck Bunny* (BBB) file, simply click Object and select the object named rabbit. There may be many child objects that make up the rabbit object, and you may want to select them instead. When you click Load Library, the selected assets are either appended (a clone copy is made and put into your current blend file) or merely linked, depending on which option you have selected in the header. A link allows the original owner to update the original file with the latest version, and then when you open your file, your work is refreshed with the latest updates automatically.

When you append a parent object, all the child objects and related items are brought in as well (parent and child objects are discussed shortly, in the "Parenting" section). Using our rabbit example, you would see that the rabbit itself, its materials, armature, fur settings, (particle systems), and so on are also brought in.

> *The BBB asset files use groups to group many of the complex elements together, so check the* Group *asset class first. Groups are discussed in the upcoming "Groups" section.*

Layers

A whole scene works together, and a complex scene will have many elements that all need to align in order to look right. However, you may want to work on one or a few related elements at any one time. Blender provides a means of displaying a very complex scene in manageable chunks by allowing you to assign an object to up to 20 layers. Every object in the scene belongs to one or more layers.

> *What Blender calls a* layer *is very different from what is a layer in image-editing programs like Photoshop, Illustrator, and GIMP. In those packages, an element is assigned to a layer, and then those layers are stacked up. Blender has an infinite number of those kinds of layers, because objects are "layered" by being positioned in 3D space relative to the camera, and there is no (what I consider to be) clumsy interface for stacking layers. In Blender, a layer is simply an organizational tool for relating similar objects together for a logical purpose.*

When you create an object, it is automatically assigned to the active layer (the last layer you selected to display). To see or change which layers an object belongs to, select the object and press M in the 3D view window, or select Object ➤ Move to Layer from the 3D view header. You will see a pop-up window like the one in Figure 3-20. By convention, the layers are numbered 1 to 10 across the top, and 11 to 20 across the bottom. They are divided into groups of five just for ease of visually distinguishing them.

Figure 3-20. Layers pop-up window

You can then click (and Shift-click) to select layer(s) to which you want the object to belong. These layer buttons are toggles, so to remove an object from a layer, just click that layer again. An object must belong to at least one layer.

On the 3D view header, the layer panel is repeated, but with a slight twist. If there are objects on a layer, a small dot appears in the layer button. To select only a single layer, click it. To select additional layers, Shift-click the button. To deselect a single layer, Shift-click it. In other words, the button is a toggle.

While in object mode, if you press a number key at the top of your keyboard, you select that layer (0 gives you layer 10). Hold Alt and press the number for layers 11–20. The tilde key (~) selects all the layers. Just like Shift-clicking, holding down the Shift key while pressing number keys selects multiple layers. These keyboard commands also work with the layer pop-up control (Figure 3-20).

Layers are an incredibly powerful way to organize your work. Start planning which elements you are going to put on which layers as soon as you start your project.

Over the years, I have developed a set of informal standards for the use of layers, as shown in Table 3-1. These conventions handle pretty much any size project, big or small.

Table 3-1. My Layer Assignments

Layer	Objects
1	Lead actor, main elements
2	Supporting actor, other elements
3	Supporting crew (background actors)
4	Particles and effects (vortex, wind)
5	Cloth
6	Main stage
7	Main backdrops and panels
8	Main props (tables, chairs)
9	Little props, fillers, decorations, trappings
10	Cameras, lights
11	Lead actor's armature
12	Supporting actor's armature
13	Crew armatures
14	Alternative clothing
15	Mesh work in progress (WIP)
16	Different stage setup, dimensions
17	Different backdrops
18	Big props that clog up the scene
19	Props WIP
20	Additional lighting

I have also supplied a Layer Manager script to help you manage your layers. This script, written by BlenderArtists user Mariano, allows you to name and lock layers, as well as save standard layer-naming conventions for easy reuse. From the lib/scripts folder on your DVD, copy the libmgr.py script into your scripts folder. This script should be part of your user defaults. To activate it, use the Scripting screen layout, or just change a window pane to a scripts window by selecting Scripts ➤ Misc ➤ Layer Manager.

Figure 3-21 shows the Layer Manager script UI. In this figure, you can see a portion of the 3D view header above the scripts window. Notice how the Layer Manager has layers 2, 9, 10, and 12 selected. As they are selected in the scripts window, they are selected in the 3D view as well. Notice that in the 3D view header's layer buttons group, layers 2, 9, 10, and 12 are selected. These two windows work together.

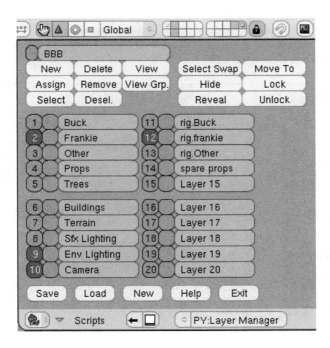

Figure 3-21. Layer Manager UI

The best available user manual for this script can be found through the scripts library wiki or by visiting the BlenderArtists forum, currently thread 65719 (http://blenderartists.org/forum/showthread.php?t=65719). Briefly, you can name the layers, and save these names to a standard template. Other functions allow you to swap all the objects from one layer with another, and select all the objects on a layer with one click.

Groups

Often, groups of objects work together to accomplish a unit of work or achieve an effect. You can expand groups to show the inner workings, or collapse them to hide their complexity and work with them at a higher abstract level of consciousness. Like integrated circuits, groups build up a lot of little parts into a higher-functioning mechanism.

Just remember that **gr**een is for **gr**oups. Groups are shown in green-bordered boxes. Groups can be appended and linked as a unit across projects. There are many kinds of groups in Blender, and some are relevant to compositing. Groups of compositor nodes are discussed in Chapter 12. Groups of video strips (called *metastrips*) are discussed in Chapter 13.

To see how groups work, let's make a group from the Camera, Plane, and Suzanne objects. Go ahead and unclone Suzanne so her mesh shape is back to being a monkey. Shift-select each of these three objects in 3D view, and then select Object ➤ Group ➤ Add to New Group. You should see all of them change to have a green outline. In the buttons window, change to the Object-Object context, and in the Object and Links panel, you should see a GR: field. Change that to Compo, as shown in Figure 3-22.

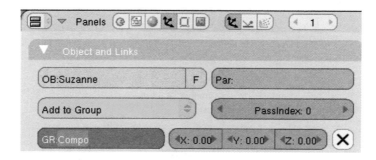

Figure 3-22. The object is a member of group Compo.

Now, if you save this file in your library, as perhaps Compositing.Blend, you will find it super easy to import these three elements together as a group in one easy step. (Importing is discussed in the "Importing elements" section a little later in this chapter.)

Parenting

Along with grouping as a way to associate like things together, *parenting* provides a way to establish a movement relationship for a bunch of elements. In a parent-child arrangement, when you move the parent, the child moves with it (just as in real life). If you rotate the parent, the child rotates with it, but keeps its offset (distance and angle) relative to the parent.

Making parent-child relationships is done in the 3D view window. You can create a parent-child relationship at one of two levels: at the object level and the vertex level.

To create a parent-child relationship at the object level, select Object Mode in the 3D view header. Select the child by right-clicking it. If you wish to make many elements fall under a parent, Shift-select them as well. Next, Shift-select the parent object, and then press Ctrl+P or select Object ➤ Parent from the 3D view header.

Parenting objects to a vertex is useful in animation when you want to tie the location of an element to the deformation of another mesh. For example, you can make a boat "float" on the water. As the water mesh is deformed—by a bone, a modifier, a shape key, a fluid simulation, or whatever—the boat will move up and down in the waves, or move downstream by however that vertex moves. Another use is moving the eyes, eyebrows, and lips of a cartoon "face," such as one on a soda can. As the soda can bends and stretches, these features move, even though the soda can itself does not move.

> *Parent your key light to the camera, just like mounting the key light on a frame to a real camera. I like to position the key just slightly above and to the left of camera, facing the direction of the camera.*

To create a parent-child relationship at the vertex level, select any children and Shift-select the parent, press Tab to enter edit mode of the parent, and then select the controlling vertex. Next, press Ctrl+P or select Mesh ➤ Vertices ➤ Make Vertex Parent.

To destroy a parent-child relationship, select the child that wants to move out on its own and press Alt+P or select Object ➤ Parent ➤ Clear Parent from the 3D view.

> *In Blender, holding down Alt while pressing a key generally undoes whatever the key did originally. In this case, pressing P in object mode establishes a parent-child relationship, and pressing Alt+P destroys it.*

Scenes

Scenes are another way to apportion a very complex overall shot. You can spread the objects across multiple Blender scenes, and then either chain them together as sets or bring them together in the compositor or sequencer. Linked and set objects cannot be modified in the target scene; they can be modified only in the scene where the objects are local.

Adding scenes

To add a scene, locate the scene selector (SCE:) in the user preferences header and select ADD NEW, as shown in Figure 3-23. Blender will give you four choices: Empty, Link Objects, Link ObData, and Full Copy. An empty scene is just that, devoid of any objects giving you a fresh clean slate. Full Copy starts you out with what you have already, allowing you to build on or modify what you have done. Choose Empty for now. Your scene is automatically named Scene.001, but you can rename it.

Figure 3-23. Choosing to add a new scene

Every scene can have totally different render settings, objects, lighting, frame rates, and so on. Every scene must have a camera. To add one, in your empty 3D view, press the spacebar and choose Add ➤ Camera. Add a lamp, and then some other object, and move it in front of the camera. Press F12, and congratulations! You now have two scenes in your blend file. I will show you how to get the images from each scene into the compositor in Chapter 11 and into the sequencer in Chapter 13.

Linking scenes

What's really cool is that a scene can function as a backdrop, or set, for other scenes. The set linker is located in the scene render Output panel, as shown in Figure 3-24. For our example, choose Scene. In your 3D view, you will see gray outlines of everything in that scene: the light, plane, Suzanne, and a redundant camera, which you can ignore. The objects are going to be in the render of your scene, and cast light and shadows and such.

Figure 3-24. Using a scene as a set

Object visibility

Objects can be hidden from view. In 3D view object mode, a hidden object is not shown or rendered, even if it is on an active layer. In the sequencer, hidden strips are shown, but are "muted," meaning that they do not participate in the render pipeline. In 3D view edit mode, vertices (and thus parts of an element) can be hidden.

You hide objects by selecting them and pressing H (for Hide) in their respective window (3D view or the sequencer). To make the object visible again, press Alt+H. In the sequencer, hiding (muting) works for video and audio strips. (Of course, you can always just turn the volume down to zero for audio strips.)

Muting is not the same as making a strip black by, for example, turning its brightness to zero. A blackened strip steak tastes great, but a blackened video strip is just charred and will darken the result.

The other way to control object visibility is through the outliner window, shown in Figure 3-25. This window provides an easy way to limit the view in its window to objects on the selected layers, the active layer, or objects on the same layer as the selected object. This provides a quick way to filter out objects that you are not concerned with at that time.

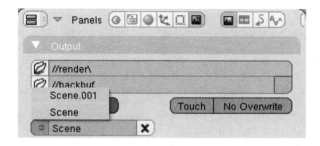

Figure 3-25. Outliner window shows assets and grouping/organization

Clicking the little arrows on the left expand or collapse a tree. The tree is the parenting or ownership lineage of the object. On the right, clicking the eye icon hides/unhides an object in the 3D view, allows or disallows you to select it, and hides/unhides it from the renderer. You can also use the hotkeys V (Visible), S (Selectable), and R (Renderable) on selected outliner elements to toggle those properties.

You can filter what you want to see using the selector in the outliner window header:

- All Scenes: **The entire file**
- Current Scene: **Everything in this scene**
- Visible Layers: **Only what is showing in 3D view**
- Groups: **Multiple objects grouped together into a logical unit**
- Same Type: **Only objects that are the same type as the selected object**
- Selected: **Only those objects that are selected**
- Active: **The last-selected, active object**
- Sequence: **Strips in the sequencer**

Right-click any element in the outliner window, and it is selected (highlighted in 3D view). A great use for the outliner is simply to find something. If you've moved something, or hidden it on some forgotten layer, use the search function in the outliner (press the F key) to find the object. Search works on partial names as well.

Importing elements

One way to get elements (or groups of elements) is to import them from another blend file or from a file created by another application. From a blend file, you usually append an object, which, in compositing, will be a mask or other computer-generated element. Let's cover importing from blend files, since that's the simplest, and then move on to importing elements from interchange files.

Importing from the current blend file

You may want to use the same element from another scene within the same blend file. This is very easy to do.

As you learned earlier, you can have multiple scenes within the same blend file. If you've been following along, you should have two scenes now. Switch back to Scene using the SCE: selector in the user preferences window, and select the plane. Now select Object ➤ Make Links ➤ To Scene and select Scene.001 from the list. Switch back to your Scene.001, and voilà! There is a clone of the projection plane. If this were an element such as a girl holding a balloon, she would be in both scenes and their composition.

You may notice that no Shading, Object, or Editing panels are available for this object. You cannot change this object, but you can move it around, scale it, and place it wherever you want. If you ever do want to make any changes, you must make a local copy via Object ➤ Make Local ➤ Selected Objects and Data.

Appending or linking from another blend file

Similar to linking an object across scenes, you can link and append objects across blend files. As you saw earlier in this chapter, using the file browser, you can bring in either the object itself or just the pattern (template) for the object.

Select File ➤ Append or Link. In the file browser window that appears, navigate to the lib\textures\ abstract folder, and notice that the Blender logo.blend file is bright white with a yellow box. Click the file name and observe that you have just drilled into the file. Also notice that the header has changed a bit from the standard file browser header, because this is actually an asset browser, as shown in Figure 3-26.

Click Object, and then click Blender Logo. The phrase Blender Logo should be copied into the second line of the asset browser (the Cancel line). Click Load Library, and the asset browser will close, and you will see the Blender logo in your scene. This is a complete copy of the object, including any children and the materials, because Append is selected in the header. You can place it in front of the projection plate, and even change its colors and shape if you like.

If you instead choose Link in the header, a clone of the object will be brought in. You will not be able to recolor or edit it (which is a good idea for corporate logos, so you don't accidentally change them from their standard). Linking links the object itself, and not any other children. In our example, the Blender Logo object is only the outside area, and the blue ball is the CurveCircle object. While Append brings them both in when the parent is selected, linking brings only the specific element requested. Linking is used extensively in more complex Blender productions like *Big Buck Bunny* and *Elephants Dream*, as an artist works on the original file independently of work being done by others.

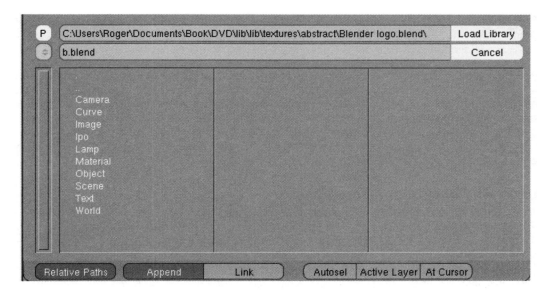

Figure 3-26. Asset browser peers inside a blend file.

When you open a blend file that has links, Blender reaches into any linked files and pulls in the *latest version* of the objects you have specified. This is a key difference between Append and Link: Append copies the object into your file and breaks any traceability, whereas Link preserves that traceability. If the object is updated by its author, you automatically get the update.

You will notice that you cannot even move a linked object, since its position may be important relative to other elements in the file, such as the precise location of the swoosh over the word "Nike." If you do want to be able to move it around in your scene, select Object ➤ Make Proxy. You will not be able to change the color or shape of the object, but you will be able to put it wherever you want in the scene.

> *Logos have a required area of isolation; they cannot overlay other elements or have other elements interfere with them. Check your legal team for more information about rules regarding compositing logos and other trademarks. Be sure to include the registered or trademark symbols on registered or company trademarks.*

Importing from another application

When you select File ➤ Import, you see a long list of interchange files that have import routines. These import routines are written in Python, and may work with only certain versions of the generating application and a certain version of Blender.

For example, suppose a team member has designed a logo in Illustrator and saved it as a Scalable Vector Graphic (SVG) file. I have supplied two SVG files on the accompanying DVD, in the lib/textures/ abstract folder: Olympic flag and Blender logo. Let's get them into Blender.

First, start with a clean slate. In 3D view, press A to select all of the objects in the scene, and then press X to delete them. To import a file from another application into Blender, select File ➤ Import ➤ Paths and choose the Inkscape SVG format. One of your windows will change to a file browser. Navigate to the file. Various formats have some import options. For the SVG file, the defaults should be fine. After it imports (check the console window for any issues or status), you should see the object in your 3D view. You can then rotate or scale the object, either manually (using the G, then R or S keys) or by editing the values in the properties panel.

Importing images as elements

To import an image as an element, you must first create the projection plane object by selecting Add ➤ Mesh ➤ Plane. You then scale the plane into the proper aspect ratio to match that of the image (assuming you do not want to distort the image). I find that simply entering the X:Y ratio (for example, 4 and 3) into the ScaleX and ScaleY fields in the properties panel is easiest. Then arrange the plane in 3D space to "layer" it. Finally, apply the image to the plane as a texture (this process is described in detail in Chapter 7). If the image has an alpha channel, just the opaque areas will appear in your 3D view, as shown in the example in Figure 3-27.

Figure 3-27. Alpha-mapped image element

Your first composite in 30 minutes or less

Your task is to take an image of a road sign at the entrance to the great state of Mississippi and composite some alternate slogans into it for a grant presentation. The road crew took a picture of a current one, which you can find on your DVD in textures/world/roadsign.jpg.

Fire up Blender with my B.blend file as the default. and load that welcome sign to Mississippi as a background image into the camera perspective window pane. With the Blend at 0, you get a full-color image on your monitor.

You can delete or hide the lights in the scene, as you do not need them. Select them using the outliner, and click the eye icon to hide them.

The first task is to figure out the orientation of the original camera relative to the main object you will be masking—in this case, the road sign. You need to work in three dimensions here. Scale the plane down and move it so that its height matches the *middle* of the sign. At this point, switch to solid view using the draw type selector in the 3D view header, just to the right of the mode selector. The plane is straight on and square, but in the picture, the sign is tilted away from you. Click the right RotZ arrow once to give the plane a 10-degree rotation. In solid view now, the gray plane should look like, well, like someone vandalized the sign with gray paint! Notice that since you are using a perspective camera, as the plane tilts away from you, the left side gets taller while the left side gets shorter.

Now that you know the plane matches the orientation of the overall sign, you can scale it down to just cover the current tag line. Press S, then Z, and then move your mouse toward the center of the screen to shrink it down vertically. Press G and then Z to grab and move it down to cover the line, centered on the line. Repeat as necessary so that it just covers the text letters, height-wise. Monitor the transform properties—a ScaleY of 0.15 is good. Notice that even though you said Z in 3D space, the plane's dimension is Y. A plane is infinitely thin and can be scaled only in the X and Y directions. Relative to the plane, X is left/right, and Y is up/down.

Now adjust in the X dimension, scaling and grabbing so that it covers the text width-wise. Your camera view should now look like Figure 3-28.

Figure 3-28. Aligned Mask

If you are completely lost by this point, you can cheat and open the tut\roadsign. blend file.

Now you want to shade this mask to match the main color of the sign. Considering the lighting (which is overcast) and texture for the sign (a flat blue color), a simple shadeless material will work. Add a material by switching the buttons window to Shading Material context. in the plane's Shading properties, click the color swatch for the diffuse color (the Col button swatch). In the pop-up color picker applet, click the eyedropper. Your cursor changes to an eyedropper. Use it to sample the sign's blue color (your background image Blend factor should be 0 to get an accurate sample), and then press Enter. The Material panel should look like Figure 3-29.

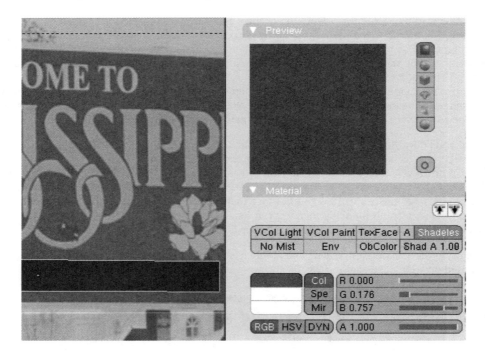

Figure 3-29. Shaded mask

If you are in shaded view with a Blend factor of 0, it should already look like there is no tag line at all. Press F12 to get a test render.

Use the image as a background buffer by clicking the file folder icon in the Output Backbuf field, finding the file, and enabling it by checking it (see Figure 3-14). Pressing F12 should give you a render that looks like Figure 3-30.

So, now you add the text. Poke the 3D view and select Add ➤ Text. A text object (with a default value of Text) will appear in your 3D view, in edit mode. Press Backspace four times to erase those letters, and type in . . . hmmm . . . something better than "It's Like Coming Home." Type in your text, and then press Tab to exit edit mode. Position it just in front of the plane, working i 3D Views to adjust the location and rotation to match the mask, but just in front of the mask between the mask and camera. Press F12 or select Add ➤ Render Current Frame, and you have it!

> *For extra credit, read Chapter 7, and then give your composite a nice, happy, orange shadeless material that matches the existing tagline color.*

You have the background buffer image, a blue mask, and text as elements in your final composition, as shown in Figure 3-31. In the Roadsign.blend file, the mask is on layer 1, and the text is on layer 2. The original plane that masked the whole sign is on layer 11.

Figure 3-30. Test render of mask

Figure 3-31. New tagline for the road sign

Saving blend files

If you have Save Versions set to a number higher than 1 in the Auto Save section of the user preferences, every time you save, Blender will trickle up the backups and save your blend file. For example, if you have triple backups specified, every time you manually save your blend file, Blender will
copy Roadsign.blend2 over Roadsign.blend3, Roadsign.blend1 over Roadsign.blend2, and
Roadsign.blend over Roadsign.blend1, and then save your current work over Roadsign.blend. In
this way, Roadsign.blend has your most recent save, and Roadsign.blend1 your next most recent,
and so forth.

When you save, Blender does confirm if you want to save over your file, even if it is making backups for
you. You can open these .blendx files at any time with Blender; they are not saved in any kind of a compressed or different format from a normal blend file. If, after saving, you discover that you have made
some terrible mistake and wish to use a backup, you can simply open the backup file (such as Roadsign.
blend2) and save it as Roadsign.blend. Then each time you save, the new line of backups will trickle up.
You can also rename the files manually using your file system, for example, by deleting the Roadsign.
blend file and changing the file name extension from Roadsign.blend2 to Roadsign.blend.

The first part of a blend file is the version of Blender that was used to save the file. This way, if the internal file format changes, Blender can automatically convert the file to its new structure. This way, Blender maintains backward-compatibility to a very large degree.

Summary

In this chapter, we explored Blender from a hands-on perspective. You learned a lot about the raw capability of Blender, including how to navigate within screens and scenes. You explored the UI and saw how things are set up to work, and how you can customize Blender to your liking. We learned about the facilities Blender has to manage and organize a very complex project involving hundreds of objects and image elements. Finally, you created some objects and made your first simple composite. Congratulations!

In the next chapter, we'll look at the formats in which you can render your images and also explore the world of video, since I know you're anxious to move on from still images.

Chapter 4

FORMATS

With compositing and workflow, your main work product is an image or video, and you also hope that it's an asset that can be used not only in your current project, but also reused (licensed) in the future. Therefore, your work must be saved in some format that preserves its quality, while balancing the need for storage space with ease of access and future referencing. Unfortunately, asking a group of experts which format is best suited to these tasks will probably produce a variety of answers, each directed toward a different standard. The reason we have so many different standards for the same thing is really a story of progression and grappling with increasing complexity. By tracing standards from their beginnings through to the present, you will be able to project into the future to understand emerging standards and select standards that are most applicable to your projects.

Your goal in compositing is to create a moving image of beauty that will be admired long after you have gone on to bigger and better things. As you work, you create work products that mark your efforts. As discussed in Chapter 2, *work product* is a general term for something that is produced from your workflow by an application. Your work products are saved in a file in some kind of format (with a tinge of nostalgic regret, I am predicting the demise of cellophane). A work product is either the main result or intermediate information that is probably needed later on in the process. In compositing, you need to be concerned about several kinds of work products:

- Assets, which are things you can open natively with your application
- Interchange, which are things you can import into your application that were produced by a different application
- Images, which are pictures, composed of small dots called *pixels*, arranged in rows and columns, and compressed by an image codec
- Video, which is a sequence of images in a single file, compressed by a video codec
- Audio, which is sound, compressed by an audio codec
- Containers, which are video and audio in one happy file

Each of these is covered in this chapter.

Asset file formats

Even if you are already a wizard on digital image formats, you probably don't know about the format of the asset file. Different packages (like Blender) save your 3D work in an internal data file format. As you've learned, with Blender, your work is saved in a blend file. For example, if your project file name is called SodaCan, then when you save your file in Blender, a file called SodaCan.blend is created. (Yes, file extensions can now have more than three characters—a little known and underutilized fact.)

Each 3D application saves your work in a native format that is totally different from the native format used by another application. Some applications publish their file format, like Blender, and make the specification available for other applications to use. Others make their format proprietary and do not release information about their format; in fact, they may prohibit reverse-engineering to determine what the format is. A vendor may not choose to read in another application's format just for competitive reasons. For example, 3ds Max saves its work in a proprietary 3ds file format. Blender cannot directly open a 3ds file, and 3ds Max will not open a blend file.

Thankfully, a number of file converter scripts ship with Blender. These programs are written in Python and can be run from the scripts window or by using the File ➤ Import (and Export) menu options.

Since many non-Blender asset file formats are proprietary, or poorly documented, and the format itself is subject to change without notice, there is limited support for extracting information from a file created by another application. One application may represent an object very differently from what Blender needs to properly define it. Since the import/export program is written by someone other than the format owner, and format changes are kept secret, there will always be a lag or limited functionality in which assets can be extracted and how reliable the script is.

Figure 4-1 shows this list of file formats supported by Blender.

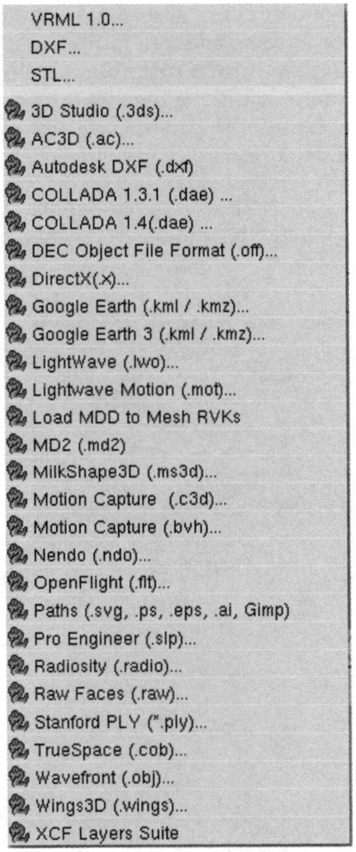

Figure 4-1. Imported object formats

Interchange file formats

Chapter 2 talked about a pipeline of different products that are created by a workflow. The issue is that each product saves its results in a different file format.

So, you're thinking, "Can I even use 3ds Max and Blender on the same project in my pipeline?" The answer is yes, it is possible to do certain kinds of work in one package and hand off the results to another. The way you get assets from one package to another is through an *interchange format* or *import/export* conversion.

Figure 4-1 shows some possible interchange formats that Blender can read in, at least partially, by executing an import script. To be a great exchange, Blender needs to have paired import and export scripts that process the same file format with similar capability, and the file format must either be usable by both applications or something that can be passed on to the next application in the workflow.

Interchange formats fall in a range between simple, open, and free to complex, proprietary, and licensed. The Collada file format is an example of an open and free format, as is the blend file format. On the other hand, the FBX format is a complicated format that costs money to obtain. As of this writing, Autodesk, which owns many 3D applications, is pushing the FBX format as an interchange format, at least between its products. Currently, because of the complexity and cost of the FBX format, Blender does not support all of its concepts and features.

A recent release of Autodesk 3ds Max has a Blender MultiChannel file option, as shown in Figure 4-2, which Blender calls the multilayer format. Hopefully, this multilayer format will gain popularity as Blender integrates into the workflow of more shops.

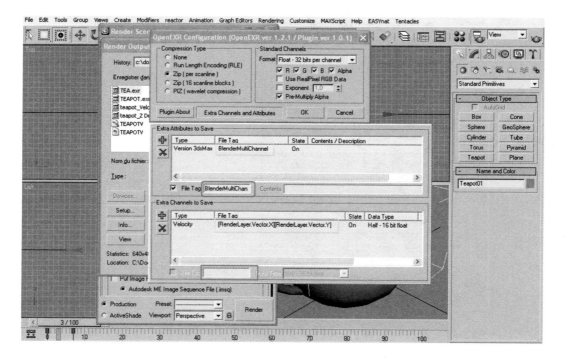

Figure 4-2. 3ds Max saves Blender multilayer files.

There are two issues with interchange: structure and concept. Structure is the order and encoding used to represent data in the file, and is easily solved by a programmer. Concept may be difficult or impossible to address.

If format A stores a color value for a pixel as a 32-bit floating-point triple (where the first number represents the red value, the second the blue value, and the third the green value), and format B stores a color value for a pixel as a 24-bit floating point quadruple (where the first represents the hue, the second the saturation, the third the value, and the fourth the alpha), a program can mechanically go through and convert and assume values to create format B.

However, as you get to more advanced concepts, like animated armature bone rotations, the idea of how to store that information evolved very differently between the two applications, and thus the data that stores that representation is fundamentally different. It is difficult, if not impossible, to simply translate a complicated concept.

For this reason, some information is easily interchanged, while other information can be "lost in translation." In general, basic information about objects and meshes translates well, while animation (armatures and shape keys) and physics simulations (like particles, fur, cloth, and soft bodies) do not.

Image file formats

Over the years, it seems like everyone has come up with their own method of saving a digitized image. This section discusses the formats supported by Blender. Figure 4-3 shows the video and image formats that Blender can read and write. FFMPEG bundles nine formats, including MPEG, DV, and FLV. JPEG 2000 support was recently added as well.

BMP and color channels support

Color TVs used red, green, and blue (RGB) as three channels of information in the broadcast signal, and that technology is well understood. So computers just digitized it, creating a packed RGB format. This format saves a color as a series of three numbers, each number representing the strength or dominance of that color in relation to the others. In many places, Blender reports a color of a pixel in terms of the RGB values. Blender also supports YUV channels, which consist of luminance (Y), chroma blue (U), and chroma red (V) components.

You can also think of color a *hue*—a value somewhere along the visible spectrum of light (remember Roy G. Biv?). If you were to drop that color ink on a paper, the saturation of the color is the amount of time the ink sets on the paper and saturates it, and the value is the dilution of that ink that is used. So color is also expressed as a combination of the hue, saturation, and value (HSV) channels. Blender supports the HSV notion of expressing color, both in materials and in postprocessing.

Save image as:
TIFF
MultiLayer
OpenEXR
DPX
Cineon
Radiance HDR
Iris
HamX
Jpeg
BMP
PNG
Targa Raw
Targa
QuickTime
AVI Codec
AVI Jpeg
AVI Raw
FFMpeg
Frameserver
QuickTime

Figure 4-3. Exported image formats

> *Roy G. Biv is a mnemonic to remember the order of color spectra using the first letter of the colors: Red Orange Yellow Green Blue Indigo Violet.*

JPEG

The Joint Photographic Experts Group (JPEG) released the very popular JPG format in 1992, primarily for use in digital cameras. This format gives the user a choice of how heavily to compress the file. Using this format, you can reduce the file size, but you lose the detail and may start to see compression artifacts, or banding, at very low-quality settings. JPG is therefore called a *lossy compression* format. JPEG released a new standard in 2000, called JPEG 2000, which saves images with a .jp2 extension and provides fantastic compression of High-Definition images. Blender supports JPEG 2000 and has several presets to choose from.

Digital cameras save their photos in the JPG format and upload them to your computer. If you want to take a high-quality photo, turn down the compression and increase the resolution. For just a quick snapshot, such as doing a location shoot where a high-quality image isn't needed, turn up the compression and use a lower resolution. The camera will have quality and resolution settings on its menus.

Blender fully supports JPEG compression in both images and video. Using the compositor rig (discussed in Chapter 10) shown in Figure 4-4, you can read in any image in any supported format, and rerender to the JPG or JP2 format while choosing your level of compression. In the Format panel in the figure, you can see that Jpeg has been selected in the yellow selector box. If you have enabled file extensions in the Output panel, the file will be saved with the .jpg or .jp2 extension.

Figure 4-4. Sample image conversion to JPG

Figure 4-5 shows an image saved without compression. The uncompressed image takes up about 1MB of disk space. If you change the Q: (quality) slider field in the Format panel (just below the selector that says Jpeg) from 100 to 30, press F12 again, and then save the file, the image takes only 10% of the original disk space, with little or no perceptible difference in quality (when viewed in full resolution on a professional monitor), as shown in Figure 4-6. Only when the quality is turned down to 10% does some visible degradation occur, as shown in Figure 4-7.

Figure 4-5. HD image at 100% JPEG quality. Without compression, its file size is 973KB.

Figure 4-6. HD image at 30% JPEG quality. Its file size is one-tenth the original size, at 95KB, with minimal artifacts and degradation.

Figure 4-7. HD image at 10% quality. The file size is 50KB, and banding is apparent.

PNG and the alpha channel

The Portable Network Graphics (PNG) format was born as an open standard to combat proprietary actions with other formats, notably GIF (which is why GIF is not supported in Blender). The PNG standard offers compression without any loss of quality and is immensely popular worldwide. (More information about the PNG format is available at http://www.libpng.org.)

PNG (and other formats, like TGA) also supports the notion of transparency, where a pixel has a certain opacity, enabling PNG images to be layered on top of one another. While color can be thought of as being stored in three channels (red, green, and blue), the opacity information is stored in an *alpha* (A) channel.

Figure 4-8 shows a computer-generated image of a dog's snout in RGBA colors on a white background. Figure 4-9 shows its alpha channel as a grayscale image. This particular example is rendered with Premul (for Premultiply) instead of Sky in the Render panel (discussed in Chapter 9). When this image is layered on top of a base live-action shot, as shown in Figure 4-10, using the AlphaOver feature in the sequencer (discussed in Chapter 13), you get the result shown in Figure 4-11.

> *A grayscale image shows values equal to 0 or less as black, and 1 or greater as white, with values in between as shades of gray.*

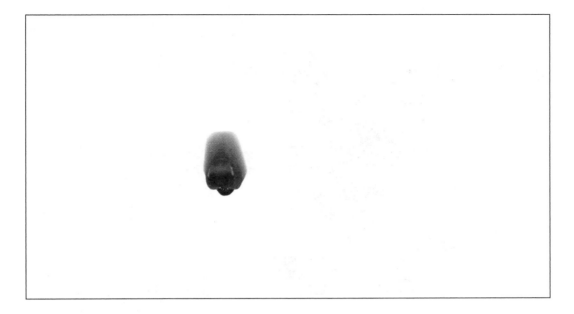

Figure 4-8. Computer-generated snout

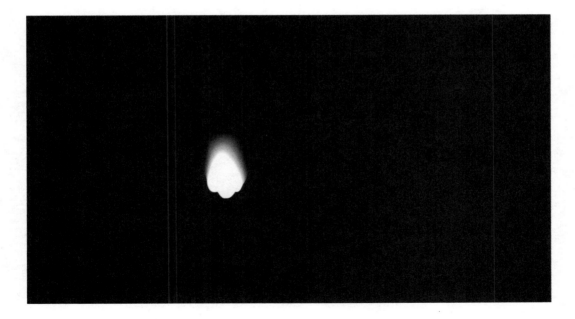

Figure 4-9. Alpha channel as a grayscale image

Figure 4-10. Base plate image (courtesy of Rob Collins Productions)

Figure 4-11. Composited image blended using alpha channel

While JPEG saves only the RGB colors (and not the alpha channel), the PNG format does and is very popular with compositing professionals.

> By animating (discussed in Chapter 8) and match-moving the computer-generated snout with the real dog's base plate, you can make the dog talk about . . . well, whatever a dog wants to talk about.

Targa and TIFF

The .tga extension indicates a Truevision (now owned by Avid) Advanced Raster Graphics Adapter format, which provides a simple and fast 24-bit color and 8-bit alpha channel file format. Still in widespread use, this format is showing its age a bit, and is being superseded by PNG and EXR.

The .tif format is common in faxing and publishing, and is a little more advanced than Targa. Many print publishers (including my publisher, Apress) still use this "trusty-dusty" format.

OpenEXR, the Z-buffer, and multilayer

3D compositing brought with it not just the image opacity (the alpha channel), but also other information like distance from the camera (called the Z-buffer). The leading computer generation and compositing powerhouse, Industrial Light & Magic, formed by George Lucas, developed an open format for the exchange of rasterized images, called OpenEXR. This format allows you to store many different layers of information about an image, including that Z-buffer, in a very large range of values, called a high-dynamic range (HDR) image. Blender fully supports the OpenEXR format, and was one of the first applications to do so.

Z-depth pixel information

In Blender, the Z value of an image pixel is a number reflecting the distance of the object from the camera. You use this information to merge two images together, like interleaving two decks of cards when you shuffle them. In Blender, this information is used to both combine images as well as give realistic depth of field blurring.

I've included a file on the DVD that comes with this book to help you visualize how the Z-buffer is saved for each pixel in the image. Open the file tut/dof.blend on your DVD. With your cursor in the node editor, press E to execute, and you will see a practical example of using the Z-buffer. Figure 4-12 shows the 3D view of a camera floating 10 units above a mask, which is shaped like a girl holding a balloon (I'll show you how to make a mask in the next chapter). Ten units in back of the mask is a curved background object that curves away from the camera for another 5 units. Therefore, the farthest point is 25 units away from the camera, and the closest is 10 units.

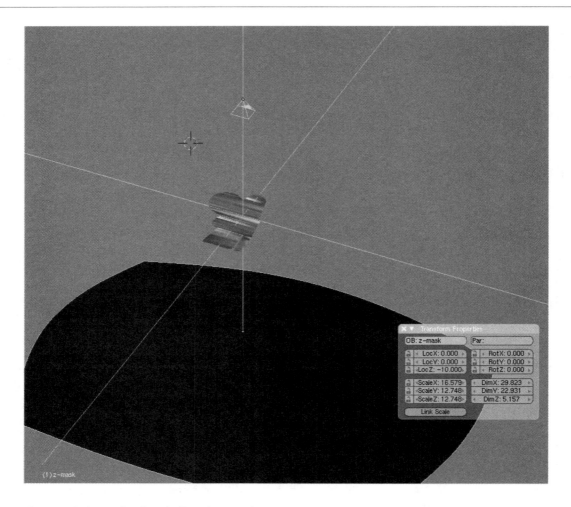

Figure 4-12. Computing the Z-buffer using a mask

The Map Value node (which we will discuss and use in Chapter 12), as configured in Figure 4-13, takes the Z values from this scene and subtracts 10 (-10.00 in the Ofs, for Offset, field). Therefore, the mask pixels are now zero, and those of the background curve are between 10 and 15. The node then divides every Z value by 20 (actually multiplies by 1/20 or 0.05, as shown in the Size field). The output is a value between 0 and almost 1. Those values are then fed to a viewer, and they show up as a grayscale image.

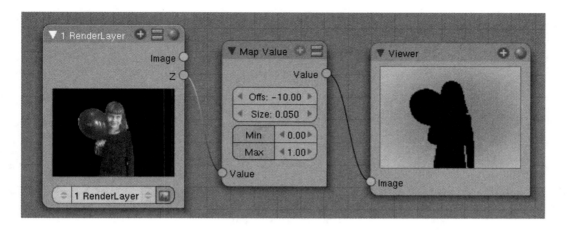

Figure 4-13. Visualizing the Z-buffer

Multilayer format

OpenEXR native format supports only RGB, alpha, and Z information. However, the OpenEXR specification allows applications to add on to these basic layers and create their own additional layers of information. In fact, the Blender Foundation proposed the OpenEXR multilayer/multipass format specification, which is currently in use. Blender has released the specification for these additional layers to the general public, as well as the software to create and use this format extension. This multilayer open format allows you to store any render pass for later compositing and postprocessing.

In Chapters10 through 12, we will dive into the use of different kinds of render layers to postprocess and composite images. If you need to save your passes in an intermediate file store, tell Blender to use the multilayer format to save your images and Blender render passes, such as speed, reflections, and even object masks, from the 3D view.

Video formats

Video is a sequence of still images, called *frames*, which are shown to you rapidly. Your brain detects changes and perceives motion. Blender allows you to construct a video from a frame sequence.

NTSC and PAL formats

A modern TV broadcaster sends out an image as either a progressive scan of all horizontal scan lines of image pixels one after another or as a set of interlaced lines. With interlaced rendering, a frame of video is sent as two images, and the TV set puts them back together. There are two standards: NTSC for North and South America, and PAL for the rest of the world. Because of differences between these standards and your PC monitor, a frame rendered for TV broadcast will be distorted when viewed on your monitor, but will look fine on the TV.

To improve the product seen by the consumer in the European Union, a PAL format was extended to be a different aspect ratio. Instead of the viewed image being 4 units wide and 3 units high, the image is stretched to 16 units wide to 9 units high. This is the 16:9 ratio and is also called *widescreen*. Blender supports this format through the PAL 16:9 preset in the Format panel, which changes the output image size (resolution).

Table 4-1 shows the Blender controls and settings you need to properly process or create DV for either NTSC or PAL broadcast.

Table 4-1. Blender Settings for Broadcast Video

Panel	Setting	NTSC	PAL
Render	Fields	Enabled	Enabled
Render	Odd	Enabled	Disable
Format	Preset	NTSC	PAL
Format	FPS	30	25
Format	Divider (/)	1.001	1.0

The PAL or NTSC preset setting in the Format panel sets many things, like pixel aspect ratio and resolution. The Render and Format panels, set for NTSC output, are shown in Figures 4-14 and 4-15, respectively.

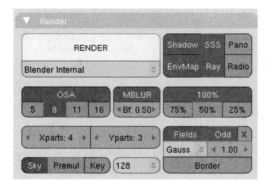

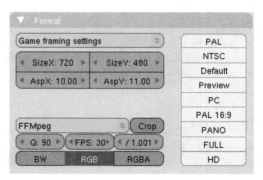

Figure 4-14. Render panel set for NTSC, with Fields and Odd enabled

Figure 4-15. Format panel set for NTSC

HD formats

To improve the product seen by the consumer worldwide, the broadcast community upgraded the video standard to digital high-definition (HD) quality. HD essentially quadruples the amount of information shown on the TV screen, and changes many other aspects of the video and how it is transmitted. While an NTSC image is 4 pixels wide for every 3 pixels high, HD is 16 pixels wide for every 9 pixels high, called a 16:9 image aspect ratio.

HD changes the way in which colors are represented. A color is value of brilliance (Y) and two chrominance difference values (blue and red), known as YCbCr. An HD video may be interlaced (denoted by an *i* following the resolution) or progressive (denoted by a *p* following the resolution). For compositing, you have your choice of HD output formats:

- 1920×1080p (maximum)
- 1920×1080i
- 1920×720p
- 1440×720p
- 1280×720p

The HD preset in the Format panel sets the 1920×1080p format. If you want one of the other varieties, you will need to change the values in the SizeX and SizeY fields in the Format panel.

As you can probably tell, HD images take up a lot of space and memory, which slows down response time. So, when working with HD video on a modest machine, Blender supports the automatic creation of a proxy, discussed in Chapters 9 and 13.

Frame sequences

Instead of a video being in one big file, compositors commonly use a *frame sequence*, which is a numbered sequence of individual image files, where each file is one frame of the video (if using fields, then each image is actually half a frame). Each of the image files uses any of the still image formats (JPG, PNG, and so on). Frame sequences show up in two places in Blender:

- Any time you are reading or writing images, you can use a frame sequence instead of a video file.
- When using proxies in the sequencer. Instead of slowly slogging through the huge video, Blender uses the small proxy image to give you fast response time, even when working with HD. Making and using proxies in the Sequencer is discussed in Chapter 13.

Let's make a frame sequence from a video. On your DVD, in the lib/images/NASA folder, open 4-Sequence.blend. This is a video of the liftoff of the one hundred twentieth mission of the space shuttle. (This and many high-quality videos are available from http://www.nasa.gov for educational purposes.) The file should open to the make sequence scene, in the sequence desktop shown in Figure 4-16. This is the main workspace you will be using for sequencing, and it's described in detail in Chapter 14. For now, I just want to show you a practical example of making a frame sequence, because this process throws off a lot of newer users.

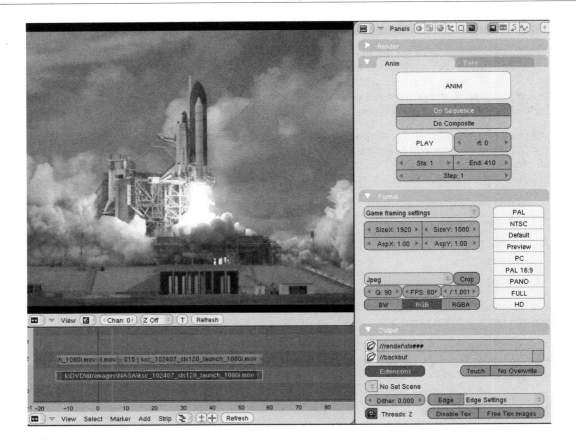

Figure 4-16. Sequencer desktop

The buttons window on the right allows you to control the render process, and three panels are showing. In the top Format panel, notice that the output format is set to Jpeg. In the Anim panel, Do Sequence is enabled, which means the image to be rendered is pulled from the sequencer, and the frame range is 1 to 410, which means that 410 JPEG files will be created when you click the ANIM button. The Output panel specifies where the files will be put, and the top line there reads //render\sts###, which means that the images will be put in a render subfolder, and their file name will begin with sts, followed by a three-digit frame number. So, frame 123 will be named sts123.jpg, as shown in Figure 4-17, which is a snapshot of my file browser.

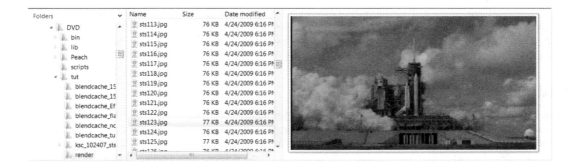

Figure 4-17. An example of an image sequence

Click the ANIM button in the Anim panel to start the process. Assuming you have optimized your user preferences for video compositing and have a modest PC, the 400 frames should be rendered out as images in about 2 minutes. You can use the console window to watch the progress. When complete, each image represents a frame from the video.

> If you ever need to interrupt the animation process, simply press the Esc key in either the render window (if there is one) or the interface window. To resume an animation, picking up where you left off, enable No Overwrite in the Output panel, and Blender will skip over any files that already exist.

As you've seen, the default file name for images in a frame sequence has three digits at the end. At 30 fps, a 30-second TV commercial uses 900 frames. A 5-minute documentary uses 30×5×60, or 9,000 frames. Thus, four digits would be needed for any shot or even a medium-sized project. In practice, with commercials, even an hour-long TV show is interspersed with commercials every 5 minutes, so each sequence needs to be only (and must have a breaking point every) 5 minutes.

A 75-minute feature length movie will have a total of 75×24×60, or 108,000 frames. If sequenced as one continuous video, it will need to use six-digit frame numbers. The epic *Lord of the Rings: The Return of the King* (2003), extended edition cut, ran for 251 minutes of glorious imagery and drama, thus needing 360,000 frames—still only six digits. If it were rendered at 4KB horizontal resolution in a 2.35:1 aspect ratio (4096×1743), it would need about 5MB per PNG image, and the final composited frame sequence would need about 2TB of disk space, give or take a few gigabytes. Try backing that up to floppy!

To change the default number of frame digits saved, simply enter a # for each digit of the frame number in the top line of the Output panel (see Figure 4-16) as part of the file name. For example, the file specification Cut-Dir-###### would indicate that this is the director's cut and would enable an 11-hour continuous epic movie. Bring your own popcorn for that one.

Blender can also work in reverse, and construct a single video file from a frame sequence, which is discussed in detail in Chapter 14. To do this, you simply tell Blender that you want to load an image, but then highlight multiple frames, and they will be brought in as one strip. You then change your output format to a video file format.

Codecs

A video is just a series of images, and many computer algorithms have been devised to compress and encode them into a single file, usually compressing that image sequence into a series of keyframes and changes. A keyframe, or actual image, establishes a group of pictures (GOP) as a starting image. Subsequent frames then need to save only what has changed from the previous image. Similarly, you need a companion algorithm and program to decode that file back into an image. This **co**mpression-**dec**ompression program is called a *codec*.

Codecs implement a video-compression standard. A modern example of a compression standard is H.264. This particular standard was developed by ITU and MPEG, and has been recognized by the ISO. It provides a far more efficient algorithm for compressing video than any previous standards, and is the best available at the time of this writing. Compared to MPEG 2, H.264 provides a threefold improvement with regard to file size and quality.

To use a codec for your video, you must have the compression part on your machine, and your viewer must have the decompression piece on their computer or player.

Codecs are not part of Blender, but instead are used by any video program or player on your operating system. Many codecs are available, and a lot of them work well. Some work well on Windows, but not on Apple or Linux. Some are lossy; some are lossless. Some work well when running inside media player A, but crash media player B because they are not coded exactly right. Some codecs properly handle all variations of a format standard like H.264; some do not. A codec may say that it can handle a video stream when, in fact, it cannot, and simply stops working or crashes. Can you tell I've spent many frustrating hours with codecs?

Codecs provide a lot of control over the output video, and each one is different. I commonly use the QuickTime container with the H.264 codec via the FFmpeg format (discussed in Chapter 9). QuickTime is available from http://www.apple.com/quicktime. The DivX codec, available from http://www.divx.com, is very nice. The DivX standard, which is proprietary, is a popular choice for commercial work. The Xvid codec is an open source equivalent, and can be obtained from http://www.xvid.org.

Many codecs are obtained automatically when needed by some players using the Internet, or you can search for them. Each codec has basic settings for speed, GOP, and quality. Generally, I set a keyframe every second, so for a 24 fps film-like render, I would set GOP (keyframe) to 24 as well.

Audio file formats

Not to be outdone by the myriad of image formats, the audio people have been busy devising ways to compress the largest amount of audio information into the smallest possible digital file as well. One of the first formats was .wav, or wavelength-encoding, which stored the voltage value (8 or 16 bits number) at some sample rate. Blender supports .wav files sampled at 44.1 kHz or 48 kHz. The 8-bit mono format at 44.1 kHz is 352 Kbps, which represents the bandwidth needed to play the file without any pauses or gaps. The 16-bit stereo format is four times that, which may become a pipe hog.

To overcome the problems with .wav files, some wizards borrowed run-length encoding (RLE) schemes from the JPEG in connection with the motion picture industry—the, yes, you guessed it—Motion Picture Experts Group (MPEG). This group's first specification, MPEG-1, laid out how to encode audio and video. The first version of the audio specification was not that good, the second better, and the third time was the charm. This is the MPEG-1 Audio Layer 3 standard, or MP3 for short. The MP3 standard caught on like wildfire and is the most commonly used audio compression scheme. While some quality is lost, you have a wide array of compression choices, some of which (depending on the kind of audio) result in a very small file size. Small file sizes therefore need much less transmission pipe (bandwidth) to be transmitted or stored on the playback device. A fairly simple decompression algorithm makes it very easy to reexpand and play the audio track back to the consumer. I have had good success using the MP2 and MP3 audio encoders inside a MOV container. In Blender, you set the audio codec on the Audio panel, which is revealed when you choose the FFmpeg format.

The audio track may be saved or processed separately from the video track, although most modern digital cameras record them together. Digital compositing is mostly concerned with video postprocessing. Other tools, such as Digidesign's Pro Tools or Magix's Audio Studio, are used to process audio in postproduction. At some point, the audio track must be merged with the video for playback. During a live-video shoot, a clapper (also called a slate) is used to establish a point in time when the audio and video align. The clapper is a hinged board that claps in front of the camera. That clapping sound is matched up the image of when the two hinged pieces come together on the video to synchronize the audio with the video. As long as either audio or video is not cut from the middle, or if both are cut out for the same duration, and the video frame rate is stable, words spoken a minute into the audio clip will still match up with the mouth movements seen on the screen.

> For the extremely budget-conscious producer, you can simply clap your hands on camera.

Blender provides the ability to layer and mix multiple audio tracks. You can, for example, import a voice-over as one track or strip, some background music, a foley sound effect, and export the combined result as the audio track in an audio-video file. How to do this is discussed in Chapter 14. All of the audio tracks will be mixed down and compressed, and then integrated into the video container file.

Container formats

So now you have a compressed video stream and a compressed audio stream that need to play back together, and be shipped out on a DVD together. To accommodate this, several container formats predominate: AVI, MOV, and MP4, and Blender supports all of them.

Audio-Video Interleaving, or AVI, is an oldie but goody standard that intersperses parts of the audio track with the video frames, so that playback can begin immediately. AVI was supported early on by Microsoft. Not to be outdone, Apple developed its standard, MOV, and began distributing the QuickTime Player, which is now ubiquitous.

To support TV video and audio transmission, the motion picture experts improved their first version and produced MPEG-2. This standard is widely used in DVDs and video files. With the arrival of DVDs and HD, the motion picture experts got back together a third time, but really could not come up with anything better. This fourth and latest time, the experts addressed digital rights management and 3D content. Practically speaking, Blender supports both MPEG-2 and MPEG-4. Blender supports these containers through the FFmpeg library of routines.

For example, to render a QuickTime movie, you can either choose the format directly from the format selector on the Format panel or choose the FFmpeg format. When you choose FFmpeg, two more panels appear, one for video where you choose QuickTime and then another for selecting the H.264 codec. If you choose the QuickTime container format directly (not through FFmpeg), you won't be able to integrate audio into your output, and you need to click Set codec in the Format panel to con-figure the container to use the H.264 codec.

I wish I could wrap up this section with a clear and simple answer as to which codec and container work the best. My best advice is to make a lot of trial runs with an image the size you wish as the final result, and record your results regarding file size and playback quality. The ultimate goal is to create a quality file in a reasonable file size. For HD output, the H.264 codec inside the QuickTime or FFmpeg MOV container seems to work very well. You can check video help sites on the Internet, as well as DVD authoring forums, to get support. Services, such as Youtube and Vimeo, which I use to post work, convert your container to something suitable for streaming. Different formats convert differently, with varying quality (see Chapter 9).

Players

Any player must be able to open the container, and recognize the video and audio that is compressed inside. Therefore, it must be able to understand the container, the video codec, and the audio codec in order to play back the movie. The player must also be able to deal with any delays or errors in the file, accommodate the power of the playing device so that it plays without skipping (hopefully), and when it does get behind, catch up and keep the audio and video in sync.

The leading players for PCs include VideoLan Compressor (VLC), DivX Media Player, QuickTime Player, Windows Media Player, Totem (which I use on my Ubuntu box), and Xvid players. VLC is the most reliable open source video player I have found. It works very reliably with a variety of codecs, plays more formats than my Windows Media Player, and provides a set of video-manipulation features. I have included VLC on the DVD that comes with this book, in the bin\VLC directory of the DVD for Windows and OSX. You can also get VLC directly from http://www.videolan.org. Linux varieties are readily available through apt-get, and there are versions for each specific flavor and release.

Summary

A myriad of formats needs to be supported for a viable worldwide video compositing tool, and Blender supports most if not all of the major ones. Static (still) image formats, of any size, can be gen-erated. Video, in all of its different formats and standards, can be used and generated. For HD video and other large formats, Blender provides automatic proxy generation. Blender can split a video out into a sequence of individual image files, and construct a video from a frame sequence. Audio can be encoded into the container to provide a complete movie.

Chapter 5

3D ELEMENTS

This chapter focuses on working in 3D view. You'll learn how to work with objects and images, and arrange them in 3D space. This includes creating masks, using Blender's empty object as a guide, and adding text. Special effects (such as particles, smoke, and dust) use 3D objects, so this chapter will give you the foundation for adding these into your composition (as discussed in Chapter 8).

Blender objects are created in the virtual world by modeling them in the 3D view. Blender offers hundreds of modeling tools and features. In this book, I'll present only the essentials of modeling specific compositing elements. The good news is that you don't need to be an expert modeler to be a great compositor—those are two separate specialties. If you want to learn more about modeling, I recommend that you refer to resources devoted to the subject, such as Essential Blender, available from the Blender e-shop at `http://www.blender3d.org/e-shop/product_info. php?products_id=96`.

Working with objects

For creating, changing, and moving objects, the 3D view is where it's at. When you work in a 3D view window, you need to pay close attention to the current mode, so we'll look at that first.

To begin, make sure you are in a screen that suits the modeling tasks. In the B.blend file on the DVD that comes with this book (introduced in Chapter 3), SR:1-Model, which has one big 3D view window, is a good choice. The file also has an SR:2-Model 4-up view, which splits that big window into four panes, each with a different perspective.

Object modes

In the 3D view, the modes available depend on what you are able to do with the currently selected type of object. Select the plane, and then choose a mode to work in using the Mode: selector on the 3D view header, as shown in Figure 5-1. Your choices are as follows:

- Object Mode: **Works with the object as a whole**
- Edit Mode: **Allows you to change the shape and definition of the object**
- Sculpt Mode: **A different method for changing the shape of a mesh object**
- Vertex Paint: **General mesh painting, by assigning a color to a vertex**
- Texture Paint: **More accurate mesh painting through a UV texture**

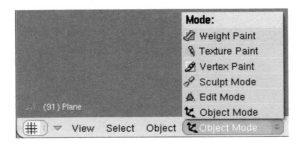

Figure 5-1. 3-D view modes

The sculpt, vertex paint, and texture paint modes are not used in compositing, and we covered basic object mode manipulation in Chapter 3, so that leaves edit mode to be discussed in this chapter.

Hotkey commands

Hundreds of hotkey commands are available to speed your editing workflow. To see the full list, select Help ➤ Hotkey and MouseAction Reference, as shown in Figure 5-2. When you choose this menu item, one of your windows will turn into a script window with a script application that shows you all of the hotkey commands and lets you search for specific functions.

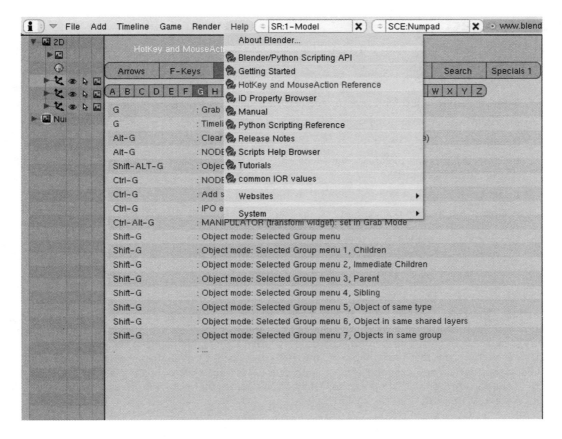

Figure 5-2. Hotkey help

Most commands are mnemonic and start with the first letter of the command. As mentioned earlier, holding down the Alt key while pressing a hotkey often is the "un" equivalent, undoing what was just done. For example, pressing H hides the selected object from view, and pressing Alt+H makes it visible again. The Ctrl key is often used in conjunction with a hotkey when multiple objects are involved.

> *The same hotkey may do different things, depending on the current mode, object type, and window type. For example, pressing X in the 3D view in object mode will delete the selected objects, but X in the text editor will type an X in the text file. Pressing X when editing a text object in the 3D view will add an X to the text string, whereas when editing a mesh object in the 3D view, pressing X will delete the selected vertices.*

Adding objects

Each kind of object is used for different things, and several already exist in your scene. To see the objects you can add, press the spacebar in 3D view and select Add. The following kinds of objects are commonly used in compositing:

- **Mesh**: A solid object with several varieties; used mainly as a projection plate
- **Grid**: A special mesh plane that is already divided for you
- **Curve**: Useful for masking an organic object or to act as guidelines
- **Camera**: Takes the picture of the scene and sends it on to the compositor or sequencer, or saves the image directly
- **Lights**: Used to light non-self-illuminating meshes and curves
- **Empty**: A reference point used to control other objects

> *While 3ds Max has a teapot as a "test" object, Blender has Suzanne, the beautiful monkey. Needless to say, while I enjoy a cup of tea, I favor the monkey.*

The plane object is commonly used as a projection plate to hold an image as an element in a 2D or 3D composition. Meshes and curves can also serve as the starting point in making a mask (plane for very angular or irregularly shaped objects; curve for rounded organic objects). Mesh objects can be 2D or even 3D shapes that can be morphed into different shapes through shape keys (discussed in the "Changing image shapes" section later in this chapter). Mesh objects are the only kind of object that can spout particles for special effects (as described in Chapter 8). Figure 5-3 shows an example of a Bezier curve as the start of a making a mask.

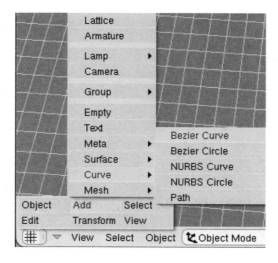

Figure 5-3. Adding an object in 3D view

Setting Edit Methods preferences

When you add an object, like a plane or a mask, it is created at the location of the 3D cursor. The 3D cursor is where you last left-clicked in 3D space. The object may be in edit mode, depending on your Edit Methods user preferences, as shown in Figure 5-4.

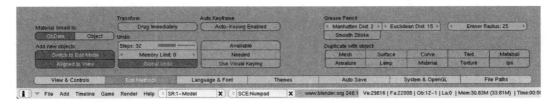

Figure 5-4. Edit Methods user preferences

This context of the user preferences provides seven areas of customization for how Blender behaves when editing and duplicating objects. The Add new objects section has two features I like to enable for compositing:

- Switch to Edit Mode: This puts the 3D view into edit mode when an object is added. For example, after you add a text object, you can immediately edit the text. If you prefer to place objects first and edit later, disable this option.

- Aligned to View: This orients the object to "face" the orientation of the view you used when adding it. For example, when you add a text object in camera view, it is automatically rotated to face the camera.

I'm not that perfect, so I also enable Global Undo in the Edit Methods user preferences, so that any errant commands can be undone by pressing Ctrl+Z. Any undone command can be redone via Ctrl+Y. Once you have executed some commands, you can also press Alt+U to bring up a list of the commands and actions you have recently done. Selecting an entry brings you all the way back to that state (so you don't have to repetitively press Ctrl+Z).

Editing 3D objects

Select an object by hovering your cursor over it and right-clicking. When you edit an object, you work with the individual parts that make up the object. For a Bezier curve, those parts are called handles, which control the shape of the curve. For a mesh object, the smallest part is called a vertex. These vertices connect to form an edge, which looks like a line, and two edges can connect to form a face. While in edit mode, you can work with vertices, edges, and faces by toggling selection modes, as shown in Figure 5-5. You can Shift-select to work with multiple parts.

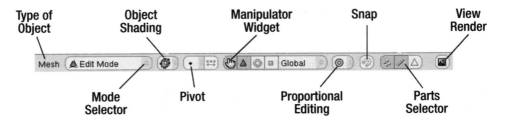

Figure 5-5. 3D view edit mode header

The manipulator widget puts a multiple-axis widget around the selection. You can click and drag the heads of the widget to move the selection. The three options next to the manipulator widget let you grab, scale, and rotate an object, respectively. Enabling the snap option aligns things to each other or to the grid.

> *If you use the 3D manipulator widget, the axis orientation will be shown as red, green, and blue arrows pointing in the global X, Y, and Z orientation, respectively. Click and drag on an arrowhead to move an element in that direction. Hold Ctrl while dragging to snap the element to grid units.*

You can render an image of any 3D view by clicking the view render icon on the far-right side of the 3D view header. The image is not a formal render, but just a snapshot of the window pane from the current perspective, which you can use for reference purposes. It is very fast, especially for animations and test shots (if you click it from a 3D view in camera perspective). Holding Ctrl and clicking this icon renders a snapshot movie consisting of all the frames in your animation.

Working with images

In Blender, you have many ways of compositing different elements together. Most of the time, those elements will be an image in some form. Images are used in all sorts of ways in Blender, including the following:

- As a background to your 3D view, to serve as a reference image (covered in Chapter 3)
- As a background buffer to a render of the virtual world (also covered in Chapter 3)
- As a texture to the world settings (covered in Chapter 6)
- As a texture to some object (covered in this chapter)
- As input to the compositing nodes for a scene (covered in Chapter 10)
- Added as a strip in the sequencer (covered in Chapter 13)

In addition, you can just inspect an image by loading it into the UV/image editor, as you will see shortly. You can also use the same image in multiple places.

Compositing most often involves arranging alpha-mapped images to make a final result. Once you have brought an image into Blender, you use it to texture an object, which I call an element. I am borrowing the term element from packages like Adobe After Effects, even though Blender cannot work with an image in exactly the same way as After Effects. However, both After Effects and Blender use the same alpha-mapped image, such as a PNG image, as the basis for an element.

UV mapping

In Blender, you create an object, specifically a mesh plane, and then texture the image to the plane through a process called UV mapping. In this way, you can orient the image however you want on the plane, without moving or rotating the plane. You can then rotate the plane in 3D space to give a correct three-dimensional look to a two-dimensional image when the image is taken with a perspective camera, or a skewed look to the image if you use an orthographic camera (types of cameras and their effects are discussed in Chapter 6). Since the image is mapped to the object (like a plane), you have three kinds of options: what shape of object to map to, how to map the image to the object, and how to orient the object in 3D space relative to camera.

> *It's called UV mapping because a pixel of an image is mapped to appear at some XYZ coordinate. That pixel is located at a coordinate on the image, and since X and Y were already taken, we geeks just backed up few centuries when UVW was the coordinate system, and few centuries when UVW was the coordinate system, and few centuries when UVW was the coordinate system, and picked U and V.*

In compositing, your 3D object is most often a rectangle or grid. Let's do a simple UV mapping now to see how it works.

Start with a new blend file, which with my template (B.blend on your DVD) consists of a projection plane. Select the 4-UV screen, which has a 3D view and a UV/image editor window. Select the plane and tab into edit mode. Press U (for Unwrap, the default). The UV/Image editor now shows you a square outline of a plane, which is your UV map. Also, a UV Texture slot, named UVTex, is added to the plane's Editing Mesh. There are four UV coordinates, shown as yellow dots in the UV/image editor, and each UV corresponds to a vertex of the plane.

> *Blender has one of the best UV unwrapping subsystems out there. If provides many options that are very handy for unwrapping complicated objects.*

In the UV/image editor header, choose Image ➤ Open and use the file browser to load lib\images\ people\rebe\balloon premul.png (from your DVD). Your UV/image editor window should now look like Figure 5-6.

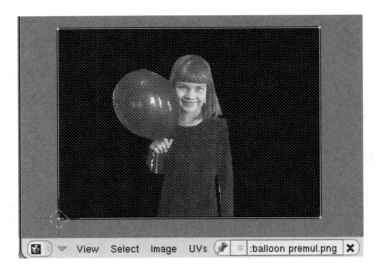

Figure 5-6. UV/Image editor with image loaded

Now that you have a UV texture for this plane in edit mode, locate the Texture Face panel in the Editing context, and enable Alpha in the Active Face Alpha Blending section. This allows the 3D view to show transparent areas of the images as, well, transparent. I also like to enable Twoside, so that I can flip the object around and view it from the back side, which flips the image in camera.

> *Many thanks to BlenderArtists user "forTe" for the Active Face tip!*

Ensure your 3D view is in solid mode, and you should see the image in 3D view as well. If not, ensure Solid Tex is enabled in the View Properties panel. If the image is upside down in the 3D view, you can reorient the plane or the mapping. You could rotate the plane in 3D space, but I prefer to rotate the UV coordinates. If you took the image with the camera held sideways, the image may be off by 90 degrees. This can also be corrected by rotating the UV coordinates.

With your cursor in the UV/image editor, select View ➤ Update Automatically to get a real-time inter-active display for this next step. Then press R and move your mouse. (The G, R, and S hotkeys, with or without Ctrl or Shift, work the same in the UV/image editor as they do in 3D view.) You will see the coordinates start to rotate, and the degrees of rotation are in the header. Hold down the Ctrl key to control rotations to 5-degree increments, and move your mouse until you have rotated the coordinates by 180 degrees. As you move your mouse, notice what happens in the 3D view: the image rotates since you have real-time display enabled, as shown in Figure 5-7. (If the coordinates do not rotate, make sure they are all selected by pressing A once or twice in the window until they are all highlighted in bright yellow.)

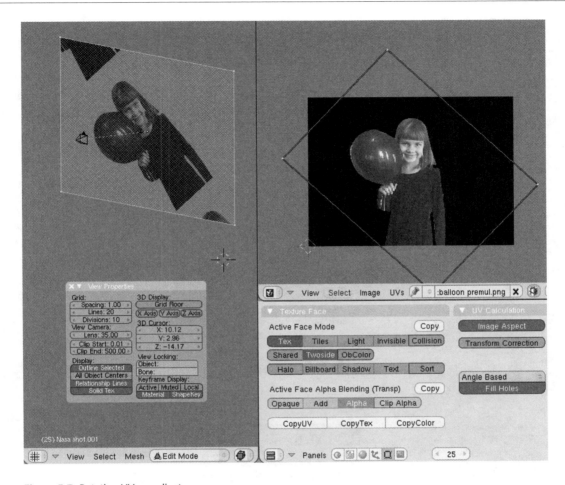

Figure 5-7. Rotating UV coordinates

As a professional touch, name the mesh (ME:) Element and the object (OB:) Balloon in the Link and Materials panel. You can go ahead and pack this image inside the blend file by clicking the package icon (next to the image selector) in the UV/image editor header.

You can now see this mapping in 3D view, but to be able to render this mapping, you need to apply the mapping as a texture that affects the color and alpha of the plane. Tab out of editing mode. In the Shading Materials context of the buttons window, locate the Texture panel and click Add New. In the newly revealed Map Input panel, enable UV. and enter the name of this set of UV coordinates, UVTex, in the UV: field on that panel. In the Map To panel, enable Alpha (Color will already be enabled).

> *UVTex is the default name assigned to a UV texture map. You can find/change this name in the Mesh panel of the buttons window.*

In the Texture subcontext of the buttons window, select Image as the image type. In the Image panel, use the selector to select the image. Ensure Use Alpha is enabled in the Map Image panel. The complete set of options you should enable is shown in Figure 5-8.

> *Yes, it takes a little work (maybe ten clicks or so) to get elements into Blender, because there are so many possible uses. But after you do it a few dozen times, it becomes quite easy. A macro feature is being discussed by the Blender community, and this would be an ideal application for a macro.*

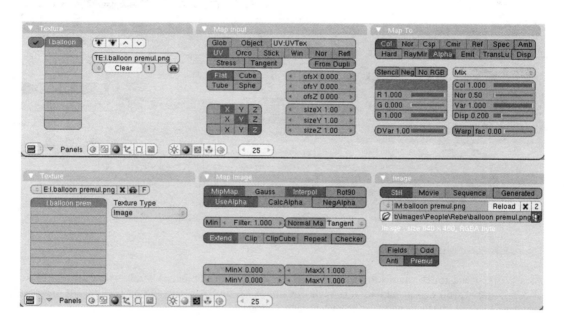

Figure 5-8. Material and texture settings for an image element

Now save your work in your library, in the lib\images\people\rebe folder, as balloon.blend. You may want to fix a relative path to the image. You will be using this object as an element in the other examples in this chapter.

Changing image shapes (morphing)

Do you remember an application called Goo by Kai Krause, which provided localized image stretching and distortion, and was quite innovative when it came out? Nowadays, you can the get same effects with Blender. Practical applications include envisioning what someone will look like after plastic surgery, distorting landscapes or elements for a kind of Salvador Dali surrealist expression, or just making someone look goofy.

Let's try out some morphing. With your previous exercise open in the UV/image editor, select Image ➤ Replace and choose the Becca.JPG image in that same directory.

In either window, you can scale the image, thus remapping the location of those pixels. So, a simple scaling action by a slight amount can make a person look thinner (X axis), taller (Y axis), and so on. Too much leads to distortion, of course, but a slight amount can take off a few pounds.

For finer control, you need more control points to work with. If you were doing this from scratch, you could add a mesh grid for this. However, it's easy enough to convert your plane into a grid. In edit mode in 3D view, press W to bring up the Specials menu, and select Subdivide Multi. Click into the Number of Cuts field and enter 30 to get a fairly fine grid.

> *This Specials menu has a lot of very nifty editing features. Take some time to explore them.*

Lock in this shape by clicking Add Shape Key in the Shapes panel in the Editing buttons. The first shape is called the Basis shape, and should be the basic shape before you do any editing. All other shapes are based on this basis shape. Press Tab to leave edit mode, which locks in that shape key. Click Add Shape Key to add a second key, and press Tab again to return to edit mode.

> *Other packages use the term morph target rather than shape key. Each shape key is like a target for a morphing kind of action to take place. If you animate this morphing action into a video, the viewer can witness the transformation, which I am sure you have seen in weight-loss commercials.*

When modifying faces of people, I find that it is very important to use proportional editing. To activate the proportional tool, press O (the letter O, not zero). Figure 5-9 shows the proportional tool activated in the 3D view header, in the middle of selecting the falloff, which determines how much to move nearby vertices. Proportional editing works with all vertex-movement commands: Grab, Scale, and Rotate. Localized editing allows you to stretch or shrink any portion of an image.

> *Before you press S or R (Scale or Rotate), position your mouse cursor farther away from the center to give you finer control of the scaling or rotation.*

Figure 5-9. Proportional editing aids in distorting a UV-mapped Image

First, let's play with a little rhinoplasty (a nose job). Select a vertex just to the right of the bridge of the girl's nose, and then press G. A circle should appear in your display. If you cannot see it, roll your mouse wheel in to shrink the circle. This is the circle of influence, and any vertices inside the circle will be proportionally affected by the movement of the selected vertex. Move the vertex a little to the left, as shown in Figure 5-9. Her cheekbone becomes more pronounced, and her nose shrinks.

Now that you have a good image, tab out of edit mode to lock in this second shape. You will notice that the image in your 3D view reverts back to the basis, but that's OK. Rename the shape key from Key 1 to Nose Job. Locate the Influence slider on the line below the shape key name, and drag it to the right, as shown in Figure 5-10. The Min and Max fields determine the minimum and maximum values of the influence slider. You can exaggerate the morphing by setting Max to a value greater than 1.

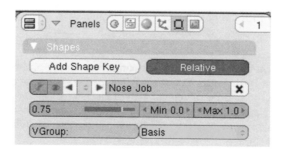

Figure 5-10. The Nose Job shape key with 75% influence

Shape keys work on any mesh object. So, for example, if you want the text "Growing" to literally grow, you need to convert it to a mesh (Object ➤ Convert Object Type), and then apply shape keys.

Rotoscoping with shape keys

Shape keys apply to video as well as to images, and can be useful for extracting specific movements, which is done through a process called rotoscoping. For example, If I had a video of my daughter (Becca) holding a balloon (instead of the image used in the previous example), I could extract her movements to make a video of just her and the balloon.

> *Rotoscoping was invented decades ago as a way for artists to trace live-action film, to get ultra-realistic animation. This was before the days of blue and green screens, and the artists literally went frame by frame, tracing the outline of the actor.*

In Blender, to rotoscope a series of frames, create a mesh mask and lock in the shape for the first frame of the video. Then create shape keys to change the shape of the mask from frame to frame. For rotoscoping, name each shape key based on the frame number that it masks. If the actor or camera does not move in a frame, then you got lucky, and you don't need a shape key for that frame. Otherwise, edit the mesh to cover the actor in that frame, tab out of edit mode to lock in the shape, advance to the next frame, create a new shape key, name it, and then tab into and edit the shape to match the outline.

After you have created a shape key for a frame, slide the influence to 1.0 for that frame. As you work through the video then, that frame's shape will change the shape of the mask for that frame. Yes, it's very tedious work, which is why a lot of thought and effort have gone into blue and green screen support in both the Blender compositor (Chapter 12) and sequencer (Chapter 14).

Layering elements in 3D space

Any element, including the camera itself, is free to move in the 3D space. After selecting an object (by right-clicking it), you can move it in several ways:

- Click and drag the manipulator arrows.
- Press G to grab it, and move your mouse. When it is where you want it, just click again to drop it (right-click to cancel the move).
- Press N and change the values in the pop-up Transform Properties panel.
- Gesture by swiping your mouse cursor (click and drag) left or right in a straight line. When you release the mouse button, the object will be rubber-banded to your mouse cursor. Move your mouse to position the object, and click to drop it in place.

As I mentioned in Chapter 3, although Blender has some 2D sections like the compositor and sequencer, it is a native 3D application. It does not work like After Effects, PowerPoint, or Photoshop, where you arrange things on top of one another through layers that have some precedence over others. Instead, you have the complete freedom to arrange elements in a virtually unlimited 3D space. You then take a picture of that arrangement with a camera. Any opaque element standing in front of another is thus "layered" on top of that element. If you have done any stage work involving a camera, the way Blender works will be intuitive, because it is exactly how you do it in the real world.

Figure 5-11 shows an example where I have three "layers" of elements (this is the Elements scene in the tut/5-Layers.blend file). It has five elements and a camera arranged in 3D space, for two pictures and three text objects. The frontmost layer, which would be the "top" in Photoshop, is the Spring Stimulus Special text object; the second layer is Balloon, and so on. Each element appears as a vertical line in side or top view. To layer the elements, simply alter their Y location, if you are using the front view orientation of the camera.

Figure 5-11. Stacking elements in 3D space

Go ahead and open the tut/5-Layers.blend file on your DVD and play with rearranging the layers. Notice that how you stack them and what the camera sees are two different things. Thus, when arranging elements, always check the camera view to make sure they are getting on camera. I've deliberately arranged them to look good in front view, but if you render this scene (press F12), you will see that some elements are not in the camera view. You can bring up the properties panel (press N) and observe the X, Y, and Z changes as you move the objects around. Select various elements (right-click) and observe the Transform Properties panel Y value. I chose these Y values just to keep some physical separation between them, and give me some room if I wanted to insert something in between them. As you can see, by using the Y value as a layer, you can have an infinite number of layers.

Using an orthographic camera, all elements in front of the camera, regardless of the distance, will be rendered as long as they are in the clipping range (as discussed in Chapter 6). Anything you move to a Y value in back of the camera will not be rendered. In this file, the camera is at -3. To include a wider "angle" shot of the scene, with an orthographic camera, change the Scale value in its Editing context Camera panel.

The 3D view shows your elements that are being layered. When you look through camera view (by pressing 0 on the number keypad), you will see what is being rendered. Normally, when doing 2D work, you use an orthographic camera (discussed in Chapter 6). This kind of camera does not distort the view of any object based on its depth, or distance, from the camera. The view label, in the upper-left corner of the window workspace, will say Camera Ortho, as a reminder of the view perspective you have chosen.

Masking

One of the most common tasks in compositing is to make a mask to either select or avoid a section of an image. In the example in Chapter 3, you created a simple mask. Here, we'll look at masking in more detail.

Setting up the 3D view and camera for masking

Before creating the mask, you'll need to set up your view and camera. For this exercise, start a new file and use the SR:1-Model screen layout. Change the 3D view to camera perspective (press 0 on the number keypad), and you can delete the plane and lights (but not the camera!). Load the images/People/Rebe/balloonee.jpg file from the DVD as a background image in the 3D view. To get nice sharp outlines when masking, change the Blend value on the Background Image panel to 0. You can use the View Properties panel to clear the grid floor and axis selectors. While they are handy in doing detailed modeling, you really don't need them in compositing, and they clutter the display. Roll your mouse wheel to zoom in your display so that the girl and/or title safe area fills the whole screen.

By default in my B.blend file, the camera is rotated and translated to work in front view. In this example, you will be working solely in 2D, so you need to use an orthographic camera. Press F9, and your buttons window will change to the Editing properties for the selected object. In this case, the camera has two panels: Link and Camera. In the Camera panel, click Orthographic and Passepartout, as shown in Figure 5-12.

Notice that the reference image is 640×480. To ensure that your mask lines up perfectly with the image, you need to change your render settings to match the image aspect ratio. Press F10, and the buttons window will change to the Scene context. In the Render context, locate the Format panel and click the PC preset. Figure 5-13 shows the Background Image panel with a Blend factor of 0, reporting the image resolution, and the buttons window showing the Format panel of 640×480, a PNG output format, with RGBA enabled (you want to save the image with that alpha channel!), and Premul enabled (you don't want any sky, world, or background color altering your output—these settings are discussed in Chapter 9).

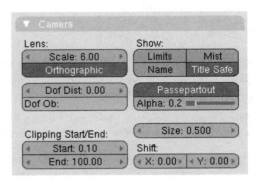

Figure 5-12. Camera properties panel

Figure 5-13. Setup for masking

Of course, the girl (my daughter) is cute, but the background is absolutely horrid (those are my son's LEGO kits cluttering the background). Let's make a mask of just her and the balloon, so that you can use them as a compositing element.

When masking, you have your choice of any Blender object type that has a renderable surface. Closed curves and meshes are the most commonly used. Let's start by making a Bezier curve mask.

> *For people and organic objects, I like to use Bezier curves to make my mask objects, since they have rounded outlines. For straight-edged objects like buildings, meshes are the obvious choice, since vertices are connected by straight edges You can use any 2D object, or if it's something worth your time, model a 3D object. For some challenging masking projects, I have made a 3D replica of the object I was masking. Refer to a Blender book on modeling for more information about 3D modeling.*

Masking with Bezier curves

Now you're ready to make the mask. With your cursor in 3D view, press the spacebar and select Add ➤ Curve ➤ Bezier Curve. This adds a two-point open curve with an object center wherever the crosshair cursor is located. An open curve does not have a surface until you close it, but you will do that last. For fun, you can press C now and see an ovoid shape. The idea is that you add points (handles) to trace the outline of the girl and balloon.

A Bezier handle consists of a triple set of points. The center point is the actual vertex (edge connecting point), and the outer two are control points that control the slope/shape of the connecting edge. The handle acts like a stick, in that if you move one control point, you twist the handle. This provides a very smooth transition of the edge through the control point. By moving the control point closer to or farther from the vertex, you change the slope of the connecting point. Notice that you are in edit mode, so you are working on individual points, as shown in Figure 5-14.

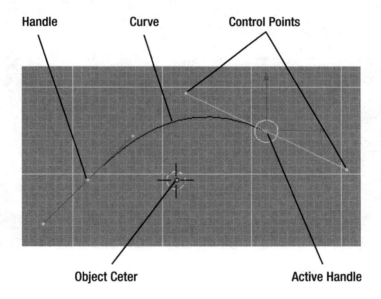

Figure 5-14. Components of a Bezier curve

In edit mode (press Tab to cycle into/out of edit mode), select (right-click) the left handle vertex, and move it to below the girl's dress on the left side. You can "break" the handle by pressing V with the vertex selected. There are actually four types of handles, as listed on the Transform Properties **panel:** Auto, Vector, Align, and Free. You can change any handle type by clicking the appropriate Transform Properties **panel button.** Auto is handy when tracing an object, as the handle orients to fit the curve. Align **aligns the handle with the previous vector, sort of in parallel.**

Click Auto in the Transform Properties panel, then Ctrl-click while moving your mouse, and you can see how the handle automatically rotates based on where you have clicked before. Now select and move the second handle to just under her right elbow. Press R to rotate it about 90 degrees, so that the connecting edge lines up with the edge of her dress. Notice that you are rotating only that point, not the whole object, since you are in edit mode. Adjust the control points slightly outside the edge

127

so that they curve the edge to match the outline of her dress. Figure 5-15 gives you an idea of what you should have at this point, with the second vertex selected. (I've turned down the Blend factor so you can more easily see the curve.)

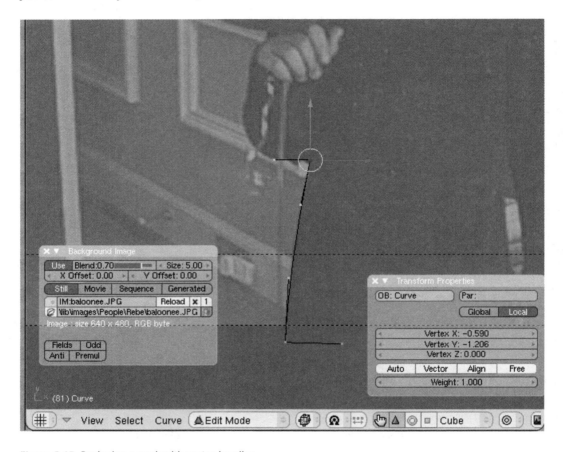

Figure 5-15. Beginning a mask with vector handles

Now you have a couple of choices. Do you mask the folds in her sleeve there, or just cut them out? Do you mask the dangling ribbon? For the ribbon, you could use another mask object or simply omit it, since it isn't important to the overall element—in fact, it may be distracting. A lot of masking is an effort-to-quality ratio based on the time you have available to complete the job.

> *Don't think your mask has to be only one thing. A mask can be a combination of many objects parented together, so that they act in unison. If you were masking a man with a spear, you could make one mask for the man and another for the spear, especially since one is organic and the other is a man-made object. You might use a NURBS or Bezier curve for the man to follow the organic curves of his outline, and a mesh for the spear, where a few simple polygons will match its shape.*

Next, position your mouse cursor at the girl's elbow and Ctrl-click. You just extruded another point, automatically connecting it to the previous one. Notice that the vector handle was duplicated as well, which you don't want since you are going into a rounded area around her elbow. Click Auto in the Transform Properties panel, or press Shift+H. This turns that handle back into a normal handle. Now press R to rotate it so that the curve edge matches the outline of her elbow. Next, Ctrl-click near her wrist, rotate, and press S to scale that point down a little.

> The best way to model in Blender is with one hand on the keyboard and another on the mouse.

Use a mix of vector and auto handles to continue tracing the outline of the balloon. The only disadvantage is that Auto handles cannot be immediately rotated after being created, but you just need to move one control point to twist the whole handle. Figure 5-16 shows the outlining in progress.

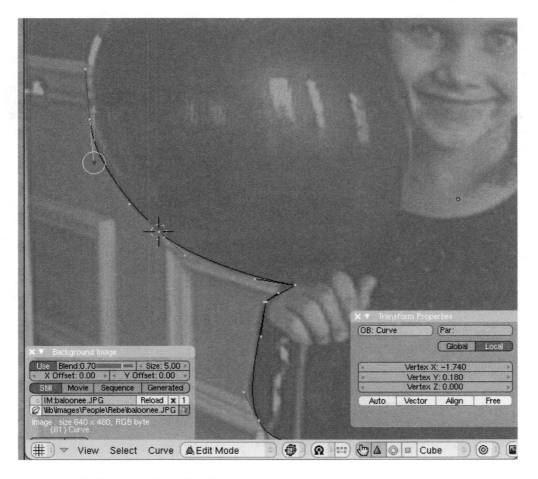

Figure 5-16. Masking around the balloon in progress

Continue on around the girl's head in a clockwise fashion, tracing her arm until you reach your last point of the image, as shown in Figure 5-17. Then press C to close the curve.

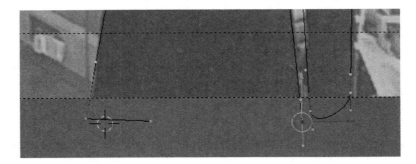

Figure 5-17. Last Bezier point before closing the curve

So far, you probably have been working in wireframe viewport shading mode, which is clean, simple, and fast. Unfortunately, you cannot see the objects as solid: only their outlines and mesh structures are shown. Using the viewport shading selector on the 3D view header (just to the right of the mode selector), choose the solid box. You should have a mask like that shown in Figure 5-18. It's perfectly OK if your mask extends beyond the image/camera boundaries, as it will simply be cropped by the camera. Your mask might be gray, but the color in the 3D view does not matter at this point. What you want is a opaque surface with an alpha value of 1, which the default material has. I colored mine red (Chapter 7 examines all the shading options) to contrast with the blue and green of the image.

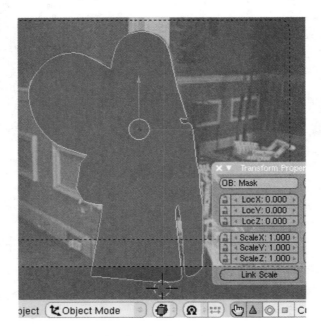

Figure 5-18. Completed mask using Bezier curves

Creating elements from masked images

Now that you have a mask, let's use it to extract that portion of the image, creating a nice image element to use in later compositions. All you need to do is map the image to the mask, which is accomplished by assigning the image to the mask as a texture, and selecting Win in the Map To panel, as shown in Figure 5-19. Win (for Window), in this case, refers to the viewport 3D view window.

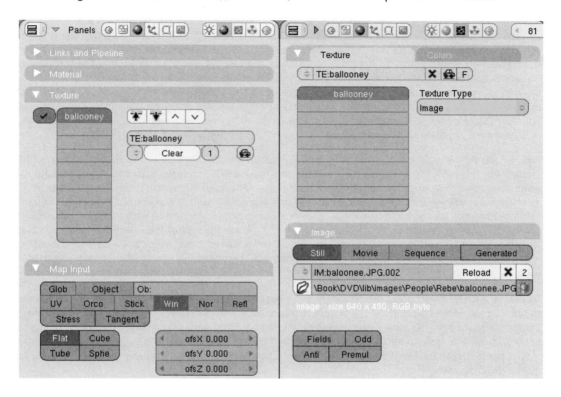

Figure 5-19. Mapping an image to a mask

To begin, click Add New in the Shading Material context Texture panel, which creates a generic Tex texture. I renamed the texture from Tex to ballooney by editing the TE: field. In the Map Input panel, select Win.

Now hop over to the Texture context (the right column in Figure 5-19). Select Image as the Texture Type, which will reveal a bunch of image-specific panels. In the Image panel, just click the yellow selector and choose the JPG image.

With the appropriate image format (covered in Chapter 4) and render settings, pressing F12 yields an image of just the girl and the balloon against a transparent black background. Save this image (press F3) in lib\images\People\Rebe\balloon premul.png (to indicate that it has a premultiplied transparency channel).

Masking with meshes

When working with straight-edged objects like buildings, desks, parking lots, or other squarish items, it can work to your advantage to use 3D objects as masks even in simpler cases. However, you must be careful to correct for camera lens distortion, or use a Blender nonorthographic camera and model the image correctly, and then adjust the Blender camera to match the real-world camera used.

For example, in the balloonee image (my daughter affectionately named the balloon Balloonee, and yes, it was a melancholy day when Balloonee accidentally flew up to heaven), consider the edge of the door on the left. The door is straight (trust me), but appears curved because of the camera lens distortion. Furthermore, it is an irregular curve, since the camera was tilted down and the top part of the door was a little closer to the camera than the bottom. Understanding this effect is critical to camera match-moving programs, like Voodoo and Icarus. A real camera lens with a long zoom is almost orthographic. Only when the camera is close do you get a bulging effect on objects close to camera. For this reason, never take a close-in shot of your girlfriend, or her nose will look, er, bulbous, and she may never let you take another picture of her again (there's that voice of experience again).

Figure 5-20 shows an in-progress view of modeling a simple 3D mesh object to mimic what is in the picture—in this case, the front of a house. Later, this mask can be textured with an image of the house using projection texturing, allowing different computer-generated elements (in this case, a front stone garden was envisioned) to be superimposed. In this example, I kept the grid floor as a guide to indicate the driveway location and give me a reference point. I knew the person who took the picture, so I could accurately guesstimate the height of the camera. I knew the wall of the house was perpendicular to the garage wall, so I modeled it that way, and then adjusted the camera angle so that the edges aligned, further refining and making my virtual camera alignment with the real one that was used. I used the edges of the windows, since I knew they were rectangular, as further guides.

To create a mesh mask, press the spacebar and select Add ➤ Mesh ➤ Plane. Then extrude the plane to create more edges, and move them into position, using the different views. I like to use a four-up configuration of four 3D views, with windows aligned to front, top, side, and user/camera, to speed my workflow. The neat thing about masking in Blender is that you have a 3D workspace, so you can model the actual thing, like a dog's snout, and then position the camera and the snout in 3D space to match the real world.

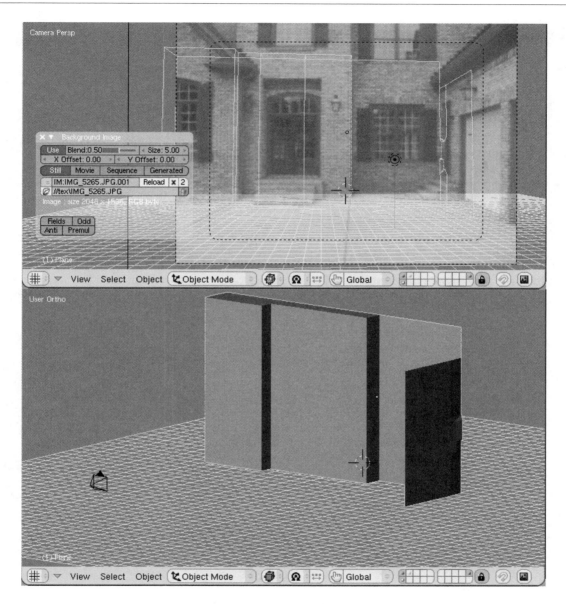

Figure 5-20. Mesh masking

Using empty targets

A deceptively simple but incredibly useful object is an empty. An empty is just a point in space. It appears in 3D view as just a mini-axis. An empty can be moved, rotated, and scaled. Since it does not have a renderable surface, it does not interfere with any rendering. It is simply used to guide and direct other objects and textures. Let's try that now.

Start with a new file (File ➤ New), and with your mouse in 3D view, press the spacebar and select Add ➤ Empty. If the empty is not at (0,0,0), use the Transform Properties panel (press N to pop it up) to move it there. By default, the first empty you add to a scene is called Empty, but you can change that name. As always, I suggest giving objects names that imply their purpose. In this case, you are going to use the empty to point the camera, so click Empty in the OB: field in the Transform Properties panel to highlight it (if your cursor ends up somewhere in the editable field, just use the Delete and Backspace keys to erase the existing name), and type Focus to rename this empty object.

Now select the camera, and press F7 or select the Object context in the buttons window. You will see a Constraints panel. In that panel, click Add Constraint and select Track To. The panel fills in with the fields that are relevant to this kind of constraint. Notice that the Const field is red, which means that there is a problem with the constraint. In this case, Blender is hinting to you that the Target: OB: field is blank. Click the OB: field and enter Focus (this name, like all names in Blender, is case-sensitive).

> Blender offers many types of constraints. For details on each, refer to the online documentation in the wiki at http://wiki.blender.org.

You should see your camera instantly rotate to somewhere pointing down, and the Const field change to gray. The constraint overrides the rotation settings in the Transform panel. This constraint (as it is configured now) says, "Hey, camera, point your Y axis to that Focus empty over there." (Recall that with the camera, the Z direction is from/to the camera looking out through the camera, X is left/right, and Y is up/down.) If you switched to side view now and moved the empty to above the camera, it would act as a stick marionette, but that is not too useful. It's better is to make the camera focus on the empty all the time. In the Constraints panel, click To: -Z and Up: Y, as shown in Figure 5-21.

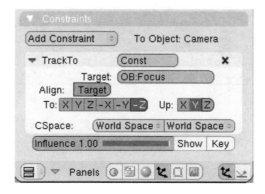

Figure 5-21. The Track To constraint selected in the Constraints panel

Now grab and move the empty around, and you will see that the camera tracks its movements, always pointing at the empty. Go ahead and move the camera to (0,-10,0). If you switch to camera view now (press 0 on the number keypad), select the empty, and move it, you will see that you are rotating the camera around to look in different places in the scene, just as in real life. If you grab and move the camera around, you have what other packages called an orbit camera, since the camera is orbiting around in space, but automatically tilting to always look at the empty in the center. Depending on the relative (layer) distances between the objects, they appear to move proportionally to one another.

We are setting up what I call a "flying camera" rig in order to configure Blender to operate similarly to Adobe After Effects. To enable this rig to feed the compositor fully, enter the name Focus in the camera's DofOb: field in the Editing context's Camera panel. If you are using a four-up modeling layout, part of your display should look like Figure 5-22. Notice that I hide the grid floor in one view, and also the XYZ axis in the other views. This is strictly a personal preference.

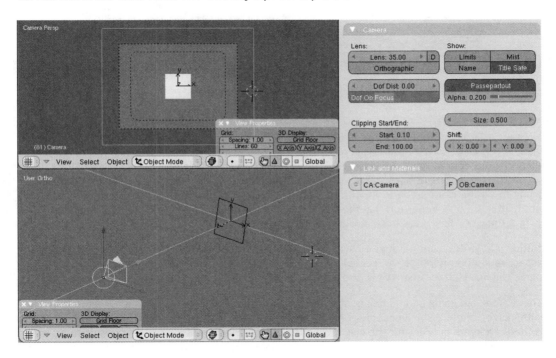

Figure 5-22. Making the camera stay focused on an object

When you move something in Blender, you can click to drop it in place, or right-click to cancel the move and put it back where you found it.

Next, select the camera in camera view by right-clicking the big box that is around the passepartout (the area of the camera view that will not be rendered). For this and later exercises, add a billboard by pressing the spacebar and choosing Add ➤ Mesh ➤ Plane. Press Tab to leave edit mode, and snap the selected plane to the cursor (press Shift+S). Assuming you have not repositioned the cursor, the plane should now be centered at (0,0,0) and in the middle of the camera view. If it isn't, use the transform widget or panel to get it there. Use the Transform Properties panel to scale the plane to a 4:3 aspect ratio and rotate it 90 degrees to face the camera, as shown in Figure 5-23.

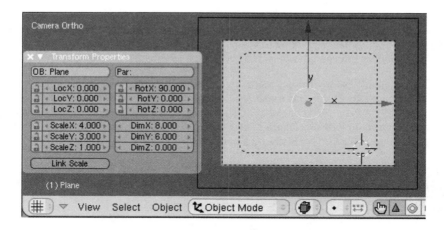

Figure 5-23. 4:3 Aspect ratio projection plane

Switch to an orthographic camera (because you are setting up to work only in 2D, and you do not want artificial distortion) and change the camera to a scale of 8. The plane will now fill the field of view. This is an important ratio to keep in mind: the scale of an orthographic camera is the number of Blender units across that the field of view encompasses. Therefore, a unit plane scaled to 16:9 needs an orthographic camera scaled to 32, since the orthographic camera scale is twice the X scale of the plane to fill the plane of view. As with all orthographic cameras, the distance from the camera does not matter. It's only important that the element is in front of the camera and within the camera's clipping settings. A 16:9 rig is shown in Figure 5-24.

Notice that in the scene settings, I have chosen HD 1920×1080 and RGBA. Thus, my projection plane aspect ratio and my render aspect ratio match, since they are both 16:9. If there is a mismatch, the plane will not fill the camera view, and you will get a letterbox or cropping (which you may want).

The reason I am going on and on about the plane and scales is that you are going to texture this plane with images, and the plane becomes what is known in packages like After Effects as an element, which is then rendered. In order for the element not to be stretched or distorted when it is textured to the plane, the plane needs to be in the same aspect ratio as the image. You then stack these planes (and text and other computer-generated elements, as described earlier in this chapter) in 3D space to make a composite image.

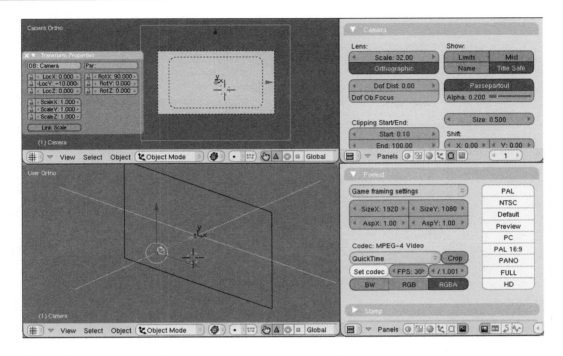

Figure 5-24. Camera aspect ratio matches projection plane aspect ratio

Working with text

Text is very commonly used in compositing for titles and credits, and in normal 2D artwork. The text object is a special kind of element with a multitude of font properties and controls. To add one to your scene, press the spacebar and select Add ➤ Text. The default value for the text itself, creatively called Text, is displayed. You now are in a special editing mode, where X does not delete a letter, but is instead a real letter. Use Delete, Backspace, the arrow keys, Home, End, and Enter as you would in a standard text editor. As you type, your text is created directly in the 3D view.

Setting text properties

The properties for a text object are shown in Figure 5-25. These properties are split among four panels: Link and Materials, Curve and Surface, Font, and Modifiers. The Link and Materials panel in this example says this is a curve object. (The Link and Materials panel also has a setting for material, which is discussed in Chapter 7.)

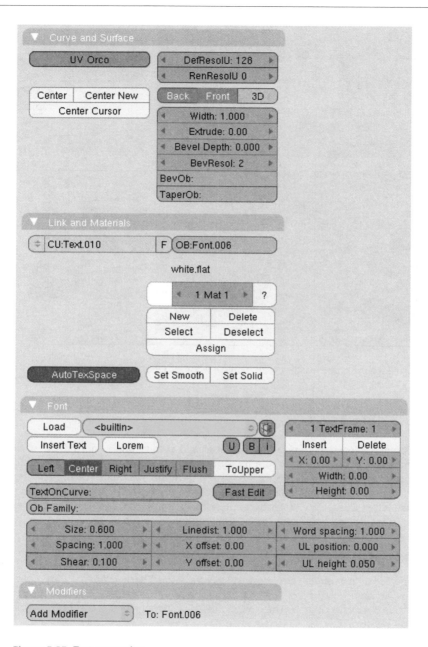

Figure 5-25. Text properties

Because text is just a special kind of curve, you also see the same type of panel that you saw when you made the Bezier curve mask. With text, the Extrude value is relevant, and it gives text some 3D thickness. When used with a perspective camera, deep text can be very dramatic. Text can be beveled to give the edges some roundness. In Figure 5-26 (in the DeepText scene in the tut/text.blend file on your DVD), I extruded the text 10 units, set up a world with mist, filmed the scene with a wide-angle lens (10mm), and offset the shot for a perspective shift. (Chapter 6 discusses how to add mist and offset camera shots.)

Figure 5-26. Extruded text on a curve

The Font panel is unique to the text object. You can load fonts from your PC, and Blender can use any normal font installed on your system. You point Blender to your default fonts directory in the user preferences window's File Paths tab (on Windows PCs, it's usually c:\Windows\Fonts). Once the font is loaded, you just select it using the <builtin> selector in the Font panel. Fonts can be packed into the blend file by clicking the package, which is very handy when sending blend files between PCs that may not have the same fonts installed.

The Lorem button inserts placeholder text. Text is fit into frames (not to be confused with video frames), very similar to how text is handled in other layout applications like Illustrator. Create frames by clicking Insert, and offset the frame from the object center by the XY values (in Blender units).

Text does not need to be in a straight line. To have it follow a curve, create a Bezier curve and enter the name of the curve in the TextOnCurve field. I used this in making the SuperBlender example in Figure 5-26.

You can create a family of objects that each serve as a "letter" using the ObFamily field. First, create a mesh object that stands for each letter—for example, MyFont.x for the letter x. Be sure to enable DupliVerts (on the Object Animation panel) for all font objects, including the text object itself. Then create a text object, and enter the starting name of the font family (MyFont. in this example). Then for every x in the string, Blender will substitute the mesh object MyFont.x. In this way, you can create your own reusable 3D font object library, say, with letters that look like they were carved from stone (*Ice Age* comes to mind).

The group of nine controls at the bottom of the Font panel affect the spacing and slant of paragraphs of text. Finally, the text can be modified, for example, by a wave modifier that makes the letters wave. This modifier was also used in the SuperBlender example in Figure 5-26.

Getting text files into Blender

Often, you will have text provided for you for use in your composites. Instead of retyping all of that text in the 3D view, you can import plain text files into Blender. Using the Scripting layout and the text editor window, select File ➤ Open and open your text file. Blender can read in ASCII text files. Now convert the text to 3D space via Edit ➤ Text to 3D Object. A pop-up menu allows you to convert each line of text to an object or to convert the whole chunk as one object. Once the text is a 3D object, you can change the font and arrange it into frames.

Animating text

In a video, you often want text to scroll, pop into/out of view, or fade in/out. A great example of using text for credits is in Peach\production\scenes\dvd\menu_credits.blend on your DVD. Many of the text elements are arranged in a 3D space as children to a huge box kind of object called Plane, which is animated to slide slowing down in front of camera, dragging all the text with it. To the viewer, it appears as though the text scrolls. Additionally, the material (covered in Chapter 7) of other elements is animated to fade in and out using the alpha channel, and thus some text characters can fade in, while others can scroll. Other text, such as Font.005, is animated to jump from an unrendered layer to a layer that is rendered, and thus "pop" into view. A perspective view of the scene is shown in Figure 5-27.

Summary

In this chapter, we dove into the use of the 3D view and how to arrange objects and elements. You learned how to use masks and shapes, and how to morph those shapes from one to the other. You also learned how to bring in image elements and arrange them with other objects in 3D space. Since you can arrange any object anywhere relative to camera, you are not confined to a set of "layers," as in other packages. You learned about the importance of the camera, a topic we will explore in depth in the next chapter. Finally, we took a look at the text facility in Blender, which is used quite a bit in compositing.

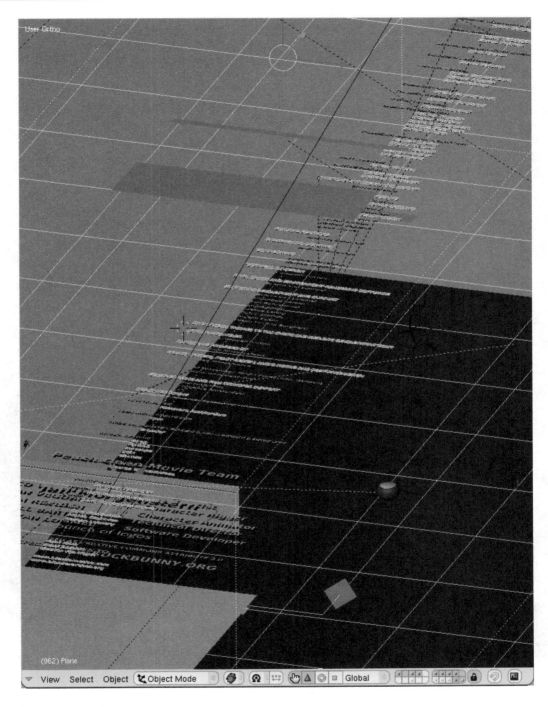

Figure 5-27. Peach credit text objects

Chapter 6

CAMERA AND WORLD

In order to render an image from 3D view, you need a camera and something to shoot. You may think I'm being silly, but when you get a Black Render of Darkness, you will know what I mean. The camera needs to be on an active layer as well, and be visible to the Render panel.

Blender's camera object provides the focal point and framing for any image that you render. In this chapter, we will explore how to use the camera effectively. We will also look at the world in Blender, which provides a backdrop to your compositions.

Blender cameras

In Blender, any object can be a camera, but only the camera object type gives you fine control over the render. With a camera, you have control over the following:

- Perspective (three-point, two-point, or orthogonal)
- Depth of vision (mist and clipping)
- Depth of field (focal plane, full-screen anti-aliasing)
- Position (target and animation)

You can have many cameras in a scene, on various layers. If you do not have a camera on any visible layer, Blender will try to use the active camera to make the render.

However, for accurate results, and to avoid problems, be sure to have the camera visible in the 3D view before making a render.

In Figure 6-1, a 3D view window is set to camera view (by pressing 0 on the number keypad) and shows what the camera sees. The yellow rectangle is the camera object itself; yellow indicates it is selected. Other figures throughout this book show that from another perspective, the icon for a camera is a pyramid with an up arrow indicating orientation. The lightly shaded area inside the dotted-line area is what will be included in the render output, since Passepartout is enabled on the Camera panel.

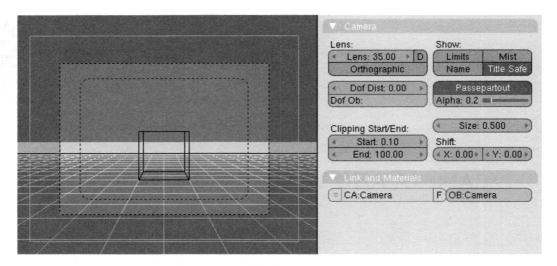

Figure 6-1. Camera perspective display and properties

When looking through the camera, and when compositing, X is left/right and Y is up/down. Z is the vector straight out through the lens, which is also the distance to whatever is being photographed. This information is saved in a Z-buffer in the OpenEXR format. Some real cameras also have a transponder that records this information, for use with compositing live action.

Camera properties

The Camera panel, shown in Figure 6-1, contains many controls:

- Lens: When using a normal camera, this controls the lens focal length, which simulates the distortion caused by a real lens. A 35mm (35.00) lens is standard. A 16mm lens is wide angle, 50mm is closer to human vision, and 120mm is a long lens.

- D: Makes the Lens field use degrees to define the field of view.

- Orthographic: Switches between a perspective camera and an orthographic one. While a perspective camera "bends" the image based on the Lens size, the orthographic camera captures the image as if it were viewed by a large backplane through a flat lens (without any depth distortion).

- Scale: This setting replaces the Lens setting when Orthographic is selected. It controls the scale, or area of the scene that is covered by the orthographic camera.

- **Dof Dis:** This is shorthand for Depth of Field Distance, which is used by the defocus compositing node to determine how far from the camera (called Z-depth) that objects are in focus. This is a manual setting in Blender units.

- **Dof Ob:** Rather than setting Dof Dis, you can have the camera stay focused on an object by entering its name in this field.

- **Clipping Start/End:** For very large, dense scenes, render times can get huge. If the camera were allowed to see out to infinity, it might spend infinity trying to calculate the color of something way off in the distance that really does not matter much. For this reason, Blender offers clipping values. Set the End clip value to the maximum distance from the camera, called the *Z distance*, that you want the camera to see.

- **Limits:** One of the Show controls, this displays a ray that ends where the clipping starts and ends. When the scene is viewed from the top or side, you can see the range of objects that will be rendered.

- **Mist:** When enabled in the Material World subcontext, this visually shows the mist start and depth. Mist is discussed later in this chapter, in the "Mist and stars" section.

- **Name:** This displays the name of the current camera when in camera view in a 3D window. If you have multiple cameras in a scene, this can be handy for checking which one is active.

- **Title Safe:** This shows dashed lines around the TV safe area. If you are composing a scene for eventual TV broadcast, keep important elements within this safe area to avoid clipping due to overscan.

- **Passepartout:** A French term for blocking (darkening by the amount) the area of the camera view that will not be rendered.

- **Shift:** This shifts the frame (the view that is rendered) of the camera by X,Y units in camera space.

Tracking the camera to an object

Sometimes it helps to just tell the camera to stay focused and follow a certain object in the shot. However, to simulate a cameraman's delay when things are moving, you don't want the camera to follow the object exactly. For example, in Pixar's movie *Cars*, the camera lags the cars as they accelerate, which emphasizes the acceleration, because the audience can see the separation occurring in the frame. Tracking the camera exactly to the car would not look the same; in fact, it might give the optical illusion that everything else is moving backward. Therefore, you want a kind of rubber-band effect between the center of the camera and the object that is accelerating—a slight lag so that the audience can see the object speeding up or slowing down within the frame.

You can track an object with the camera in three ways. The first is to manually create keys while looking through the viewfinder, which is very tedious. The other ways are to parent the camera or to use the Track To constraint.

Parenting the camera

Using the parenting approach, you position the camera directly facing a frame, and then parent the camera as a child to the frame. Figure 6-2 shows an example of positioning the camera using a 16:9 grid that shows the rule of thirds (discussed later in this chapter) such that the grid fills the view.

I have given this grid a transparent material (discussed in Chapter 7), so although it's visible in 3D view, it will not show up in your render.

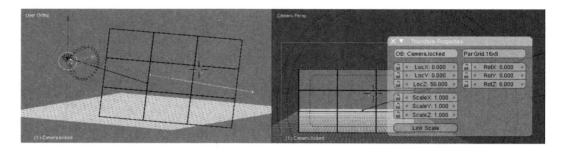

Figure 6-2. Parent the camera to a control frame.

Now you just move this frame around, and the camera will move along with it. Twist (rotate) the frame, and the camera swings around through space to be properly positioned. Rotate the frame vertically to get a kind of see-saw effect, if you rotate based on the active object's center. As an analogy, imagine a (well-behaved) small child walking beside her parent.

You can experiment by reversing the parent-child relationship, making the camera the parent of the grid. Then if you rotate the camera, the grid will swing through space to align. You can then use the grid as a sort of focusing frame to direct the camera. With either rig, the camera and frame stay far enough away from each other to capture everything inside the frame (use your camera view), but you always have the frame's guideline to guide your shot composition.

Using the Track To constraint

Another way to control the camera is to set up a Track To constraint, which was introduced in Chapter 5. The example in that chapter used an empty object named Focus to direct the camera's orientation.

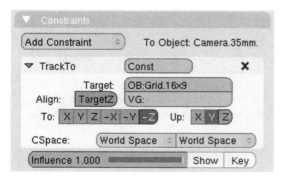

Figure 6-3. Constraining the camera to always look at the object

Figure 6-3 shows an example of a Track To constraint set in the camera's Constraints panel. It tracks to the 16:9 grid. You can have the camera stay focused on this grid by entering the grid's name in the Dof Ob field in the Camera panel (see Figure 6-1). Now, when you move the little grid around, your camera will rotate to follow it, and stay focused on it—kind of a focal plane that you can see and touch. Notice that I said "rotate." The Track To constraint will not slew the camera, as the parent-child relationship does.

In Figure 6-3, Influence is set to 1.000, which means that the camera will override its normal rotation and spin to perfectly stay looking at the grid's center. If you animate this influence ramping up from 0 to 1 over time (as discussed in Chapter 8), the camera will go from its "rest" orientation to face the object. You can see this by clicking and dragging the slider manually.

When controlling a camera, you need to think like a cameraman and make the camera do what a good director of photography would do. For example, when tracking a decelerating object, you want the camera to start to lead the object as it decelerates, so that the object travels backward in the frame, simulating a cameraman's delay to this real-world change. We call this "lazy" tracking. In Blender, you track the camera to the grid, and animate the location of the grid to follow the object. You can also orient the camera and then animate this Influence slider to get lazy tracking (animation is covered in Chapter 8).

Perspectives and vanishing points

In the real world, we see in what is called *three-point perspective*. Figure 6-4 shows a wide-angle lens picture of a cube on a table illustrating three-point perspective. Here, I've added lines that trace each edge of the cube and table in the three dimensions (X, Y, and Z). The lines from each dimension intersect into what is called a *vanishing point*. This point can be in the image (as shown in the figure for the X and Y dimensions), just outside the image, or located way off in the distance (as with the Z dimension). The farther out the vanishing point, the more those edges appear parallel. The location of these points depends on the camera lens settings and the location of the object relative to the camera.

Figure 6-4. An angled perspective camera gives a three-point perspective.

Let's explore the settings for Figure 6-4. Open the /tut/camera.blend file on your DVD to the Perspective scene. This is the scene used to generate the image in the figure. The 3D view window should be in camera view. Select and move the table or cube more to the center of the camera, and notice what happens to the vanishing points in the camera view window: they don't move! Now move the camera, and you'll see that they still don't move! Now in the Camera panel, change the Lens size setting. As you increase it from 14 upward, notice how the image zooms, but the vanishing points do not change their relative position.

This means that for a certain lens size and camera rotation, the vanishing point for any object is fixed. Press Alt+A to see the cube move and twist on the table (but it stays flat on the table), and notice what happens to its vanishing points relative to the table. They stay aligned, and travel in a straight line between them as the cube rotates 90 degrees.

You may ask "Why should I care about vanishing points?" When compositing computer-generated elements on top of live video, for things to look like they fit together, you must match your vanishing points to those represented in the live picture.

Matching vanishing points

Vanishing points are introduced by the lens and rotation of the camera, which means that you need to match Blender's virtual camera to the real-world camera that was used. For objects to look aligned, their vanishing points must be in the same spot. Every shape of object has these edges, called a *bounding box* in Blender, which you can use to align your object (as viewed through Blender's camera) with the background image.

Even though it can be very tedious to properly position your virtual camera to match the real world, it is essential to good results. If you do so, you can keep your computer-generated world oriented logically as well.

Let's work through an example. Suppose you have a background image of the Panama Canal, and you want to put another ship in front in the upper lock. You know that the water is level, and that the lock outline is a rectangle. Here's how you could match the vanishing points:

1. Initialize the camera to an approximate position, with a 90-degree X angle (looking out at the horizon). If you are using real-world units, position the camera accordingly. For example, if your eyes are 5 feet off the ground when you take a picture, you should place the camera five units above the "ground" in your virtual shot in Blender.

> *Blender is real-world unit agnostic, which means it could care less if a unit is a foot, a meter, or a mile. Blender has been used to model microscopic and galactic real-world situations. Your choice of real-world units of measure to Blender units is up to you. A Blender world is a 10,000 Blender unit cube.*

2. Load the live-action plate as a background to camera view. For this example, open \lib\ images\places\Panama Canal.jpg on your DVD. Notice the vanishing lines of the sides (which are going away from the camera) of the upper lock that is full of water.

3. Position a reference plane at *exactly* the height of the camera, pretty far away from the camera (but within clipping distance!).

4. In camera view, rock the camera left/right to match any tilt in the image. In the Transform Properties panel, lock in RotY.

5. In side view, rotate the camera up/down to match the horizon line in the background image, and lock in RotX. At this point, your setup should look something like Figure 6-5. In the figure, the red line is my horizon reference, and the Transform Properties panel shows my camera rotation and position settings. Now you have a good horizon reference and a general orientation for your scene.

Figure 6-5. Camera setup to match vanishing points

6. Position a plane in front of and slightly below the camera, say at a height (Z) of 8. Note that the left side of the levee's vanishing point angles to the right, whereas the right side angles to the left, which means that the vanishing point is somewhere in between. This also means that one edge of the plane will be to the left of camera, and the other will be on the right of camera.

7. In the Camera panel, select an approximate Lens size, based on how distorted the image is (35 is a good starting value). Images that show more rounding of straight edges near the limits of the view will have lower values, and vice versa.

8. Using some nicely delineated edges, position the plane somewhere in 3D view that matches the area, placed roughly relative to where it was with respect to the real camera. In this case, the plane should face up and roughly cover the area of the filled lock.

9. Scale the plane roughly to fit the dimensions of the real-world area. In this example, the lock is about eight times longer than it is wide, so a scale of 4 in the X direction and 32 in the Y location is about the right aspect ratio of the lock area. Put the plane in front of but below the camera. A good location for the plane is (-2, 34, 8).

10. Move and rotate the plane to match the area in camera view. You will see that you can rotate the plane to get one edge to align to the bank of the lock, but not the other. That is because the perspective distortion does not match. To fix this, make the Blender virtual camera a Lens size of 34, and readjust your X angle so that the horizon matches up again.

> For less distortion, use a longer lens (a bigger Lens value).

11. Now it's a matter of rotating and positioning the plane so that it overlays the water area of the lock. As you get closer to a finished product, you can see that you can almost slide the plane over the surface of the water. As you move it around in top view, in camera view, it will look like a shadow on the ground (or water, in this case). Figure 6-6 shows my results (which you can view by opening \tut\camera.blend). Your results may be different based on how close you want the plane to the camera (the relative scale of things in your computer-generated world).

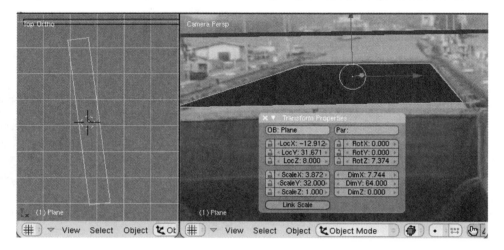

Figure 6-6. Matched vanishing points

12. As a final touch, square up your virtual world by selecting everything (press A twice), and then Shift-select the camera (again) so that it is the active object. With your pivot center (the control located on the 3D header to the right of the draw type selector) in active object mode, rotate everything in top view so that the plane is "square" relative to the 3D view grid. Everything will be off in camera view, but you can fix that by deselecting the camera and sliding everything in the X direction until it lines up again in camera view.

You now have a virtual workspace where you can place and move around computer-generated elements, and they will align with and integrate into the background plate. As they recede away from the camera in the computer-generated world, they will be properly distorted and look exactly as if they had been in the real world. You can even try this with the plane, moving it in top view out into Gatun Lake (which this lock opens out into, as shown in the distance in the background image). If, while watching the plane move in the camera view, it looks like your plane is a raft that floats out into the lake, you've done a good job of matching the perspective.

If you did not tilt the camera, then everything in your computer-generated world would have to be tilted, and most 3D models are made with a square orientation to the XYZ axis.

The *coup de grace* is placing your 3D model. In Figure 6-7, which is taken from the file tut\camera-matched.blend, I have duplicated that matched plane to match the other two locks and the gate house, and put a boat model by Kator Legaz (distributed herein under the Creative Commons Attribution license) into the lock in front of the ship.

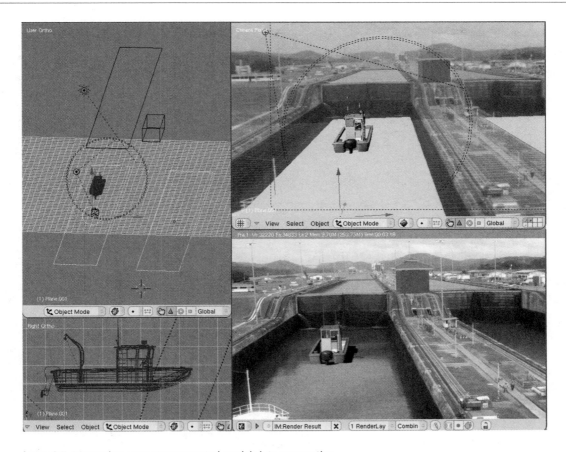

igure 6-7. Integrating computer-generated models into perspective

Using two-point perspective

One of the issues with three-point perspective is that the vertical line vanishing point, when looking up at something, is above the object, and so tall buildings look pointy at the top. When looking through a camera at something off center, it looks tilted. In fact, the Greeks figured out that if you shape the columns of a building to taper above head height, they look taller than they really are. This trick is used in set design to this day. For example, in the special features of *Hellboy II*, the director shows how a shallow alcove appears deeper by using smaller furniture and the trick of perspective. Architects and clients, however, don't like their buildings tapered at the top, and especially do not want them to look like they are falling over as the camera rotates. Therefore, they want vertical lines to be parallel, but use perspective for the other two axes. This type of rendering is called *two-point perspective*.

The trick in getting a two-point render is knowing that a camera, facing some object whose one vanishing point axis aligns with the camera's, will be rendered "square," or parallel in the image. If you have ever used parallel rulers, you will understand how this works in the real world.

An example of two-point perspective is in the 2-point scene within the /tut/camera.blend file on your DVD. The properties for this camera rig are shown in Figure 6-8.

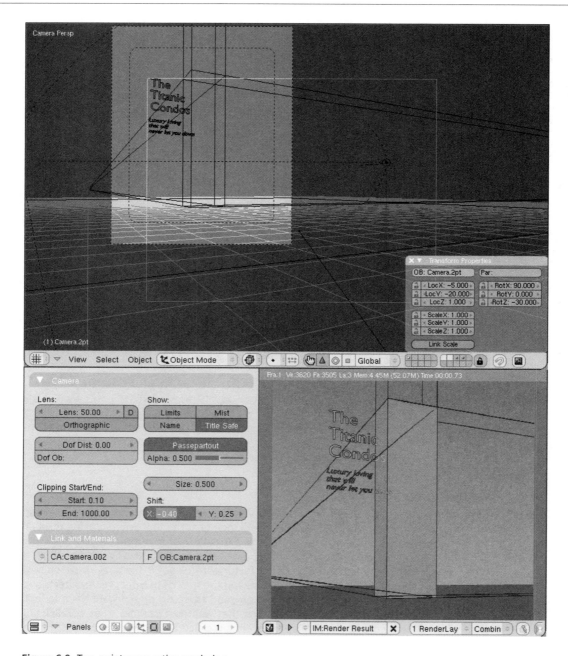

Figure 6-8. Two-point perspective rendering

In this example, you have a building whose front you want to show square. Thus, you *rotate* the camera so that it looks square on to the front face of the building, but *move* it off to the side so that it can "see" the side of the building (and thus give you that one vanishing point). That side, however, is outside the passepartout. You now use the X offset in the Camera panel to move the camera view "over," without actually moving the camera. Since you are not actually tilting or moving the camera, the perspective does not change, so vertical lines remain parallel, while the other two perspectives—the X and Y—retain their vanishing points. You also slide the view up a little to center the building vertically in the composition.

Two-point perspective is nice, but it can make the building appear to slide off to one side. Another perspective is called *one-point perspective*, which as you might have guessed by now, has one only vanishing point.

Using one-point perspective

The trick in getting a one-point render is knowing that a camera, facing some object directly, will render that object square. An example of one-point perspective is in the 1-point scene within the /tut/ camera.blend file on your DVD. The properties for this camera rig are shown in Figure 6-9.

In this case, you have a building whose front you want to show vertical, and you want the horizontal lines to be parallel as well. The vanishing point on receding lines thus gives a feeling of depth, while the front of the building looks all neat and orderly (squared). Figure 6-9 shows you how to achieve this. The virtual building is square and not angled, and so the camera isn't angled either; it's looking straight out at the horizon. Without rotating the camera, slide it in the X direction off to the side, and shift the view to bring the building (and text elements) back into the composition.

Using zero-point perspective (orthogonal)

So, by now you must be asking, "Wow, we went from three to two to one! How low can he go?" And I shout out, "Yes, folks, this is low, low Louis, who can go all the way to zero!"

Zero-point perspective, also known as *orthographic rendering*, is where all three axes are parallel. With orthographic rendering, all of the light rays from the scene appear to come into the lens in parallel.

By far the easiest way to achieve zero-point projection is to click the Orthographic button in the Camera panel. When you do so, the Lens setting no longer applies, and thus changes to a Scale control, which allows you to set a relative scale of the area being rendered. In the tut\camera.blend file on your DVD, the 0-Ortho scene shows the building example shot with an orthographic camera.

A special variation of orthographic projection is isometric view, which is through an orthographic camera that looks down and left/right, so that the top of a cube has 120-degree and 60-degree angles. In isometric view, the orthographic camera is rotated by 45 degrees on the Z axis, and looks down by 35.264 degrees. An isometric view of a building is in the 0-Isometric scene of the tut\camera.blend file. This view is used a lot in sprite-based video games to give depth or almost a 3D look, and thus is also know as *three-quarters perspective* or *2.5D*. For the X rotation, enter 90-35.264 as a formula to get the correct angle of the dangle.

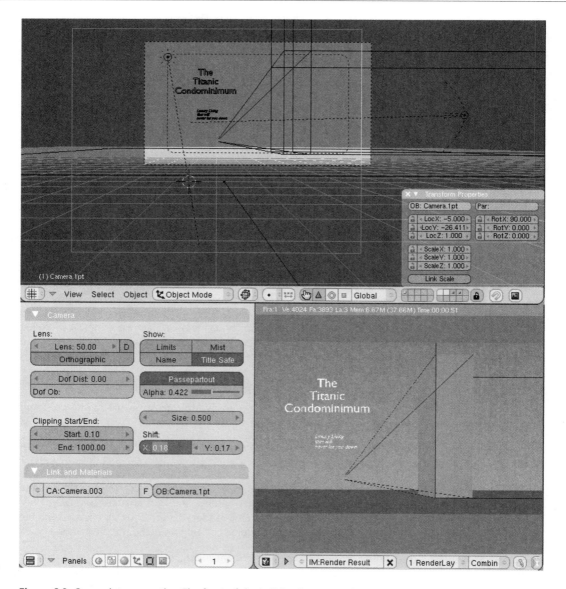

Figure 6-9. One-point perspective. The front of the building is a rectangle.

The rule of thirds

I often parent a grid that is divided into thirds to the camera. I use this grid in positioning the camera to give a balanced composition. This guideline is called the *rule of thirds*, which says that a viewing area or image can be divided in thirds, giving nine quadrants. The middle four intersections are called *power points*, and they should align with points of interest or focus.

In the tut/camera.blend file on the DVD, in the thirds scene, I have constructed a rig that I use often. This is a plane that was converted to a wire grid using the Solid Wireframe script that is bundled with Blender. There are two grids: one 16:9 and the other 4:3. When I am working on an HDTV display, which is the 16:9 aspect ratio, I hide the 4:3 grid. (To unhide it, press Alt+H.) The horizontal slices for both grids are the same, but the vertical slices are a little different because of the different aspect ratios. They both are placed about 30 units from the camera, so that they should be behind most things.

I use these grids as guides to give a stronger composition. Before rendering, I deselect layer 20 so that the grid does not show up in the render. As a safety precaution, I have given them a fully transparent material.

In the thirds scene, I wanted to render the building in two-point perspective, but use the power points. As you now know, rendering in two-point perspective requires a frame shift, yet my grid is tied to the camera view. I wanted that receding vanishing point to align with the bottom of the building (perfectly horizontal). When using a perspective camera, as you've learned, the camera must be aligned with that point in 3D space. Since the base of the building was at zero Z in 3D space, the camera had to be at zero Z as well in order for the vanishing point to be horizontal with the base. The camera could not tilt up to look at the building, because if it did, I would gain a vertical vanishing point. Therefore, the camera needed to have an X rotation of 90 degrees.

I adjusted the location of the vanishing point by rotating the camera, and moved the vanishing point closer to or farther away from the building by shifting the camera left and right. To test alignment, I moved the grid to where I will eventually shift the frame. The results, with some random text placement, are shown in Figure 6-10. In this example, I gave the grid a slight opacity so you could see it.

> *When drafting layouts, use the* Lorem *button on the* Font *panel to quickly fill in some placeholder text.*

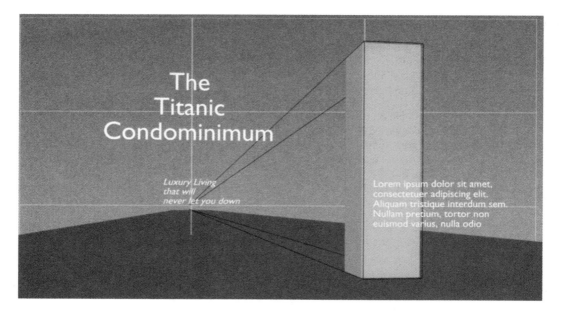

Figure 6-10. Use the rule of thirds for layout.

The Blender world

You may have noticed that Figure 6-10 has a blue background. This backdrop is called the *world*, and it is controlled through the virtual world settings. To find these settings, select the Shading context, and then the World subcontext. Within this subcontext are some panels that give you ultimate control over your virtual world.

The first control on the main World panel is the selector, which allows you to add a new world, shows you the number of shared uses, and lets you to delink these world settings. Blender will not save a set of settings that you delink unless you click the F control to give it a fake user.

World colors

The three sets of color controls on the World panel allow you to set the RGB values of the horizon (Ho), zenith (Ze), and ambient light (Am), respectively. The horizon is what you see when you look straight out. The zenith is overhead, when you look straight up or down. In the real world, the sky's horizon and zenith are different colors, because as you look out, you are looking through more atmospheric fog, mist, and dust (and pollution), so you see more light scattering. When you look up, you are looking through fewer atmospheric elements into space.

The net color of the horizon and zenith can also be affected by a sun lamp's Sky and Atmosphere settings, as shown in Figure 6-11. Enable Sun to reveal the controls on the left side of the panel, and enable Atmosphere for the controls on the right side of the panel. The Sky setting affects how much light different objects receive as they get farther from camera. Use Atmosphere to simulate pollution and spectral effects due to atmospheric scattering.

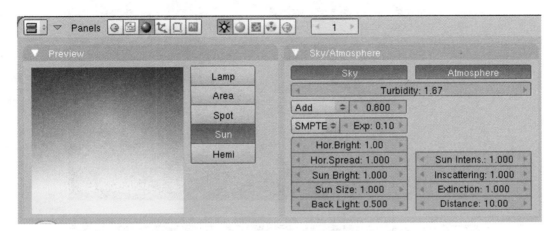

Figure 6-11. Sun lamp's Sky and Atmosphere settings affect the world backdrop color.

In reality, the color of ambient light depends on your surroundings and the general climate (and pollution in the air, unfortunately). Generally, I like a sunny clime, so I use a yellowish, warm light. For a man on Mars, you might use a gray-red color to reflect the environment. On a spaceship, harsh white light might be appropriate. In a volcano deep in the center of the earth, a deep, angry red would be a good ambient light color. You do not see this light directly, but it does affect the shading of objects in the scene through the use of the ambient (Amb) slider in the Shaders panel (shading is discussed in Chapter 7).

Exposure and dynamic range

The World panel also allows you to vary the exposure (Exp) and the dynamic range (Range) of light in the environment. If an image has too much light, your render will have washouts. In those cases, you want to increase the range, so that the overall range of visible color is bigger—the maximum brightness of the image has a wider range. If the image is underexposed and black, you want a range of less than 1, so that the overall contrast in the image is increased. When you change the Range setting, pure black remains black, but the dynamic range is increased. This is also referred to as making a high-dynamic range image.

Figure 6-12 shows an overexposed scene. If you render this image from the tut\world.blend file, Range scene, and drag your mouse over the washed-out area, you will see that Suzanne's head and the icosphere (a geometric term for a soccer-ball shape) are too white, with RGB values greater than 1.0, in the 2.4 range. You could spend a lot of time fiddling with the lights. But since the overall balance between all the lights and materials is about right, and the problem is that the whole image is overlit, simply increasing Range to 3.5 produces an acceptable result.

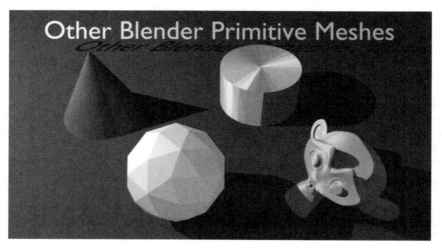

Figure 6-12. Render with a World panel Range setting of 1.0 (default) and 2.5 to correct overlighting

In the Exposure scene in tut\world.blend, you see the opposite problem: not enough light. As with normal photography, if there isn't enough light, you need to increase the exposure (by keeping the shutter open longer). By increasing the World panel's Exp setting to 0.4, you get a nicely exposed render.

> When adjusting the exposure or range, you want to compare the impact of your change on current render to the render with the previous settings. In the render window, press J (Jump) to go to the previous render before making your next render. The first time you do this, the window will go blank, but when you render, it will be filled in with the current render. Then you can jump back to the previous render by pressing J, switching between the two each time you press J.

Mist and stars

In compositing, you may want to make things appear to fade away as they get out to the horizon. The trick here is to make them turn to alpha 0 as they get farther away from camera. This effect is called *mist* in Blender. In photography, you will often angle a ground cover up to the backdrop to achieve the same effect, so that there isn't a hard (distracting) line in the background. In Blender, you can do the same thing with a mesh or use mist.

Figure 6-13 shows mist used to make the mountains fade off into the distance. In the tut\sky.blend file on your DVD, in the Badlands scene, you'll find a generic matte constructed with Mist enabled on the Mist/Stars/Physics panel.

Figure 6-13. Mist fades objects out to the horizon.

The Mist/Stars/Physics panel has the following settings for mist:

- Mist: Enables the mist effect.
- Quad, Lin, **and** Sqr: These stand for quadratic, linear, and inverse square root, respectively. This selection sets the rate at which things fade away. In real life, things fade off in a quadratic fashion, since the obscuring effect of dust is cumulative.
- Start: Nothing fades until it is this far from the camera.
- Dist: Over this distance, the object fades out to nothing.
- Height: Fog normally hovers over a river or in low-lying places, and this setting allows you to simulate that.

In compositing, you can use the Height setting to fade out an element from the bottom up. To simulate a 2D fade in, you can use the Lin (Linear) setting and just angle the object away from camera. This gives you an element that has a linear blend with the background. Figure 6-14 shows how you can use this effect to make rolling text fade away, as was done in the introduction to *Star Wars*. I've included this scene on the DVD in the Mist-Linear scene of tut\world.blend.

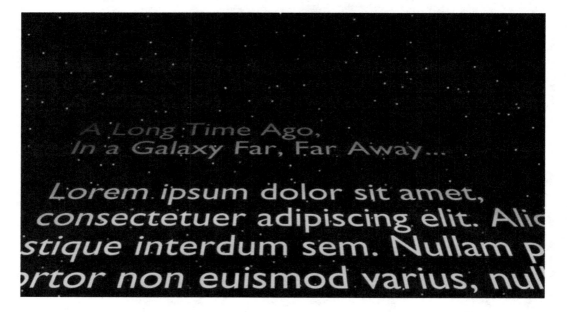

Figure 6-14. Using mist to fade out a title

In Figure 6-14, notice the black space background filled with stars. Blender has a simple special effects feature, called *stars*, which fills the background with simple dots of light. You won't get any galaxy clusters or anything fancy—just something to fill in a night sky quickly. The stars are infinitely away from you, so they do not have any "depth" to them. To use stars, enable the Stars setting on the Mist/Stars/Physics panel. You can adjust their distance, size, and color variation.

> *For nebulas and galaxies, consider using portions of the Hubble images available from* `http://www.NASA.gov.`

World textures

You can use a few kinds of special world textures. The most interesting are sphere maps and angular maps. These image textures provide a seamless 360-degree view. You apply a texture to the world in two basic steps: create the world and map the texture, and then create the texture.

Sphere maps

Sphere maps look like a big wall map that you typically see of the earth, but are usually of the sky, like that shown in Figure 6-15. This sphere map is included on the DVD in `lib\textures\world\sphere\sky_escape2.jpg`.

Figure 6-15. Sky :Escape, courtesy of BlenderArtist M@dcow

> *The sphere and angular map examples (Figures 6-15 and 6-19) were created by BlenderArtist M@dcow. Check out the sticky thread "Sticky: Free high res sky-maps" in the Composition, Visual Effects, and Rendering forum on* `http://www.BlenderArtists.org` *to see more of his work.*

To access textures for the world, you need to go from the Material World subcontext to the Material Texture context to assign the texture to the world. The specific process from a new blend file is as follows:

1. In the buttons window, select the Shading World subcontext by pressing F5 and then clicking the little globe subcontext icon. In the World panel, click Add New if you want to add a new world. In the Preview panel, enable Real.

2. In the Texture and Input panel for that same subcontext, click Add New. This loads a texture in the top texture channel, and reveals some mapping options. In that panel, enable Sphere, since you will be using a sphere map image. In the Map To panel, enable Hori, because you want this sphere map to replace the horizon color, as shown in Figure 6-16.

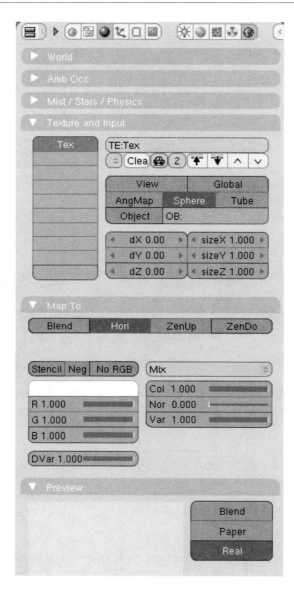

Figure 6-16. World with sphere map texture loaded in the first texture channel

3. Now you need to load the image texture. Click the Texture subcontext icon, and note that the Preview panel has World enabled, indicating that you are loading a texture for the world. In the Texture panel, click Add New. Select Image as the Texture Type. In the Image panel that appears, load the image by clicking Load. One of your windows will turn into a file browser, which you

use to navigate to the image file. When you click SELECT IMAGE, the image will appear in the preview. Click the auto icon in the Texture panel to rename this texture based on the image name. You should now have the settings shown in Figure 6-17.

> *On this and all world textures, enable* Real *on the* Preview *panel to "lock in" the texture, so that if you rotate the camera, the background pans as well, just as it would if you had a real camera taking a picture of the real horizon.*

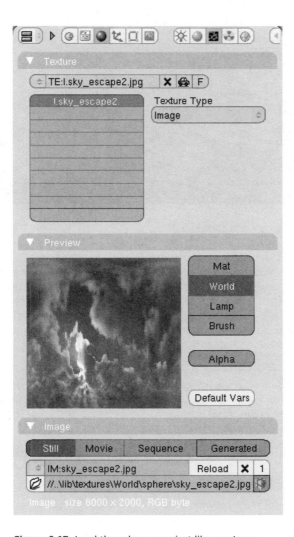

Figure 6-17. Load the sphere map just like any Image

Figure 6-18 shows the sample condo ad with something a bit more exciting than the flat blue background.

Figure 6-18. Compositing over a world background

You can use this image as is, or blend in other colors, such as the zenith color set in the World panel. by enabling Blend in the Preview panel, ZenUp in the Map To panel, and then sliding down the color influence of the texture using the Col slider (also in the Map To panel). You can have many layers of textures, blend in stars (if you use an image with an alpha channel), alter colors, and use an animated texture (video) for a moving clouds background (for example, a time lapse). You can also animate a static image, varying the dX component in the Texture and Input panel to simulate moving clouds (animated textures are discussed in Chapter 8).

> *While this example uses a still image for the world texture, you can also use a video as a background. Depending on how the video is constructed, you map it to either a view or a sphere. For example, if you go out with your camera and shoot a video of a sunset and want to use that in your composition, simply load it as shown in Figure 6-17, but in the* World *settings, map it to* View *instead of* Sphere.

Angular maps

Angular maps are a little stranger way of representing a complete wraparound environment. If you can imagine taking a picture of a chrome sphere, or using some sort of monster fish-eye lens, you've got it. I've included an angular map in the library on the DVD (lib\textures\world\angmap), which is shown in Figure 6-19.

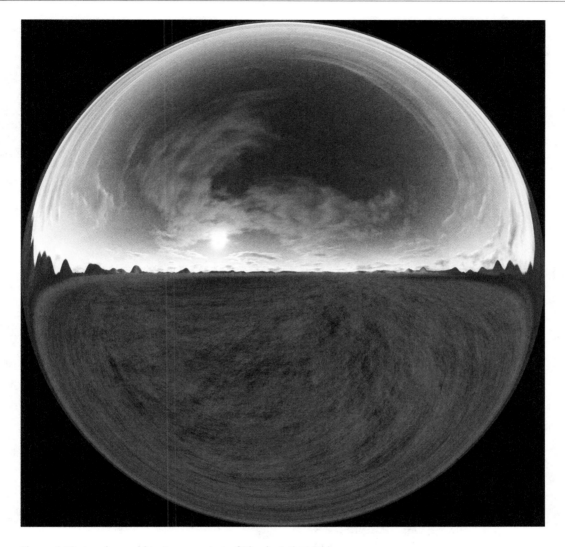

Figure 6-19. Angular world texture, courtesy of BlenderArtist M@dcow

Angular maps can be horizon-based, like the one shown in Figure 6-19, or can just show the sky or ground. Depending on the image, you want to set the horizon (Hori) and zenith up and down (ZenUp and ZenDown) accordingly. Almost always, you will want to set Real as well, unless you find a particularly nice background piece that you always want to use, and you will not be rotating the camera.

Load the image as a texture, and then in the world's Texture and Input panel, apply the image as AngMap (and not a Sphere, as for a sphere map).

Here are a few notes about using angular maps (and sphere maps as well) convincingly:

- **Apparent sun**: For angular maps that represent an outdoor image, you should look around with the camera to find the sun in the picture, and place your sun lamp in the same position. Angle the sun lamp so that its rays track to the center of the computer-generated scene (0,0,0). This way, any shadows that are cast will be accurately computed, and lens flares will be accurate when the sun comes into view.

- **Ambient light**: The color and intensity of the ambient light is "built in" to the angular map floor, so it is important to "extract" the ambient light. Look at the ground (or anything in the image), figure out its true color, and calculate an appropriate ambient light color. This way, any computer-generated elements will fit into the scene much better.

- **Ground plane**: Now that you have the sun shining in the sky and lighting elements as they would normally, you need shadows. Unfortunately, the angle map is just an image of the ground; it is not an actual flat ground on which Blender can "cast" shadows. To solve this, Blender has a special material that shows only shadows, but is transparent otherwise (the OnlyShad setting on the Shaders panel, as discussed in Chapter 7).

A Big Buck Bunny world compositing example

Let's look at an awesome example of world compositing in the movie *Big Buck Bunny*, and investigate what the compositors did and how they did it. From your DVD, open Peach\production\ scenes\01_intro\04 works.blend, which is a file that I have created based on scene 1, shot 4 of the movie. (Note that this blend file links to assets in 15 other blend files.) The world settings for this shot are shown in Figure 6-20.

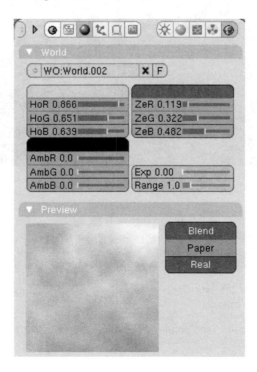

Figure 6-20. Basic world settings for *Big Buck Bunny*, Scene 01 Shot 04

Examining the world textures

Look at the matte scene and the Material World subcontext, as shown in Figure 6-20. You see two colors, peach for the horizon and blue for the zenith, which are blended together. However, the Preview panel shows a mottling kind of effect. Where does this come from? To find the answer, you need to look at the Textures and Input panel, which shows that this world uses three textures stacked in the top three texture channels, as shown in Figure 6-21.

This first texture maps the texture in the first channel to the world in "plain-vanilla" fashion, mixing in a light shade of blue with the sky (horizon to zenith, both up and down) color. The Col (Color) slider is set at 30%, so this will have a slight effect on the overall color. Recall that the sky color is a blend of peach and dark blue. Great, but that light blue is not blended evenly—it's mixed according to the texture. Clicking the texture subcontext icon (the square mottled icon in the buttons window header) reveals the information shown in Figure 6-22.

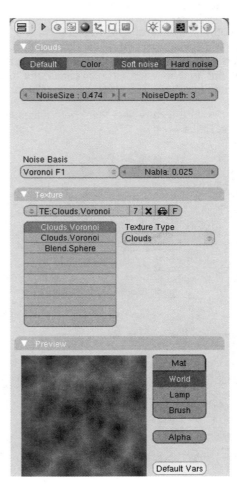

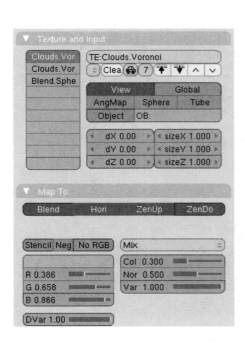

Figure 6-21. World texture channels, with the first (top channel) selected

Figure 6-22. First world texture in the *Big Buck Bunny* scene

Aha! It is a simple Clouds texture, but with a bit of "puffiness" introduced via the Voronoi noise basis, shown selected in the Clouds panel. The Clouds texture is a general-purpose texture for varying a color in a random but somewhat regular kind of way. Dr. Georgy Voronoi developed this algorithm over a hundred years ago as a way to compute cells and points in space. When I look at a Voronoi structure, I am reminded of cells (like skin cells or brain cells) under a microscope. If you open the Noise Basis selector, you will see many other algorithms that the Clouds texture can use as a basis for computing the texture pattern. As applied to the *Big Buck Bunny* world, where this texture is black, no light blue is blended; where it is white or gray, that proportional amount of light blue is blended in.

Referring back to Figure 6-22, note that sizeX and sizeY are 1.0. This means that one repetition of the texture will be spread across the entire view, and then only a 30% variation will be applied. This tells you that this texture gives very subtle graduations of color. Now switch back to the world shading and move down to the second texture by clicking the second channel, as shown in Figure 6-23.

Here, you see that the second texture channel is mapped to white, and again, sizeX and Y are 1.0, which means that the whole graduation is spread across the entire view. However, this one is mixed a little differently than the first texture. The mix mode is Add (as shown in the Map To panel), so this texture will lighten the existing background by adding white where instructed by the texture pattern. If you click the Texture subcontext, you will see that the same texture has been reused (that Voronoi cloud), but (in the Texture and Input panel), this texture channel shifts that pattern left a bit (notice the dY setting) to offset it. This trick gives the illusion of sunlight lighting the side of the "cloud."

Finally, the third texture uses the sphere mapping discussed earlier, adding in a light-orange color, as shown in Figure 6-24.

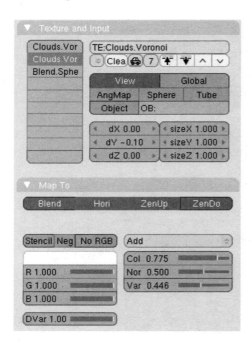

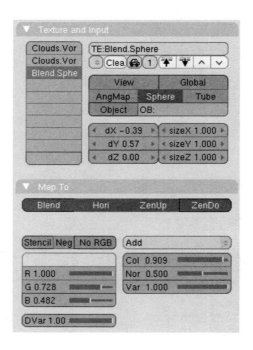

Figure 6-23. Second world texture in the *Big Buck Bunny* scene

Figure 6-24. Third world texture channel in the *Big Buck Bunny* scene

Notice that this texture is offset both downward and to the right. This is so it adds a glow, like warm sunlight, to the upper-right corner of the camera view, based on those dX and dY settings. When you look at the texture itself, shown in Figure 6-25, you see that it is very different from the Clouds texture. It is called a Blend texture, because it blends very gradually from nothing to full strength.

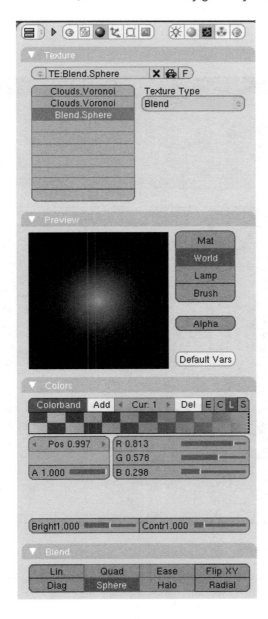

Figure 6-25. Previewing world texture 3

This Blend texture has a few varieties as well. The variety used here is called the Sphere texture, since if you looked at this texture in space, it would look spherical, almost like a candle in a fog bank.

Using matte paintings

Looking back at the 3D view of the *Big Buck Bunny* scene, the large ring you see is a matte painting of a tree line. This very long and thin image is mapped to a ring that extends around the set, providing a panorama. In the outliner, you can see that it is called matte_forest. Looking at the list of library files (reported in the console window), you see the linked file //..\..\mattes\sky-hills.blend as the only matte file linked. Open this file from your DVD (Peach\production\mattes\sky-hills.blend) to see the original matte_forest object, as shown in Figure 6-26.

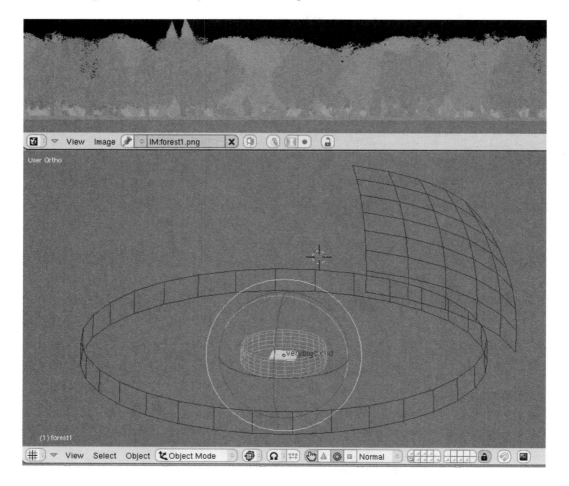

Figure 6-26. Matte painting applied to a panorama ring

In this scene, there's another object standing up like the screen in the old-time drive-in movies. It's textured with an image of a very big cloud. To see this, right-click the object and look at the Shading Material Preview panel. Each of these images has a transparency channel to allow the textured world to show through. As you can see, not all image elements are mere flat planes, but can be of various sizes and shapes, and used for various purposes.

Combined with the world settings, you just saw an interesting use of world texture channels and a matte painting to produce a very professional background. In plain English, you overlay two cloud textures, the second one offset a little, and then blend in a sunny orange to brighten the overhead sky. Lastly, you put a matte image in front of all of that. Press F12 to render, and you will be rewarded with a nice, flat, unobtrusive but Easter-sunrise pastel image, as shown in Figure 6-27 (I've altered the colors a bit so you can see them in the printed book).

Figure 6-27. Matte with textured world

Summary

In this chapter, you learned how to use the camera (and all of its options) to take a picture of your composition. You saw how to make a composition using zero-, one-, two-, or three-point perspective, and when to use each one. I also introduced the rule of thirds as an important tool for designing a pleasing layout, and a few ways to float a grid in front of the camera to give you those guidelines all the time. We discussed a few cameraman techniques, including how to do lazy tracking and how to set up the camera for depth of field and focus.

We then looked into the beyond, exploring the world settings. A not-insignificant part of compositing a good-looking image is coming up with an interesting yet unobtrusive background or backdrop, to complement the main message. In Blender, you combine matte images and world textures to construct this backdrop. We've explored three kinds of special-purpose images—angular maps, spherical maps, and matte paintings—that can be used to provide photo-realistic virtual worlds or just something to make a horizon. Blender gives you different ways to use different types of matte images and textures, alone or in combination with one another, as the backdrop to your composition.

Chapter 7

SHADING

This chapter adds some color to your life! In Blender, almost anything can be colored—meshes, lights, environments, whatever—and they're all configured in a similar manner. You were introduced to shading in Chapter 3, when you shaded the mask to match the sign, and in Chapter 6, which covered the world background color and textures. This chapter focuses on compositing shading, which is a subset of all possible shading.

Shading categories

In total, there are five broad categories of shading in Blender, and these form the subcontexts for the Shading properties. These categories are selected by clicking the appropriate icon in the Shading buttons window header, as shown in Figure 7-1:

- **Lamps**: Accessed by clicking the first icon (which looks like a light bulb) in the subcontext.
- **Materials**: Accessed by clicking the second icon (which looks like a red ball). This type of shading is covered in this chapter.
- **Textures**: Accessed by clicking the third icon (the square dotted icon next to the materials icon). Texture shading is also covered in this chapter.

- **Radiosity**: Accessed by clicking the icon that looks like a radiation sign. This is an important topic in making photorealistic renders, but it isn't that relevant to compositing.
- **World**: Accessed by clicking the rightmost icon (which looks like a globe). This type of shading was covered in Chapter 6.

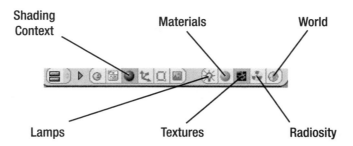

Figure 7-1. Shading contexts

Shading can be thought of as the process of coloring a textured material. The color of every computer-generated object with a renderable surface needs to be computed in order for the virtual camera to see it. This process happens at two places:

- All the time in your 3D view if you are in any of the solid, shaded, or textured drawing modes. The 3D view uses an OpenGL rendering routine to make a fast approximation of the final output.
- It happens during a preview or render operation. The preview operation invokes the Blender Internal render routines, and the full render output invokes the renderer you have chosen, which is also the Blender Internal by default. Preview occurs in the 3D view when you use the View ➤ Render Preview panel, and in the Shading Materials or Textures Preview panel (to make that image of the box, sphere, and so on).

If a surface is not self-illuminating, then it also needs some light in order to be seen. You can override all of the shading in a render by entering the name of a light and/or material in the respective field in the Render *panel (discussed in Chapter 9).*

Materials

The basic definition of how a surface looks in Blender is called a *material*. A ton of options and features are available for material shading. Here, we'll go through the ones that are relevant to compositing.

Adding a material

With your object selected, access the Material subcontext and click Add New in the Links and Pipeline panel. A generic material is created and initialized for you, as shown in Figure 7-2.

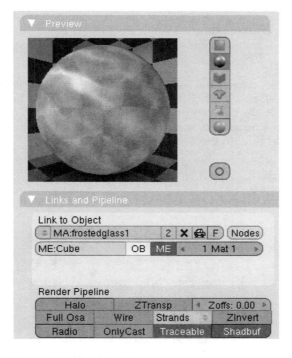

Figure 7-2. New material

In the Links and Pipeline panel, you can click into the MA: field to rename the material to something meaningful, or click the little auto icon to automatically assign a name based on the base color of the material. The up/down selector allows you to pick a material that is already loaded, so you can reuse the same material definition for many objects in you scene. As in other panels, F assigns a fake user to the material so that it will be saved in the blend file.

The next line of controls beginning with ME: show you the selected object. You work on a material for an object by selecting the object in 3D view. When you select the object, these panels change to reflect that object's material settings.

The Render Pipeline section of the Links and Pipeline panel allows you to choose which family of materials to work with. You can, by enabling the options shown, configure the following types of materials:

- **Normal**: The kind of surfaces we touch (the default, when nothing else is selected).
- Halo: **Blobs and sparkles of light.**
- Wire: **A wireframe of the object.**
- OnlyCast: **The object itself is not visible, but it casts shadows.**

I'll describe these materials later in the chapter, in the "Defining a material" section.

Another button in the Render Pipeline section of the Links and Pipeline panel allows you to select ZTransp (Z transparency), which makes transparent areas of the object see-through, without distortion, and not ray-traced. Z transparency is essential to the compositor when working with alpha-channel image elements.

Above the Links and Pipeline panel is the Preview panel. This invokes the renderer to show you what this material (and any textures) will look like when applied to any one of six different simple objects (plane, sphere, cube, and so on). Click any icon in the vertical list to make a mini-render. Transparency (ray or Z) will automatically be applied to let the grid box background show through based on the material's transparency (set through the Material panel).

Defining a material

The main definition panels for a material are the Material and Shaders panels, as shown in Figure 7-3.

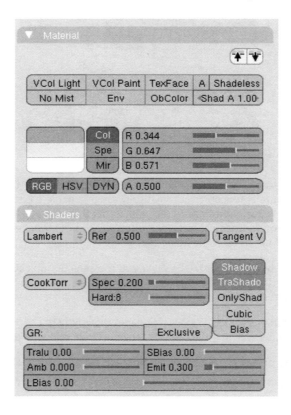

Figure 7-3. Material and Shaders panels

Materials used for compositing can broadly be classified into shaded (normal) or shadeless (the Shadeless button is the last one in the top row of the Material panel). Blender's shadeless material is akin to self-illuminating in 3ds Max, and is not affected by any lights in the scene, as discussed in more detail in the upcoming "Shadeless material" section.

Material colors

The next set of controls on the Material panel allow you to set the three main colors that define a material:

- Col: The diffuse or base color of the material
- Spe: The specular color of the sheen that is radiated when light hits the surface
- Mir: The mirror color of the reflective surface that colors reflections

To set a color, select the color type by clicking the corresponding blue button. The R, G, and B sliders will change to reflect that color. Either slide the sliders or click the number to manually enter a value. If you want to use HSV values instead of RGB, click the HSV button. Alternatively, click the color swatch itself to bring up the color picker.

Anywhere you see a color swatch, just click it to bring up the color picker:

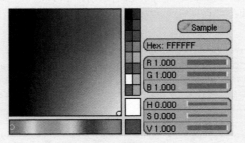

The color picker provides a simple color-selection system. With colors, when designing a color scheme for a composition, you want complementary colors that both go well together and reflect the mood of the composition. The site http://kuler.adobe.com has a searchable database of thousands of five-color combinations.

In the color picker, notice the central column of tiny swatches. You set these to be the colors for your session. In the example here, I have set these to be the theme used in the Blender logo. To set a color in that column, simply select the color through sampling or entering the values, and then Ctrl-click the swatch. It will turn the active color. Now, for your Blender session, those 16 colors will be available anywhere you need to pick a color in Blender, since clicking a color swatch brings up this picker, and you can just click the mini-swatch to activate it when selecting a material color, brush color, lamp color, and so on.

To save these colors, you need to render an image of them (a simple set of shadeless planes will suffice), and then either load that image as a background or into the UV/image editor, and resample and set the swatches the next time you start Blender.

Last, but not least, the A slider at the bottom of the Material panel sets the base alpha (opacity/transparency) of the material: 1.0 is fully opaque, and 0.0 is fully transparent. In the example in Figure 7-3, the material was a frosted glass, so the alpha is 0.5. Note that textures (discussed later in this chapter) can modulate this alpha value; this slider provides the base alpha value. The ZTransp option provides a distortion-free transparency, as with image elements. Ray transparency accounts for all the physical properties and distortion of light passing through transparent objects.

Shader algorithms

Some really smart geeks have come up with algorithms to compute what light does to a surface and how it looks. These are available on the Shaders panel (see Figure 7-3). Two major algorithms are used: diffuse and specular. Blender codifies five diffuse and five specular algorithms, and you can use any diffuse algorithm with any specular one, so there are 25 combinations. The Lambert diffuse algorithm is shown selected in Figure 7-3, and the main control for it is the Ref (Reflective) slider. This slider sets how reflective the "paint" is. Do you want it to be dull and "dead" (a low value), or vibrant and lively (a higher value)? The higher the value, the more of the diffuse color is given off when light hits it.

The specular algorithm (CookTor, for Cook-Torrence, is selected in Figure 7-3) computes the sheen color you see as light glances off the surface. The main controls for this algorithm are the amount of the light (Spec slider) and the diameter, or hardness, of the sheen (Hard slider). A very hard, epoxy paint on a flat metal surface will have very high specular and hardness values, whereas a piece of worn yarn will have a very low specular value and a hardness in the single digits. In general, real-world materials have very low specular values.

Select a different diffuse and/or specular shader algorithm by clicking the selector arrow next to the current setting and choosing it from the pop-up menu. The Toon shader diffuse/specular pair of algorithms is worth special mention. Use this shader pair to give a cartoon look, as was done for the well-mannered bear character created by Rebecca Wickes, shown in Figure 7-4. While the bear is a 3D object, the Toon shader gives it a 2D feel.

Figure 7-4. "Bukequi" using the Toon shader, courtesy of Rebecca Wickes

Shading a solid material

Blender has many ways to shade solid surfaces, which fall into two main categories: shadeless (unaffected by computer-generated lamps) and shaded. Shadeless was introduced in Chapter 5, and is commonly used for images that are textured to an object, usually a plane used as a projection screen. You can choose a Halo material, which looks like blobs of light, and Wire, which looks like a wireframe. At the bizarre end, we have the OnlyShad (Only Shadows) material, which renders only the shadows that fall on it. This is very useful when compositing a computer-generated element over a picture to give it that extra sense of realism. Practical examples of using these materials are presented throughout this chapter and book.

Shadeless materials

As you saw in Figure 7-4, the Toon shader removes that smooth gradient of shades of color normally seen when you look at an object. You can completely remove any gradient by setting a material to Shadeless through the Material panel. You'll notice that the Preview panel shows a flat, evenly colored sample.

These materials are called *shadeless* because Blender will not alter their shades of color as it normally would when computing the effect of lighting, and instead will transfer the diffuse color directly to the render. You will use shadeless materials for images most of the time. For the examples so far, you've used shadeless materials to color the mask in Chapter 3 and in Chapter 5, when making image elements (a shadeless material is initialized for the projection plane).

Choose Shadeless whenever you want a perfectly flat, even shade of the same color. The most common use of shadeless materials is for text overlays. Most of compositing is for TV commercials, print commercials, web flash commercials . . . I think you see the trend. Even film uses shadeless text for titles. When composting image elements (image-textured planes), select the top plane as the preview to give you an accurate rendition.

> Use a shadeless material to color anything you want to key on later in the compositor or sequencer, such as a light saber. A shadeless material is easy to key when pulling a matte.

Only shadows materials

One of the issues when integrating computer-generated elements over a live-action plate is shadows. Figure 7-5 shows an example of compositing a car model over an image. You expect to see the shadow of the car on the driveway, yet how do you get one there? You could make a mask that looks like what you think the shadow should be, but that would be a lot of work. Not that I am lazy, but using a simple ground plane set to OnlyShad (on the Shaders panel) and ZTransp (on the Links and Pipeline panel) does the job for me.

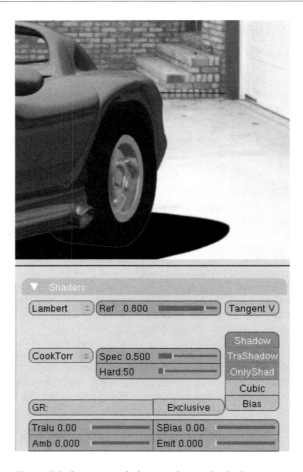

Figure 7-5. Set a ground plane to show only shadows.

Halo material

The Halo material (selected from the Links and Pipeline panel) can simulate energy particles, lens flares, fairies, snow, and whatever that was floating in the air after Hellboy killed the elemental forest god in *Hellboy II: The Golden Army*. Halo is not really a material in the traditional sense of the word. For each vertex of a mesh object, it renders the vertex as a sort of sparkle, as with the cube shown in Figure 7-6.

There are a few ways to control the "glint" from the Shaders panel: Rings draws those circular rings around the vertex, Lines draws the lines out from the center, and Star makes the center like a star. The controls on the Shaders panel let you vary the overall size of the Halo material, its intensity, and the number of lines and rings.

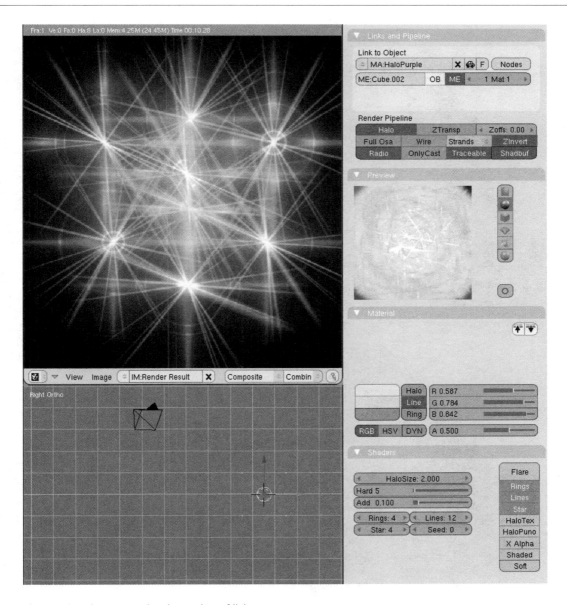

Figure 7-6. Halo turns vertices into points of light

"Halo is cute," you say, "but how do you use it?" Well, chances are you've actually seen it in a TV commercial for toothpaste, car wax, or floor cleaner. An example of a Halo material setting for a diamond production is shown in Figure 7-7. Very often, the Halo material is used for just a brief second (see Chapter 8 to learn how to blink or animate a material) and in combinations with the light passing overhead. Particles using the Halo material simulate dust and smoke (also discussed in Chapter 8).

181

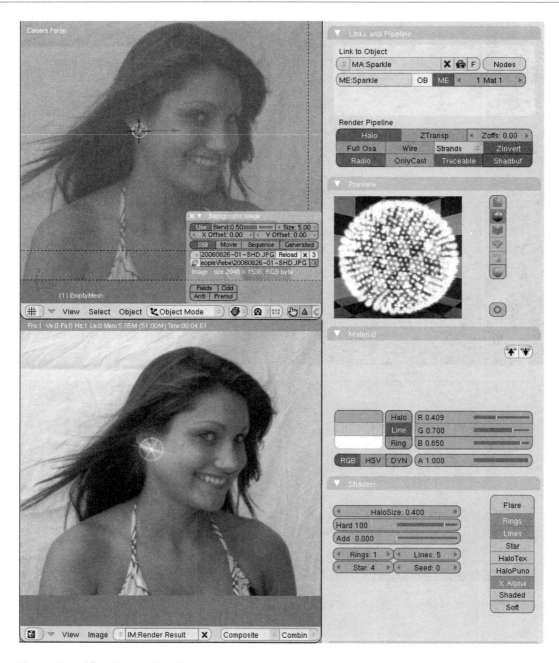

Figure 7-7. Adding that sparkle with Halo

A special case of Halo is the lens flare, set with the Flare option on the Shaders panel. This control, when enabled and used in conjunction with the proper Halo size and intensity, produces the spots of light caused by elements in a real camera lens when looking directly into the light. To use this convincingly, you must match up the location of the flared object with the sun lamp, and point the sun lamp at the camera. When enabled, as in Figure 7-8 (taken from tut\sky.blend on the DVD), additional Flare controls become available, enabling you to control the size of the flare, the number of flares (which would simulate the number of lens elements inside the barrel), and how pronounced (Boost) to make the flare. As the camera rotates, these flares will track across the frame, just as they would in real life, as long as the sun is visible in the frame.

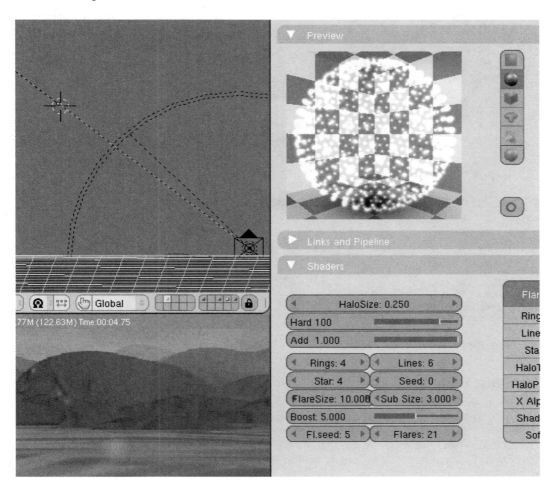

Figure 7-8. Lens flare in action

Wire material

In the title sequence to *Quantum of Solace* (2008), I noticed the use of a wireframe texture for a UV sphere, as shown in Figure 7-9. As you can see in the figure, just enable Wire in the Links and Pipeline panel, and the edges of the object are rendered. To enhance the effect, enable Edge rendering in the Output panel, and you can then use the Eint settings on that panel to make the wire little thicker. For an interesting camera angle, put the camera inside the sphere looking out (which was done a few times in *Quantum of Solace*).

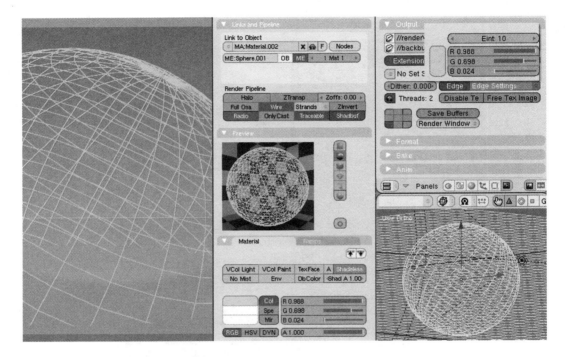

Figure 7-9. Wire material with edge enhancement

OnlyCast material

OnlyCast is another material type available on the Links and Pipeline panel. For a practical example of its use, I'm reminded of the *Star Wars* poster, where Luke is standing in front of his dome home, but his shadow is that of Darth Vader. In the Links and Pipeline panel, be sure Traceable is on, so that the ray-tracer can "see" this material, and that ShadBuf is on, so that it can cast buffered shadows. The actual object will not be rendered, but its shadow will.

Textures

After you add and define your material, you're ready for textures. First, you add a texture, orient it, and specify which aspect of the material it should affect. Then you create the actual texture, generally as either an image or some sort of computed procedural texture.

Adding a texture

In the Materials context, Textures panel, or the Texture buttons Texture panel, click Add New to add a new texture to the selected channel. Blender creates a new, blank texture and makes two more material mapping panels available, Map Input and Map To, in the Materials context, as shown in Figure 7-10.

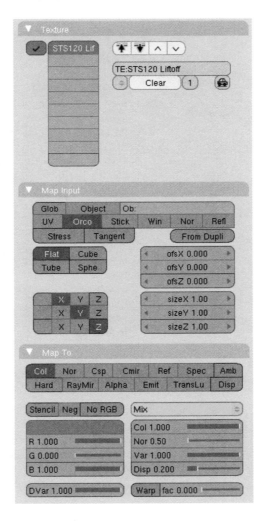

Figure 7-10. Texture and mapping panels in the Material subcontext

When you add a new texture, you need to choose which kind of texture it is through the Texture Type selector on the Texture panel, as shown in Figure 7-11. Textures can broadly be classified into two types: procedural and image-based. Procedural textures are math functions that generate the texture during the rendering process. Image textures are created ahead of time and loaded from a file. I'll talk more about each type in the "Working with image textures" and "Working with procedural textures" sections later in this chapter.

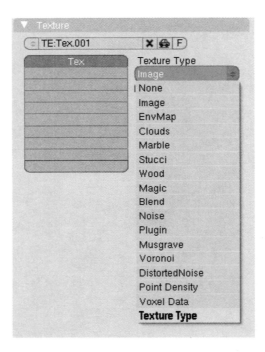

Figure 7-11. Selecting the texture in the Texture subcontext

Mapping textures

Textures are patterns of colors. They must be positioned over a material surface in some manner. They affect some aspect (usually color) of the material, and are layered on each other.

Orienting a texture

The orientation of the texture is specified in the Map Input panel. You map an alpha-channel image to the UV coordinates of the plane in order to make an image element, or to the window coordinates when texturing a mask. In the example in Figure 7-10, this movie is mapped as a texture using the original coordinates of the object. In this case, the object is a simple plane, and there is no need for UV mapping. Later on, in the "Blending computer-generated elements into photos" section, I will show you how to map a texture to an object—to put a tattoo on a shoulder, for example.

In the Map Input panel, you can map to the following:

- Orco: Original coordinates—for normal, nonalpha images; regular application.
- Win: For images on masks.
- UV: For alpha-channel images on projection planes, and images on complex meshes. For UV mapping, the name of the UV texture is UVTex by default.
  - OB: To use an object as the center of the texture. For OB mapping, you must enter the name of the object to use as a reference.

With image elements, you almost always use Flat mapping. However, if you are texturing a planet from a sphere map, you want to use a sphere (Sphe) mapping. The little XYZ grid of blue buttons maps the input to the output, like a patch panel. Swap X and Y to rotate the texture 90 degrees.

To offset the texture across the surface enter values in the ofsX, ofY, and ofsZ fields to shift the location of the texture center. To scale the texture across the surface, enter values in the sizeX, sizeY, and sizeZ fields to scale the texture this number of times across the surface.

Mapping to a material aspect

Now the texture must be mapped to affect some aspect of the material, which is set in the Map To panel in the Material subcontext using the blue buttons across the top of the panel. Click a button once to enable it in a positive manner. Some buttons (like Nor) can be clicked again to swap the selection so that it has a negative effect, and a third time to turn it off. The following are the texture mapping options commonly used for compositing:

- Col: Color of the underlying material
- Nor: Bumpiness of the surface; minor surface irregularities
- Ref **and** RayMir: The reflectiveness, such as a foggy mirror
- Spec: The specular intensity, such as paint imperfections
- Amb: The amount the ambient light affects the coloration
- Hard: Affects the hardness, like uneven paint thinner will cause
- Alpha: The transparency
- Emit: The diffuse color emission

Mixing textures

The base material of a texture can be augmented by one or more layers of textures to make it look more real or different. The top texture, channel 0, overlays on top of the base material. The second texture down the list (and successive texture channels) layer on top of layers above them, working down the list of slots in the Texture panel.

The way the layer is applied to either the base material (in the case of slot 0) or to the net result of all prior slots is through the Mix method, which is selected on the Map To panel. Most of the time, Mix is just fine. However, if you want the texture to totally supply the alpha channel, Add (if the base has no alpha) or Multiply (if the base has an alpha of 1.0).

Of course, an object (such as a plane) is not limited to only one texture. As you have seen, you can have many texture channels, and these can be mixed in many different fashions. In pop and op art, for example, you can screen one image against another, darken one and layer it on top of another, or use a texture to vary the color saturation—the possibilities are endless.

Blender supports the blending modes shown in Figure 7-12. These modes are the same as those supported in the compositor and sequencer, and invoke different color math functions that perform special operations. You can think of it as *net result <operation> this channel*. In the example in Figure 7-12, for this first Tex texture, I take the base material color and Mix (the operation) in a magenta color. I use the texture itself to indicate where to mix in more or less of the magenta color. If the operation were Lighten, I would be lightening the magenta hues in the base color by the amount specified in the texture itself.

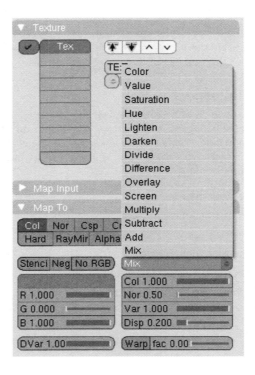

Figure 7-12. Blending modes

For example, you can subtract an image from white material to make it look like its negative, for those of you feeling nostalgic for the old school days of physical film. Mixing in a video strip in the negative gives a very jarring effect. Darkening the sky of an image can have a foreboding effect.

Working with image textures

Now it's time to work with the texture itself. To access the textures in the blend file, within the Shading context, click the little leopard skin icon to access the Texture subcontext.

You worked with image textures in Chapter 5, when you textured "balloonee" to the default project plane. Figure 7-13 shows another example of compositing—a NASA promo, in this case. It uses two projection planes, each textured with a video that shows a shuttle takeoff. Each video is an image texture of the takeoff video (included on your DVD, in the lib\images\NASA folder, redistributed for educational purposes only).

Figure 7-13. Compositing a NASA commercial

Let's see how to work with one of these NASA videos as an image texture. Starting with our default blend file, change the projection plane in front of the camera to 16:9 aspect ratio using the Transform Properties panel. Press 7 on the number keypad for top view, and move the plane off to the left. Tilt it away from the camera at a 30-degree angle. Scale it down a little. The initialized material for the plane should already be Shadeless. Now reveal the Texture panel and click Add New. For this example, all of the defaults are fine, but here's a review of the important settings:

- Map Input **panel**: Use the original coordinates (Orco); the image will fill the whole surface (size in the XYZ axis is 1).
- Map To **panel**: This texture will affect the Color of the surface, and will Mix (yellow selector) 100% (the Col slider is at 1.0).

Now click the Texture subcontext button. Choose Image from the Texture Types pop-up menu. Then click Load on the Image panel that appears, and find the STS120 liftoff video on your DVD, in lib/images/NASA/ksc_102407_sts120_launch_1080i.mov.

Blender automatically tags the file you specified as a Movie, and you should recognize this panel's options from the discussion of the 3D view Background Image panel in Chapter 5. You almost always want the proper frame of the video to be shown to you, so click Auto Refresh. This video has a fade-in that lasts for 17 frames, which should not be used in this example, so specify a 17-frame offset. The video seems a little washed out, so in the Colors panel, set the Brightness to 0.9 (darkened a bit) and crank up the Contrast to 1.2. (If you needed to make any color correction or further refinement to the video, you could use the compositor or sequencer to preprocess the video, but just making those brightness/contrast adjustments here works fine for this example.) All of these settings are shown in Figure 7-14.

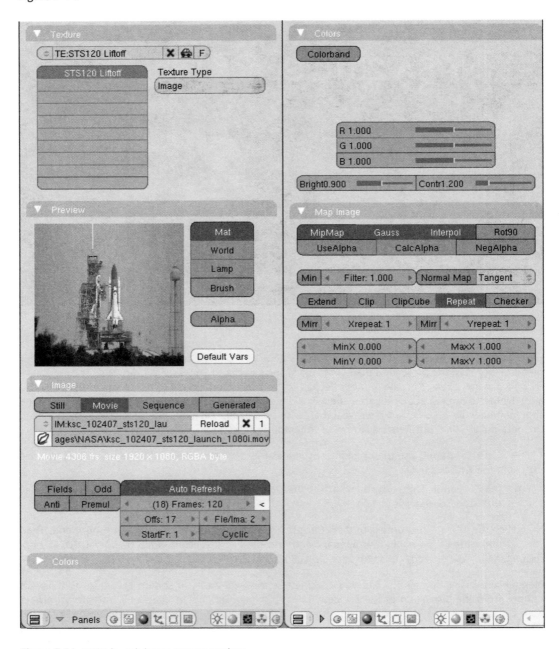

Figure 7-14. NASA launch image texture settings

You can add another plane on the right side, angle it, and texture it with another video. In this case, I cheated and used the same video, just offset by 480 frames. Add some text and a background buffer, and that's it! The result that I obtained is in the NASA scene of tut/roadsign.blend, if you want to compare your work with mine.

Recoloring image elements

You normally use Shadeless when working with image elements, but it isn't always necessary. For example, you could take a picture of a street during the day, disable Shadeless, and then light the scene with lamps to make the image look like it was taken at night. Here, we will look at an example of using light to add false color to an image.

In general, when doing postproduction with image-textured surfaces, you do *not* want any specular flare to show. Blender offers two methods to avoid specular highlighting: by setting the material's specular to 0 in the Shaders panel or by enabling No Specular in the Lamp material settings. I usually choose the latter, as I have other elements in the scene, and I just don't want to fiddle with each material's settings.

Open tut/sunrise.blend on your DVD to see a completed example of using what we have discussed so far, and to add light. If you render the file right after opening, you should see frame 180 of an animation. Don't let that throw you (animated compositing is covered in Chapter 9).

> You do not need to use the whole element in your composition. In the tut/sunrise.blend case, you can see how I moved the plane to crop the man and the chair out of the image.

I thought the image was very blue. To introduce the pinks and purples of sunrise, I gave it a deep red specular color, as shown in Figure 7-15.

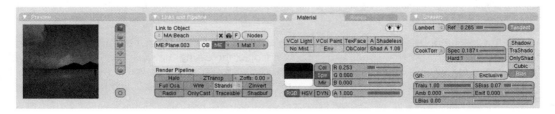

Figure 7-15. Shading an image element

In the scene, select each of the three lamps. One is the sun, which is just rising, and is angled to cast light onto the image, as a real sun would at that time. Another lamp is the area light on the water, which gives that ray of light on the water that you would expect to see. The third is a wide spotlight that casts a rosy bloom up into the sky. I added a simple mesh UV sphere, gave it a shadeless material, and cut it off (using the box mesh editing tool) to make it look like the tip of the sun coming up over the horizon. These lamps interact with the base colors of the image, giving the result shown in Figure 7-16. Basically, I "painted" with light!

Figure 7-16. Sunrise at the beach—a recolored image

Placing very tiny sharp lights in the mountains here, lighting the beach, and adding very soft moonlight light could transform this image into a nighttime scene as well.

Interpolating image texture

If you really zoom in on an image, or render in HD, especially on a low-resolution image element, you can start to see the individual pixels that make up the image, and the composite looks blocky. Also, an image element may be underexposed (too dark) or lack contrast. Blender has some quick-and-dirty features to counter this.

With a low-resolution shot, if you zoom in on the image, you can readily see the individual pixels in the image. On the Map Image panel, with Interpol enabled, increasing the Filter value blurs the image and blends those pixels a little, which gives a better-quality image when viewed at normal resolution. Keep in mind that if you are going to print with this image, the paper fiber will naturally blur the image as well.

Figure 7-17 shows a Filter value of 1.5, which I feel gives the right amount of blending without excessive blurring. To overdo the effect, try setting Filter to 4.

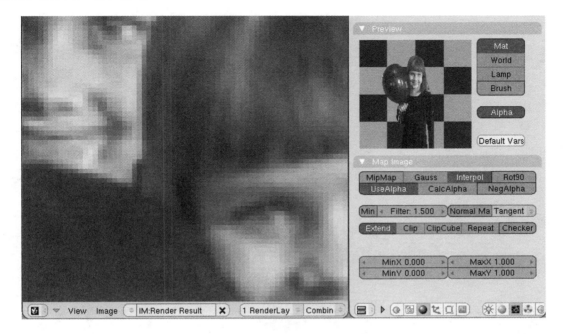

Figure 7-17. Interpolate low-res elements.

You will also want to enable UseAlpha if the image has an alpha channel. If the image is against a black background but does not have an alpha channel, click CalcAlpha, and the image will be treated like a mask. If it has a white background, use NegAlpha. Note that even if you click UseAlpha here, that alpha must be transmitted to the base material by enabling the Alpha aspect in the Map To panel as well, and must be mixed successfully with the base material alpha.

Stretching an image

Blender will try its hardest to fit the whole texture on the object (based on the scaling that you specify in the Map Input panel). This can cause issues with images, if the object (the plane) is not the same aspect ratio as the image. For example, the beach image in Figure 7-18 is in a 4:3 aspect ratio, yet it is mapped Orco to the plane in Figure 7-19, which has a 16:9 scale (aspect ratio). So, the image is actually stretched out in the X direction, which makes everyone in the picture look fatter, and also makes the clouds in the sky look less puffy. The advantage, with this image at least, is that you can do this without it being very noticeable, and it makes the beach look longer. To maintain the proper aspect ratio, though, you need to rescale the plane to be the correct ratio, and then float the plane however you want so that the appropriate crop appears inside the passepartout.

Figure 7-18. Actual image aspect ratio

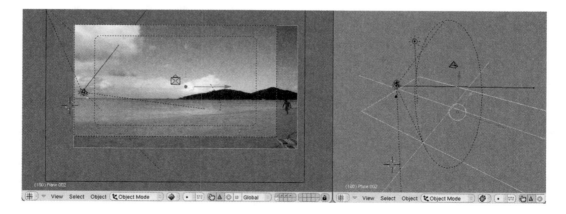

Figure 7-19. Stretched (distorted aspect ratio) image

Blending computer-generated elements into photos

Blending computer-generated and real-world elements works for humans as well, as shown in Figure 7-20. Here, I created a simple mesh as a virtual model of the shoulder. I then added an empty object, named Tattoo, and placed it near where I wanted the tattoo to appear. Next, I created a Shadeless material for the shoulder, added the texture of the Olympic rings, and mapped the input of the logo texture to the empty, treating the image of the Olympic rings as a decal that bends around the arm, since it lays on the surface of the shoulder model. While it is a fresh, new tattoo that I want you to be able to see, I might tone it down just a little for a convincing real-world fake.

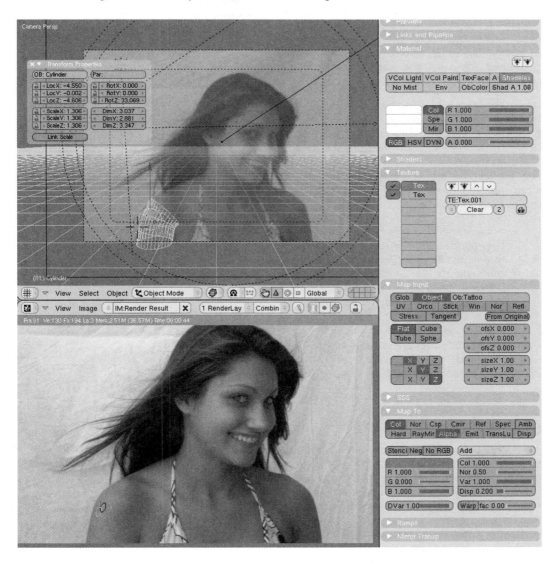

Figure 7-20. Adding an Olympic rings decal

Working with procedural (computed) textures

Blender provides dozens of computed textures, and you can get even more plug-in textures. These are used by texture artists to paint and give objects realistic surfaces. Version 2.49 (included on your DVD) even features node-based texture definition. In compositing, two are commonly used: Clouds and Blend.

Using a Clouds texture

Using a simple Clouds texture (choose Clouds instead of Image), you can add slight (or dramatic) color variation, as you saw in Chapter 6's example of adding the cloud texture to the world. When positioned over a wall and mapped to a gray color, Clouds dirties the wall, for example.

When you select the Clouds texture, you can change the basis for the randomness. You get a random blending of puffiness when you select Blender Original or a Voronoi option for Noise Basis. Figure 7-21 uses the Voronoi Crackle formula, which is perfect for ice fractures, porcelain crackles, cellular structures, and so on. Change this to the Blender Original, and you have a good lava texture.

> Colorbands and color ramps are used throughout Blender. Click Add to add a color and use the Cur selector to cycle between the colors in the band. Inside the band, click and drag on a vertical line to position that color within the band, or adjust the Pos control. Click the swatch to set the color or use the R, G, and B sliders. Use the A slider to adjust the color's opacity.

Using a Blend texture

The Blend texture is used to blend two objects together. In Figure 7-22, I've used the Blend texture to create an alpha channel for the image texture, fading out the image as it is applied to the dog's snout. Thus, the snout blends into the background image because the snout literally fades away. Without it, there would be a readily visible seam, which would spoil the effect.

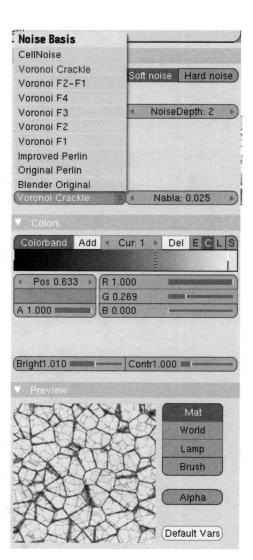

Figure 7-21. Clouds texture using Colorband

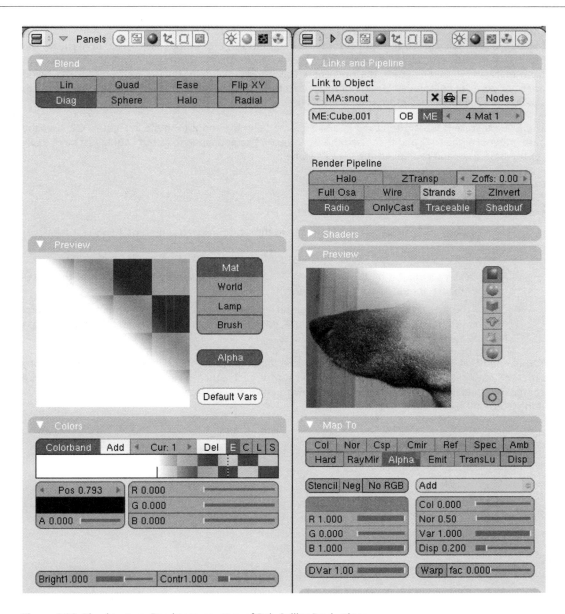

Figure 7-22. Blend texture. Dog image courtesy of Rob Collins Productions.

The Blend panel offers a lot of options for controlling the texture. Usually, the texture runs from left to right, transitioning from black to white in a linear (Lin), quadratic (Quad), or spline (Ease) transition. You can select Flip XY to make it run vertically, or Diag to make it run diagonally, Sphere (which was used in the *Big Buck Bunny* example in the previous chapter), and so on.

Using the Colorband option gives you precise control over where the blending occurs. In my use, I was blending alpha, so I wanted my right color swatch to be transparent (notice the A: 0.0 underneath the black swatch), but you can blend any kind of colors you want. Without Colorband, the texture runs from black to white. By setting the brightness (Bright), you can vary that as well, so that the blend does not go from completely black, but instead from some base level. By increasing contrast, you can squeeze the blending area more toward the center.

The Blend texture is most often used in a Multiply mode. In the snout example in Figure 7-22, I set the base material alpha to 0, and then used the Blend texture to add alpha to it, but I could just have easily set the base to 1, and multiplied the blend's alpha.

Summary

In this chapter, you saw that there are a few steps in the workflow to use materials and textures:

- Create a new material. Set the kind and type of material, and its base color and alpha.
- Add a texture. Orient it on the object (Map Input panel), and specify which aspect of the material the texture should affect (Map To panel).
- Create the actual texture, generally as either an image or some sort of computed procedural texture. When you create the actual texture, you can control the brightness/contrast, as well as filtering to help with low-resolution textures.

You learned that the same texture can be oriented and applied to many different materials, in many different ways, and that these textures layer on top of each other, mixing and combining to form a composite, shaded material. Now let's learn how to change things over time, by exploring the animation system in Blender.

Chapter 8

ANIMATED EFFECTS

Blender has several facilities for adding animated effects to your composition; these facilities fall into two broad categories: manually established and automatically computed. The manual animation system in Blender uses interpolated curves that establish certain property values at certain keyframes. In Blender, you key the starting property of something (such as the location of the camera), move in time, change the property to a new value, and then key the ending property. Blender then creates a curve to connect them. Blender also contains a very advanced simulation engine that can automatically compute the location of an object (and even thousands of objects) and can be used for compositing smoke, fire, and even flocks of birds, examples of which you will walk through in this chapter.

A core concept of animation in Blender is the interpolation (Ipo) curve, shown in Figure 8-1 animating the location property of an object, specifically, the location along the global y-axis. Blender uses a continuous Bezier type of curve (very similar to the 3D curve used in Chapter 5) to compute the *tweens*, meaning the values in between the two keys. Figure 8-1 shows the parts of the Ipo window.

The Ipo window shows Ipo curves for the selected object. The value (y-axis) is in Blender units, in a percentage (such as 0.6 for 60%), or in tens of degrees (such as 4.5 for 45 degrees), whichever is applicable to the kind of channel you have selected.

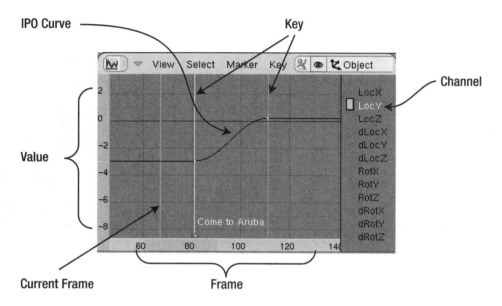

Figure 8-1. Animation anatomy in keyframe display mode

The window in Figure 8-1 is in keyframe mode; press K to toggle between keyframe and curve modes. In keyframe mode, you can select the yellow keys and grab them to move them, or you can press X to delete them. In curve mode, just like in 3D view, you can select a curve and tab into/out of edit mode to edit individual points on the curve. When animating, you have to consider the following:

- The object you want to move (such as a text element)
- The property of that object you want to change (such as the location)
- The starting and ending values (such as (0,0) to (2,4))
- How you want it to get there (such as fast, with a little shake at the end, through a few way-points, and so on)
- When you want it to move (such as starting at 2 seconds into the animation and ending a half second later)

In addition to the location, which is what you probably normally think of when animating, you can change many properties of an object, such as its rotation and size. In addition, you can animate certain properties of its material, such as its color, opacity, texture, and so on. Depending on the type of object, you may even be able to change additional, special properties; for example, you can animate a lamp's energy level (brightness). Although you could group these effects in several ways, let's examine them according to these categories:

- **Object animation**: This type of animation includes moving an object around, following another object around, following a path, or animating some aspect of an object (such as its shape).
- **Camera animation**: This effect principally comes from or looks like it was caused by or involves the camera.

- **Shader animation**: This is when the object's material or texture, such as its opacity or color, changes over time.

- **Lighting animation**: In the case of a lamp, this is changing its energy or color over time, such as to simulate lightning or sunrise.

The goal of this chapter is to show you how to use Blender's animation tools when making a composite video, such as a TV commercial, with professional results. It is not going to teach you about character animation or other noncompositing animation topics like that. However, an interesting crossover between animation for compositing and animation for characters is in shape keys, or what other packages call *morph targets*. In compositing, you can use shape keys to change a mask's shape because it needs to morph to properly mask out an element from a video where you cannot pull a key. As you saw in Chapter 5, you can UV map an image to a shape, and now in this chapter you will see that, by changing that shape over time, you can distort the image in convincing (or funny) ways.

All of the animation in this chapter occurs on the 3D side of Blender. The compositor (Chapters 10–12) animates its effects through the use of a Time node, which is discussed in those chapters. The sequencer (Chapters 13–15) animates its effect through the same Ipo curve discussed in this chapter, but the use of that curve in sequencing is discussed in Chapter 14. Where there is a direct crossover or alternate way to accomplish an effect using either the compositor or the sequencer, I will attempt to provide you with a link.

Open the file tut\8-anim-obj.blend, and locate the Ipo window. Notice that it is in object mode. You can pan and zoom the window or scroll the channel list by clicking and dragging with the MMB. Each property of an object, such as the location, is broken down into one or more channels of information, such as LocX, LocY, and LocZ. You assign a value to these channels at a certain frame, and Blender will work its magic to make sure the object is there when you want it.

The shapes of the Ipo curves shown in Figure 8-1 are controlled by the Bezier handles, which are identical to those used in a Bezier curve (Chapter 5) in interpolation mode (Curve ➤ Interpolation Mode). To tweak the shape of the curve, and thus those in-between interpolated values, first leave keyframe mode by pressing K so that you see the curves themselves. The curves are color-coded to correspond to the channel for which they provide values. Select a curve by right-clicking it, or select that particular channel from the channel list by clicking its colored box. The control points should now be white (highlighted). Press Tab to enter edit mode, and you will see the yellow Bezier handles. Just like 3D view curves, you can grab and move the whole point, or the ends of the handles, to change their influence over the curve. If interpolation mode is linear, then there will be a straight line between the points (no curve). If interpolation mode is constant, then the connection is like a stair-step function.

You can also, just like in 3D view, press N to see and edit the numerical properties directly. With Ipo control points, the X value is the frame number. You can delete points by pressing X, add a point by Ctrl-clicking, or move a point by pressing G to grab it. You can also change the handle type (to a vector, for instance).

A neat thing about Ipo curves is that you can extend them (Curve ➤ Extend Mode) to infinity in one of three ways: Blender can put out a final constant value, interpolate the curve based on a trend, or even extend a cyclic value based on an established pattern.

Object animation

When assembling a composite, it isn't just about the final placement but also how it got there (adding in the time element). When animating objects, first you have to choose the look you want, and then you can choose the most appropriate technique for making that effect happen. The properties of an object that you can animate are listed on the side of the Object Ipo curve.

Navigating in time

You can use the arrow keys on your keyboard to move through time in your animation. The left and right arrow keys advance and back up one frame, respectively, and the up and down arrow keys advance and back up ten frames, respectively. Try them now to see the text elements move.

You can also click and drag any frame indicator left or right (there is one in the timeline window header and another in the buttons window header) to scroll through time, or click and enter a specific frame number in the field.

In addition, the timeline window header has playback controls for (from left to right) rewinding to the beginning, rewinding to the previous keyframe, and playing and/or jumping forward to the next keyframe and end.

You can also click anywhere in the timeline window or Ipo curve window's workspace (the "grid" area) to position you to the indicated frame. The vertical green line shows you the current frame.

The start and end of the animation are set in the Start and End fields in the Scene Render Animation *panel fields or in the timeline window header.*

Moving an element into view

We discussed some considerations in Chapter 5 when you were arranging your objects in the camera frame, and you should consider the following issues if an object can be viewed by the camera:

- Is it in the field of view of the camera?
- Is it opaque?
- Is it hidden by some other object?
- Is it a member of at least one selected layer?
- Is it a member of the active render layer?
- Is it within the clipping distance of the camera?
- Is it in range of the world mist (Chapter 6)?
- If it is not shadeless, is it lit by a lamp?
- If Do Composite is on, is it a member of an input render layer, and has it been mixed in using nodes (discussed in Chapters 10–12)?
- If Do Sequence is on, has it been mixed in using the sequencer (discussed in Chapters 13–15)?

I hope you can tell that I've been (somewhat) methodically working my way through these issues in this book. Figures 8-2 through 8-4 show a selection of 3D views for selected frames from an animation. In this TV commercial, you lead off with the company name as a header over a textured projection plate (Chapter 7).

When you opened the file, you were positioned on frame 91. Press the up arrow on your keyboard (not the keypad) to advance ten frames, and you will see how both the scale and the location of the "Grand Opening" text element are animated. You can also press the right arrow to advance one frame. The down arrow and left arrow do the opposite, rewinding ten frames and one frame, respectively. You can also use the playback controls in the timeline header.

At frame 91, the text is large but off-camera. During frames 91–121, it scales down and moves up, coming to rest in front of the projection plate, and then it hangs there until frame 191, which is when it recedes to the back of the plate. Since it crosses behind the plate perpendicularly, it pops out of view. Since it is using an orthographic camera, an element is rendered the same size no matter how far it is from the camera.

Another example of object animation is the image element of the girl with the balloon; that element rises into the view (as if the balloon were floating up) between frames 361 and 391. Figure 8-2, Figure 8-3, and Figure 8-4 give you an idea of what the opening 10 seconds look like.

Figure 8-2. Frame 1

Figure 8-3. Frame 121

Figure 8-4. Frame 391

The screen layout in Figure 8-5 shows you the timeline window and the Ipo curve's window.

Figure 8-5. Animation screen layout

A storyboard is a series of very simple (line art) sketches that portray keyframes during the animation. I recommend that you always develop your animation based on a storyboard. Simply take a blank sheet of paper, and split it down the middle and laterally into four sections. This will give you a grid that is roughly a 16:9 aspect ratio, where you can sketch eight keyframes. Annotate each frame with what is happening and approximately when in the video you want this frame to appear. For more information on using Blender during the storyboarding process, consult the two online tutorials I have written at http://wiki.blender.org/index.php/Doc:Tutorials/Sequencer/ Animatics and http://wiki.blender.org/index.php/Doc:Tutorials/Game_Engine/ Storyboards.

Using the timeline window

Like all Blender window types, the timeline window, shown in Figure 8-6, has a workspace and a header. The workspace shows you the current frame as a green vertical line and shows you any keyframes for the selected object as yellow vertical lines. The header has a menu and some media controls that help you navigate in time.

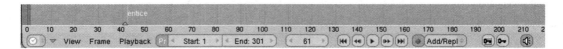

Figure 8-6. Timeline window header

The View menu essentially replicates the media playback controls, allowing you to jump to the previous/next keyframe or to the beginning/end of the animation range. You can also change the x-axis from frames to seconds, and vice versa. The current frames per second is set in the FPS field of the Scene-Render panel's Format area.

The Frame menu allows you to set markers in the timeline. Markers are very helpful in annotating what is supposed to happen in the animation. You first set the marker and (if you want) name the marker. You can rename a marker by navigating to its frame and then choosing Name Marker. You can also set the start or end frames of the animation to the current frame by using the Frame menu. In Figure 8-6, the "entice" marker is set at frame 41, marking when you want the enticement to pop in.

> A keyframe *is a "key (important) frame" where the exact position or some other property of an object is explicitly specified.*

The Pr (preview) button, to the left of the Start/End fields, darkens areas in the Ipo window that are outside the animation preview start/end (if set) or the full animation range indicated in the Start/End fields. When working with an animation, you may want to preview a fairly narrow range in time, say a few seconds. Pressing Ctrl+P in the timeline window lets you drag a box-type selection of a range of frames to define a scrub range. This helps you keep the scrub on a narrow animation range. Now when you press Play, the animation will play into the scrub range and, when it hits the end of the scrub range, will jump back to the beginning frame you set with the Ctrl+P operation.

You can change the full animation range by deselecting the Pr button and using the numeric controls (click the arrows to advance/rewind by a frame, click and drag to scroll through numbers, or click and then type in a number manually). The current frame number is shown in the numeric control between the end frame and the playback controls.

The playback controls allow you to rewind to the start of the scrub or full animation (depending on whether Pr is enabled), skip back a keyframe, play the animation in the range indicated, or fast-forward to the next keyframe for the selected object or to the end of the animation.

The red record button greatly simplifies the whole keyframing process. When enabled, you do not have to press I and select the channel to key a new object location. When the red record button is enabled, all you have to do is move the object, and in add/replace mode, a new key is added when you drop the object in place. If you have the timeline fairly locked into place, then use replace mode to avoid creating new keys, and instead just update keys that are already there.

The key icons ease the task of managing keys and channels. The left one inserts a key, essentially doing the same thing as pressing I in 3D view. The right one, which is just a key icon, actually deletes the key for the selected channel. For example, you may want an element to visit several locations in your composition but while rotating at a constant rate. In those cases, you want to key each location but have only two rotation keys (the starting rotation and the ending rotation). If you accidentally key the rotation in the middle, you can use this key icon to delete just the keyed rotation values at that frame.

Last but not least, the speaker icon turns on sound and plays the sound file loaded in the sequencer. This feature is essential when match moving, lip-syncing, or otherwise making sure your animation matches up to the sound track. In this example, I recorded a sample 30-second script and loaded it into the sequencer (Chapter 14), so you may hear me doing the voice-over (yes, I know, I am not a professional announcer), but it gave me a framework for timing the animation while I made the commercial.

Using the Ipo (animation) window

I introduced the anatomy of the Ipo window in Figure 8-1. Let's go over it in detail now. The Ipo window is the workhorse of animation, showing you any kind of Ipo for any object and allowing you to link Ipo curves to objects. The workspace for the window is in two parts: the workspace that shows curves and keyframes and the channel list on the right. In Figure 8-7, the location property is first, with its three channels LocX, LocY, and LocZ, and so on, down the list.

In the workspace, the actual curves are shown for each selected channel. In Figure 8-7, three curves are shown in the workspace as black lines since the workspace is in key display mode. The x-axis of the workspace is numbered 0, 20, 40, and so on, and indicates the frame number in the animation. If there are 30 frames per second, then the 60th frame is 2 seconds into the animation (assuming the animation starts at frame 1). The y-axis of the window is the value, and the y intercept of the curve indicates the value for that channel at that frame. That value may be something explicit set by you (called a *key value*) or may be computed by Blender in interpolating the value of the curve, which is why they're called *interpolation curves*, or Ipo for short. The value can be in Blender units, a percentage, or tens of degrees (for rotations).

The window header contains four menu items: a type selector, Ipo selector, copy/paste buttons, and window zoom and lock buttons.

The View menu has some very nice features for helping you edit more efficiently, such as the lock view area that prevents you from clicking to a frame that is outside your animation range. The Channel Properties panel (also available by pressing N in the workspace) shows you the exact values of each curve point, allowing you to precisely (but manually) adjust any value of the selected control point.

The Select menu allows you to select keys or curves. Keys can be selected like objects in 3D view: by pressing B and box-selecting or by right-clicking and then holding down Shift while you right-click for multiple keys. If your display is in curve mode, then dragging over a curve selects the whole curve.

The Marker menu is the same as the markers in the timeline window and in the sequencer. It allows you to set and name placeholders along your timeline; this can be a handy reference and visual indicator/reminder as to when things are happening.

The next menu item is either Curve or Key, depending on what view mode you have active (press K in the window to switch display modes). You want curve mode if you are going to change the shape of the curve, which changes the object's rate of transition from one value to another.

Figure 8-7 shows you the Ipo window's header in key mode.

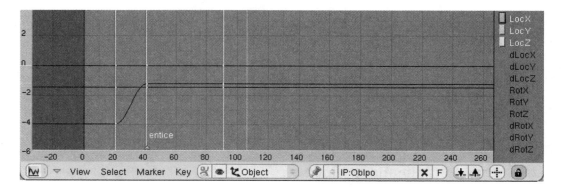

Figure 8-7. Ipo window header

The Ipo type selector allows you to view the different types of Ipos that may be defined for an object. These types are discussed in the remainder of this chapter, and available entries vary based on the type of object you have selected.

The Ipo selector (the next control with the pushpin and IP prefix) associates the selected object with an Ipo. Click into this field to name the Ipo (I frequently use the name of the object or a logical name for the action). The X icon delinks the Ipo from the object. Unused Ipos are not read in from a file. In some cases, you may want to preserve the Ipo "just in case" you need it for a different object, so the F icon allows you to fake a user of the Ipo. When enabled, even if no object is actually using that Ipo, it will be saved.

At the far right of the header, you can use the up and down arrow icons to copy and paste a curve (not a key) to the buffer (which is somewhat analogous to Ctrl+C in Windows) and then select another object and paste the curve (using the down arrow icon) to that target object. The + icon allows you to zoom in on a frame range.

The lock icon, located on the far right side of the header, should be enabled; it causes other windows to update in real time as you make changes in this window. For example, if you select the "balloonee" element in 3D view and then select, grab, and move the keyframe from frame 40 to 80 in this Ipo window (with your current frame at frame 55), you should see the element move in real time as you drag the keyframe back and forth. With the lock icon disabled, the other windows are updated only when you drop the keyframe in place.

Making things change

Every TV commercial, webcast, film, and presentation involves movement or animation of an object or many objects in some coordinated fashion. Depending on what you want to animate, you start out by inserting keys (for example, a color key), which creates an Ipo of a certain type (in this case, a Material Ipo). That Ipo contains animation information for one or more channels that pertain to that type of Ipo (in this case, the red, green, and blue color component values). Each channel has an Ipo curve that controls the values for that channel. You select the type of Ipo using the Ipo selector, shown in Figure 8-8.

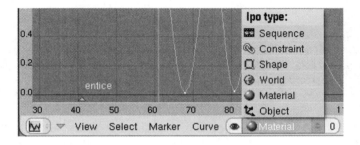

Figure 8-8. Ipo types

The list of available types varies based on what is appropriate for an object. For example, a camera does not have a material, so that type of Ipo is not available for that type of object. These are all of the types of Ipos you can create:

- Object
- Material
- World
- Texture
- Shape
- Constraint
- Lamp
- Camera
- Sequence
- Path

Figure 8-8 showed a Material Ipo, and Figure 8-7 showed an Object Ipo. On the right side of the Ipo window, you see the channels that are available for the Object Ipo. There are a lot of them, but it starts off with the first three, which are in color (indicating they have values): LocX, LocY, and LocZ. The color of the channel matches the color of the curve line in the workspace when the workspace is in curve display mode.

The Material and Texture Ipos allow you to animate certain material properties for an object. The World Ipo allows you to animate changing horizon and zenith light and mist as time goes by. (World settings were discussed in Chapter 6.) Changing the shape or constraint of an object is discussed later in detail, but suffice to say that this set of Ipos allow you to set the influence of a particular shape or constraint at any time. Sequence strip effects can be animated and will be covered in Chapter 13.

You can select individual channels to work on and display by clicking the channel name, or you can select multiple channels via Shift-click. Channels with values always have a colored square in front of their names, but if they are not selected, their names will be black (not white). For example, in Figure 8-7, the remaining channels do not have values, telling you that you have only an Ipo controlling the location of the object. All other values are fixed at whatever their values currently are. For example, the text element Fun! Free Food! Is rotated 25 degrees along the z-axis. Since that RotZ channel does not have an icon, it won't change, because it therefore does not have an Ipo curve.

> *The Ipo curves for an object are shown automatically in the Ipo window as soon as you select the object in 3D view. If there are more channels than will fit in the window pane, click the MMB over the channel list and drag up and down to pan the display to reveal the other channels.*

The names of the channels are pretty self-evident, and there is a channel for each individual value of an object's property. For example, LocX is the location in the X direction in the 3D view space, RotY is its rotation, and ScaleZ is the scale of the object in the Z direction. Each channel is a different color, and you can click to select/hide channels from view. Note that when you hide a channel, any operation you make, such as deleting keyframes, does *not* affect that channel.

> *With your cursor in the Ipo window, press K to switch views between keyframes and curves. If you want to specify what a property should be at a given time, you will want to work with keyframes; other times you may want to change the transition curve shape. If you want an object to arrive at a location at a different time, use keyframe mode to just select, grab, and move the whole key and all three location channels at the same time. If you want the object to start moving faster, you have to edit the curve(s) controlling the how fast the channel values change over time.*

Animating an object

To set a new keyframe, simply navigate to the frame that indicates when you want the object in a specific location. Then in 3D view, position (grab and move, rotate, and/or scale) the object where you want it to be at that moment in time. Then, with your cursor in 3D view, press I, and from the pop-up select which channel set (properties) you want to key, such as the location and rotation. If you select the location, Blender will create a key for each of the LocX, LocY, and LocZ curves in the Ipo window. For example, play with the Fun! text element. At frame 450, position it in-camera, and key its location and its rotation and/or scale. While it is moving into frame, key the Spring Stimulus Special text element to rotate and fly out of the frame.

> *Press K in the 3D view to see a yellow outline of the location, rotation, and scaling of any object for each of its keyframes.*

You work with keyframes in the Ipo window the same way you do with objects in 3D view. Right-click to select a keyframe, and then press G to grab it and move it in time (holding Ctrl to snap to whole frames) or press X to delete it. You can even border-select multiple keyframes to move them as a bunch, and you can scale them to make the object move faster/slower through them. Press A to select all or none of the keyframes. You can duplicate selected keyframes via Ctrl+D; just be sure to move your mouse before clicking to drop them. Otherwise, you will have two keyframes on the same physical frame, which can be very confusing.

You can disassociate (delink) an Ipo curve from an object by clicking the X next to the Ipo name in the Ipo header. You can rename the Ipo curve to indicate what it is doing. You can also have objects share an Ipo. If you have an Object Ipo that, for example, rotates only the object, you can share that Ipo with another object (select the second object, and then select the Ipo from the selector instead of clicking Add New). Then, the rotation (but not the location or scale) will be controlled consistently by the same curves.

As I discussed in Chapter 6, Blender has a concept of *parenting*, which is a relationship between a *parent* object and one or more *child* objects. You set up a parent-child relationship by selecting one or more children, then Shift-selecting the parent, and finally pressing Ctrl+P. Remember that if you animate the movement of the parent, the children will move along with the parent, just like real life. They keep their relative distance and orientation, but they are directly affected, as objects, by the parents. You can animate a child as well; they are free to move around on their own and do not affect the parent's location, rotation, or scale.

Animating a layer

In the previous section, you learned how to move an element into camera view, thus making it visible. You can also use a technique to animate the layer(s) to which an element belongs. If an object is on a "hidden" layer and it jumps to a layer that is rendered, the object will pop into view. There are two ways to make a layer not rendered. The first is simply not selecting it in 3D view, as shown in Figure 8-9, which shows the 3D view header with only layer 1 selected.

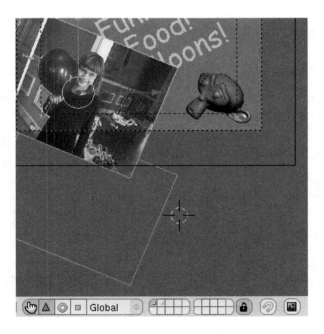

Figure 8-9. 3D view with only layer 1 selected

Blender is telling you that something is on layer 2 by showing a little dot in the layer 2 button. Even though the object is in the scene, since it is on a deselected layer, it will not be rendered. Therefore, one way to exclude an object from rendering is move it to a layer that is not selected.

Another way to make something disappear is to change it to a layer that is not selected by the render layer. By default, a render layer includes all layers, so you will have to change it so that it does not include that layer. In Figure 8-10, you can see that even though layers 1 through 5 are enabled at the scene level (the top-left set of scene layer buttons), in the Render Layers panel's layer button set, layer 2 is not selected, and therefore any objects on layer 2 will not be included in the render.

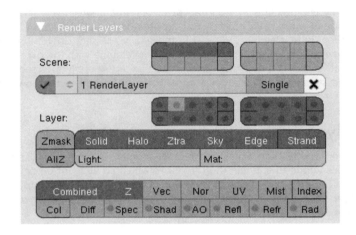

Figure 8-10. The render layer excludes layer 2. Layers 1, 3, 4, and 5 will be rendered.

Consider a skateboarding commercial, where you want to show a couple of skateboarders, one going left to right and another going right to left. The video of each skateboarder is textured to a projection plane, and you animate the location of these planes to fly in front of the camera. You start out the first image element on the left side (when looking through camera view, called *house left* or *stage right*) and have it move across the screen, but before it goes out of frame house right (also known as exiting *stage left*), you want it to pop invisible. Popping elements in and out of view is spunky and keeps the viewer's attention.

Let's assume that layer 2 will not be selected during rendering so that it can hold our "invisible" objects. In the 3D view header, select layer 1, and Shift-select layer 2. Add and texture the plane, and ensure it is on layer 1. At frame 1, with your cursor in 3D view, press I, and select Layer from the pop-up Insert Key menu. Then go to frame 31, and move the plane to layer 2 (press M in 3D view and click the layer 2 button). Then press I, and select Layer again.

If you deselect layer 2 (Shift-click the layer 2 button in the 3D view header), the plane will pop invisible as you scrub through frame 31. In the Ipo window, select the Layer channel, and you will observe a constant kind of interpolation curve (actually a horizontal line) for each layer that the object belongs to, where the Y value indicates the layer number.

You can also do the opposite and have an object pop into view. Start with the object on an invisible layer, and key that. Move in time to the frame where you want the object to pop in. At that frame, press M, and select layer 1 only. The object should still be visible since the 3D view shows you objects on layers 1 and 2. Key this layer membership as before.

Now, deselect layer 2 in 3D view by Shift-selecting the layer 2 button (the button is a toggle button). If you rewind a frame by pressing the left arrow on your keyboard, you should see the object "disappear." Figure 8-11 shows the Layer Ipo.

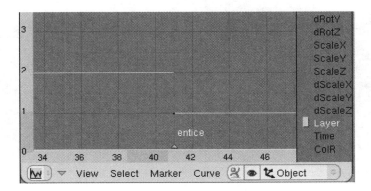

Figure 8-11. The object jumps from layer 2 to layer 1 at frame 31.

> *Note that this can get a little tricky since you cannot key an object that is not visible. You may have to select that hidden layer in 3D view, just so you can select and key the object out of that layer and into a visible layer. Just remember to deselect that layer prior to rendering.*

Moving elements into range

Next up is making an element appear at some point in the animation by moving it into range of either the world or the camera.

Camera clipping range

Like a layer animation, moving an object into camera range has the effect of popping it suddenly into view. The camera has a clipping range defined by a start range and an end range from the camera. Objects closer to the camera that start, or farther from the end, are not rendered, even though they may be viewable for all other reasons. Figure 8-12 shows a practical use for this with an orthographic camera.

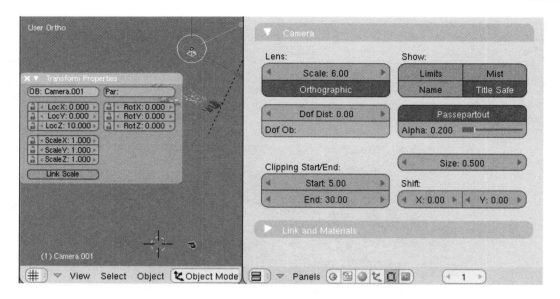

Figure 8-12. Using camera clipping

As you can see in the figure, the camera has a clip start of 5 units and a clip end of 30 units. The camera is at 10 units above Z, and the monkey is at –30, so it is 40 units away, as shown in the partial side view. Even though it is in the camera frame, it is not visible to the camera view since it is more than 30 units from camera.

As you move the object closer to the camera (or move the camera closer to it), the object will pop into view as it crosses that clipping boundary. It will be clipped out of view when it gets too close to the camera, which in this example is less than five units away. You have to be careful with this technique, though. If an object is only halfway outside of the clipping range on a rendered frame, the object's faces that remain inside the range will be rendered, making it appear that the object has been sliced in half.

> The 3D view has a clipping range as well, usually set to a large number like 500 units.
> Set this range via View ➤ View Properties.

World (mist) range

The world can have a range of visibility defined by mist, described in Chapter 6. Moving an object into this range gradually makes it more visible. Figures 8-13a through 13c show an object moving from a Z-depth distance of 30, 20, and then 10, where the mist start was 10 and the depth was 20. As you can see, as the object progresses through the mist, it becomes more visible. Note that an orthographic camera was used, so it stays the same relative size.

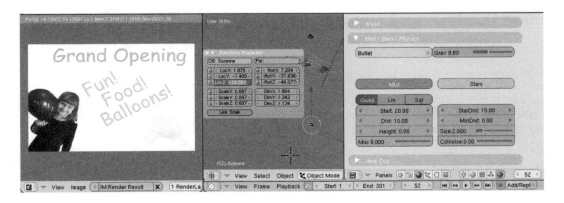

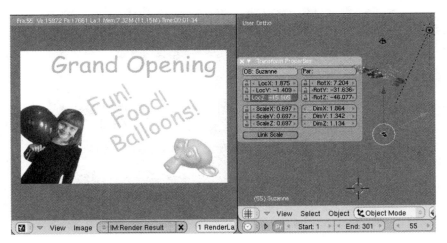

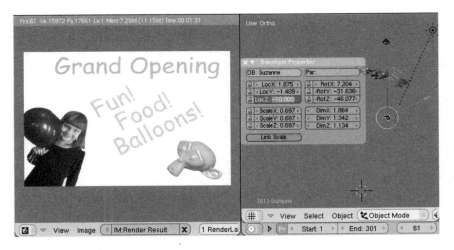

Figure 8-13. Suzanne becoming visible, partially faded, fully visible

217

Adding the finishing touches to element motion

This section includes just a few notes on making things animate as the audience expects them. If something comes to a sudden stop, you expect it to overcorrect and back up just a bit as it comes to a stop, just like your vehicle if you brake hard (imagine a tire screeching sound). When something drops into view (imagine a popping sound), you expect it to jiggle a little as it stops. In addition, it may puff up a bit (*scale*, in Blender terms) or stretch as it comes to a stop. Another finishing touch is adding a jiggle to the element as it pops in and out, like it's on some sort of magical spring (imagine a springy "boiiiing" sound). The editing workflow you can use is to Ctrl-click to form a sinusoidal curve.

To make something come to a sudden stop, you need to edit the Ipo curve to make it look like that shown in Figure 8-14, which shows the curves for the third cube in the file `tut\8-touche.blend`. Notice their shape; they decelerate quickly.

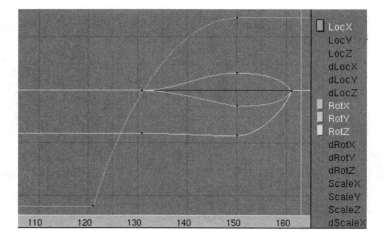

Figure 8-14. Finishing touch after editing an Ipo curve

Open the file, and press Alt+A in the 3D view to watch the show. The first red cube is the normal curve. The second green cube is a decelerating cube, which looks like there is friction and is a little more realistic. The third cube skids to a stop, partially upending (which is why you see the rotation curves).

To get that deceleration, I changed the ending handle to a vector type (recall this handle type and working with Bezier curves from Chapter 5). The principles of editing an Ipo curve are the same as discussed when making a mask using a Bezier curve in Chapter 5, so there's no need to repeat them. To make these changes, select a curve (not a keyframe), tab into edit mode, select one of the handle's control points, and change its type (press V) or move it by selecting the middle point. Or you can select and move one of the control points, thus changing that point's influence over the curve.

> *To make an object appear larger when using a standard perspective camera, all that you need to do is to move it closer to the camera. With an orthographic camera, your only option is to actually scale the object.*

Camera animation

A camera is an object, so you can move and rotate it in time just like any other object. Therefore, you use the Object Ipo curve to animate the location and/or rotation of a camera. When you move the camera, you can get some very neat effects.

Flying the camera through a field of dreams

Observe the movie on your DVD called lib\images\things\splash-0000-0661.mov, which was an advertisement done for an up-and-coming security company. The emotive is that you have all these issues coming at you (in alarm red) from seemingly nowhere, and then the solution arrives in calming blue. To achieve this look, simply fly a perspective camera down through the words, arranged so that the camera flies "through" some of them, and use a world mist (Chapter 6) to make distant letters invisible.

Animating a camera is a little tricky, in that you can do two types of animation with a camera: you can animate it as an object, and you can animate its special settings through a camera type of Ipo. I used both kinds of animation here: moving the camera as an object and then animating the clip end. Figure 8-19 shows the Camera Ipo used in the video clip. By shrinking the clip end, the tag line disappears even though nothing moves.

The camera itself is a special object and has its own special set of channels in the Camera Ipo (Figure 8-15):

- **Lens**: The angle or length of the lens, in mm, where 35 is the normal value, 16 is considered wide-angle, and 210 is a very long lens. Shorter lenses introduce more spherical distortion.
- **Clip Start and End**: The Z-depth range that is visible to the camera. The camera clips off any object (or portion thereof), which is outside this range and is not rendered.
- **Apert and FDist**: Aperture, or size of the iris, and focal distance, both used by the depth of field (DOF).
- **Shift X and Y**: Used to shift the perspective of the camera so that you can composite architectural perspectives (see Chapter 9).

Other object animation can affect the camera. Within the Camera properties panel, if the camera's DOF distance is tied to another object, the camera's DOF distance changes as that object moves, even though nothing specifically about the camera itself is animated. This information is picked up by the Depth of Field node.

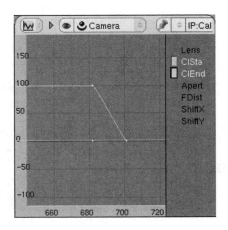

Figure 8-15. Camera Ipo channels

Creating camera shake

KaBOOM! You want your audience to feel, see, and hear that explosion going off, and you expect to be shaken by the shock wave. To see that explosion, in addition to the flash and fire and smoke, you expect the camera to shake. An example of this is the opening sequence of Halo, when a banshee flies close by, and the air pressure shakes the camera. I've used camera shake when a dragon roars at the camera and stomps the ground, and I've used a slow roll when backing away from the dragon to simulate the rocking that would occur with a handheld camera as the cameraman backs up to save his life.

There are a few ways to shake the camera: by shaking the camera, by shaking everything that the camera is looking at, or by doing both, depending on the size of the explosion. In the compositor and the sequencer, you will see that you have to jiggle the image, since the camera has already done its job. In 3D view, you can shake anything you want.

Generally, producing camera shake just means animating the location and rotation of the camera by a little bit, using a sinusoidal location curve, as shown in Figure 8-16.

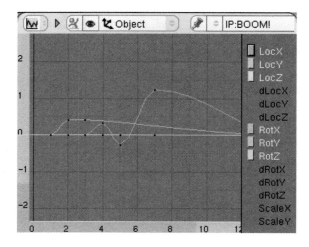

Figure 8-16. Camera shake example

In this method, and with this particular curve set, the camera is knocked back and rotates up, vibrates, and returns to where it was looking. If you were trying to simulate the shake from, say, a train passing close by, you would go sideways. In general, pretend how you would react to the boom as if you were holding the camera, and emulate that with the camera motion. Another kind of camera shake is to simulate a handheld, as was done with the *Battlestar Galactica* series. You can also texture a non-shaken video to a plane and then shake the plane.

Another method of doing camera shake is to use one of Blender's physical simulations, the soft body, and tie the camera to the simulated object. This can generate some extremely realistic shaken camera motion in simulating handheld reaction and overcorrection. You can find a tutorial on this method at http://blenderartists.org/forum/showthread.php?t=116699.

Following a path

Often it falls to the compositor to put up simple animated overlay or graphics over a background. Using the simple editing tools you learned in Chapter 5, you can animate them. Figure 8-17 shows a model of an arrowhead parented to a curve in a CurveFollow relationship.

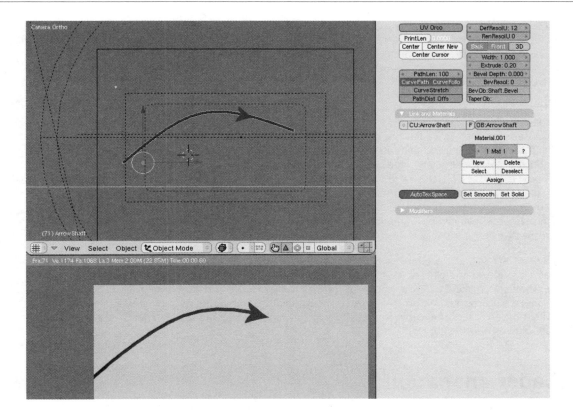

Figure 8-17. Arrowhead following a curve

To assist you, I've provided just such a solution on the DVD in tut\CurveFollow.blend. You can easily create this in a few steps:

1. Create a curve that traces the completed path of the arrow's shaft. If this were overlaying a chart showing sales, this shaft would trace the "line chart." When you open the file, this shaft is selected and named ArrowShaft.

2. Extrude the curve so that it is solid and renderable, and match its camera perspective to the background chart so it will trace the path you would like. In the example file, the Curve and Surface panel (in the buttons window's Editing context) shows an extrude of 0.20. The camera is looking directly at the curve.

3. Model an arrowhead. Select the arrowhead, then Shift-select the curve, and press Ctrl+P, making the curve the parent of the arrowhead. In the pop-up confirmation box, choose Path follow. The arrowhead will now travel along the path for 100 frames, from start to end.

4. Give the path a material with a blend texture that is half transparent and half white, and map that texture using the arrowhead object as input. Set the texture to affect the alpha using a multiply mix method. In the sample file, press F5 to switch the buttons window to the Shading context, and observe the Map Input panel. Refer to the previous chapter on shading to review how to inspect and change materials and textures.

The yellow background is transparent, and you can key that over any background chart. Notice that I've told the arrowhead to turn to follow the tangent of the path (named *arrowshaft*) by clicking CurveFollow in the parent path's Curve and Surface panel, so it (and all children) always point "forward" along the path. To change the overall duration of the animation, simply change PathLen in the Curve and Surface panel of the parent path.

The other (and more modern) way to accomplish this motion, instead of parenting the arrowhead to the path, is to assign a FollowPath constraint to the arrowhead, providing the name of the shaft in the Constraints panel. To switch this example to using the constraint method, delete the parent relationship by clearing the Par field in the Transform Properties panel, press F7 to access the Object panel, add the Follow Path constraint in the Constraints panel, enter ArrowShaft in the Target field, enable CurveFollow, set Fw:Z (forward) and Up:Y, and then rotate and move the arrowhead to align with the curve. You can now animate the Inf (influence) channel in the arrowhead's Constraint Ipo to allow the arrowhead to veer off the curve. By using the constraint method, you can have multiple constraints in place, and you can have multiple paths influence the motion of an object, each governed by their respective Constraint influence curve.

Behind the scenes, Blender has enabled a Path Ipo type, which has a speed curve that controls the acceleration of the camera as it traverses the path. Initially it is blank, but you can create one, for example, to make the arrowhead accelerate as it gets to the end of the path if you were trying to convey a project getting off to a slow start but building momentum as it progressed. In the example file, I have created this curve for you, so you can readily experiment with effects on the animation, should you edit the curve.

Shader animation

Another way to make an element appear in a composition is to animate its opacity from fully transparent to fully opaque. You can also change its color like an octopus or chameleon. Instead of keying in the 3D view, you key a material setting by pressing I while your cursor is in the buttons window in the Material context. Doing this provides you with an entirely different set of channels, which form an entirely different set of Ipo curves. To view these curves, select Material in the Ipo window header, changing from Object to Material, shown in Figure 8-8. They are still curves, however, so they can be edited just like all the other Bezier curves and displayed in keyframe mode as well.

The workflow is also consistent with objects; you navigate in time to the frame you want the change to take effect, make the changes, and then key those changes. You have to press I each time you make a change with your cursor in the Material panels in order to see the material's channels. If you press I with your cursor in the 3D view, Blender assumes you want to key the object, not the material/texture. You can also manually set a value by working in the Ipo window to select the channel and then Ctrl-click to set the control point.

To change an object from transparent to opaque, move the Alpha slider in the Shaders panel to 0. With your cursor hovering over the panel, press I, and select Alpha from the pop-up menu. Navigate in time to where you want the object to be opaque, slide the slider to 1, and press I again, choosing Alpha again. Figure 8-18 shows an example Ipo curve. The curve in this figure results in an object that fades in and out of view repeatedly.

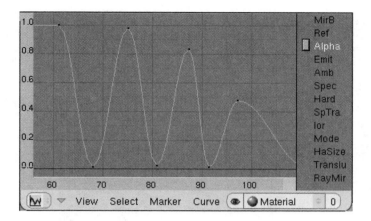

Figure 8-18. Alpha channel Ipo curve

> *You need to enable either Z or ray transparency in order for the rendering engine to compute transparency. If using ray transparency, ensure* Ray *is enabled in the* Render *panel.*

Animated textures

The only really tricky thing when animating textures for a material, such as if you want a crackle texture to appear as your character turns to stone, is to select the proper texture channel. Since a texture is applied to a material through a stack of texture channels, numbered 0 at the top through 9 at the bottom, animating that texture's application is achieved by selecting the Material type Ipo in the Ipo window header and then manually indicating the texture channel by entering a number right next to the selector (which is 0, or top channel, by default).

You saw how you can animate the material's alpha channel directly. Since a texture can be mapped to influence the alpha value and you can animate the texture's influence on the material, you indirectly can control the alpha channel. In the tut\8-Anim-Obj.blend file, examine the material for the projection plate. You will see that it has two textures. In the top slot, slot 0, is an image of the island from offshore. The second texture, in slot 1, is an image of the beach. These are placeholders for the video that will come when the camera crew gets back from the resort after shooting their B roll and getting a nice tan. I still can't figure out why they needed two weeks in Aruba to shoot one minute of B-roll. Although we only have static images now, you can still animate the crossover from one to the other, get all the animation done, and then simply swap the image texture for a video later.

Figure 8-19 shows the color influence channel (not the material's color RGB) for the first texture (number 0) and, right below it, the same channel but for texture channel 1. Notice how one is dropping off in influence as the other comes up. This provides a nice smooth transition from one to the other.

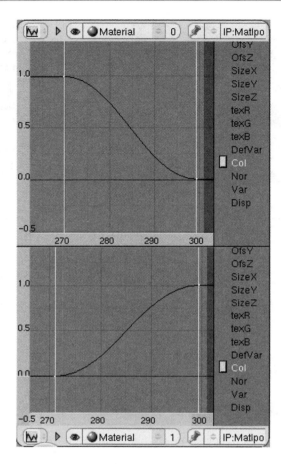

Figure 8-19. Material texture Ipo to cross-fade two
textures; channel 0 (top) and channel 1 (bottom)

As you can see from that channel list, you can animate many things. As a compositor, besides the color
factor, you may need to animate the size or offset of a texture. For example, animating the offsetX
property of a texture will slide it left or right.

Blender provides ray-traced transparency. If a transparent surface is bent and has an index of refraction (IOR) greater than 1.0, then any light that passes through it is bent as well. You can shape a lens,
as shown in Figure 8-20, and it will magnify or reduce and distort the image behind it.

In Figure 8-20, I have shaped a convex lens (actually half of a convex lens) and placed it in front of a
floating plate textured with a scene from *Big Buck Bunny*. The lens is formed by simply adding a UV
sphere (one of the simple mesh shapes available from 3D view) and editing in side mode to box-select
the back vertices and delete them. Alternatively, I could have scaled the sphere in the Y direction (S,
Y, move mouse) to make a more precise convex lens.

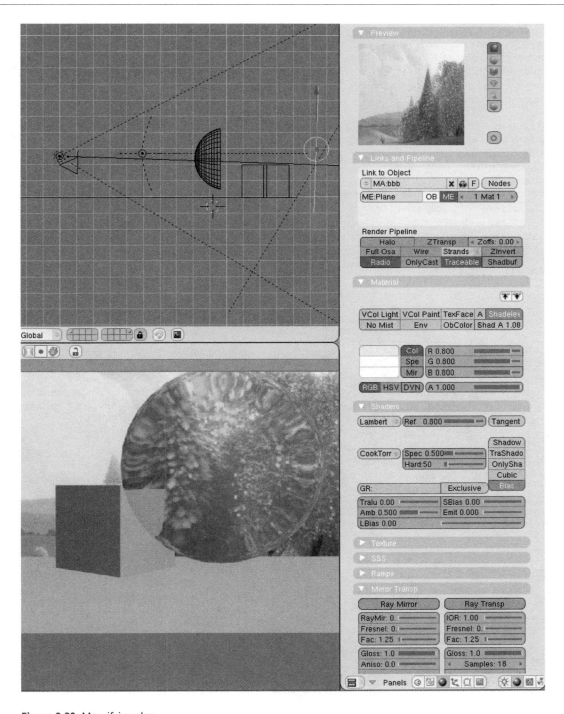

Figure 8-20. Magnifying glass

By animating the location of the lens, various parts of the image are distorted as well. When combined with an actor "resisting" the pull or scaling the lens larger over time, you can produce quite interesting effects. You can also scale the lens to 0 in the Y direction, making it flat, or you can animate the material settings so that the lens initially has no effect on the plate image. Then, by animating it, it can gradually start sucking up the city (or the actor) or start a force field ripple or discontinuity in the space-time continuum.

As you will see later in this chapter, you can shape a sphere into something else, for example, a head, and save those two shapes. By animating the influence of one shape key over the other, the net effect over time is to morph into that other shape. If the image is transparent (or mirrored), the effect can be, well, anything from subtle to startling. Please exercise caution when altering our continuum.

In summary, you can create a localized image distortion that looks like, well, a worm hole forming or a gravity well or simply someone looking through a magnifying glass or porthole into another dimension. When animated, either by changing the position of the lens/mirror or by varying the strength, all kinds of neat interdimensional effects are possible. Your imagination is the limit!

Moving subtitles

You can animate text sliding to the right, as in a ticker tape or news summary. Usually you use a background plane, such as black, so that the rest of the image or background can be displayed. You will work through a subtitle example in Chapter 13.

You can also animate a simple sphere to be the bouncing ball over the lyrics of a song, as shown in Figure 8-21.

Figure 8-21. Follow the bouncing ball and sing along.

Lighting animation

Since a light is an object as well, you can animate the location and rotation just like any other object. I see animated lights as objects all the time in TV show announcements and headers. Although you do not see the light directly, since the light itself does not render, you see things get brighter and shinier. For example, you might see the name of a company, and then you can tell that a light crosses in front of it, from left to right. However, there are other properties and uses for light in an animation, discussed next.

Fake light

In Chapter 2, you saw how to float a shadeless plane in front of the camera, textured with the image or video. With shadeless shading, no light is needed, no lights affect the surface, and the image is rendered exactly as it was filmed. You can make gross adjustments to the brightness and contrast in the texture's Colors panel.

So, the question becomes, what happens when Shadeless is disabled? Well, two things come into play. First the Diffuse setting specifies how bright the original colors are, and the Specular color says what kind of sheen you get when light bounces off the plate at an angle. Figure 8-22 shows an image of the beach rendered shadeless, then shaded to match shadeless, and finally shaded to introduce some false lighting. The file tut\8-light has the four images. The top row is a shadeless plate, and the right plate has a Diffuse setting of 1.0, has a Specular setting of 0, and is lit by a lamp delivering an energy value of 1 at the surface. (The lamp is 10 units away from the plane but has a half falloff of 10 and thus an energy of 2. The falloff value of a lamp is the distance at which half the energy is delivered.) In the bottom row, the left plate is slightly yellow and the light is a little brighter, whereas the right plate has a Diffuse setting of 0.5 and a Specular setting of 0, lit by a few lamps to simulate a purple sunrise, a flashlight, some island home and radio tower lights, and a clear night sky. For fun, I've included lib\images\places\sunrise.wmv that shows lamps animated.

As you can see, using CG lights to light an image can have dramatic effects on an image, and you can add lights to mimic streetlights, headlights, moonlight, and sunlight, with appropriate coloration, to light an image however you would like. Use color to set the mood: pink for girly, blue for cold, yellow for sunny, and so on.

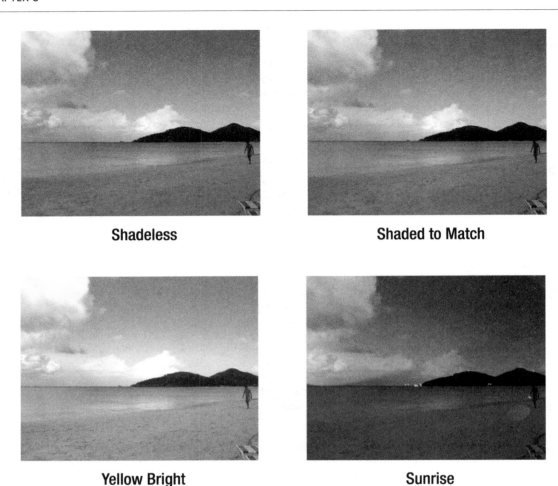

Figure 8-22. Fake lighting of a background plate

Matching a live-action plate

When integrating CG and live-action video, it is very important to match the lighting that was in the real world with your CG scene so that any objects you composite over the scene will look like they fit into it. This also goes for any shadows the objects might cast and any ambient occlusion. Figure 8-23 shows a magic ball floating in front of me, an obvious composite of a sphere on top of me acting. There are two elements to making this look "good" (well, three if you consider superb, convincing acting as an ingredient). First, the shader for the material, texture, and world was set up to react realistically, including ambient light:

- An appropriate diffuse level considering the light level using the Oren Naur shader and a high surface roughness
- Fairly low specularity and very low hardness with the Phong shader

- Ambient light to match the ceiling color (a light tan)
- An appropriate amount of ambient mixing (it was indoors with lots of ambient light, so 0.2 was used)
- A pleasing, fairly neutral color for diffuse and a lighter (nonwhite) specular color
- A texture to give color irregularities

Second, three lights simulate the real light that was coming in from the sides, as would be blocked by my body, and were animated to mimic shadowing and ambient occlusion that would occur as I open my hands. Hemi lights provide soft, shadowless lighting, and one simulates the light bounce from the ceiling as well as directly from the windows stage left. A big area light simulates the very diffuse light from stage right. I've given you a background image to play with on the DVD in lib\images\People\ Roger\magic-plate.AVI.

> To make this image very convincing, the CG image should be gamma corrected (see the gamma node information in Chapter 11) so that when composited on top of the photo (which is gamma corrected), the color spaces match.

Figure 8-23. CG lights mimic reality.

On another occasion, I was filming a live-action plate and had my choice of filming times. I chose the time when the sun was setting and was occluded by the buildings; thus, the real scene was bathed in ambient light, which was very easy to simulate in the CG world using hemi lights. So, if you can avoid filming where there are lots of hard shadows to mimic in CG, by all means do so, or you will have to construct a virtual set of walls and floors set to receive shadows and spend a lot of time tweaking them to look real.

Fairy light

"I hold in my hand the glowing fairy light of enlightenment." OK, maybe it is really just a Halo material assigned to a single vertex mesh object that is animated to float around (Chapter 7). The lamp adds light to the image, which is a textured plane flying in front of the camera to simulate the light that should be given off by the halo, if it was really there. Animate the color of the halo, or halo size, to make it "dim" as it passes behind objects or goes farther away from the camera. Since a Halo material does not emit light, if you want the fairy light to cast light (for example, to light up my hand), then parent a weak lamp to the object, and that will cast light onto the projection plate (and thus the part of the image it is near).

I've also seen this used to show "knowledge" coming out of an open book (much to the amazement of the reader). As the book opens, animate the energy of a yellow lamp to shine on the video.

Lightning

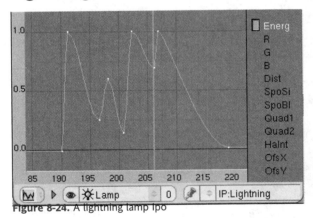

Figure 8-24. A lightning lamp ipo

There are many types of lightning, such as cloud lightning, which arcs within a cloud or between two clouds (sometimes called *heat lightning*), and ground lightning, which is the dramatic lightning that gives off a lot of light. Figure 8-24 shows the energy animation curve for a lamp that simulates a lightning flash. Repeat that curve a few times to simulate lightning flashes of varying intensity (to simulate lightning strikes occurring over a wide area) and position. If the image is a video, you can simulate a time lapse or, in the case of Figure 8-24, animate a lamp to give off indirect storm lightning.

Glowing orbs

You can combine lamps moving around as objects, as well as having lamp energy (brightness) Ipos, tracked to the gaze of the person. All the person has to do is imagine seeing this magical mystical light swirl about (much like I acted as if there was a magical floating ball), and there you have it!

Animating masks

As we saw with the road sign example in Chapter 1, a shape (in that case a rectangle) takes on a different projection when rotated in 3D space. Since we were compositing over a still image, that mask did not have to move. However, more complex and precise video masks for more complex shapes may be needed, and this section explains how to do that in Blender. There are two topics I'd like to cover here: moving a mask as a whole and changing the shape of an object. You can even do both at the same time, like was done with the hole in Goldie Hawn in *Death Becomes Her* (Robert Zemechis, 1992).

Why move a mask? Well, usually it's because the object being masked is moving in the video and your mask has to keep up with it. In Goldie's case, as she turned, the hole had to change shape as well. If the object is something like a hand, then the mask has to change shape to cover the finger movements. Moving a mask is no different from simply animating the location, rotation, and scale properties that I discussed earlier in the chapter, so I won't bore you with repetition here. I will bore you with a special case of animating the location and shape of a mask, which is called *rotoscoping* or *match moving*.

Match moving and rotoscoping

The process of making CG elements match real-world movement is called *match moving*, and when a mask is used to cover up a piece of the image in a precise way, it is called *rotoscoping*. I should warn you that it is not glamorous; it is tedious, time-consuming, painstaking work. Rotoscoping was invented more than 90 years ago as a way for an animator to create realistic motion for a cartoon character by tracing the movement of a real character frame by frame. A favorite question of Blender users relates to lightsabers, and the interested reader should google the technique, because it was used on all three *Star Wars* movies. Briefly, you animate the saber by replacing the prop with a glowing tube, moving the CG tube to cover the prop, frame by frame.

In the digital age, some tools can help by analyzing the image stream and trying to mark key points from frame to frame. Open/free examples include Voodoo Camera Tracker (which helps you when the camera is moving) and Icarus. An open source library of image and pattern recognition routines is also being developed and may find its way integrated into Blender. The root of the problem is that you have a two-dimensional image of moving objects in a three-dimensional space with a camera that itself may be moving while the lighting conditions change. SynthEyes is a commercial product that has been used with Blender as well.

The file `tut\magic.blend` features a mask, called Mask, that I rotoscoped to hide some of my fingers. Why? Well, there is a portion at the start of the picture where my CG ball should have been behind my fingers. In order to tell Blender what portion that was, I had to make a simple mask (starting with a curve Bezier circle; see Chapter 5 on making masks) that matched the outline of my fingers, as shown in Figure 8-25.

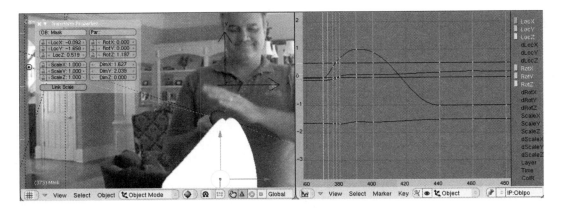

Figure 8-25. Rotoscoping a mask

As you can see, the mask can cover more than my fingers, since in compositing I will just texture that mask with the original video, and thus my fingers (and part of my belly and other stuff) will be in front of the ball. Starting with the frame where you envision the ball popping into existence, position the mask (adjusting the location and rotation) to cover the part of my fingers that should be in front of the ball, and of course position the ball where you want it to be. Laboring intensely (OK, maybe not that intensely), arrow right to advance a frame or two, and then move the mask to cover my fingers, repeating this until you envision that the ball will be clear of the hand. The only real important part of the mask is the intersection between the ball and my fingers. The "mask" white area will be replaced by the background image layered on top of the ball, thus partially hiding the ball. You can now define a render layer as described elsewhere to pull only the mask layer and use that to composite that portion of the image over (in front of) the ball, thus blending the background plate, the ball, and then the finger-mask matte, in that order, to arrive at the composite image. If the object happens to be a dog's snout, as I showed in Chapter 4, then moving the snout (or, to be more exact, in the case an armature controlling the snout) and aligning with the dog's movements creates the effect that the snout is part of the dog. Remember, the movements have to be exact, or you get a kind of "sliding Halloween mask" artifact that takes you out of the illusion.

Animating shapes

I think we have all seen those TV commercials that say "Lose weight in seconds!" where a chubby person sheds a few pounds in a magical onscreen shrinkage of the waistline. I have also seen cosmetic surgery ads where portions of an image are distorted (shrunken or enlarged). Let's look at this as an exercise in 2D shape changing. Recall the rhinoplasty exercise in Chapter 5 where you created two shape keys for a grid object that was UV textured with a picture. Opening the Ipo window, select the grid object, and, since there are shape keys for the grid, switch to the Shape key Ipo type, as shown in Figure 8-26.

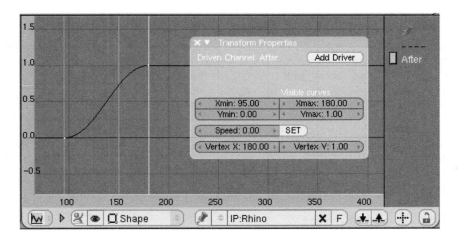

Figure 8-26. Shape key animation

You can think of each shape as a property of the gird, and the shapes are listed down the side. The basis shape is "---" because you are using relative keys, so the "after" shape internally saves changes to that basis shape. Here, 3 seconds into the commercial (frame 90), the "after" shape starts influencing the basis shape. The simple way to set that key is to navigate to frame 90, use the left/right arrows in the Shape panel to show that shape, move the Influence slider once to make the key, and then slide it back to 0 (where it started) to update the key. Then navigate to frame 180, and set the slider to 1.0. Doing so creates the selected key shown in the figure.

Alternatively, as with any Ipo, you can Ctrl-click in the Ipo window to set a value for the active property. Pressing N brings up the Transform Properties floating panel, shown in the figure. In that panel, at the bottom, Vertex X refers to the frame number, and Vertex Y refers to the property value at that frame.

Animating shapes in this way is exactly what I did for the talking dog examples running through this book. I defined a shape key for each mouth shape and then, scrubbing through the audio track (Chapter 14), asserted the influence of that shape at that frame.

Particle effects

Blender has a very robust particle and volumetric system that was recently greatly revised to provide a fast yet sophisticated tool for artists to create clouds, fire, steam, dust, smoke, fireworks, and sparks. A boids system enables you to simulate community-intelligent flocks of birds, swarms of bees, schools of fish, and swirls of magical mystical fairy charm, and we will work through a practical example later. Particles are emitted and then travel on their merry way until they are either affected by a force, deflected by colliding with an object, or simply expire (die). A particle can be a semitransparent halo, a mesh shape (like an ice crystal), or even an animated mesh like a bird flapping its wings.

Throughout any CG film, once you recognize them, you will see tons of uses of particles. If Pixar used Blender in making *WALL-E* (Andrew Stanton, 2008), they would have used particle boids in the very opening sequence to simulate seagulls flying around the trash heaps, halo particles with a vortex force when Wall-e hitched a ride on the spaceship and held his hand into the light field, mesh particles for the scene when Wall-e was dancing with Eve using the fire extinguisher, and so on. In this chapter, I'll walk through each of those effects using the particle system. Of course, you are limited only by your imagination and creativity in applying these tools to your challenges.

An entire book, *Bounce, Tumble, and Splash! Simulating the Physical World with Blender 3D* (Tony Mullen, 2008), is dedicated to presenting the full Blender simulation systems (including the particle system), so you can explore that resource as well. I will cover essential composting effects such as smoke, boids, steam, mist, and clouds, but Tony's book goes into much more detail.

Generating particles

Let's examine the basic particle generation tool. Smoke is physically millions of microscopic particles that swirl around in the air. Obviously, you cannot simulate that exactly, so you have to use a little bit of fake stuff. Ken Perlin (http://mrl.nyu.edu/~perlin/) has created many special effects systems, and one of his ideas was to create a few particles and then blur them together. The blurring will create slight variations in uniformity and provide a convincing effect. In our case, you can use the Blender particle system and can use the Halo material shader to provide the blurring.

Creating a new particle system

You can access the particle system from the buttons window's Object context, in the Particle subcontext; it has several panels. When you select a mesh shape (particles are emitted only from mesh shapes), you will see the blank Particle System properties panel, as shown in Figure 8-27.

Figure 8-27. Particle System panel

Click Add New, and in 3D view, the mesh will "disappear," and only its vertexes will be displayed; this is a visual cue that the mesh faces are not going to be rendered, but the particles will be rendered instead. Therefore, it can be difficult to select (so use the outliner window to select it).

One of the first things I'd like to point out is that part selector. Each mesh can have multiple particle systems, each configured separately from another. So, for example, you can have a fire shape emit both sparks and smoke at the same time. When you click Add New, a new system is initialized, and the part selector will increase to 1 out of 1. To add your second and third system, simply keep clicking Add New, and the part number becomes 2 out of 2, and so on. The first number tells you which system the properties are displayed for, and the second says how many systems have been initialized. You can scroll through the list in order using the arrows.

Blender has three types of particle systems:

- **Emitter**: Emits lots of little things
- **Reactor**: Emits things that react and interact with other objects
- **Hair**: Grows hair and fur and fine strands

It may be daunting at first, but it becomes pretty easy to understand. The color of any of these is controlled by the shader system (materials and textures).

Each particle system is named by clicking and editing the PA: selector field, which is also used to select a system by name (instead of using the part scroll selector). To delink a particle system from a mesh, click the X icon. You can link a delinked system to other meshes, and delinked systems will not be destroyed until you reopen the file. As with all other objects, delinked systems are shown in the list with a zero in front of their names.

Blender's emitter particle system

Let's start with the simplest, the emitter system. I noticed this system used in the film *Hellboy II: The Golden Army* (Guillermo del Toro, 2008, who also directed *The Hobbit*) when Big Red kills the elemental Forest God and a bunch of Halo particles floated in the scene. In this example, the particles just lazily floated around while the actors acted mystified. Figure 8-28 shows the main panel.

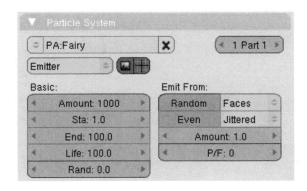

Figure 8-28. Main emitter Particle System panel

This panel has three parts:

- **Particle System definition**: Allows you to select a particle system that is already defined (to share particle systems), add a new one, or delink the particle system. The Part scroller allows you to scroll through multiple particle systems assigned to the same object. For each particle system, you choose the type of particle system; select Emitter, Reactor, or Hair. The two buttons to the right of the selector enable the system during rendering and during interactive 3D view, shown both enabled. If you have a weaker PC, you can disable 3D view to keep your system responsive during modeling.

- **Basic section**: These fields give you control over the amount, starting frame, ending frame, life span, and random number seed used to generate the particles. The start frame can be a negative number, which allows you to have particles premade and in the air on frame 1. Particles are emitted in a uniform rate across the time span (from Sta to End). The density of the particles is controlled by the amount. In the example, 1,000 particles will be emitted over the 100 frames, and therefore 10 more particles will be emitted every frame. In our example, there is 1 particle on frame 1, 11 on frame 2, 21 on frame 3, and so on. When a particle is emitted, it lives for the number of frames in the Life field, or until it is destroyed, and then disappears. In this case, the last 10 particles emitted at frame 100 will last until frame 200. Although it may look like the particles are randomly generated, a problem arises if you want to regenerate only a few frames in the middle of a sequence. If they were truly random, the frames from simulation run A would not match the location of the particle shown in simulation run B. Therefore, you can provide a seed number so that, if nothing else changes, the particles will be in a consistent location between renders on a per-frame basis. This random seed solution, however, introduces a different kind of issue. If you have multiple particle systems that use the same seed, they will generate in the same place, which will look fake. Therefore, be sure to use a different seed for each particle system so that two particles from two systems do not follow the same path and space (unless of course you want that effect).

- **Emit From settings**: These controls allow you to control where the particles are emitted. Normally, particles are emitted from the faces of a mesh, in a prescribed order, from a jittered distribution. If you select Jittered, then the Amount field lets you vary the amount of jitter. Normally, places per face = 0, and the particles will emit from all over the face of the mesh. However, you can simulate a pinhole kind of effect by setting P/F to a number equal to or greater than the number of particles to be emitted per frame. If you do, then the particles will emit only from those locations.

Go ahead and enter 1000 particles and the other settings shown in Figure 8-28. The next Physics panel controls how the particles act once they are spawned. Figure 8-29 is nearly identical for all the types of particle systems.

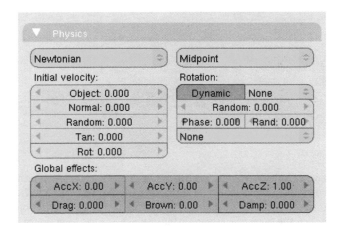

Figure 8-29. Physics panel

There are four physics "engines," or ways to calculate the movement of the particles. Based on the engine, the Extras panel options change as well. The default is Newtonian, and the options include the following:

- Boids: Swarms and schools
- Keyed: Waypoints
- Newtonian: Particles behave according to Newton's laws, conserving momentum and having acceleration
- None: No intelligence

For a particle to have motion after being emitted, it must have some speed, or be acted on by some force, or it will be spawned and then just sit there. For this simple example, notice that AccZ, or acceleration in the Z (vertical) direction, is 1.0 in the figure, so the particles will accelerate upward. Other options for giving the particles speed include using the object's speed (if it was animated to move), the normal (away from the faces of the object), purely random, tangent, or rotational.

In the smoke scene, we have poor ManCandy (an excellent training mesh and rig by Bassam Kurdalhli) trying to keep warm by starting a fire in a drum. A simple mesh circle has been added inside the drum (it should be selected when you open the file) and has been given a simple Newtonian physics particle emitter system, as shown in Figure 8-30.

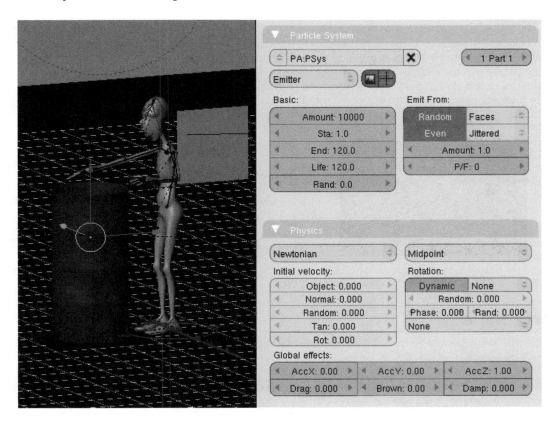

Figure 8-30. Example particle system

A total of 10,000 particles will be emitted over 120 frames (about 4 seconds), and they will be emitted in a random order from the faces of the circle inside the can.

Particles are calculated on a frame-by-frame basis, and you cannot skip frames the first time you create a system, because the computer uses the previous frame to compute the next frame. Ensure you are on frame 1, and press the right arrow on your keyboard, or press Alt+A to animate for your current animation range; you will see dots appear in your 3D view window. Dots are the normal visualization for particles, but the Visualization panel gives you all sorts of options.

You will see particles get generated and fly out of the can. They don't go up in a straight stack because they are being deflected by the can and being affected by force fields.

> *The big rule is that a deflector and a force field must share at least one layer with the particle emitter so that the emitted particles can "see" the effector.*

Colliders

A collider deflects and/or absorbs a particle when it hits it. In the example file, the drum and ManCandy are colliders. Figure 8-31 shows the settings for the drum. Enable Collision to reveal controls for damping (how much the collision slows down the particle): Friction (as the particle slides across the surface, how much it is slowed down), Kill (absorbs the particle), and Permeability (what the chances are that a particle will pass through the object). The collider object must share a layer with the particle emitter object.

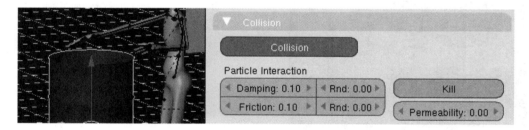

Figure 8-31. The trash can is a particle collider.

Force fields

Blender has a complete array of kinds of force fields that can act on a cloud of particles to produce realistic effects. In our example, we have used a few. Figure 8-32 shows the big field that is annoyingly blowing the smoke in ManCandy's face. You can also animate the strength of these fields to simulate a wafting breeze or a gusting hurricane. Besides Wind, there is a Magnetic field behind him, which will catch some of the smoke as it rolls off him, simulating the wind tunnel kind of draft effect that would occur naturally. A positive strength "blows" the particles, whereas a negative strength attracts the particles. Different falloff bounding areas give you more flexibility as to what degree particles are caught in the field.

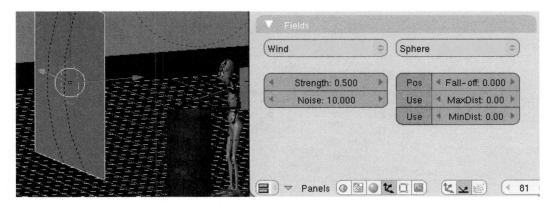

Figure 8-32. Example force field

Enable the Positive-Z and other buttons to set the distances (Fall-off, Maximum, and Minimum).

Blender's boids physics engine

Boids is a term from the late 1980s when the movement of flocks of birds and schools of fish were studied. In Blender, a boids system allows the particles to act like a swarm that has a focus and intent, almost like a collective consciousness. For example, watch the movie on your DVD called lib\ images\things\flock.mov, which was generated from the file tut\15-boids.blend. This movie shows a flock of seagulls flying as a general flock, some diving into the water to catch fish and others generally doing what birds do, which is to fly around with a general direction and intent.

With boids, particles within the swarm have a set of priorities, as shown in Figure 8-33, such as to avoid collisions with each other, crowd around, and seek a goal (an attractor). When combined with other objects that act as a target, the spawned particles follow the object while at the same time observe other "rules" you have set up, such as other deflectors.

Notice that I've set the particles to spawn negative frame 30. This gives them some time to get all "sorted out" after spawning and find a sort of pattern. They have a long (1500 frame) life so that they don't start disappearing during the movie.

In the tutorial file, run the simulation by positioning to frame 1 and pressing Alt+A. You will see a flock of birds launch into the air and follow a ball. Press Escape to stop the playback. Let's break it down.

First, there is a simple bird mesh, the basis shape of which is shown in Figure 8-34. Since the birds are going to be very tiny on the screen, you don't have to be very exact. I formed this by doing some simple proportional editing on a UV sphere. I then clicked Add Shape Key to establish the *basis* shape.

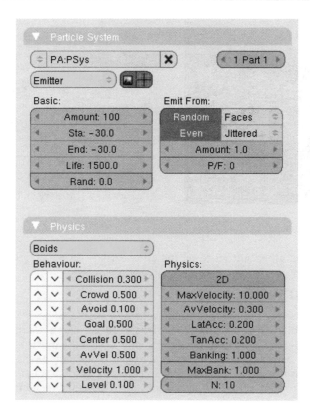

Figure 8-33. Boids settings

Figure 8-34. Seagull basis shape

I then added a new shape key, renaming it from Key 1 to Flap. I then tabbed into edit mode, dragging down the wing tips in proportional mode, raising the body a little bit to simulate lift, and exiting edit mode. Exiting edit mode locked in that shape. That Flap shape key is animated using an extended cyclic extrapolation curve so that the bird continuously flaps its wings. Figure 8-35 shows the shape key and its animation.

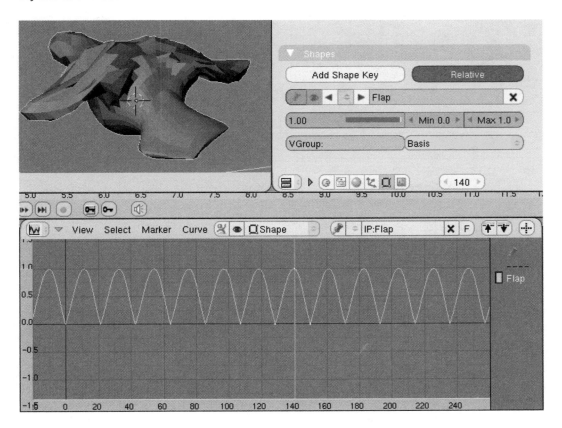

Figure 8-35. Flap shape key animation using cyclic extrapolation

> *This example ties together the 3D view editing, shape key, and animation systems in Blender.*

Next you create the Flock object, which is a simple UV sphere animated to fly around in space and acting as a spherical attractor. Figure 8-36 shows the settings, including the spherical force field effect and the object animation Ipo curve.

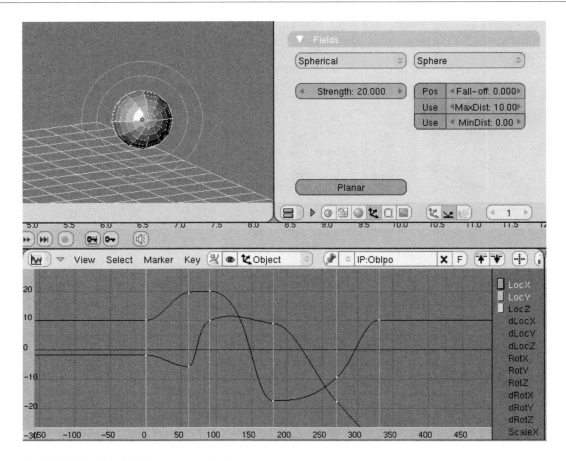

Figure 8-36. Particle (boids) attractor animation

Now you tie the flapping bird to the Flock object by creating a big box where the birds will launch from, as a boids emitter. Create the box, and then create a new emitter particle system. In the Physics panel, select Boids, and set the options shown in Figure 8-33. The key is to link the bird as the mesh object to use as a particle, highlighted in Figure 8-37.

Birds emerge from the box and flock around the sphere, taking care to avoid each other and turning and swooping as controlled by the acceleration parameters in Figure 8-33, yet all the while being attracted by the sphere. Put the boids on, for example, layers 1 and 11 and the attractor on layer 11, and exclude layer 11 from the render layer so that the sphere is not rendered. As long as the sphere shares a layer with the particles, it will influence the boids.

To composite this over your movie, remove the ocean surface plane, and save your animation as a keyed RGBA frame sequence. Then, load the sequence and AlphaOver using the compositor AlphaOver node or sequencer AlphaOver blending mode (Chapter 14).

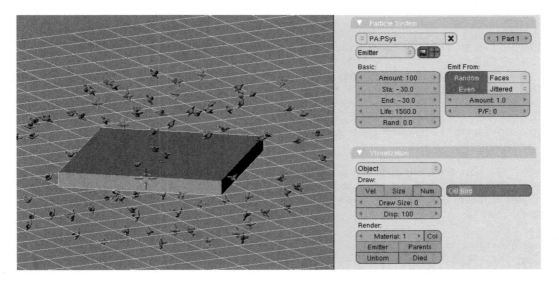

Figure 8-37. Boids settings

Combining particle effects

In many special effects shots, I notice that the talented artists used many kinds of particle systems in composing a single shot, so you should learn how to use each one, like a type of brush, and then how to use them together in making your composition.

I am reminded of many "energy balls" that gather in front of a hand. The energy gathers and then is shot out from the actor's hand. This effect is a few simple emitter systems with a hand mask as the attractor and a lamp that increases in intensity. Open tut/Effects-Particles.blend, and in the energy ball scene, render the animation (or just watch the animation); you will see this kind of effect, ready to be match moved and composited over a video of our heroine blasting her enemies into oblivion.

To make this effect, I have combined several particle systems and animation effects that you have learned:

- One particle system to be the gathering energy
- Another particle system to be the beam
- A hand mask as a force field to swirl the energy
- Animated material for the hand to glow red
- Animated movement of the hand mask

Baking

Blender uses an automatic cache system that saves particle location information. You may notice a "cache" folder named after the particle system that saves this information. The system starts with the first frame and successively computes the location of the particles, saving that information in the cache. The first time through, you must proceed frame by frame, in order (pressing Alt+A is the simplest way to build the cache). Sometimes, especially if a particle system does not start emitting at frame 1, the particles will show up anyway because of a "dirty" cache. If a particle system needs to be reset (to clean up a dirty cache and thus force Blender to recalculate the particles properly), click Free Cache on the Bake panel.

When you have the particles behaving the way you want, you should bake them by using the Bake panel. This locks in the locations of those particles and makes everything consistent and repeatable, as well as speeds up compute time. Be sure to set the appropriate start and ending frames numbers to calculate for.

Coordinating your animation

Dust, smoke, rain, snow, ash, sparklers, fireworks, and rocket engines (and exhaust) are all possible by varying the material used (recall that you can animate the material color and brightness as well) to vary these particles along their lifetimes. Most often, especially with smoke, you'll make a standard "plume," render it with an alpha channel, and then use the animation to add texture to a plane and composite that plume over whatever you want, wherever you want it to appear as though some distant fire is burning. There are many kinds of smoke, depending on what is burning; tires burn very black, and wood burns gray. Moving more into the special effect category, you can fake (and composite) fire and explosions to make a full range of visually amazing effect shots. I know this has been a long chapter, but let's work through a short example. I have many fond memories of firing off model rockets with my son, Alex, so I'd like to use that as an example.

Open tut\liftoff.blend from your DVD. There are four objects and two materials animated in this file, and they synergistically bring together many of the individual concepts I covered in this chapter. The net result of this is in the video lib\images\Things\liftoff-0001-0210.mov, a simple CG rocket lifting off. The set consists of a simple ground plane and a textured world (Chapter 6).

First, look at the outliner window. It shows you the particle systems (the dot icon) and the animations (a squiggly arrow icon) for each object in the file. When you click an entry in the list, it is selected in 3D view, and the rest of the screens change to show you information about that object.

In the outliner window, click the rocket itself, which I have christened Beyond. When you do, the rocket is selected, and the top Ipo window shows you its Object Ipo, which I have also named IpoRocket. This Ipo has a vector handle at frame 1, and it rapidly climbs and then decelerates, reaching its maximum height, and then falls back to Earth. Note that this Ipo has a LocZ and rotation channels, but not LocX or LocY. This is so that I can place this rocket anywhere I want on the ground plane. I simply keyed the location once, which created all three channels and, then in the Ipo window in curve mode, selected those two curves and deleted them via the X icon.

Next, click the camera. Notice that this has an Object Ipo curve, but only the rotation channels. It exhibits the lazy tracking I discussed earlier; the rocket gets ahead of the camera on rapid liftoff, the cameraperson overcorrects a little as the rocket zooms up and away, and then the reverse happens during descent.

Now let's look at the fire, which is the light from the rocket engine itself. Notice in your buttons window, the shading says that this is a halo. The flame object (which is actually just a little mesh square) shares the IpoRocket, and it also has a Material Ipo. Change the Ipo type from Object to Material to see this Ipo. This Ipo varies the halo size, which, when rendered, looks like the intensity of the flame that varies from nothing, ignites, sputters a bit, and then burns out. If you tab into edit mode, you will see that even though the object center is at ground level, the vertices for the square are just above it and just under the rocket body. This way, they start glowing above the ground but can share the same Object Ipo as the rocket.

Last but not least, we have a particle system that makes the exhaust. The emitter object is also a square, and it shares that same IpoRocket and has a Material Ipo that tells the particles to start off red, then fade to gray, and finally fade out while increasing in size. That's what steam and smoke look like as they disperse into the air. The Material Ipo for particles does not apply to animation frames; it applies to each particle throughout its lifetime. So, when the particle is emitted, it is red, and it then turns gray and finally transparent as it ages.

By sharing Ipos where needed, you have the exhaust move right along with the rocket, emanating from the tail, and there's no disconnect. Realistic camera motion goes a long way toward giving a more natural feel, but of course this is more work than a simpler Ipo. By combining all these effects, we get a decent-looking result.

> *True volumetrics are scheduled for inclusion in an upcoming release of Blender. I have already tested and documented it, but it is still being polished and was not available for standard inclusion at the time of this edition of the book. I can tell you that it will give photorealistic results using particles and volume rendering, so get smart on using particles to prepare for it!*

Summary

There are a ton of manual and computed animation possibilities, and I have the space to explain in detail a few effects only. The goal within Blender is to allow anything to change over time and thus be animatable. In this chapter, I've described what animation means to the compositor and how it can be used as tool to make great video. Now that you have all of this motion going on, you'll learn how to make a video of it all in the next chapter.

Chapter 9

RENDERING

Rendering is the process of making an image from information in the 3D view, compositor, and/or sequencer, alone or in combination with each other. If you are using 3D view in your final image, Blender takes all the computer-generated elements in a scene, computes their colors, and blends them together to make an image. When you ask Blender to render a scene, based on the options you choose, a *render pipeline* of rendering functions come into play to compute the image and spin off any render passes you have requested. Those passes are made available for use in the compositor. That scene output may be merged with other images in the compositor and/or sequencer into a final output that you see. Finally, all of that is saved in a format that you specify, possibly in a container file, using compression options you choose in order to save space.

This chapter introduces rendering based on the two steps you encounter in the real world: rendering a still image, and then rendering a video. Rendering a video is just like rendering an image, except that you have even more options. However, you can't just jump into rendering a video without understanding the basics of still image rendering, so let's cover that first.

Rendering an image

A still image begins as an idea and ends as a single image, usually a combination of image and graphic elements, overlaid with special effects and composited over a background. Let's examine the logical thought process of creating an image from the perspective of a (fairly) logical workflow, and talk about how to perform that workflow using Blender's myriad of render panels and settings.

Start with the aspect ratio

When I am compositing, the first thing I think about is the ultimate medium that will show this work. If it is a TV commercial for normal broadcast, or a video for webcast, I immediately know that it will be in the 4:3 aspect ratio, as all normal TV and normal webcast resolutions reduce down to 4:3. If my work is destined for the HD channel, then 16:9 is the required aspect ratio. As discussed in Chapter 4, aspect ratio is the lowest common denominator for the resolution of the image.

Also identify any template that will be used in the final broadcast. TV shows, especially news and talk shows, reserve the lower third or fourth of the display for scrolling or roll-on graphics, and you should not put any critical elements in that area.

For print, the aspect ratio depends on the layout of the graphic on the page and the artistic direction. The aspect ratio for print could be the same as for TV or HD, square, full-page, or something like a sidebar—long and thin (1:4). A full-page image follows the page format of the magazine, which, by tradition, is a 5×7 or 8×10, so aspect ratios for them are 5:7 or 8:10. In this book, for example, the aspect ratio for a full-page color image is 7.5:9.

Determine the resolution

After you decide on your aspect ratio, you need to compute what Blender really cares about: the size of the image in pixels, also called the image *resolution*. You set this on the Format panel, shown in Figure 9-1, which is the nexus for selecting the kind of output you would like from the rendering process. It is a rather hodge-podge collection of various related elements.

The pixel information section is what we are concerned with right now. When you click a preset (try the NTSC one now), the SizeX and SizeY fields fill in with the values shown in Figure 9-1. To compute your needed size for online media, use the standard for that medium (NTSC broadcast TV is fixed at 720×480, no matter what size TV screen it is shown on). For flavors of other media, such as HD, check with the TV station to see what resolution they use for broadcasting.

For print media, multiply the physical image size times the print resolution. Print resolution is expressed in terms of dots per inch (dpi) and is typically 150 dpi. Multiply the resolution times the physical dimension of the paper/image to get a reasonable maximum image resolution. Offset printer shops also like an image that is a little bigger (around 0.25 inch or 9 millimeters) than what will actually be printed for a full-page image, giving them a little "bleed" area of 0.125 inch on each margin.

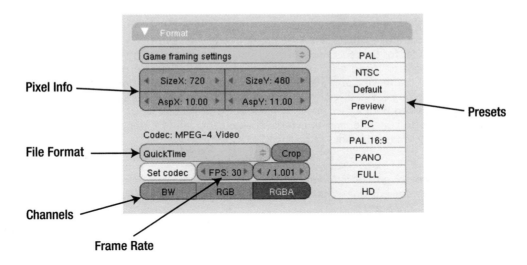

Figure 9-1. Render Format panel

For example, a full-page image in my favorite magazine, *Popular Science*, runs 7.5×10.5 inches (which is a 5:7 image aspect ratio). Multiplying 150 dpi by those dimensions, you find that you need an image that has 1125×1575 pixels. If you were doing a full-page ad for *Popular Science*, you would enter those numbers in the SizeX and SizeY fields, and use 1 for the AspX and AspY. Again, this is the maximum resolution, since the printer cannot print a unique dot for more than one pixel. Printing software can, of course, take a higher-resolution image, but will end up blending the multiple pixels down to one dot color.

> The AspX and AspY *fields in the* Format *panel do not refer to the aspect ratio of the image, but of the pixels themselves, as discussed in Chapter 4.*

You can render an image of any size, limited only by your PC's memory. You should choose a size based on your final output media, and how that media is going to be produced. A photograph may print on glossy high-quality paper at true 300 dpi, requiring an image of 2KB×3KB for a full 8×10 at full resolution. You may be able to render an image with only half that and still get acceptable results (effectively printing at 150 dpi). A poster or banner 16 feet (3 meters) across may print at 10 dpi, so even though it is physically larger, it may need only the same number of pixels to cover the area. Don't think that a huge poster needs a huge resolution. A billboard, like the kind by the side of a road, may be 42 feet wide, but it is printed at only 7 dpi, so an entire image rendered for a billboard needs to be only by 3KB×1KB.

Proxy rendering

A proxy is a stand-in for the real thing, and I use the term *proxy render* for any render that is a stand-in or interim placeholder for the real thing—in other words, a test render. As you make these interim renders, you don't want to spend a lot of time computing detail that you may not be concerned about. Therefore, you can make a proxy render that is a smaller-sized render of the final output. You invoke proxies by selecting 25%, 50%, or 75% in the Render panel. Figure 9-2 shows a 25% proxy setting. Since the % refers to both a percentage in the X and Y directions, a 50% proxy has one-fourth the number of pixels to compute, and thus renders about four times faster than a full-size image. Similarly, a 25% proxy renders 16 times faster.

> Blender can make proxies automatically and use those in order to speed up responsiveness when, for example, sequencing HD video strips together. Automatic proxies are covered in Chapter 13.

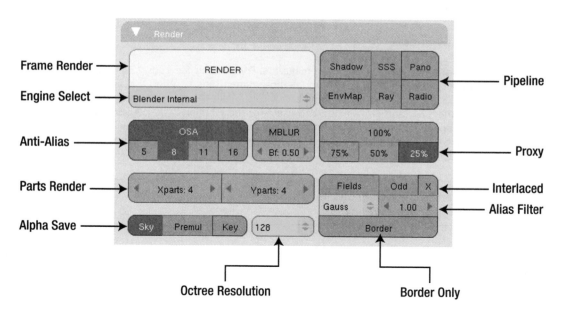

Figure 9-2. Render panel

OpenGL rendering

As discussed in Chapter 3, if your 3D View is oriented to the camera, a very fast alternative to invoking the render engine (F12) is to click the Render This Window button on the far-right side of the 3D view header. Doing so will render the current viewport in whatever shading mode you have set. This will also render objects in the 3D view that are normally not rendered, such as empty and bone objects, which may be helpful.

Border rendering

If you are adjusting one portion of a large and complicated image, you can save time by not including the whole 3D view image every time you render. In a 3D view window, press 0 on the number keypad to switch to camera view. Press Shift+B to start a special border box operation, and drag a box shape in camera view somewhere within the passepartout (the area of the camera view inside the viewfinder). As you drag, a red dashed box will be drawn, and an overlay will tell you the location and dimensions of the border. When you release the left mouse button, Border on the Render panel (Figure 9-2) will be enabled, and the red border in 3D view shows you the portion of the image that will be rendered.

When you press F12, only that small portion of the camera's view will be rendered. Disable Border in the Render panel when you want to rerender the whole image again. You can redefine the border at any time by simply redoing the Shift+B operation.

Pipeline components

In the upper-right corner of the Render panel is a mini-panel of six selections that engage major functional chunks of render processing that are relevant to scene rendering:

- Shadow: Opaque elements (masks, image elements and other objects) can (even if they are shadeless and thus cannot get shadows), cast shadows onto other objects. Shadows are essential to depth and 3D perception, but can take time to render (and you may or may not want a 3D look depending on your current compositing task).

- SSS: Essential to photorealistic rendering (but not that germane to compositing), subsurface scattering fakes the situation where the surface of an object may allow light to permeate into the stuff in the middle. That stuff scatters and colors the light before some of it reemerges and colors the surface.

- Pano: Panoramic rendering allows a stitched kind of effect for wide-angle landscapes.

- EnvMap: Enables the creation of environment maps, a specific texture type that quickly simulates reflections. Environmental mapping enables textures that are mapped to the environment (world) to be reflected in the environment.

- Ray: Ray tracing is required for any accurate transparency or mirroring, as well as precise (non-buffered) shadow calculation.

- Radio: Enables radiosity coloring to be added into the scene (discussed in Chapter 6).

When doing simple layered compositing of image elements, most the time you won't need any of these rendering options. However, as I pointed out in Chapter 7, sometimes you need to composite a shadow for realistic computer-generated element integration. I generally keep Shadow and Ray enabled.

Alpha channel rendering

When you want to save an image using the alpha channel (introduced in Chapter 4) of an image, be sure to enable RGBA on the Format panel. An issue with reading in and using alpha-channel images arises when using a world (colors and/or maps) or buffer background. If not enabled correctly, you will get bad results, as shown on the left in Figure 9-3.

Blender provides you with three choices when saving a rendered image that has an alpha channel:

- Sky: The fully transparent background and any semitransparent objects are colored with the sky color, and a transparency equal to the material. Therefore, a pure red material against a pure blue sky background, with an alpha transparency of 0.5 (50%) will be saved as red: 1.0, green: 0.0, blue: 1.0, and alpha: 0.5 for the RGBA channels.

> *Pixel values are normally expressed in terms of a number between 0 and 255 (the maximum 8-bit number), so if you drag your cursor over the render or UV/image editor window, you will see both 8-bit and decimal values for the pixel color.*

- Premul: The Sky color is not used, and the semitransparent pixels are saved with a color equal to the material color premultiplied by its alpha value. So, a pure red semitransparent pixel becomes RGBA: 0.5, 0.0, 0.0, 0.5. If you did not know it was premultiplied, you would think that the pixel was a dark red that is semitransparent.

- Key: The issue with Premul is that the pixel color has been altered from its true color, which could throw off the color value further when that pixel is later mixed with other semitransparent pixels. A better solution is Key, where the Sky color is not used, and the semitransparent pixels are saved as their true color and alpha value, which is RGBA: 1.0, 0.0, 0.0, 0.5 in this example. When you look at a keyed RGBA image layered against a white background, you see the image as you would expect it to look.

When you load in a premultiplied image, you must enable Premul in the Texture Image panel, Alpha in the Preview panel, and UseAlpha in the Map Image panel. Otherwise, you will get an outline, or "halo," around the object, as those off-color pixels are merged with a different color background, as shown in Figure 9-3.

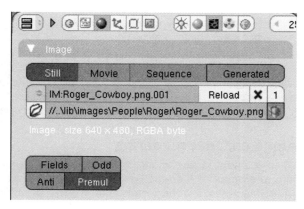

Figure 9-3. Premultiply disabled (note white edge)

> *If a nonalpha channel image is saved against a white background and is a dark image, you can enable* CalcAlpha *and* NegAlpha, *and Blender will use the colors in the image to determine an alpha value. However, this is really not that good for pictures of things, and is better used to turn a black-and-white mask image into an alpha mask.*

Test render

When I work in Blender, I am always making test renders, as these give me constant visual feedback as to the impact of my latest changes. I advise you to do the same, so that you don't make a lot of changes, run a render, and then see that something you did a while ago caused an issue.

The big RENDER button in the Render panel (Figure 9-2) invokes the selected render engine and, together with all the other options chosen, computes your image for the current frame. The default blend file that is loaded when Blender starts has a camera, a light, and a cube against a blue world, so you can immediately test that everything is working right off the bat by clicking RENDER. If you are using the default compositing blend file provided on the DVD that came with this book, the render will be a big gray image of an untextured plane. Alternatively, press F12 to render the current frame through the eyes of the active camera.

> *If the render window that pops up from either of these defaults is black, you may have an issue with your video card's OpenGL driver. Try moving the window, or minimizing and maximizing it, to see if the image appears. Ensure you are using shadeless materials or have lights lighting the scene, and a camera object in the scene. If all else fails, consult the web site of the card manufacturer to check for latest driver updates.*

Pleasantries for rendering

In addition to computing the basic image, Blender features a few niceties to dress up the render. These include anti-aliasing, motion blur, edge rendering, and information stamping.

Anti-aliasing

When a render is computed, Blender makes its best guess as to which object occupies most or all of a pixel, and colors it according the shading for that object. Since pixels are essentially square blocks of color, you can sometimes see what is called an *alias*, or a jagged edge, which may look like a tiny stair-step. Blender gives you a couple of tools to make the render look better.

Oversampling computes the pixel color a few times, each time jittering the camera just a little. Blender then averages the pixel values, thus blending in the edges. To use oversampling, enable the OSA option on the Render panel and choose how many times you want the image oversampled: 5, 8, 11, or 16. Figure 9-4 shows a blow-up comparison of no oversampling and the OSA 8 setting (as enabled in Figure 9-2).

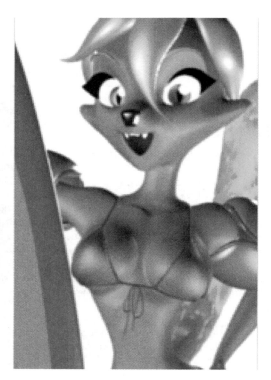

Figure 9-4. No oversampled anti-aliasing (OSA) and eight times oversampled (Kitty B! character design by Max Hammond)

At very high resolutions, especially HD, normal oversampling still can leave some "jaggies," or stair-stepping. Also, when you have a very big distance between a foreground and background element (and especially when one or both elements are partially transparent), you may see some aliasing even when using oversampling. Aliasing can also occur along object edges when they are overilluminated.

A great general-purpose, all-around solution is to use full-screen sample anti-aliasing (FSA). To enable FSA, you must first enable Save Buffers on the Output panel, so that Blender can write out intermediate results to a small OpenEXR file. When you enable Save Buffers, the Full Sample button appears on the Output panel, right next to the Save Buffers button. If you enable that, then the OSA settings on the Render panel switch over to FSA, and you can select your desired FSA level. FSA takes a little more time to compute than oversampling, but if you find yourself fighting very fine aliasing issues, this could be the cure.

Motion blur

In real film, a fast-moving object will blur on the film because it moves while the shutter is open. Blender offers a few ways of introducing blur into your composite image: through the 3D view and through the blur nodes in the compositor (discussed in Chapter 12).

When enabled, the MBLUR button on the Render panel computes 3D view blur based on object and camera animation. MBLUR has a Blur Factor (Bf) setting, which varies how far ahead and back in time to look when computing the blur (0.5 is half of a frame). This simulates how long the shutter is open relative to the frame speed. Even when rendering a still image, motion blur is essential in portraying speed and action. To motion blur your central object, animate its motion as described in Chapter 8. To give motion blur to background (stationary) objects, animate the camera object. For much faster blurring of your central object, use the vector blur node described in Chapter 12. Note that motion blurring takes a lot longer, because of the number of images that must be computed and combined.

Edge rendering

Cartoon edges, like that shown in Figure 9-5, outline the outside of 3D view objects, just as in cartoons and comic strips. To use edge rendering, enable Edge in the Output panel. Set the color using the RGB sliders, and set the thickness of the outside line using the Edge Intensity (Eint) number field.

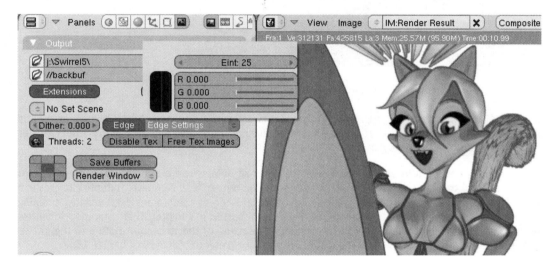

Figure 9-5. Edge rendering. "Kitty B!" Character design by Max Hammond

Information stamping

As you make intermediate renders, either for your own reference or for review, you should stamp them with some basic information so that you have some traceability. *Traceability* means "can you trace back to the origin?" Your file system gives you the file name and the date that the image was made, but if you e-mail that file or image, the date information is lost. Furthermore, the recipient may change the file name, and thus traceability is broken.

Another situation where stamping can be useful is when you are making a few alternative looks to a composition. Consider Figure 9-6, where I am playing with a Halo material for that sparkly diamond earring, and I want to pass a few alternatives to the client for review. I stamp the render with a note (overlaid in the upper-left corner) indicating the basic Halo settings I used, so that I can quickly re-create that look and feel.

Stamping is also effective when reviewing test animations and composites. If there is a problem, you can easily see from the stamp on which frames the problem exists.

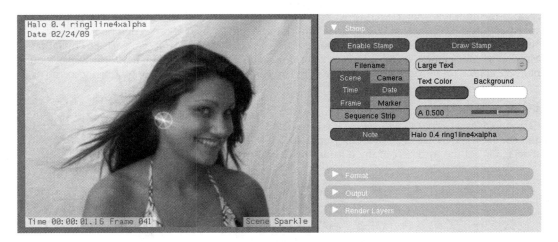

Figure 9-6. Stamping renders with information

Stamping is accomplished through the Stamp panel (see Figure 9-6). First, choose Enable Stamp and enable/disable the information to be stamped by clicking the relevant blue buttons under Enable Stamp. Then add the stamp by choosing Draw Stamp.

Most of the stamp options are self-evident. Recall that all objects can be named, so Camera stamps on the name of the camera that was used to generate the render (you can have multiple cameras in a scene; for example, if you are investigating or evaluating different camera angles). Similarly, enabling Marker adds in the name of those elements. Markers (discussed in Chapter 8) are stamped for a few seconds upon reaching them. Sequence Strip stamps the name of the strip contributing to the image, and is relevant only if Do Sequence is enabled on the Anim panel (discussed in Chapter 13).

Note that you can click into the field next to Note and enter your note, but you must also click the Note button to add that element to the stamp. The alpha (A) slider controls the opacity of the stamp overall, and you can click the little swatches to use the color picker applet (introduced in Chapter 7) to choose the text color and background color.

Each stamp element has a predefined corner as to where it is drawn. Multiple corner elements are stacked, as in Figure 9-6, where the note appears above the date.

Which image standard to use?

Now you need to pick which image format to use. The file format selector on the Format panel covers four fundamentally different kinds of file formats: image, video (no sound), FFmpeg (video and sound), and frameserver (used for a special render farm).

Run-of-the-mill image formats were presented in Chapter 4. Here, I'll go into more detail about the OpenEXR and multilayer formats, because they are the newest and highest quality image formats supported. Figure 9-7 shows this format selected in the Format panel.

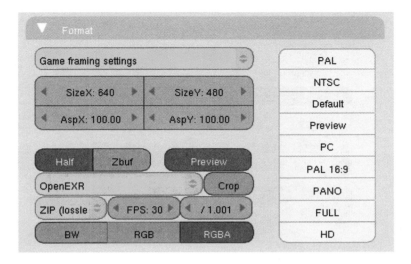

Figure 9-7. OpenEXR format options

The OpenEXR format is a single-image format that is also kind of a hybrid container. While full OpenEXR is 32-bit color depth, that is quite a lot and not necessary for most purposes, so Half (16-bit) is also selectable on the Format panel (enabled in Figure 9-7). You can also enable saving the Z-buffer by enabling Zbuf. Since most file systems cannot show you previews of an OpenEXR image, you can enable Preview (as in Figure 9-7) to make a small JPG image as a companion to the OpenEXR image (they will share the same file name, but will have their respective extensions). The JPG version can then be previewed in your operating system file browser as a thumbnail. Since the files can be huge, you can compress them using the ZIP, RLE, Pixar 24-bit, and other compression algorithms. Only the Pixar 24-bit (Pxr24) format may result in some image degradation, as it is lossy, like JPG.

The multilayer format builds on the OpenEXR format. It is also a single-image format, but contains multiple render passes that are selected in the Render panel. Most passes are an image that contains the coloring for that pass; other passes, like Z-buffer and vector, are just numbers that correspond to each image pixel. Using render passes enables you to save these passes for later compositing, as discussed in Chapter 10.

A place for everything . . .

One of the last steps in rendering is to visit the Output panel, as shown in Figure 9-8. Here, you set up some locations and general rendering parameters for where things should go,

The top field in the Output panel is used for video output, so it's described with the video rendering options later in this chapter, in the "Choose your destination" section. The second field indicates whether to use (and where to find) a background image to use as a matte), as discussed in Chapter 3.

You should always enable Extensions so that Blender adds the appropriate file name extension to your file. Otherwise, you might mistakenly name your image with the wrong extension—for example, use helloworld.jpg when the image is actually in the PNG format.

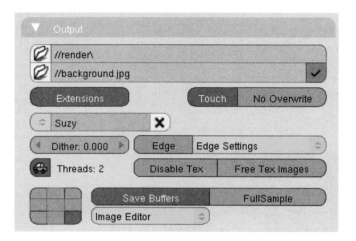

Figure 9-8. Render Output panel

The Touch and No Overwrite options on this panel are relevant only to video, so they are covered in the "Render the video" section later in this chapter.

For big, hairy HD-sized renders, you need to enable Save Buffers, so that as a tile or image is computed, it can be written out to disk in a kind of virtual swap file system, freeing up memory for other uses. Full Sample anti-aliasing, discussed earlier in this chapter, requires this, since full renders of the image are computed and merged.

As discussed in Chapter 3, when your blend file has more than one scene, you can choose that other scene to integrate with the current scene. Like combining two sets in a stage play, you select the other scene (Suzy in the example) to link in using this control. When linked, all the elements from that other scene are added to the current scene (including any linked by that scene, and so forth in a daisy-chain fashion). Thus, a set of linked scenes (and all the objects in them) make up the composite render The elements from the linked scene become visible in your 3D view, but are shown in a kind of gray outline in wireframe display. An object from another linked scene cannot be selected in the current scene. To move or edit the object, you need to trace back to its scene of origin.

The Threads indicator shows how many CPU cores are being used for the render, as described in the next section.

If you choose Render Window from the selector list at the bottom of the Output panel, a pop-up window will show up on your display to show you the render. Where it pops up is controlled by clicking one or more of those elements in the 3X3 grid in the Output panel. Otherwise, the render can be sent to one of the Blender window panes (which turns into a UV/image editor window type), or be shown as a full-screen image.

Multithreaded rendering

Blender is able to use each processing unit or core on your CPU chip to render different tiles of the image in parallel. If you have a dual-, quad-, or even eight-core CPU chip, you should split the render up into multiple parts. To do this, on the Render panel, set Xparts and Yparts to some value greater than 1, and the render will be split up into X times Y parts. Each part will be assigned to a core for rendering in a round-robin fashion.

Figure 9-1, earlier in this chapter, shows a render split into four X parts and four Y parts. With these settings, Blender can break up the image into 16 tiles, and assign the computation of each tile to the next available core. On a quad-core machine, each core would render, on average, four tiles and the render would finish four times faster.

Each of these parts can be kept in memory, or, if you enable Save Buffers on the Output panel, can be written out to disk in order to free up RAM for processing other parts.

Rendering curves

A curve in Blender is used for masks, text, and other simple shapes, like arrows. They do not have infinite resolution, however. Their resolution is set in the Curve and Surface panel of the Edit buttons, under DefResolU, as shown in Figure 9-9. As you can see in the 3D view, the curve can start to look "chunky." If you run into this, simply increase the RenResolU setting, which controls the rendering resolution. In Figure 9-9, I've set RenResolU to 100, as you can see that the final render of the curves is nice and smooth. Text is a special case of a curve, with the same issues regarding resolution. Text resolution is set in the same panel.

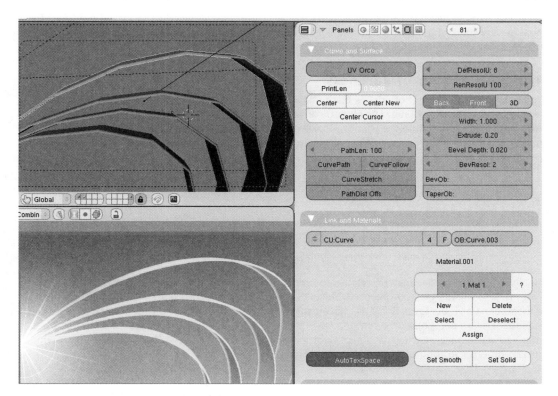

Figure 9-9. Set a high render resolution for curves.

Curves (including text) can be converted from a curve to a mesh. When they are converted, they lose that curve resolution; instead, that resolution is used to compute the mesh's edges. Once converted, there is no going back to a curve. However, you can increase the resolution or roundness of a mesh object via the Subsurf modifier, added in the Editing Modifiers panel. This modifier interpolates an edge in between existing edges, once for every level of resolution that you add. The modifier has two algorithms: simple and CatRom. When using the CatRom algorithm, named after the mathematicians who developed it, the modifier places this phantom edge based on where it thinks the curve was headed, by looking outside the two edges to the edges before them. It then can get a feeling for how the slope of the surface was going, and properly insert an edge to match the "roundness" of the surface. Thank Mr. Catmul and Mr. Rom for their math algorithm, which figures that out. You can keep this modifier as a virtual modifier, where it places phantom edges, or you can apply it, which creates real edges for those phantoms.

> Before converting, go ahead and duplicate the curve object (Ctrl+D), and move the copy to a nonvisible layer, so that you have a backup just in case something goes wrong.

Dealing with rendering issues

Sometimes things just don't turn out as you expected. After answering a few thousand questions from new users, I think you might want to know about the most common mistakes and errors that might occur during rendering.

The black render of darkness

You press F12 and get . . . nothing—a black image. First, don't despair. I get this on my new laptop quite regularly, and it's not my fault. The OpenGL drivers for that particular machine have a refresh problem. All I need to do is minimize the window, maximize it again, and like magic, my render is there. So, first make sure it isn't a driver issue. When it gets too annoying, using a UV/image window to display the render result works flawlessly.

Another possible cause is that there is no camera on a selected layer, or that can be seen by a render layer. The quick check for this is twofold:

- Be sure you can select and see the camera in 3D view.
- In the Render panel, make sure that the render includes a layer that has a camera. My convention is to always have the camera on layers 1, 2, and 10, or simply have it on all layers.

Finally, the black render may be related to hidden objects. As you've learned, Blender allows you to hide (H) and unhide (Alt+H) objects. Objects that are hidden in 3D view are still rendered, if they are a member of a visible layer. So, if you have a mystery object showing up in your render, chances are it is hidden. If you get a black render, or a large part of your render is black, press Alt+H just to be sure that you don't have a renegade object right in front of the camera lens (analogous to the infamous "inside of lens cap" photos that we old-timers have taken).

> Word of warning: H is right next to G, so if you think you are grabbing something, and it "goes away," you might have pressed H by mistake.

Broken links

A second cousin to the black render of darkness is strangely shaded (pink, white, or black) elements, where there should be a pretty picture of something. This is caused by a broken link to a texture; Blender simply cannot find the image file and load it. Check the UV/image editor for that element in edit mode, and make sure you can see the image. If it is mapped through the material texture, check the image texture to see if it appears in the Preview panel.

Overly bright or miscolored elements

When you look at your render, if an image element is overly bright (brighter than the image itself), you have forgotten to set it as shadeless, the texture brightness is set above 1.0, or the overall exposure is high (see Chapter 6 for exposure controls). Another possibility is that the object is shaded but has a high ambient value (0.5, the default when creating a new material, is very high), and there is a world setting with a color that, because of the excessive ambient value, is throwing off the color.

Also, keep in mind that a hidden light will still add light to the scene. If you are using any non-shadeless materials, and they render too bright in your scene, check for hidden lamps.

Render crashes

After churning for an hour on a very complicated 3D view scene, the dreaded operating system window tells you that Blender has stopped working. If you are using a console window (introduced in Chapter 3), check it before closing Blender and see if the message is malloc() returns nil or calloc() returns nil. The nil means nothing, and malloc or calloc is a request to allocate memory to the renderer. So, malloc returns nil is a geeky way of saying that there is no more memory available to allocate to the renderer, and so it cannot continue. If you're experiencing seemingly random crashes after a long period of rendering, the odds are that you are reaching the limit of your available system memory.

Because Blender runs on a wide variety of PC/server platforms and their power varies widely, some scenes and images cannot be rendered in their ultimate, highest quality and size across all machines. The biggest factors across platforms are random access memory (RAM), the physical chips in your computer, and virtual memory—your operating system's ability to make, manage, and allocate it to Blender. The full HD 1080p images for *Big Buck Bunny* were rendered on multicore workstations with 8GB of RAM. While the scene will render fine on that workstation, when you try to render that same scene on your 512MB Windows 98 machine, there simply isn't enough physical and logical RAM available to render the scene. Therefore, you will have to work a little to get that scene, or an approximation of that scene, to render using your PC.

By enabling and disabling certain options, you control the processing power needed to produce the image. Conversely, not including some elements eliminates the ability to produce or integrate that render aspect, which may be critical to accepting the final image. You need to balance render time (the amount of time needed to compute the image) with the complexity you are asking the computer to deal with. Complexity, in render terms, is expressed and controlled in several ways:

- **Size**: How many pixels and channels need to be computed
- **Pipeline**: Major chunks of computing some aspect that affect which render technologies are actually employed, such as subsurface scattering (SSS) or strand (hair) rendering
- **Objects**: The things to be rendered, and their texture image size
- **Compositing**: Processing nodes that need to be executed to modify passes

To address the problem of render crashes, first enable Save Buffers on the Output panel and use more Xparts and Yparts (set on the Render panel). If that does not solve it, reduce the particle systems, and then the size (pixel resolution) of the image. You can also split up the render into logical components that can be rendered to multilayer images, and then use a new blend file and the compositor to combine those images into a composite.

> The Blender Render Benchmark site at http://www.eofw.org/bench has a standard blend file that you can download. If you open that file, with nothing else running (no gadgets, no file indexer, and so on), and press F12, and wait and wait, eventually you will be rewarded with a render window. In the top of the window is the elapsed time it took to produce the render. You can then register your results, and compare your render time with other PCs listed there to evaluate how your machine stacks up. You can also use the listing to evaluate the cost/benefit of various PC operating systems and chip sets if you are considering the purchase of a new PC.

Also, for test renders, you can try to reduce image texture sizes. High-resolution textures slow down renders, or may even cause renders to crash. For example, a PNG image that is 4,096 pixels square can take 48MB of RAM. Enable the Disable Tex button, located on the Output panel, and those image textures will not be used. Free Tex Images (also on the Output panel) cleans out memory after rendering each frame. The advantage is that if an object goes out of frame and is not rendered, its image textures are cleared out of memory, allowing room for other image textures of other objects entering the frame. The disadvantage is that the image textures must be reread back into memory for each frame. For 99% of compositing, you do not need to do this.

You can also consider using proxy textures for test renders. Have a 1KB×1KB proxy texture (which takes only 3MB), saved in a folder named something like Tex1K, and then the 4KB×4KB "real" texture, say in folder Tex4K. For the test renders, copy the Tex1K folder to the Tex folder. When linking to textures, link to the image in the Tex folder. Then, for final renders, copy the Tex4K over the Tex folder, replacing those low-res textures with high-res elements.

> I have started a dynamic list of solutions and work-arounds for render crashes and memory problems at http://wiki.blender.org/index.php/Doc:Manual/Render/Performances.

Rendering video

Now we get to rendering your actual video, TV commercial, or film project! In this section, I'll present a general workflow that takes you from concept to production.

Develop your storyboard

Generally, first you plan your video by developing a storyboard. I often take a blank piece of paper, orient it landscape, and divide it into 12 squares, 3 across and 4 down. Then I sketch what I want representative frames to look like throughout the animation—about one keyframe every 3 seconds for a 30-second commercial. Once I have these keyframes sketched out, I start modeling and animating.

The 6-P rule: Prior Proper Planning Precludes Poor Performance.

Plan how you are going to use layers, and which elements belong to which layers, as discussed in Chapter 3.

Set frames per second

The first overriding factor is how fast you want the images to be shown, one after the other. The rate, or speed, of the video is in frames per second (fps), and is usually dictated by the output medium, such a TV or film. You set the overall frame-per-second rate and the divider in the Format panel. The most popular choices are 10, 24, 25, and 30 fps. Anything less than 10 fps results in a noticeably choppy video. A rate of 10 to 15 fps is common for video capture utilities like CamStudio, and is fine if you are compositing video tutorials of that ilk, especially if they will be uploaded to YouTube or Vimeo. A rate of 24 fps is the standard for film, 25 fps for European (PAL) TV, and 30 fps for NTSC (North American) TV. To be ultra precise, enter 1.001 in the 1/ field in the Format panel to give a precise frame rate of 29.97 fps for NTSC video.

> The speed of the movie is embedded in the video, so any player will play back the animation at whatever speed you set.

Set the duration

Now consider how many seconds of real time your video should be, and multiply the seconds times frames per second, which gives the overall number of frames, or length, of the video. Set the start and ending frame numbers in the Sta: and End: fields in the scene render Anim panel or in the timeline window header. So, for a 15-second NTSC TV commercial, 15 seconds * 30 fps = 450 frames, which you enter in the End: field. Remember that you can enter numbers or simple equations in any numeric control.

Now, annotate your storyboard with the frame number of each key storyboard image. Suppose you lay out your storyboard, and determine that your keyframes will be at frames 30, 140, 280, and 390 (just as a wild example). In Blender, in the timeline window, add markers (discussed in Chapter 8) at these frames as well.

Most of the time, you will leave the starting frame at 1. When using some of the physics simulations, you may wish to give them time to "settle down" before you begin rendering. In this case, you want to set start to a number such as 60. Be sure to then increase the ending frame number by the same amount. If you later change the frame speed but want the video to be the same duration, be sure to revisit these fields and update the calculation.

> You can also use the speed effect in the sequencer to change the speed of a video in postprocessing, as discussed in Chapter 14.

Trade off quality with time

A video or any real length goes through a few iterations, and the amount of time you have to make it is usually a key factor. First, you want to block out basically *what* happens *when*, usually through some sort of storyboard. Then you refine the timing, and finally focus on making it pretty. During the first few iterations of rendering, you want the video rendered *fast*, so that you don't waste your day waiting to see the latest iteration. Blender has a few neat options in this regard, which can be used in addition to all the image rendering tips given previously. Overall, disable the rendering pleasantries discussed earlier, like OSA on the Render panel, to make draft renders.

Step rendering

Step rendering (set in the scene render Anim panel) renders every other or every *n*th frame of an animation. It allows you to make, essentially, a storyboard kind of render of the final product. When you render steps out to a video format, the final video will have the intended duration, and thus everything will seem to move choppy, proportional to the step size. For example, if you set a 300-frame animation to render at 30 fps, which will result in a 10-second video (300/30=10), but set the step size to 10, the final video will still play at 30 fps, but the advantage is that the entire video will render ten times faster.

Watching the video will give you an overview of the whole strip, which is really the purpose of a storyboard as well. It will help you block out animation, time dialogue and foley sound effects, and quickly show the customer your basic idea for the video.

Override shading

In addition to a smaller size, and/or a step render, you may also want to make an even faster render of a video by overriding the lights and/or materials, sacrificing image quality for speed, because you really want to focus on the timing of the animation, and could care less (at that point in the workflow) about exact colors.

Calculating multilayered textures takes CPU time, and it can add up to a significant render time. Assuming you are just testing the timing of your animation, you really don't need it to look pretty—you just want it to render quickly so you can judge the animation. For example, if you are working on a TV spot, at some point in your workflow, you will want to focus on the timing of the spot, to ensure that the right elements pop in at exactly the right time (usually to match the voice-over). In these cases, timing is critical, but the lights and/or materials don't matter, and you really do not want to waste a lot of time with pretty renders. The solution is to override the lights and/or materials in the Render panel with a basic lamp group (a three-point rig does nicely) and/or a basic white material, by entering their names in the Render panel. These simpler lights and/or materials will render faster, allowing you to work with high iteration and fast refinement.

Interlacing (fields rendering)

As discussed in Chapter 4, interlaced broadcast sends out frames in pairs, with each member of the pair containing alternating lines of the display. The TV then shows each frame in rapid succession. Since each frame is slightly forward in time than the previous frame, fields rendering provides a smooth transition from frame to frame, for a kind of hardware motion blur effect. DV cameras also record interlaced frames, and captured images look like Figure 9-10.

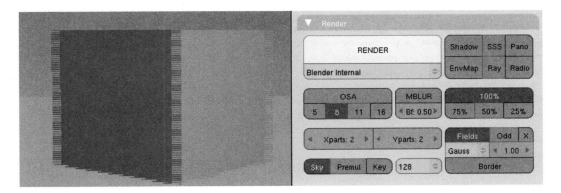

Figure 9-10. Interlaced render of the cube in motion

To enable interlaced rendering, click Fields in the Render panel. Now, even if your format is say 720×480 at 29.97 fps for NTSC, each frame rendered will really be two renders: lines (Y value) that are even-numbered (lines 0, 2, 4, and so on) will be the image at an even time mark, such as an even one-thirtieth of a second, but the odd lines will be the result of a render taken one-sixtieth of a second later.

In Figure 9-10, the cube is moving left to right. The even lines (because Odd is not enabled in the panel) occur at the frame indicated, but the odd lines are displaced to the right, since that is where the cube will be 1/60 second later. When viewed 60 times per second (faster than your eye can discriminate individual images), the brain blurs them together in a smooth image. Thus, with regard to interlacing at least, Blender can output the same image format as a DV camera. When rendered to a movie, it can be sent directly to the TV station, or burned to DVD, and be displayed on a TV in full quality. Warning: without interlacing, rapid motion will look choppy on a real TV.

Enabling Odd switches which scan lines are displayed on the even time tick, which is the standard for European (PAL) TV broadcast. Enabling the X disables the time offset, effectively disabling the motion blur effect.

> *Your computer monitor is probably not interlaced, and is probably much higher resolution than a TV. An interlaced movie, designed to be broadcast, will not look good when played on your monitor through a media player.*

Select sequence or container

For any meaningful project, I leave my image settings to refer to a still image format. When I render my animation, Blender will create a series of files, numbered according to the frame number they correspond to, in a sequence. So, file 0240.JPG will be the image for frame 240. At early iterations, you can use a format that is small and lossy, such as JPG, but I prefer just to use PNG from the get-go. As you get closer to your final product, upgrade to a lossless format, such as PNG, while at the same time increasing your proxy size to 50%, 75%, and finally 100%. Only at the very end of the process, when I am happy with the frames, do I switch to a container file, such as QuickTime or FFmpeg container.

Why use frame sequences if you're going to eventually render a single video file? Why not go straight to video? Well, first of all, if you render a frame sequence, you can stop the render at any time by pressing Esc in the render window. You will not lose the frames you have already rendered, since they have been written out to individual files. You can always adjust the range you want to continue from where you left off or use the No Overwrite option on the Output panel (discussed shortly in the "Render the video" section). Most important, you can switch between different codecs and codec settings (to get different file sizes and quality), experimenting to see which result works best. Since you are using the same image sequence in the sequencer, and not having to compute what each frame looks like, rendering to the container is very fast. Also, while one frame is rendering, you can inspect the previous frame using your favorite image previewer at your leisure to ensure you are getting the quality results you desire.

Choose your destination

Set the output path and file specification in the top line of the Output panel. For example, enter //render\my-anim-, and save your file in a project directory (so that Blender knows where // is). The folder location and file name template are used to specify where to put the output from the render. Clicking the file folder icon on the left changes a window to a file browser, where you can navigate your hard drive or network to find the relevant folder. As discussed in Chapter 4, entering a template here controls how the file is named. In the example, frame 31 will be named my-anim-0031.exr and will be in the render subfolder. If you will be rendering or working with more than 9,999 frames (more than 7 minutes of film, for example), enter a # in the template for each digit of the frame number. A full-length feature film contains about 130,000 frames, so my-movie-###### (six pound signs) would enable each frame to have a unique file name.

With this example, when you start rendering and saving rendered images, Blender will automatically create a render subfolder if one does not exist. As a general rule, do not mix files in frame sequence folders with other kinds of images, because it makes selecting them later on (to bring into the sequencer) a little more complicated. By convention, I use a render subfolder to contain my rendered image sequence.

> *Even though you press F12 or click* RENDER *and see a rendered image pop up on your screen, it is not saved to hard disk unless you manually select* File ➤ Save Rendered Image *or press F3 and complete the save image process. Only when you click* ANIM *are the files rendered and automatically saved, one after the other.*

Complete the animation

Prepare, collect, and add your 3D elements, and arrange them as they should be for each keyframe. Make a lot of test renders to ensure everything lines up as you want. Animate your elements to transition between keyframes—in location, visibility, size, shape, bounce, and so on, as in the examples in the previous chapter.

Render the video

In a somewhat climactic moment, click the *huge* ANIM button in the Anim panel, shown in Figure 9-11, to kick off the rendering of the frame sequence, instead of the big RENDER button to render a single frame. You can watch the console window for progress messages. Unless you tell it otherwise, Blender will render the first frame, save it, and proceed onto the next until it hits the end.

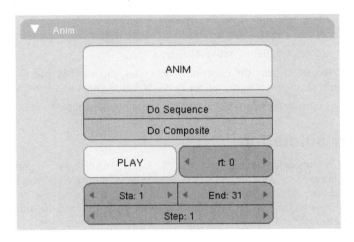

Figure 9-11. Animation panel

Some important Output panel options come into play here:

- Touch: When Touch is enabled, Blender creates an empty file before beginning to render. I recommend this, so that if you run into security privilege violations or broken network links, those issues are reported early—*before* you would otherwise waste time computing the render and *then* having it fail because Blender cannot write out the output. Also, when you are using multiple PCs to render a sequence, creating this empty file signals the other PCs that someone else is working on the file (when used in conjunction with the No Overwrite option).

- No Overwrite: This prevents Blender from overwriting an existing file of the same name. It is very helpful when recovering from a render crash or otherwise resuming the rendering of a frame sequence. Simply enable this, and rendering will fill in any frame(s) not previously rendered. Also, if you have deleted a few bad frames, or a middle section of perhaps ten frames, they will be rerendered, as Blender will simply skip over any files that already exist.

Once the animation is finished, use your computer's file explorer to navigate into the output folder (".\render in this example). You will see a lot of images that have a sequence number attached to them, ranging from 0000 to a maximum of 9999. These are your single frames.

Click PLAY in the Anim panel to preview the animation. The sequence of images will play in a window, looping until you press Esc.

Package it

When you are happy with your video as a frame sequence, you are ready to use the sequencer to pack those images into a single file, optionally with an audio track. How to do that is discussed in Chapter 13. Here's a quick summary:

1. In the sequencer, choose Add Image from the Add menu, and select all the sequenced frames from your output folder that you want to include in your animation.

2. Add in an audio file as well. It will be added as a strip to the sequence editor.

3. In the scene render Anim panel, activate Do Sequence.

4. In the Format panel, choose the container and codec you want to use (for example, FFmpeg and H.264), and configure it as described in the "Of containers and codecs" section.

5. Click the ANIM button. Blender will render the sequencer output into your movie.

Play back your animation

Once the rendering is complete, you can click the PLAY button on the Anim panel to play back the animation in a special playback window. While the animation is playing back, you can click in the window to pause the playback, and the current frame number will be shown in the header. Click and drag left/right to advance/rewind the playback, or hold the left/right arrow keys on your keyboard. Pressing +/- on the number keypad expands or shrinks the window for a close-up view.

While playback is active, the Blender UI window will not be responsive. To get back to blendering, press Esc to end playback, or simply close the window.

Of containers and codecs

We touched on containers and codecs, in theory, in Chapter 4. Now let's put some meat on the bones and use these practically.

As you may recall, instead of having each frame in a separate file, you can condense all those frames into a single file by using a compression-decompression algorithm (codec). Blender can create a video-only file in the QuickTime or AVI format, and an integrated video and audio file using the FFmpeg library of routines to create an MPEG, a QuickTime, or an AVI format file.

> If you want a sound track to your video, you must use FFmpeg format, load the audio track in the sequencer, and interleave the audio using the Audio panel. Chapter 14 covers using audio.

There is no single right answer in choosing a codec, and the correct choice may depend on the player or host that you use. YouTube and Vimeo, for example, have specific recommendations about what they favor, for both normal (640×480) and HD resolutions. When using a codec, you must be fairly confident that the viewers have that codec on their system, or that their player can automatically obtain that codec so that they can view your video. You can also convert your video to another format, such as Flash, using any variety of external converters.

QuickTime container

For the QuickTime container format, select QuickTime from the format selection list on the Format panel. You can then choose which installed codec to use by clicking Set codec. When you do, Blender will call on that container processor (QuickTime), which will take over and present a pop-up window that allows you to choose and then tailor the codec processing.

I have had good success with the QuickTime container using the MPEG-4 video codec (as well as the H.264 codec). While the QuickTime player is not available for Linux-based users, Blender on Linux can create these files, and the VLC player (included on your DVD) can play MOV files.

AVI container

Blender's AVI container format has three menu option flavors shown on the pop-up Format panel menu:

- AVI Raw: The raw format does not compress any of the images, preserving the original quality exactly, but results in a huge file.
- AVI Jpeg: This format compresses each image using a JPEG codec. You pick a Quality setting, which is just like the still-image JPEG quality setting.
- AVI Codec: This format uses any of your installed codecs to compress all the frames into a single file.

In general, you always need some compression, since the savings on each frame really adds up to save quite a bit of space. For this reason, AVI Raw is seldom used.

As with QuickTime format, when you select an AVI codec, you need to click Set codec in the Format panel to pick from the installed codecs on your system.

FFmpeg container

Selecting an FFmpeg container invokes the Fast Forward Motion Picture Experts Group (yes, that's really what FFmpeg stands for) library of routines that provide support for a wide variety of containers, codecs, and settings to tune playback. When you select an FFmpeg container, Blender is able to not only use a wide variety of video codecs, but it also can encode an audio track and use an audio codec.

When you select FFMpeg from the Format panel, two additional panels appear: Video and Audio. On the Video panel, because there are so darn many options, there is a Preset selector list. Figure 9-12 shows the FFmpeg settings resulting from choosing the H.264 preset. While there are a ton of options below the Codec selector field, I never touch them and so have omitted them from the figure.

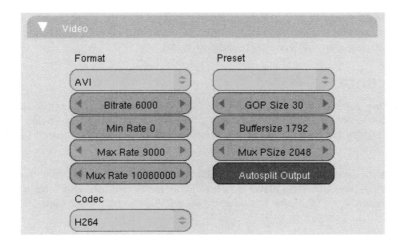

Figure 9-12. FFmpeg Video panel

The Bitrate setting in the Video panel is the bandwidth of the player. If you are packaging a video for playback and distribution over the Internet, you should keep this as is. The GOP setting is the number of frames in between keyframes, and there is a trade-off between the time it takes for the player to "reconstruct" the image based on changes versus just using the fresh image. Fresh images take more bandwidth. In general, I like to set GOP to one or two second's worth of video, so normally I use 30 (not the default 18), which cuts file size without adding a huge burden on the player.

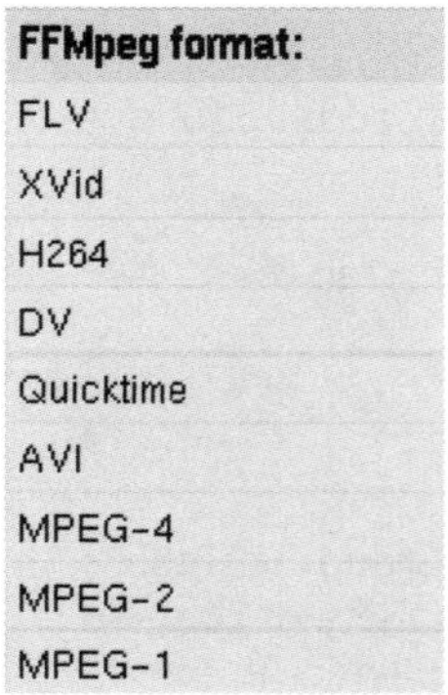

FFMpeg format:

FLV
XVid
H264
DV
Quicktime
AVI
MPEG-4
MPEG-2
MPEG-1

Figure 9-13. FFmpeg codecs available from the Video panel

Your operating system probably limits file sizes to 2GB. Movies can exceed that (based on run-length and low compression). Autosplit Output, when enabled, chunks up the movie into multiple files, to avoid exceeding the file size limit.

The FFmpeg library is open source software that supports many different (and sometimes obscure) formats. Blender has chosen the most popular ones, as shown in Figure 9-13.

The only way to load in an audio track is to use the sequencer. When you do, FFmpeg can encode that track into the final output file using an output audio codec, such as MP2, MP3, AAC, or AC3. On the Audio panel, the Bitrate setting affects the quality of the sound: 128 is fairly low quality, while 256 is better, and 384 is maximum. Low bitrates give sound a "tubular" quality and reduced dynamic range. I like MP3 with 384.

Render farms

A *render farm* is a bunch of PCs, networked together, that each renders a frame at a time. Solutions range from free and homegrown to commercial (paid) farms of hundreds or thousands of servers. What you need depends on your budget and time frame available to complete the entire render.

I have a few PCs hanging around the house, and they are networked to one another through a Public folder. My simple approach is to fire up Blender on each machine, load the networked blend file, ensure that Touch and No Overwrite are enabled on the Output panel, and click ANIM in the Anim panel on each one in succession. The first PC starts by creating the file for frame 1, and then actually starts rendering frame 1. The second PC sees that the file for frame 1 exists, so it starts with frame 2, and so on, in round-robin fashion. Each PC produces a subset of the frames, and they all balance the load by staking out and working on the next unclaimed frame as they finish with their current one. Different PCs of different computing power can be used this way. The only thing I need to deal with is render crashes on the very old PCs, as they cannot handle the complexity.

> *Make sure all image texture and file references relative paths and the folders are shared, so that each PC can access all necessary resources.*

Farmerjoe (http://farmerjoe.info/) is a distributed rendering system for Blender that provides a central system for managing the rendering system. It also provides a web server/HTML page that you can tap in order to remotely check on progress. There is also a Python script called Multiblend (available at http://stuvel.eu/multiblend) that chunks up the render sequence across multiple PCs.

The Big Ugly Rendering Project (BURP) is an external service that uses the BOINC (http://boinc.berkeley.edu/) distributed network computing platform. BURP is a compliant plug-in that uses the global distributed computing system developed by UC Berkeley and is a network of volunteers who have signed up their PCs to perform computing tasks by receiving jobs via the Internet. The SETI project uses the BOINC system, for example, to process radio signals. Any BOINC platform can log in to the BURP project and help you render your images. In practice, I found the BURP plug-in to be a compute hog, so I recommend using it on dedicated PCs or only at night.

Green Button (https://www.greenbutton.co.nz/) and the Sun grid (http://network.com) are examples of pay-as-you-go rendering farms for commercial work. They charge a few cents for each CPU minute to use their computers to do your rendering. As mentioned in Chapter 2, Sun graciously donated its grid for rendering *Big Buck Bunny* in all of its full glory. ResPower (http://www.respower.com/) offers economical farm rendering for Blender users, and their developers occasionally contribute to the Blender sources. Thanks guys!

Summary

This chapter showed you how to transform a virtual computer-generated scene, with or without the compositor and/or sequencer, into a single image, a frame sequence, or an integrated video file. Rendering produces an image or video based on what you feed it: your scene of elements, your compositor output (which may or may not be based on your scene), and your sequencer output (which also may be independent of the scene and/or the compositor). Because there has been so much innovation in such a short time regarding digital imaging, rendering can be one of the most bewildering aspects of compositing. However, without rendering, you wouldn't have anything to show the world!

Now that you know all the intricacies of rendering the 3D view, let's see how to process that render, along with other images, in the compositor.

Chapter 10

NODE-BASED COMPOSITING

Blender has three components that support compositing: the 3D view, the node-based compositor, and the nonlinear video sequencer. Figure 10-1 shows the relationship to these three components and their pipeline. For the purposes of this chapter, consider that the compositor may pull in image assets or the 3D view scene, manipulate those images or video, and either save its results directly to a file (creating a new image asset) or pass on its results to the sequencer.

> *You can use a formal digital asset management system to manage your image assets (still images, image sequences, video, textures, blend files) or just a simple file folder system. I use the library (lib) folder system on the DVD to hold all the assets (images and textures) used in this book. While not glamorous, a folder system does allow you to organize your image assets in a hierarchical manner.*

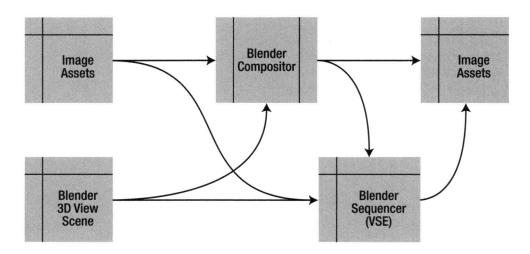

Figure 10-1. Compositor integration

As with other areas of Blender, an image in the compositor can be a still, a sequence of frames, or a movie. The compositor uses a network of nodes to process the image asset. Each node is a simple image processor, and you thread them together into a processing network. I call the network of nodes a noodle, but others call it a network or node tree. Apple's Shake program is similar to Blender's compositor, but Apple calls most of its nodes "filters". In Blender, some nodes are denoted as filters, but there are many other categories as well.

You can have the 3D view, compositor, and sequencer all activated and functionally integrated within the same Blender scene. For example, if you have some smoke simulation in 3D view, you can integrate that into rendered footage using the compositor. If you want to make changes to the smoke, such as its relative position in the frame, you can dynamically adjust the 3D view camera or translate the smoke overlay in the compositor window. If you want to change the color of the smoke or its density, you can do so in 3D view or the compositor and refresh the compositor window. Blender renders the image from the 3D view (configured in the Render Layers panel in 3D view and transmitted to the compositor through an input node called Render Layer) for the current frame. Since the 3D view and compositor are all in one package, there is no need to relink or reconnect between the two functional components.

Working with the compositor

The compositor uses *nodes*, arranged into a processing network, to create a composite output image. Just like you create and arrange 3D objects in the 3D view, you create and arrange nodes in the node editor. This node editor doesn't work by itself but is best used in conjunction with other types of windows, all of which are arranged into an efficient screen layout.

Compositing screen layout

To work efficiently, you need a good, consistent screen arrangement that supports your compositing activities. A screen is an arrangement of window panes and types to support an activity; in this case, you're using the compositor to adjust and work with images. If you open tut/.b.blend, you will have a desktop layout called SR:8-Compositing, which you can select from the Screens control in the user preferences header (Figure 10-2).

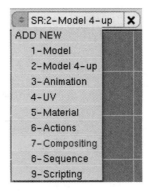

Figure 10-2. Selecting the compositor screen

Once you've selected the screen, you will see some familiar windows, as shown in Figure 10-3, as well as one new one, which is the predominant one: the node window. You have the buttons window on the right. Beneath the node editor window you have a UV/image editor on the left that displays your work in progress and an image browser next to it for selecting images to load. Beneath all of them, across the bottom of the screen, is the timeline window.

> *It's OK that some windows—such as the image editor—are relatively small. Remember that if you need more space for any particular operation, you can hover your mouse pointer over the window and press Shift+spacebar to expand it to fill the screen.*

I discussed the buttons window in Chapter 4, but I will cover a new panel, the Render Layers panel, in this chapter. I discussed the UV/image editor in Chapter 5, but you'll use it here a little differently, and I'll talk about that also in this chapter. I discussed the timeline window and how to use it when I introduced the concept of animation in Chapter 8. You can of course change this screen arrangement or the window types to whatever suits your needs. When you do, press Ctrl+U to save your user preferences.

> *I enable all the codecs on my system when working with video, which helps cut down on the "unrecognizable format" errors. This Enable all Codecs button is located in the System & OpenGL section of the user preferences window.*

Each scene in a blend file can have only one composite noodle. Recall that a blend file can have multiple scenes. A noodle in one scene can bring in the 3D view from any other scene in the blend file. Additionally, since you can link scenes (see Chapter 9), a noodle can bring in any scene from any file anywhere from your library. This gives you ultimate flexibility when a team is working on a project, since everyone can work on their specialty and refine their scene, while the compositor works in parallel to produce the final composite.

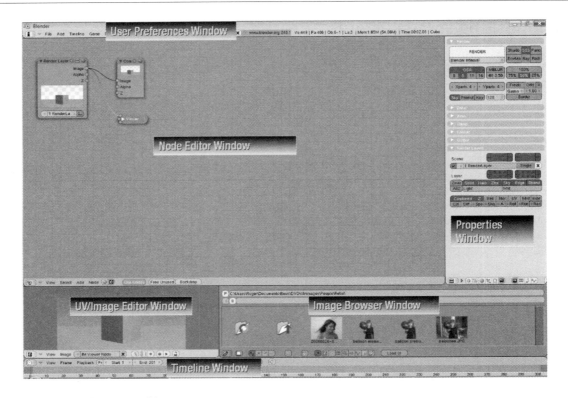

Figure 10-3. Blank compositing arrangement

The node editor

Just like all other window panes, Blender's node editor has a header, a workspace, and borders.

Node editor header

The header consists of the window type selector, an arrow to collapse/expand the menu, a menu, and some controls (Figure 10-4).

Figure 10-4. Node editor header

The header menu contains the following:

- **View**: This allows you to zoom in and out and zoom to fit (if possible) the entire noodle in your workspace. As with all menus, the hotkey is shown on the right side of the menu. In addition, a menu option allows you to invoke and use the Grease Pencil tool. This recent new feature is described in Chapter 12 and allows you to mark up your animation with a virtual grease pencil.

- **Select**: This allows you to select some or all the nodes or, for the selected nodes, all the other nodes that either feed it or are fed by it. This is very handy for tracing back to understand where this image came from (and why, to diagnose issues when you aren't getting what you want).

- **Add**: This allows you to add all sorts of nodes, each of which are discussed in this and the next few chapters. It also allows you to designate a group of nodes.

- **Node**: These choices are specific to working with a node, so I'll cover them later when I talk about working with nodes.

There are four controls on the rest of the header:

- **Node family selector**: Blender actually has whole sets of nodes, one for making really fancy materials and the other for compositing. You always want to select the face icon.

- **Use Nodes**: This causes Blender to actively reevaluate the noodle with every change that you make, which can take time and slow you down if you want to make a few changes to a complex noodle. Disable this to make your changes, and then reenable it to resume refreshing.

- **Free Unused**: Leave this disabled when you are working on your noodle, and then enable it when you have completed your noodle and are ready to render a frame sequence or video. When disabled, data is pulled from a *cache*, or temporary storage in memory, which is very fast but takes up memory. Enabling this frees up memory for final rendering.

- **Backdrop**: This shows the current viewer node image as a background image to the workspace. It is nice to see your intermediate composite really big as a background image, but I find it distracting. It reminds me of a screen saver with an activation time set too low. I prefer to use the UV/image editor window to see my intermediate results, since if a composite has black in it, it hides the threads of the noodle when used as a backdrop. The noodle itself is panned by clicking and dragging the middle mouse button. The backdrop image is panned by pressing Shift and clicking and dragging the middle mouse. The backdrop image is shown at actual resolution.

Node editor workspace

> When you open a file that has a compositing noodle and you look at the node editor window, all the thumbnails may not be shown. You need to press E to execute the noodle and refresh it before really doing any editing to the noodle.

The workspace is just like 3D view but in 2D; in fact, it works just as if you were working on a drafting table. Therefore, a lot of the actions are the same or very similar to working in 3D space. Specifically, holding down the middle mouse button and dragging pans the display, dragging the whole noodle around as if it was on your desktop. Rolling your middle mouse wheel (MMW) zooms in and out, as does holding down Ctrl and dragging up and down with the middle mouse button. Left or right-clicking selects a node, and Shift-selecting adds more nodes to the select list.

Open Peach\simple_blends\compositing\comp.blend to experiment with handling a large noodle. Note that there is a limit to how much you can zoom out and in but practically no limit to how much you can pan the workspace. Practice panning and zooming. Press E to execute the noodle to see the result (this may take a while).

Pressing B and dragging your mouse does a box-select of the nodes within the box. Be careful, though, since just dragging your mouse cuts any threads in the box. I tend to forget to press B first, so my next tip is that Ctrl+Z undoes the last (foolish) action.

Figure 10-5 shows an example compositor noodle.

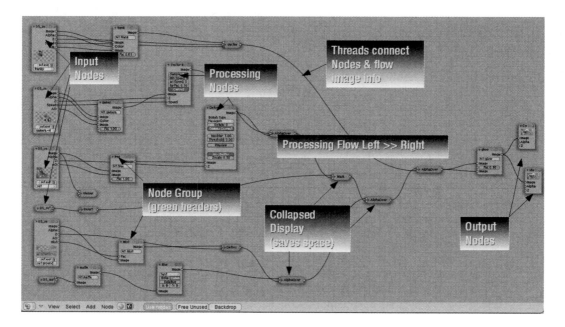

Figure 10-5. Annotated sample noodle

Don't be put off by all the complexity; all I want to show is that there are these things called *nodes*, which do some sort of image work, and they are connected through *threads*. These threads carry the image information from one node to another. Each node is a functional unit of processing that does something to an image or to data about the image. A group of nodes is shown as a node with a green header. An image (or information about the image) is brought in to the compositor by some input nodes on the left side of the window. They then pass that image, or information about the image, out through little dots called sockets on the right side of the node that are connected by threads to other nodes. That thread comes in to a socket on the left side of the node, gets processed by the node, and leaves through a socket on the right side of the node. Ultimately, all these images get combined, flowing left to right, and finally end up at a composite output node on the far right.

> *Nodes extend some visual programming concepts from software to image process-ing. In the software realm, I recall when IBM came out with a way to structure pro-grams by using input-process-output cards that you could arrange into a network diagram, called a Hierarchical Input Process Output (HIPO) chart. CSC came out with system validation diagrams called* threads, *and Ed Yourdon formalized that concept of flowing the processing. I had the privilege to meet him, work with his team, and use his Yourdon toolkit, as well as computer-aided software engineering (CASE) tools from Bachman, to draw these process models. These diagrams became affectionately known as "meatball and spaghetti" diagrams, because they would often look just like a plate of meatballs and spaghetti as the data flows started to go all over the place. That's why I call node trees* noodles.

To keep your noodles from looking like a plateful of jumbled spaghetti, always try to start with your inputs on the left, your processing in the middle, and your output toward the lower right, as exempli-fied in Figure 10-5. If you are a Shake user, then you might want to make a different arrangement, where you string your nodes from top to bottom, forming a tree kind of shape where they all con-verge down to a composite at the base of the tree. I like left to right because of the sockets place-ment, and I read left to right.

You can have as many nodes of whatever kind that you like in your compositing noodle, subject to one and only one rule:

> *Only one composite output node is allowed per noodle.*

You are limited only by your computer's memory and your ability to dream up neat effects. I have seen some really crazy noodles that are absolutely brilliant and produce great op-art with a comic-book feel, all based on a fairly simple CG scene render.

If a noodle starts to get too complicated, consider making groups that summarize the internal process-ing of a mini-network. (Groups are explained in Chapter 12.)

Typical node controls

There are many different nodes: nodes that get images, nodes that filter images, nodes that blur and distort images, and nodes that write the composite out to disk in some format. Regardless of what they do, each node has some controls and features in common with all other nodes. Figure 10-6 shows a typical node.

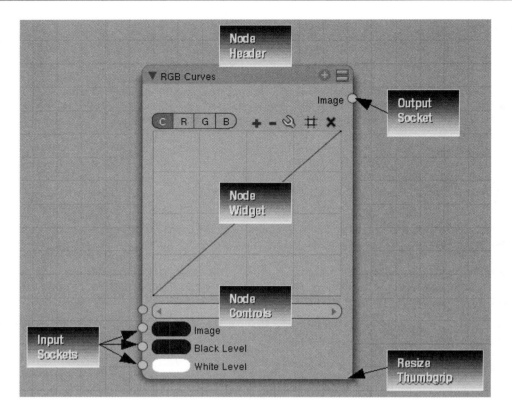

Figure 10-6. Typical node

Node header

Each node has a header and then a work area that is specific to that node. The header is either a theme color or green if a group. The other controls on the header are purely to save screen real estate and hide unnecessary information:

- **Collapse/expand arrow**: Collapses/expands the node display between normal size and bullet size.
- **Node name**: A generic or user-entered name for this node, derived from the input source or the function of the node. Change it with Ctrl+R or Node ➤ Rename.
- **+ -**: Shows/hides unthreaded sockets. This is purely to make things tidy.
- **= -**: Shows/hides the controls and widgets specific to this node.
- **Material Ball**: Shows/hides an image thumbnail area.
- **Expand**: For group nodes, expands the node out to show its contents, or collapses it.

Sockets

A *socket* is like a socket in your wall that you plug electrical devices into. In Blender, these sockets either accept (if they are on the left side of the node) or produce (if they are on the right side) image information. Sockets are different colors based on the information they transmit or expect for every pixel in the image:

- **Yellow**: RGB image channel information
- **Gray**: A number, or value, per pixel of the image, including alpha and Z information
- **Blue**: A vector or direction and magnitude information

Generally speaking, you should connect similarly colored sockets to one another, but there are exceptions that I will detail as we go along. The general exception is that gray sockets can process image information just fine.

Threading

You create *threads*, or connections, between sockets by clicking one, dragging your mouse to another socket, and releasing. As you hover your mouse pointer over a socket while dragging, it will light up, letting you know you can connect.

Threads are black when not selected, white when selected, and red when bad.

When you add a node, it is added wherever your mouse pointer is when you press the spacebar, and if the selected node (the node selected before the add) has an output socket that matches the type of primary input socket of the node you are adding, the new node is automatically threaded to the selected node and becomes the selected node. That was a really complicated way of explaining that if you add a chain of nodes, they will thread themselves to a certain degree.

Cyclic dependencies

With connections going hither and yon, it is very possible to connect a noodle back on itself, as shown in Figure 10-7.

The problem with this noodle is that the Blur node, whose result depends on the Mix and RGB Curves nodes, feeds that result back to the RGB Curves node. This is bad—very bad. Assuming the universe does not implode, you need to correct this situation right away by cutting the offending thread (simply drag your mouse pointer across the thread). As you drag, your cursor changes to a knife, just like the knife in 3D view that you use for "kutting" edges into little pieces.

To save the universe from implosion, Blender can detect these cyclic dependencies and alert you in two ways. First, in Figure 10-7 I have superimposed the console window, which is clearly screaming cyclic dependency. Second, in the noodle, the offending thread is red.

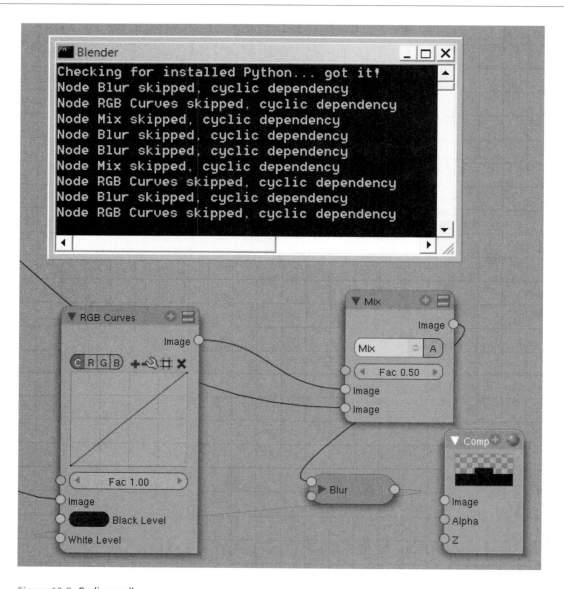

Figure 10-7. Cyclic noodle

Node editor window's Node menu

Now that you know what a node is and what it does and how it connects, let's look at the Node menu, located on the window header (Figure 10-8).

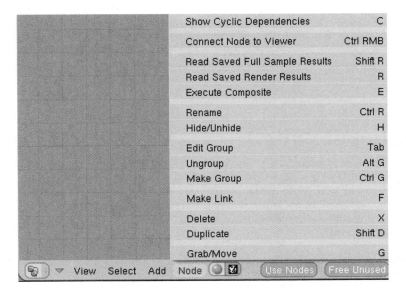

Figure 10-8. Node menu

Here's what you can do with this menu:

- Pressing C as a hotkey with your mouse pointer in the node editor window does a check for those nasty, universe-threatening cyclic dependencies.

- Using a viewer to inspect a node's output is a very common task, so instead of three mouse clicks, you can just select the node you want to inspect and press Ctrl+RMB.

- Pressing E pumps the images through the noodle, refreshing all the displays.

- Rename allows you to change the name of a node, and pressing H minimizes them or expands them.

- For working with groups of nodes, the Tab key expands the group and allows you to operate on its guts. While expanded, you can move member nodes around, change links, and so on. Pressing Alt+G destroys the group connotation and plops all the nodes back into the noodle. To make a group, select them all and use the menu, or simply press Ctrl+G. Do not include a composite output node in a group.

- To delete a node, press X, just like deleting an object in 3D view. Duplicating, Shift+D, is again just like in 3D view.

When you duplicate a node, it is placed right over the original, hiding the original. Granted, as soon as you move your mouse, it moves, but if you happen to click right away, it will drop right on top of the original and "appear" to be connected, since you will see a thread leading up to its sockets. However, it's the original underneath that is the one doing all the work, so changing the duplicate won't change the original. So, if you are clearly adjusting a node's controls but the result doesn't seem to be changing, just press G to grab that node and make sure there isn't anything hiding underneath. To move a node, you can also click and drag its header.

Feed me (input nodes)

The first thing you need is something to work with, and you bring those things in via the input node family. When you first click Use Nodes, an input and an output node are put into the workspace for you. The input is a Render Layer node that brings in the 3D view through the active camera. The output is the Composite Output node, which passes the resulting image out to a file (if Do Composite is enabled in the Anim panel) or to the sequencer via a scene strip. The input is threaded to the output through the image channel.

The output resolution of the compositor is set in the scene's Render Format panel, which is also the resolution of the 3D view camera, so it all matches up nicely. However, if you read in a different scene and it has a different resolution or if you read in an image that does not match your scene's resolution, then you have a mismatch. In these cases, Blender will attempt to center that image so the center of the input image matches the center of the output image. That way, a simple scale of the input image will allow you to match up and composite the input over the output. If you want to use the compositor to add some special effect to a 3D view but for some reason want the 3D view to render in one resolution and the compositor to render in a different one, add a new scene and set it to render in the compositor resolution. Then use the node editor in that scene to read in the 3D view (via the Render Layer node) for the other scene. If you want to position that image somewhere other than center, consult the Translate node.

Getting in the view

Since Blender is an integrated CG application, it makes sense to first discuss bringing in the 3D view. The 3D view is brought in through a selection of the scene within the blend file. After you have selected the scene, you then select the render layer. A *render layer* is a way of bringing in part or all of the image (layers) and different aspects of the image (called *passes*).

Render Layer node

The Render Layer node is the way to get the 3D view into the compositor, shown in Figure 10-9. In a multiscene file, you choose the scene using the left selector, and the image that is pulled in is taken from the camera. If there happens to be yet another composite noodle in that scene, it is ignored—the Render Layer node pulls the image directly from the renderer. The name of the node is formatted as Scene | Render Layer, so this node is bringing in the image from the bg scene via the Background render layer.

Once you have selected the scene, there may be more than one render layer used to transmit that scene to the compositor. If so, use the selector on the right (just to the left of the Render icon) to select the render layer for that scene (Figure 10-10).

Figure 10-9. Render Layer node, choosing the scene

Figure 10-10. Render Layer node, choosing the render layer

If you open Peach\production\scenes\12_peach\20.blend, you will see this node in the composing desktop. Do not press E to refresh the entire noodle, but instead click the little landscape picture in the lower-right corner of the node. That will cause that node, and only that node, to refresh itself. The render engine will go off and grab that render layer and make you a thumbnail of the image, in this case of a tree. You should be able to do this on any 2GB machine (a PC with 2GB of RAM).

This input node provides a bunch of sockets into the noodle. Which sockets appear depends on which render passes you have selected it to pass on. You select render passes in the Render Layers panel, which is in the Scene Render context.

If there are multiple scenes in the file, then the up-down selector on the left at the bottom will allow you to select which scene to pull an image from. If you've defined multiple render layers for that scene, the up-down selector to the right of the name (and just to the left of the refresh icon) allows you to select the render layer.

Alpha Channel Socket

Blender has two methods for computing transparency: ZTransp or ray transparency, and you must select either one (neither is selected by default) and use an alpha value for the material less than 1.0. If you choose ray transparency, be sure to enable ray tracing in the Scene Render panel. A material can be either ray transparent or Z transparent, but all ray transparent materials are rendered with an alpha value greater than 1.0 at the alpha socket, and they include the specular component. Figure 10-11 shows you how to isolate and process the alpha channel when you use ray tracing.

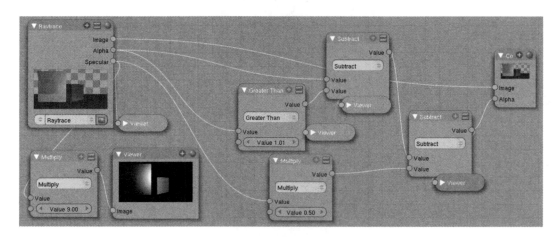

Figure 10-11. Processing the alpha channel when using ray tracing

The noodle in Figure 10-11 shows the specular pass (multiplied in the lower-left corner of the figure to show detail), which is included in the alpha socket with the ray tracer. This needs to be subtracted to get a "pure" alpha channel. Note that you can save this specular pass as well in order to get photorealistic specular coloring on glassy/transparent surfaces.

Keep in mind also that you will blend in the sky color if Sky is selected in the Render panel, which really messes up later compositing (because it adds a false color to the background). Therefore, all elements that you want to later render over other things should use the Premul or Key setting in the Scene Render panel so that the proper alpha value is saved in the image.

ZTransp (and its alpha channel) does not contain any specularity or refraction distortion, so it can be fed directly to the composite image. Note that in Figure 10-11 the processed alpha is fed to the Composite output node. The disadvantage to ZTransp is that you lose all those neat ray tracing capabilities. Once rendered, you normally lose information about that object's index of refraction (IOR) settings. However, with ray tracing, Blender can compute (and you can save) the refraction pass information. Simply enable the refraction pass in the Render Layer node (described in a moment), and save the refraction pass by using a multilayer image format.

Render passes

A *render pass* is like taking a pass through a book; you skim over to try to collect and absorb what you want to know. In Blender, a render pass is a product of the render engine, where it produces selected information about a certain aspect of the 3D view. Very often in compositing, you want to adjust these passes, or combine them in creative ways, to augment the normal rendering process, resulting in an improved image. A render layer allows you to select these passes and bundles all these passes together and sends them off (faster than overnight express) to the compositor, where this node picks them up and allows you to process them separately.

Blender allows you work on these passes separately when you select them in the Render Layers panel. These passes are as follows:

- **Combined**: The complete 3D view, including all passes and render results combined; the final image
- **Z**: The distance a pixel is from the camera

> *Z is essential to computing depth of field (DOF), a common compositing challenge. If you look at a picture taken by a real camera in dim light, the foreground and background objects will appear out of focus, because a real camera, based on the f-stop of the lens that controls the size of the lens iris, can focus only on objects within a certain range from the camera. This is nice, because it keeps the main subject, and all things within that depth of field, sharply in focus and blurs everything else, which forces you to focus on the main subject and not get distracted by that puppy in the background. In CG, however, there is no real camera, so you have to use Z-depth information (Chapter 4) to tell you how much to blur an object (or the pixels representing that object) based on how far out of the DOF that it is. The farther away from the depth of field, the more it should be blurred. Therefore, to process DOF, you need not only the image but also the Z value information. You can see this Z socket in Figure 10-10.*

- **Vec**: Vector; how fast and in what direction the geometry at that pixel is moving.
- **Nor**: Normal; the direction the geometry at that pixel is facing relative to the camera.
- **UV**: If a texture is UV mapped to a surface, the UV coordinate of the pixel.
- **Mist**: Alpha fade-out values as set in world settings.

■ **Index**: Each CG object can be assigned a pass index in its Object and Links panel. This pass allows you to pull a mask for just that object using the ID Mask node.

■ **Col**: Delivers the raw material colors, unaffected by light and shadow.

■ **Diff**: Diffuse, the basic shading of surfaces, without highlights or shadows.

The next set of passes can also be excluded from the combined pass so that you can add them manually. To exclude the pass from Combined and get it delivered separately, Ctrl+click the pass button.

■ **Spe**: Specularity; how the shine of a surface occurs across the face of the surface, based on specularity color and hardness.

■ **Shad**: Shadows, both ray-traced and buffered, are in this pass.

■ **AO**: Ambient occlusion dirties creases, corners, and light surfaces that might otherwise not receive direct light from a lamp. AO must be enabled in the Shading World settings. You must have Shadows enabled in the Render panel to see AO. If using ray-traced AO calculation, you must also have ray tracing turned on in the Render panel.

■ **Refl**: Reflection; shiny materials reflect light and the image of what is outside of them. (Ray tracing and ray transparency must be enabled.)

■ **Refr**: Refraction; light is bent as it passes through materials with an IOR value (ray tracing and ray transparency must be enabled.)

■ **Rad**: Radiosity; emitting materials color objects around them, and this pass gives you that color gradient.

Visualizing render passes

Each pass is really a number or type of number (like a vector) for each pixel in the image. In figuring out how to use those numbers, it helps to see the pass values. Depending on which one they are, they may not be readily viewable, since they are numbers. However, the Viewer node can display any pass as long as the values it gets have been normalized to a number between 0 and 1. Therefore, you have to use some math and vector converters to turn those numbers into a number between 0 and 1 that can be seen or convert them into a color to give false color using the Color Ramp node (discussed in the next chapter). Figure 10-12 provides this conversion for a sample Image input node from the Peach/simple_blends/compositing/comp.blend file.

As you can see, the handy Viewer node can give you a thumbnail of what the pass indicates. The image is the RGB image itself, and the alpha tells you the opacity of the elements. The Z socket gives you a sonar map of the image but has to be converted, either through the Normalize node or, for more specific gradients, using the Map Value node shown in the figure. As shown Figure 10-12, you can subtract 2.8 from the Z value in order to scale those Z values between 2.8 and 3.8 to a number between 0 and 1, which the Viewer node can then display as a grayscale image. Likewise, Speed is a vector (indicated by the blue socket), so you have to take the dot product of the vector to give you an idea of the magnitude (strength, size) of the vector. In Figure 10-12 you can see that in this frame the chinchilla's tummy is moving pretty fast (he is laughing) as indicated by the white value, and objects not moving are black (zero). The AO pass can be readily visualized as a grayscale factor type of pass that can be used to enhance the AO effect in post-production, without having to rerender the original 3D view.

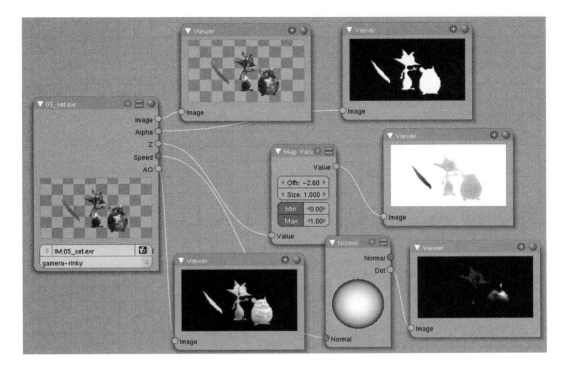

Figure 10-12. Visualizing passes

Render Layers panel

To set the list of passes, you need to refer to the buttons window, Scene Render context, and then locate the Render Layers panel (Figure 10-13). It is often tabbed behind the Output panel.

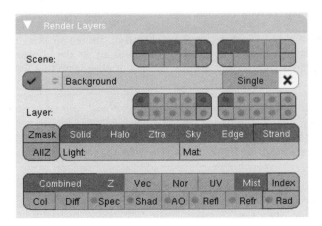

Figure 10-13. Render Layers panel

You can observe this panel in the file by selecting SCE:bg and looking in the buttons window. This panel provides you with complete control over what information to send to the compositor. In addition, changes made to the primary render layer affect what you render from the 3D view as well, even if you do not use the compositor.

In the Scene: section, the top set of layers button show you which object layers are currently selected in the 3D view header. This is just a friendly reminder that, in this case, layers 1, 2, 3, 5, and 6 are currently selected. Changes made here also affect the 3D view.

The next widget below the scene layers has five parts, which are as follows from left to right:

- **Enable**: Puts this render layer in the queue to be rendered. This is automatically checked if you select the render layer in the compositor's Render Layer node.

> *The first render layer (and not necessarily the active one showing) is used as the default render layer if you render without enabling Do Composite.*

- **Selector**: Allows you to view the settings for a certain render layer in this panel. Clicking the yellow up-down selector allows you to choose between existing render layers or add a new one.
- **Name**: Allows you to name the render layer (Background in this case).
- **Single**: Renders only this one render layer and ignores any others.
- **X**: Deletes this render layer.

There is only one render layer defined for this scene, Background.

The set of layer buttons below the selector line allows you to subset that set of active layers. This is an AND function, in that *both* an object layer and the layer buttons must be enabled for the objects in the layer to participate in the pass. Therefore, in Figure 10-13, only the objects on layers 1, 5, and 6 will be rendered and will have their combined color, Z, and mist values passed on. Objects in layers 2, 3, and 7, *even though they are seen in the 3D view, will not be rendered.*

There's the possibility that an object that is not included in the render layer is in front of an object that is. Ctrl+click a layer button to mask out that portion of the rendered objects that are behind the nonincluded ones (called a *Z-mask*), but not the shading of objects on that Ctrl+clicked layer.

> *Here is a really special note: ensure that a camera and your lights are on a render layer! Otherwise, you might get the befuddling Blank Render of Darkness (BROD), who has a distant cousin, the Blue Screen of Death (BSOD). The good news is that it is easy for you to correct BROD by Shift-selecting the layer with the active camera.*

Next on this panel begins a set of render pipeline components. The main purpose of restricting this list is to save render time when making intermediate test renders or to diagnose where a problem is coming from.

- **Solid**: Renders solid surfaces, transparent or not.
- **Halo**: Renders Halo materials for special effects.
- **Ztra**: Renders materials with Z transparency.
- **Sky**: Renders the sky (world) background.
- **Edge**: Renders any edge settings (on the Output panel).
- **Strand**: Renders hair and other strand particle types.

> *You can also disable a particle system from being rendered by deselecting the render-ability icon in the Particle system panel or the mesh object visibility in the outliner window.*

- **Light**: As you recall, light can be colored and textured and have varying intensity. Once you get a bunch of lights in a scene, they may start to conflict or cause bad image issues. Enter the name of the lamp group in here (add lamps to groups in its Object and Links panel) to override all the lamps in the scene with only the lamps in the group. Use this to simplify and speed up rendering or to start diagnosing shading/lighting issues.
- **Material**: Next, you can override all the different materials in the scene by entering the name of the material in this field. I use a simple fairly flat white material (which makes everything look shades of gray) either to isolate lighting and/or material issues or to simply give me a really fast render of a complicated scene.

At the bottom of the panel, you finally get to select the render passes described earlier. Click a pass to enable it to be passed over to the compositor. Ctrl+click to enable the pass but have its result not included in the combined pass. For example, Ctrl+clicking the Reflection pass would cause Reflection to be generated and sent to the compositor but not included in the main image. If you use this feature, you will have to combine the pass yourself in your noodle.

> *So, why have multiple render layers, if they just group the same set of passes? Well, good question, thank you for asking. The answer lies in complexity. For a complex scene, you may have objects on layers 1, 2, 3, and 4. The objects on layers 1, 2, and 3 are not moving too fast, but the objects on layer 4 are moving like a rocket, and we want to blur them and make them look hot, as if they are heating up from all the friction of going a billion miles an hour. So, just for objects on layer 4, we want to enable the Vector pass and the Color pass, so we can blur them and maybe tint them a little red. For the rest, we only need, and really only want, the Combined and Z passes. So, we define two render layers, one with combined and Z for layers 1, 2, and 3, and a second with Combined, Z, and Vector.*

Having multiple scenes pull in the same images (but do different things to them) allows you to make multiple alternative composites of the same basic scene. Usually you do this to run a few alternatives by the director to see which is preferred. When you do this, be sure to use the Scene Render Stamp option and enable Scene, as shown in Figure 10-14.

Figure 10-14. Stamp panel (activated)

Image node

This node starts off the compositing process and can load in a still, sequence, or movie. Depending on the format of the image, various channels of information may be available. Figure 10-15 shows an example Image node in the Peach\simple_blends\compositing\comp.blend file on your DVD.

Figure 10-15. Image node

The name of the node is taken automatically from the file name. The sockets are determined when the file is read in to see what channels are available based on the format of the image (Chapter 4). If the image format does not support an alpha channel, Blender will make one of fully opaque (1.0) for every pixel, which you can adjust with other nodes. These sockets provide the render passes discussed previously.

The blue up-down selector in the bottom left of the node allows you to select from images loaded into memory and already referenced in Blender. The IM: field next to it gives you the name of the image. The face icon allows you to choose the kind of image brought in: still, sequence, or video.

Sequences and movies

An image sequence (Chapter 4) provides a frame-by-frame breakdown of a movie. Using the Image node to pull in an image or sequence, as shown in Figure 10-16, reveals some extra controls.

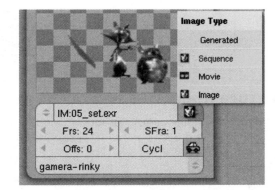

Figure 10-16. Image sequence and movie controls

The following are the options:

- **Frs**: This sets the number of frames in the shot. In this example, we were making a film at 24 fps, so this sequence is 1 second, or 24 frames long.

- **SFra:** This sets at what frame, in our animation, do we want to start reading in this sequence frame by frame and splice it into the compositing stream. For example, if you wanted the chinchilla to start laughing at frame 74, you would use 74 here.

- **Offs**: This sets the offset into the sequence to start pulling frames. When you convert a video to a sequence, there may be rollup in the front that you don't want to use. Offset allows you to offset into the middle of the sequence and start pulling frames early in your animation. For example, if there was 2 seconds of trash frames in the beginning of the sequence, you would set this to 48 since 2 seconds times 24 fps is 48.

- **Cycl**: Cyclic allows you to repeat pulling the frame sequence over and over. For example, as shown in the example, at frames 25 on, the node will supply frame 24. If Cycl is enabled, it will loop back around and begin again by pulling image sequence frame 0001 for animation frame 25, image sequence frame 0002 for animation frame 26, and so on.

- **Auto icon**: The little automobile icon enables autorefresh. This means that as you change frames in your animation, the node will go out and pull in the appropriate image for that frame. This takes time and resources, so if you're in a hurry, take the plane and leave the Auto icon deselected (a bit of geek humor there).

The bottom line allows you to select, for a multilayer image format, the render layer in the file you want to work with.

Working with different image resolutions

Normally, the resolution for a project is set at the beginning of the project, and you use that resolution in your scene's Render Output panel settings.

> *Blender cannot directly read in a vector (file extension .svg) image format as an image, but it can import it into 3D view as paths, which can then be rendered and brought in through the Render Layer node. To import an .svg file, simply have a camera view active in 3D view, and click in the middle of the view. Then select File ➤ Import ➤ Paths, which runs the paths import script; from there select SVG format, and select the file; the curve objects are then created in your 3D view space. Note they may be scaled very large or very small, and you will have to scale them to be seen in the camera view. You can then assign materials, edit them as curve objects, and rotate them for a perspective view. Then use the Render Layer node to get their rasterized image into the noodle.*

Texture node

We touched on textures in Chapter 7, and this node allows you to pull any texture (material, world, lamp, and so on) of any type (image, procedural, or map) into the composite noodle through the Texture node, shown in Figure 10-17.

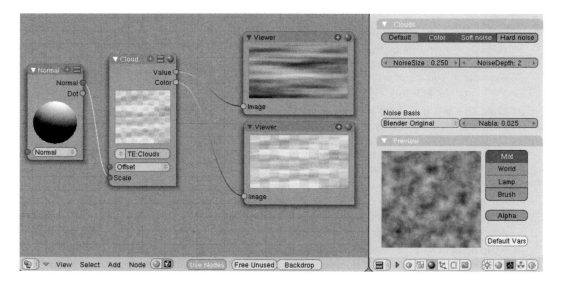

Figure 10-17. Texture node

When applying a texture to a material or world, you probably recall that you have to map the input and map the texture to something. The same sort of process applies in the compositor, but you use the normal node to control the offset and scale to offset or stretch the texture output. You then apply the texture using the Mix node.

In Figure 10-17 you can see the texture as defined in the buttons window on the right, a color clouds texture. In the noodle on the left, I have used the normal node to scale that texture horizontally. You can scale the texture manually by clicking the up-down selector and then sliding the XYZ pop-up control, as shown in Figure 10-18.

Offset displaces the 2D texture in 3D space by the specified amount, and Scale stretches the 2D texture into 3D space.

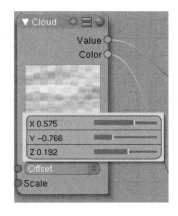

Figure 10-18. Texture control

Value node

You really cannot get any simpler than the Value node, as shown in Figure 10-19. The purpose of this node is to provide a fixed value between 0 and 1 to multiply other nodes so that they all work in a consistent manner. Use the Multiply node to scale this output to other ranges. Without this node, you have to set each receiver's node control individually. For example, you may want to adjust the brightness of several different images together or in the same amount. Instead of tweaking five different controls, threading them to the output of this node allows your one change (to this node) to propagate to the others.

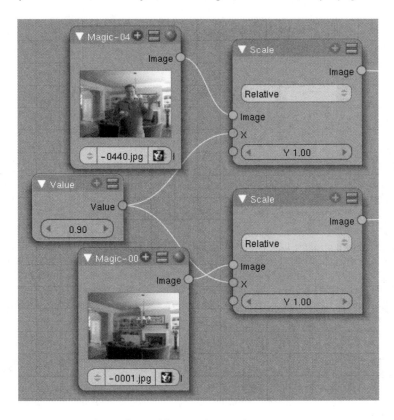

Figure 10-19. Value node providing consistent values

> *If you need a value greater than the range 0 to 1, use a* Math *node set to* Multiply *mode to scale the output to your desired range.*

Time node for animation

The Time node (shown in Figure 10-20) puts out a value between 0 and 1, like the Value node, but its output varies over time. It's also your first introduction to the curve control. For every frame in the range indicated between Sta (shorthand for "start") and End, it puts out a value between 0 and 1. The current frame is indicated by a green vertical line; frame 11 is in the example and is the (horizontal) x-axis in the graph. The output value is where the green line crosses the black curve line, which in this example is about .7.

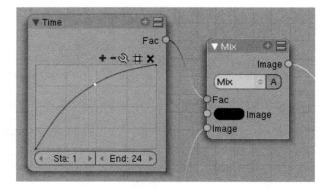

Figure 10-20. Time node

> *Normally, the* Time *node feeds the factor input of a* Mix *node, but it can be used to change the focus, for example. If you need a value greater than the range 0 to 1, use a* Math Multiply *node to scale the output to your desired range.*

The curve starts out as a straight line, which in this example would result in a linear fade in. To change it to a curve, simply click the line and start dragging. This adds a control point, shown as a white dot, that acts like a Bezier curve handle (see Chapter 5). The net effect of this curve in this figure is a 50% ease (or fade) in, which is to say that it starts out fast with rapidly changing Y values, and then as time progresses, Y (the output value) changes less and less. In this example, the output is used to control the mix node, which mixes the top image (in this example, black) with the bottom socket image. The net effect of this noodle is to fade in from black over 2 seconds.

> *There are three ways to fade in from black in Blender. There is this way, using the nodes as one. If you are rendering a CG scene from 3D view, you could alternatively animate the lamp(s) in the scene to raise their energy from 0. The third is by using a cross-fade in the sequencer.*

The curves widget

The curves widget in this Time node, as well as in other nodes like the RGB Curves node, is like a simplified Ipo curve editor (see Chapter 8). It is shown in the previous figures and is used in many nodes to give you more than just a linear control, or mapping, from input to output. It is a little graph with a line and five tools. It starts out as a straight line, mapping a direct input (a value along the x-axis) to the same corresponding output—where that X meets the line, giving a Y value, or as my son would say, y=f(x), where f() is the curve. You change this line into a curve by adding control points; simply click anywhere on the line and drag. When you click or create a control point, it becomes white and is the active point. You can then drag it around to change the curve shape.

On the top right of the widget, use the + and – tools (just click them) to zoom the graph display in/out. While zoomed in, you can use Shift and the left mouse button to pan within the curve workspace.

The wrench changes the control point handle type, just like the Ipo handles, from a normal Bezier flat handle to a broken stick vector handle, and so on. If you select an endpoint (they are there, but only half visible), you can change the extend mode to extrapolated or Horizontal. Horizontal is the default, which means that if the Time node ends at frame 300 with a value at .5, it will still put out .5 even at frame 600. However, if you choose Extrapolated, just like the Ipo curve option, Blender will extrapolate a value based on the shape of the curve. In our .5 example, if the curve was a relatively straight line from 0, the node would put out a value of 1 for frame 600, as if you kept drawing the curve out past the grid boundaries.

The little grid box allows you to enter clipping values. The numbers you enter here restrict the minimum to something greater than 0 but less than 1, and they restrict the maximum to something less than 1. When you use clipping options, the display background grays out clipped values and overrides whatever value the curve would normally provide. If you move a control point that is outside the clipped area, it snaps into the area as soon as you try to move it.

To delete the active control point, click the X tool. Don't press X on your keyboard, or you will delete the whole node. A little voice reminds me to tell you again that Ctrl+Z brings back the node if you forget (yet again) that it's X on the toolbar, not X on the keyboard.

RGB (color) node

Just like the Value node put out a fixed number, the RGB node puts out a fixed color. Also like the Value node, its real purpose is to make your noodle use a consistent color in multiple places. In the example for the Time node, we faded in from black. If there are five transitions, there would be multiple Mix nodes, all with their individual swatches. Suppose the director wanted to use, say, white, as the transition color. By using this node, shown in Figure 10-21, you have to change the transition color only once (in this node) rather than ten times.

The top color bar shows you the chosen color, which is also represented as a circle in the gradient below, that maps that hue of color (selected in the very bottom Hue gradient) across a saturation and value axis.

Figure 10-21. RGB node

Getting something out of it

Now that we've examined the "guzintas," let's look at the "guzoutas," or the nodes that bring something out of the compositor to show to you or to pass on to an image asset or the sequencer. Alternatively, there are nodes to simply show your work in progress.

Composite node

Figure 10-22 shows the composite output from Peach\ production\scenes\12_peach\14.blend, located on your DVD. While many of the peach files can be worked on with an 8GB machine only, I was able to render this file on a 2GB machine by shutting down all my unnecessary background processes and rendering each input render layer separately.

The Image socket traditionally travels the RGBA channels. You can override the Alpha value by plugging in the alpha channel socket. If you are using the EXR format, you can plug in a Z-depth map for the image as well.

Figure 10-22. Composite node

Viewer node

This node is your window into the noodle. Put this puppy anywhere you want to see what is being transmitted along the thread. In Figure 10-23, the Viewer node shows a viewer that I inserted to see the intermediate result that the AlphaOver node was putting out.

Figure 10-23. Viewer node

Split Viewer node

This handy node allows you to compare two images side by side (or top over bottom) in order to assess the changes that are made between one point and another in your noodle.

In Figure 10-24, I was examining the effect of some color adjustment by showing the original image on the left side fed to the bottom socket and the output from the defocus to the right. You can split the view either vertically into two left and right sections by clicking X or horizontally into a top and bottom section by clicking Y. The image to the top socket is shown on the right or top (depending on whether you have X or Y clicked, respectively). The slider allows you to adjust the location of the division between the two sockets in the viewer.

Figure 10-24. Split Viewer node

Using the UV/Image Editor window

An incredibly useful compositing feature of Blender is the ability to use a UV/image editor window to view, in large scale, the image information fed to a viewer or Split Viewer node, as shown in Figure 10-25. To use this, simply select Viewer Node from the image selector in the UV/ image editor.

Figure 10-25. UV/ image editor showing Viewer node

A very important trick is shown in Figure 10-25; like the render window, clicking and dragging over the window shows you the XY coordinate of the mouse cursor, as well as the RGBAZ values, in both 8-bit values and in percentages, for the image in white text at the bottom of the image. This is very handy when you need to check the resolution of an image or when you need to see what specific color a pixel really is.

File Output node

You are not limited to saving your composite only at the very end. You can use the File Output node (Figure 10-26) to save a file at any point in the noodle simply by adding and threading it in. Every time the noodle is executed for that frame, the file is updated with the current results. Be careful when using this node, though. If it contains a valid file name, it will write to that file as soon as it gets a valid input connection, possibly overwriting something and taking you by surprise.

Figure 10-26. File Output node

The distort processing nodes

All of the nodes in this loose collection distort the image in some fashion. *Distort*, as used in this sense, means that the pixels in the image are somehow moved or shifted, or the original image is changed in some manner.

Crop

Often an image will contain distracting elements, and the Crop node, shown in Figure 10-27, allows you to *crop*, or trim, out pixels from the border of the image. XY is relative to the bottom-left corner of the image, so the example shows cropping out an 850×1100 (portrait) image as a section of the 2K super high-definition (SHD) input image.

The result of the crop is scaled to fit the scene resolution if Crop Image Size is enabled. Otherwise, the output image is left in its same size and moved to the upper-left corner, with transparent areas filled in for the cropped areas.

Figure 10-27. Crop node

Displace

I like to call this the *dream node*, because it makes the image all wavy and is a common effect used when transitioning to someone dreaming, especially daydreaming. It operates two ways, with a normal map and with a black-and-white map, which is shown in Figure 10-28. Here we are using a simple wood texture to displace image pixels up to 50 pixels in an XY direction. The distortion is like we projected the image onto water and then made ripples in the water. For the vector/image input, the image pixels are shifted by the XY scale value. Set an XY value of 0, and the node does nothing.

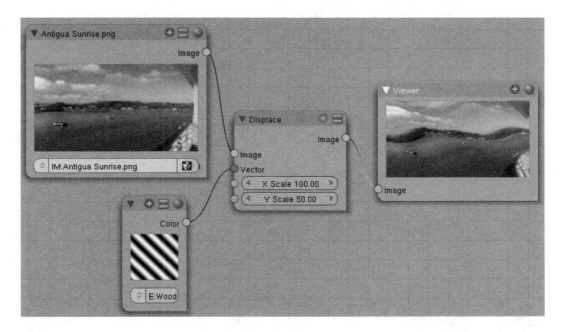

Figure 10-28. Displace node

If using a color image, then the strength of the red channel determines the X shift and the green channel the Y shift. You then scale these colors up so that the pixels are displaced.

Lens Distortion node

One of the "holy grails" of CG is photorealism, which has two issues: what is real, and what do we perceive as real? Part of that perception problem is that we view images taken from a camera, and the camera itself distorts the actual worldview as light travels through the lens, even adding lens flares (see Halo materials in Chapter 7). Other distortions are caused by the lens, such as barrel distortion, pincushion distortion, and, based on the lens coatings, chromatic aberration. Figure 10-29 shows an extreme setting, and it allows you to simulate a photo taken through a really good lens or a, um, not-so-good lens. A common use of this kind of distortion is for alien or computer vision, like HAL in Stanley Kubrick and Arthur C. Clarke's *2001: A Space Odyssey*. However, I suspect Mr. Kubrick just used a real but extreme fish-eye lens. Using this node, you can save yourself the expense!

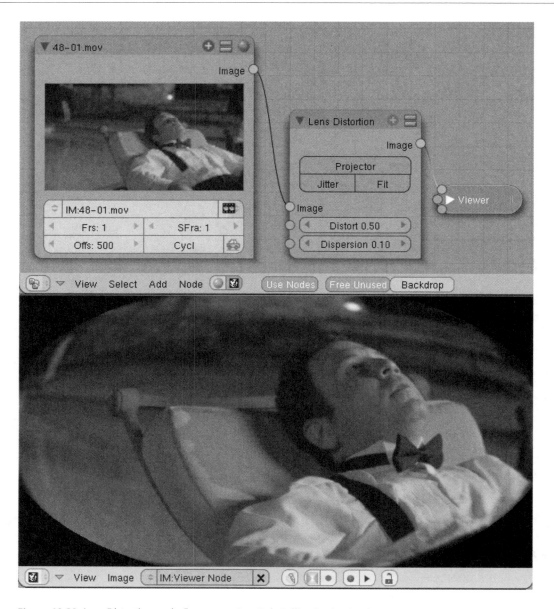

Figure 10-29. Lens Distortion node (image courtesy Rob Collins Productions)

Controls for this node include the following:

- **Projector**: Misaligns the RGB values, like a tri-lens projector out of alignment/focus.
- **Jitter**: Randomly jitters RGB values, simulating some sparkle in the lens coatings.
- **Fit**: Extends the edges of the distortion to fill in the corners.
- **Distort**: Sets the amount to distort. Positive values provide a barrel (fish-eye) effect, whereas negative values give a pincushion effect.
- **Dispersion**: Chromatic aberration (a rainbow effect), most noticeable around the edges of the distortion.

Map UV

This book does not have the space to go into UV unwrapping and texture painting, unfortunately, because those activities are really not within a normal compositor's scope. That said, Blender provides a way to retexture a CG mesh in post-production through the use of the UV pass and the Map UV node to retexture a mesh according to that mesh's UV map (Figure 10-30). As a compositor, you don't need to know how to unwrap a mesh, but you may be called on to retexture a mesh in post-production. A UV map is a texture that picks a pixel from a 2D image (bark, in this case). So, you could say that this node distorts a 2D image according to a UV map into a 3D space. If animation and modeling is complete but the texture painters are running a little behind schedule, you can start the rendering process. Then, when the painted textures are available, you can retexture them using this node. You may have to use the ID mask and pass index to pull a mask for each object in the scene that you want to retexture.

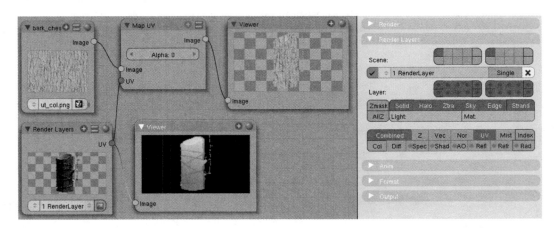

Figure 10-30. Map UV node

Rotate

Objects often aren't aligned straight, or you may just want to angle them for a dramatic effect, as shown in Figure 10-31. Degrees go counterclockwise, so negative degrees spin the image clockwise.

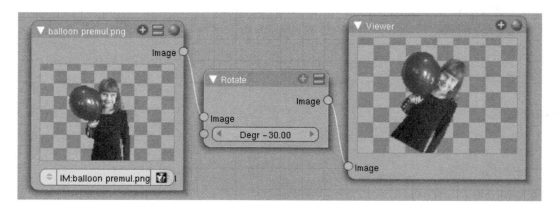

Figure 10-31. Rotate node

Scale

This node zooms in on or shrinks an image by a relative amount (think percentage) or makes the image a fixed size (resolution) and stretches/shrinks the input image to fit, both options as shown in Figure 10-32. When you initially select Absolute, the XY values are the size of the scene's Render Format panel settings (the size of the output image). Another option is to scale the image to a percentage of the screen (render) size.

Figure 10-32. Scale node

Translate

When an image is brought into the compositor and mixed with another, it is (without translation) centered over the other image. When compositing images that align, this is fine. However, you may want to composite an element that is of a different resolution (size), or you may want to put the image somewhere else. The Translate node allows you to shift the position of an image in pixels (Figure 10-33). X is left/right, Y is up/down, positive and negative, respectively. The figure shows the image shifted right and down.

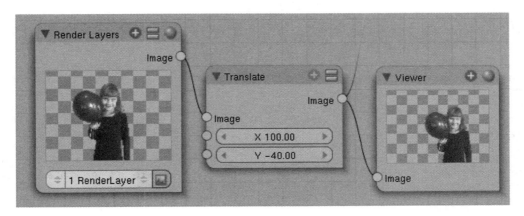

Figure 10-33. Translate node

Shake, rattle, and roll

So far, you have seen some rather simple examples of using these nodes, but the world isn't so simple. Let's get a little creative and see what we can do to combine these nodes to do some real damage.

First, we want to create a 3-second clip for TV broadcast for North America, so we click the NTSC preset button in the Scene Render context in the Format panel. Next, we set an end frame of 91, since 3*30 fps is 90 frames duration.

In the compositor, start with a 2K image so we have some pixels to work with by adding an Image node and loading the Antgua SHD.JPG image from the lib/images/places folder.

We want to crop out the railing, but by how much? To find the answer, load the image into the UV/image editor by selecting it from the active image list, and then drag your mouse around to get an XY coordinate of where the lower-right corner of the image should be. (1600,250) seems good to me, so enter those numbers in the Crop node for X2 and Y1.

Now that we know the width of the image, we need to compute how many pixels high we can go without stretching the image. We know that NTSC is a 4:3 aspect ratio and 1600 is our X, so we divide that by 4, giving us 400. That is the scale of the image from our input to our output. We do not want the image to be distorted, so 3×400 is 1200, which is how high we want the image to be. Since we are starting at 250, click into the Y2 field and enter **250+1200**. Blender calculates the Y crop to be at 1450. Since Blender's numeric fields can evaluate expressions, you could have just clicked into Y2 and entered **1600/4*3+250**.

> *Any number kind of field in Blender can accept a number or a formula. This is handy, especially for those of us who hate calculators. Be warned, though: if you enter only integers, you get a whole-number result. If you want a decimal result, like 1/3, you must enter 1./3 or 1/3. (with the period) to get a fractional (decimal) result of 0.33; otherwise, you get 0.*

Now we have our cropped image. Figure 10-34 shows you frame 91 and the completed noodle that zooms in on the image. I use an S curve here to simulate an amateur zooming in—they start by not pressing the zoom button hard enough, then overcorrect, and finally back off to a gradual finish. I feed this as the XY values to the Scale node, and thus the Scale node scales in from 0.45 to 1 over the 90 frames.

In making this the final composite output, we run into our first problem. When making the final output, Blender takes the image in process and selects the middle-out pixels for the final image. Without scaling, we get a middle "piece" of the image, not the whole image. To get Blender to use all 1600 pixels in the composite output, we have to scale the 1600×1200 image down to 720×480. To get this, we add a Scale node, and enter **720./1600** into the X and Y fields of the Scale node, which Blender tells me is 0.45. I then enter that as the Y1 clipping value in the Time node (so that the image starts out properly scaled) and adjust the curve as shown to give a zoom progression that mimics a hand-operated zoom—fast at the beginning and then slower as it nears completion.

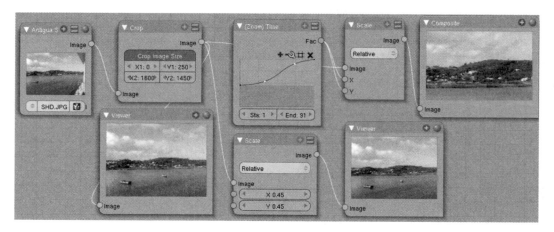

Figure 10-34. Zoom noodle frame 91

Note the mismatch between what the viewer shows you and the composite output shows. The viewer effectively ignores the zoom and rescales whatever pixels it gets to fit in its little display. The composite matches the resolution of the fed image to what you have specified in the Scene Render context in the Anim panel, pixel for pixel.

Then, in Figure 10-35, we add a little translate and rotate at the same time to zoom in on a portion of the image. This little bump gives it a handheld feeling. I did have to use the Math mode to change the 0-1 values into -.5 to .5 and then multiplied that by 50 to make a 25-pixel shift and by 5 to make a 2.5-degree rotation. The final video is in tut\render\antigua shake.mov, and the blend is in the Shake scene of the tut\nodes-distort.blend file.

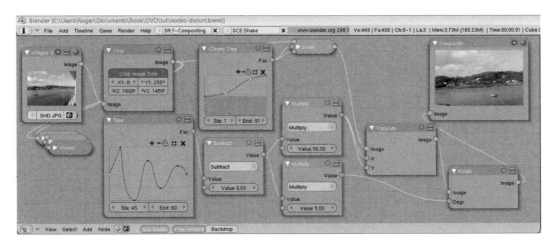

Figure 10-35. Zoom noodle frame 47

Later, we will a little blur to that shake to make it more believable.

Format conversion

As I discussed in Chapter 4, there are more than enough image formats to go around for everybody, so you might find yourself needing to convert an image or video from one format to another. You can perform image conversion quite simply using the compositor. Let's walk through a few examples.

One image to another

Using just the image input to the composite output, you can convert any image (still or movie) from one format to another. As I noted earlier, the only thing you have to be concerned about is image resolution so that you end up taking the appropriate amount of pixels. If you want to grab the whole image, use the Scale node's Screen Size scaling option. Figure 10-36 shows how to convert that 2K JPG image to a 640×480 PNG image.

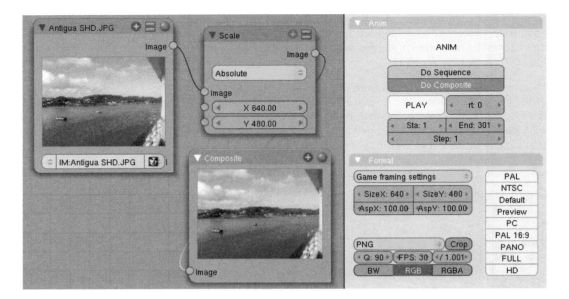

Figure 10-36. Converting to PNG

Note that the input image, Antigua SHD.JPG, in your images\places folder is 2025×1513 (you can find this by dragging over the upper-right corner of the image in the UV/image editor). If you find the lowest common denominator between those two numbers, you get 4 and 3. This is called the image's *aspect ratio*. If you take 640 and divide by 4, you get 160. If you multiply 160 by 3, you get 480. Therefore, a 640×480 image is also in a 4:3 aspect ratio. So, these two images are in the same aspect ratio (4:3), just at different resolutions (sizes).

One medium to another

An HD movie is in a 16:9 aspect ratio and is displayed on a TV with square pixels (the pixel width to height is at 1:1 ratio). An NTSC TV screen is in a 4:3 aspect ratio and has rectangular pixels at a 1:1.1 ratio. So, to convert an HD video to show correctly on a TV, we have to use a noodle and the format settings shown in Figure 10-37. In that figure I grabbed part of my compositing window to show you the noodle and also the buttons window Scene Render context to show you the format settings.

Notice that the scale Y, instead of being 480, is actually 480/1.1, or 436. When shown on a TV or official TV monitor with its elongated pixels, the image will be back to its correct aspect ratio.

The image in your Render panel may look a little squashed on your computer monitor, but that is because your computer monitor uses square pixels.

You may note that, separate from the resolution and pixel issue, I have changed formats. I am reading in a QuickTime .mov file but writing out an AVI JPEG file.

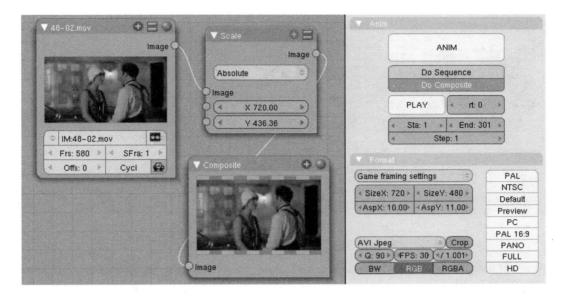

Figure 10-37. HD to TV

To change the frame rate of a video, you have to use the Speed control in the sequencer to alter the speed. In this case, if the video was shot at 24 fps, rerendering it at 30 fps will make everyone move too fast, like they need to switch to decaf. To maintain the proper duration of the action, the video should also be resampled to 30./24 or "stretched" in time by 1.25.

Cropping and letterboxing

Letterboxing is where you preserve the original aspect ratio of the media but put a black box to fill in unused areas of the medium. An example letterbox was shown in Figure 10-37. Because we scaled the entire width of the image, we had fill in the top and bottom. Blender does this automatically, and you will see a checkered background in the composite node.

Cropping is where you cut out the top, bottom, or side of an image so that it fits the size you want. If you cut off the sides of an image, you change its aspect ratio. For example, HD is a 16:9 aspect ratio, meaning that it is 9 pixels high for every 16 pixels across. HD comes in many different resolutions, such as 1280×764 and 1920×1080, but all those different resolutions are all in the same ratio, namely, 16:9. Normal TV, however, is in a 4:3 aspect ratio, such as 720×480. Operating on the theory that the left and right edges of an image are pretty useless since most or all of the action happens center frame, we can crop off the left and right sides and take only the middle for our final image.

Figure 10-38 shows that HD movie, 1248×702 10:10 pixels, cropped for TV at 720×436 10:11 pixels. 702/3=234, which is our "zoom" factor. 234×4=936, which is our desired width. (1248-936)/2=156 pixels need to be cropped from the left and right sides of the input image (assuming we want only the center). Shooting with a little wider angle does give you the option (in post-production) of moving the center of the image slightly in case the camera was not "dead on" by using the translate node.

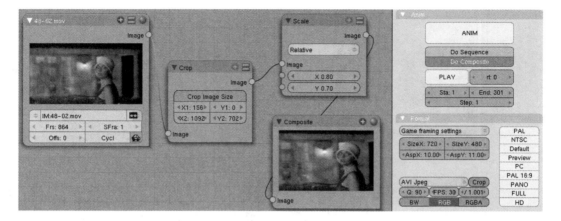

Figure 10-38. Cropped HD for TV

As a final note, some DVD authoring software will convert to the proper pixel aspect ratio format for you automatically.

Upscaling and downscaling

You cannot (realistically) convert a TV image to HD, because there are more pixels in either direction. However, you may want to rebroadcast an old reality show or sitcom over an HD channel. You need to either letterbox the old TV, rescaling for those square pixels, or stretch the image and blur what is in between. Stretching is called *upscaling*. Refer to Chapter 12 for more information on the Blur node. *Downscaling* is when you take a higher resolution image and scale it down. Figure 10-36 is an example of downscaling an image that was 702 pixels high down to 480.

When I upload a video to YouTube or Vimeo, I render in HD 1280×720p to the QuickTime container using the H.264 codec, with a GOP of 60 and an FPS of 15. This produces a file that meets the file size limitation, but with great quality. YouTube and Vimeo go through their downscaling, and their conversion preserves much of the clarity and quality but allows webcast streaming. Other settings/formats result in blackness after conversion or horrible quality.

Summary

In this chapter, you dove into nodes, learned how to get images into and out of the compositor, and learned how to do basic manipulation of the images within the compositor. In the next chapters, you will learn how to fully exploit the compositor by using different and more powerful nodes to make special effects as well as take corrective actions to improve an image or video. Next up, fill up your noodle plate with more useful nodes!

Chapter 11

MANIPULATING IMAGES

Chapter 10 scratched the surface of Blender's node-based compositor, and you saw how to bring images into and out of the compositor—from images, dynamically, or statically from a CG scene (via the Render Layer node or a multilayer `.exr` file, respectively). You also learned how to use the distort group of nodes to make basic image transformations. This chapter examines many of the wondrous things you can do to an image, alone or in conjunction with the 3D view and other functional areas of Blender.

Color nodes

As discussed in the last chapter and in Chapter 4, an image is a combination of channels that provide some net color that you see when mixed together. Therefore, Blender has a bunch of color nodes that allow you to mix, overlay, and combine these channels and other images. To add these nodes to your noodle, press the space bar with your mouse cursor in the node editor window, with compositing nodes (the face icon enabled on the header) in use (click Use Nodes in the header). In the Add menu, browse until you see Color, as shown in Figure 11-1.

As with all nodes, when you select one it is threaded to the currently selected node for you (if the selected node has a matching socket). Let's examine these color nodes. The order of presentation in this book is based on my judgment of the most simple to the most complex in this group.

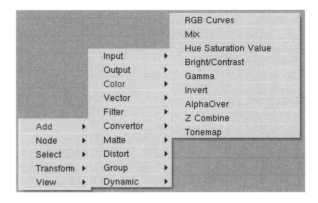

Figure 11-1. Color node menu

Invert node

This node inverts the color of the image's pixels, turning white to black, red to cyan, blue to yellow, and so on, making a negative of the image. A common use for this node is shown in Figure 11-2, which is taken from the Peach simple_blends\ compositing\comp.blend Frankie group, a group of nodes used to provide consistent color correction to Frankie, the flying squirrel. In this case, we want to use the mask of Frankie as a basis with which to add on ambient occlusion, so we need to start with a black Frankie, not a white one, which is the normal alpha channel mask.

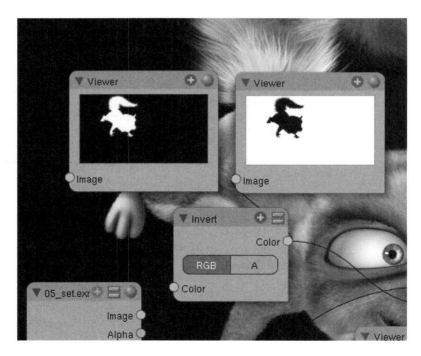

Figure 11-2. Invert node

Bright/Contrast node

This node, which is the most basic adjustment, raises and lowers the average value of the pixels (brightness) and adjusts the difference between black and white (contrast). You usually want to adjust both equally. Raising both makes the whites whiter and the blacks blacker, making an image more dynamic (great for main objects of interest). Lowering both subdues an image, making it less dramatic, which is great for backgrounds (see Figure 11-3).

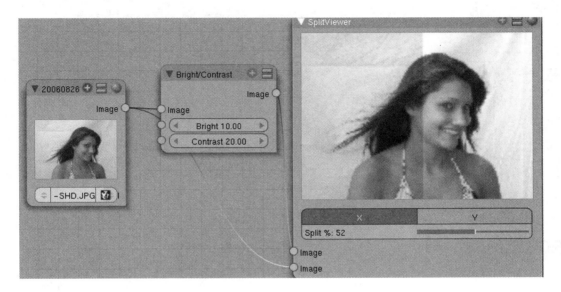

Figure 11-3. Bright/Contrast node

Gamma is a color brightness adjustment that changes CG renders to make them look more like they were taken with a camera, more "natural," or simply as expected. A computer monitor is not perfect, so it introduces some luminance distortion called gamma. Gamma is also encoded into pictures you take with a camera. The issue is that the Blender compositor and renderer compute colors in a linear, nondistorted fashion. To mix the two, you need to use a linear workflow. In this workflow, you convert all gamma-corrected images and textures to a linear luminosity before performing linear operations on them, such as brightness/contrast adjustment or mixing, and then gamma-correct the result just prior to saving (routing to the Composite Output node). Use a gamma of 0.45 to linearize an image and a gamma of 2.2 to encode it. You should adjust your CG lighting so that the final output of the gamma of 2.2 provides an appropriately lit element. You will then have to match the camera distortion (refer to Chapter 6), saturation, and contrast that reflects the real-world lighting conditions and camera quality. In tut\nodes-gamma.blend and shown in Figure 11-4, I've linearized the image with gamma of .45 before increasing saturation. I did not linearize the render layer because it is CG and already linear, but I did have to brighten it up. After compositing using the AlphaOver, I gamma-correct the result.

Gamma node

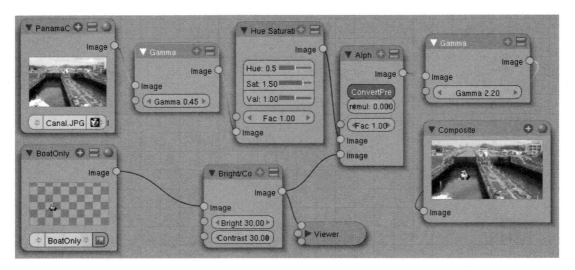

Figure 11-4. Gamma node

RGB Curves node

You will often want to adjust the saturation and value of a whole image (and/or its red, green, or blue colors). This node expands your control over the Bright/Contrast node by giving you a continuous band-value adjustment. If the Bright/Contrast node and Invert nodes are similar to a tone control knob on a radio, the RGB Curves node is a 100-band equalizer with a mixing board thrown in.

You can control the overall combined image by selecting and working on the C button; each of the R, G, and B channels by selecting the R, G, or B buttons; and remap the color spectrum using the level sockets. You can apply this adjustment to the whole image uniformly by setting the Fact: value or portions of the image by using the factor socket.

> *Increasing the red values of an image makes it look angrier and more dangerous, whereas blue makes it look colder. Reducing blue brings out yellow, which is warmth and love.*

This node has four input sockets. The Fac socket controls how much the curve affects the input image. The Fac socket can take a fixed value for a uniform application of the curves to the image, or a mask that defines where in the image the curve is to be applied. The bottom two sockets change the basis for what is considered true black and true white, respectively. For example, if you set the White Level to a shade of gray, any pixel that is that shade of gray (or whiter) will be turned white in the output, effectively brightening the image. Conversely, setting the Black Level swatch to a shade of gray (or tint) will turn pixels of that shade to black. In Figure 11-5, both black and white have been altered, and the S curve dramatically alters the colors in the image. You normally do not use the curve this way; I did this only so you could see the difference that this node can produce.

Figure 11-5. RGB Curves node

The shape of the curve determines how the input is mapped to the output. In Figure 11-6, an S-shaped curve takes lower X values and maps them to a lower Y value output, whereas upper X values are mapped to a higher Y value. This curve therefore expands the contrast of the midtones of the image.

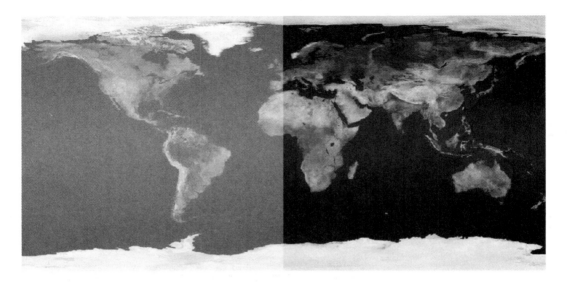

Figure 11-6. Rescaling black from original 0.0 (left) to a gray of 0.2 (right)

You can rescale the hues of an image by using a color instead of gray. Figure 11-7 shows other effects of changing the curve for various channels and levels. Going clockwise, the following appear:

1. Bright.Down: I dragged the right endpoint down in the combined channel, so all whites in the image become darker,

2. Scale.Black: I rescaled Black Level to a shade of gray, resulting in the deepening of all colors.

3. Lush Tropical: I rescaled Black Level to a dark shade of red, so any reds in the image are shifted down (less visible), thus bringing out the green and blue.

4. Contrast Up: Working on the blue channel, I curved the input so that a little blue become more blue, while still retaining the ends of the spectrum the same (bringing out the blues).

5. At the bottom, a love scene filmed at night has issues with contrast and emotion. So white is remapped to gray, which makes gray into white and expands the range, and decreasing blue brings out the warmth of yellow.

I *love* this node because it gives flexible control over any color in the image. Please experiment with this node using any of the images in your DVD library folder, threading the image socket to this node, as shown in the figures.

You can feed the factor socket from a Time node to animate the application of the node to the image(s) over time. As another example, if you feed the socket a normalized Z-buffer value, the effect will affect objects farther away from camera (or vice versa, depending on how you normalize the Z-buffer). If you feed it a texture, as when you used a spherical blend, it will have more effect in the middle of the image than at the outside edges (or reverse, if you invert the texture).

Figure 11-7. Four examples of channel adjustment and rescaling. World texture courtesy of James Hastings-Trew. Gatsby image courtesy Rob Collins Productions.

AlphaOver node

One of the most frequently used nodes in compositing is the AlphaOver node. In its simplest use, the AlphaOver node puts one image over another based on the foreground image's alpha channel. When the foreground image's alpha channel is less than 1, Blender blends in the foreground image that is fed to the bottom socket. As shown in Figure 11-8, the upper image of the field is the background, and the image of the characters is in the foreground, which feeds the respective sockets to the AlphaOver Node.

Figure 11-8. AlphaOver node

Note two things. First, recall the discussion in Chapter 9 regarding premultiplication of the alpha channel times the color value. If the images you are using are premultiplied, enable ConvertPremul control to get rid of that outline and enable the images to blend seamlessly.

Second, the factor controls how much of the foreground image (color and alpha) is mixed on top of the background. A value of 1 means the full strength of the image fed to the bottom socket (100 percent of the alpha channel of the foreground is used to blend 100 percent of the foreground's color over the background, and that pixel gets the color and alpha value of the foreground image. Values less than 1 fade the foreground image.

> *On all mixing nodes that have a factor socket and two input sockets, 0 for the factor takes from the top socket, and 1 takes from the bottom socket. If the factor is fed a texture or image, black takes from the top socket, and white takes from the bottom socket.*

It gets a little tricky when you use a number or mask/texture to feed the factor socket. If the factor is 0, the alpha channel of the top socket (background) is used; if it is in between, the two are blended to determine what mix of foreground/background to use.

Seeing ghosts

A neat "ghost" effect can be achieved by using a factor less than 1, as shown in Figure 11-9. In this case, a factor of 0.4 takes only 40 percent of the foreground pixels and mixes them over the top of the foreground, so that you can "see through" the foreground. Use the AlphaOver node to make something materialize or fade in from nothing, such as popping in a bucket of cash or (in the classic example), engaging the transporters to beam Dr. Spock to the surface.

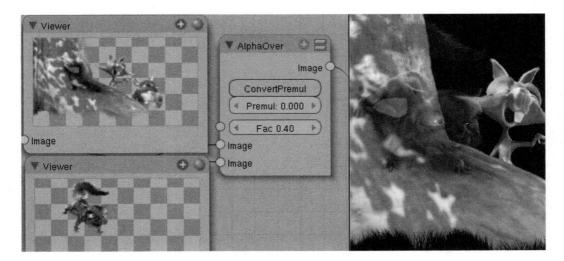

Figure 11-9. Ghost rig

Mix node

This brings us to the general-purpose Mix node, which is appropriately named because it mixes the images from the two sockets in the ratio specified by the mode and the factor. The factor is like all other factor sockets: 0 is the top socket, and 1 is the bottom socket. Unfortunately, that's about where the simplicity ends because this baby has more than a dozen different mixing modes (see Figure 11-10).

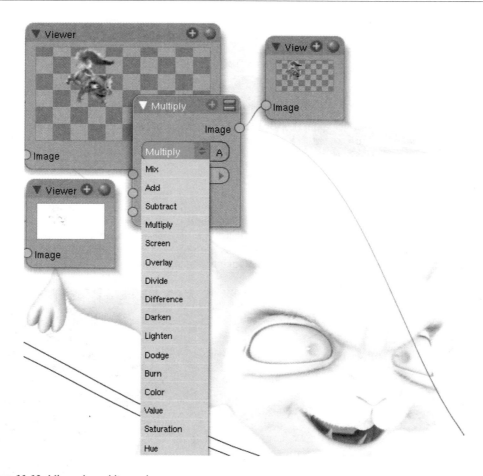

Figure 11-10. Mix node and its modes

Mix mode is usually sufficient to blend two images by using the factor mask to determine the relative weights between the two images. Enable the A button to use the alpha channel values of the foreground (bottom socket) image when mixing. In fact, using a mask as the factor, you can control which colors are chosen for the composite output. A more advanced use of the Mix node is to enhance images, as was shown in Figure 11-10, in which the colors of an image are multiplied by a grayscale to give the image more contrast in selected areas. The amount is based on the ambient occlusion pass. This use of the Mix node gives the image more pop by giving Frankie some mascara around the eyes and darkening his mouth.

Color math

The math functions of add, subtract, multiply, and divide perform what I call *color math*, which is traditionally taught in art using a color wheel. A color that you see can also be thought of as a combination of red, green, and blue. The color called *yellow* is actually red and green added together in even amounts, as shown in Figure 11-11.

Likewise, if you take that yellow and subtract out all the red, you get back to the green. Subtracting different amounts of red (50 percent shown in the lower-right example) gives a different shade of green. It is still green, just darker.

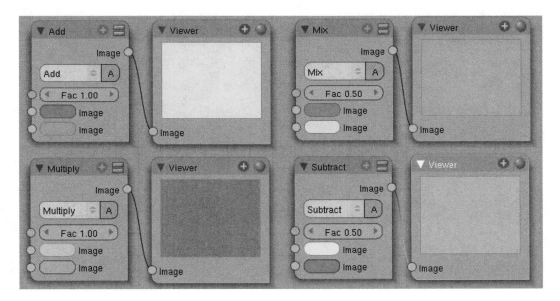

Figure 11-11. Color math using the Mix node

Hue, saturation, and value

Another common way of looking at color used in compositing is the concept of hue, saturation, and value (HSV). A *hue* is the base color—green in this case. The *saturation* refers to how dense the color is, and *value* refers to how bright the color is. The Mix node has HSV modes as well, so you can adjust any of those channels independently, as shown in Figure 11-12. Shifting hue with green, for example, adds a green tint. Increasing saturation of a color deepens that color. Increasing value by a color adds that color to everything, brightening in general but also emphasizing that color.

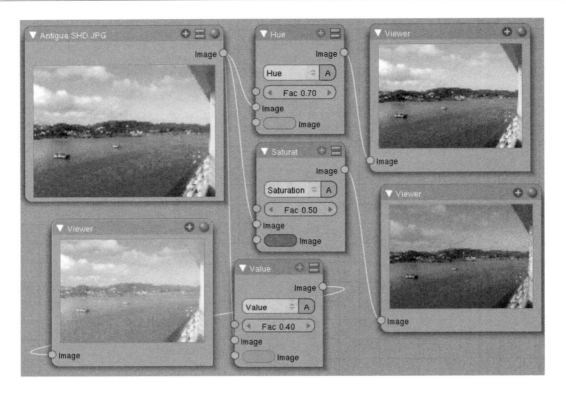

Figure 11-12. HSV mixing

Dodge and burn

I lived in a darkroom in college, and have dodged and burned and pushed all those neat and wonderful things with real paper, negatives, and fixer. Ah, the good old days of waking up to the smell of fresh fixer in the solitude of the red room.

In the old days, you would use a small round circle of paper taped to a straw. During the exposure, you would wave the circle over areas of the negative that you wanted to "dodge," which would make it darker because it got less light. Conversely, you would hold your hands together, making a circle with your thumb and fingers touching, thus masking most of the image but allowing light to pass through and "burn" the image into the paper. Because this area got more light, when you developed the paper, it would be darker and look charred or "burned-in" with more saturation. For the benefit of old-timers, the Mix node has dodge and burn modes as well, shown in Figure 11-13.

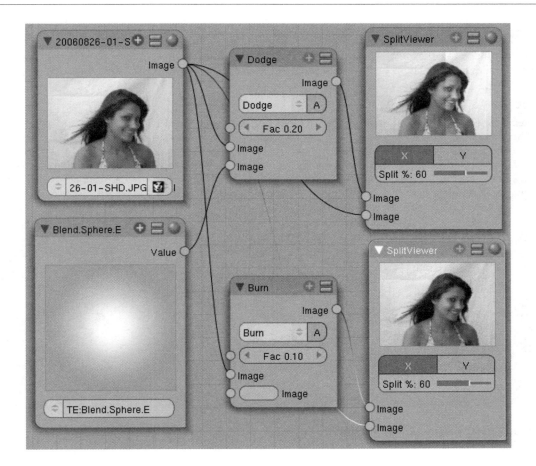

Figure 11-13. Dodge and burn

I just made a quick Blend Sphere texture and transmitted it into the compositor via the Texture node to control the dodge, making it more intense in the middle of the image. (It was already centered; if it weren't I would have to use the scale and offset vector sockets described in the next chapter.) In the burn example, I used a colored bulb to burn in the reds, giving a sunburned (or embarrassed) look.

Handy techniques

So let's blend together what we have learned into other useful techniques: adding sepia tones, making some fades and transitions in the compositor, and adjusting an image for CMYK printing.

Sepia

Sepia tones can make an image very warm by mixing orange (red and half green) into the image. In Photoshop, you add red and add yellow. Because yellow is red and green, you are really mixing lots of red and a little green, which nets orange. Because we associate yellow with the sun, our brain thinks "warm sunny tropical beach—ahhhhh happy," and we get a warm relaxed feeling when we see yellow tones (or any variant thereof) added to an image. Sepia is commonly added to black-and-white images to simulate fixer fade and to make them more pleasing, as shown in Figure 11-14. Add them to a picture of your loved ones.

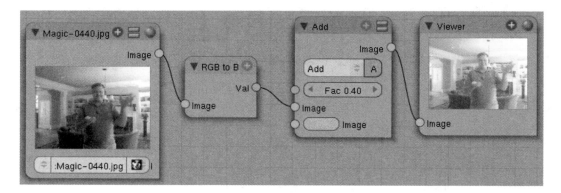

Figure 11-14. Sepia tones

Fades and transitions

Although the VSE is normally used to splice video segments together, you can use the Mix and Time nodes to cross over two video streams. Figure 11-15 shows a noodle to fade the video stream in from black over 30 frames and then crosses that over to the next video feed in frames 120–150. The second video uses the offset value so that the node starts pulling the first frame of the clip at frame 120.

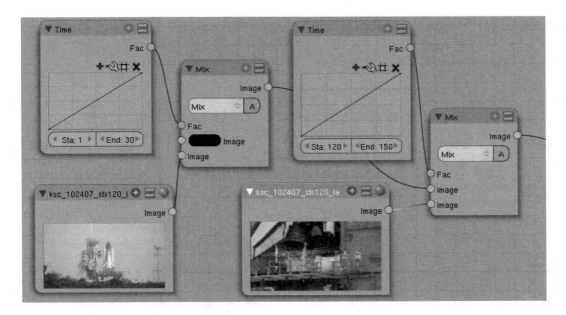

Figure 11-15. Fade and transition noodle. Footage courtesy NASA.

Adjusting for print: CMYK

In offset printing, inks of four different colors are mixed to produce a color on white paper: cyan, magenta, yellow, and black (CMYK). Cyan is an even amount of green and blue. Magenta is an even amount of red and blue. Yellow is an even amount of red and green. You can see how we just recombined the same RGB colors were recombined and then black makes the color darker. With ink, if it is more watered down, it has less color per drop, which is called saturation. The amount of ink applied to the paper, and the porosity and drying characteristics of the paper (mostly affected by how much white clay is mixed in with the fiber), determine the vibrancy of the image. If more ink seeps into the paper fiber, it blurs more with ink right next to it (muddies), and is less visible to the eye. So, if you are using Blender to prepare images for printing, and you get back your proofs from the printer and the colors don't look right, you can use these Mix nodes to bring out any particular color. They might not look perfect on your monitor, but they will print correctly.

Z Combine node

Recall that the AlphaOver node combines images based on the pixel's alpha channel value, and that the Z channel refers to the distance from the camera. The Z Combine node merges images based on their actual (in the case of a CG scene) or supplied Z value. If one pixel is closer to the camera than another one, it is picked (there is no mixing of the two pixels together).

The Z Combine node allows you to stack and combine images, as shown in Figure 11-16. The top part of the figure shows the noodle in which I use two different images with the Z buffers (taken directly from the render layer or saved in an OpenEXR image): one of a globe and another of a cage. To put the globe in the cage (and have the back bars of the cage occluded by the globe), I use the Z Combine node and then use AlphaOver. As long as coordinate systems and scales are coordinated, you can have one person model one object, another person the other, and then combine them in post-pro, as if they were in the same CG scene.

One big warning when using the Z Combine node: Z channel values are not anti-aliased, averaged, or blurred. If you rely exclusively on Z Combine to build your composites, you might see "stair-stepping" aliasing in the final product. To combat this, render at 2x resolution and downscale to do your own anti-aliasing, blur one image and remix, or use Blender's unique full-screen sample anti-aliasing (FSA).

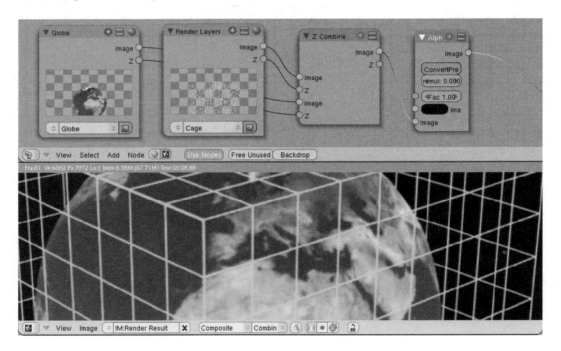

Figure 11-16. Z-Combine

Full–screen sample anti-aliasing

Let's look at a practical use of full-screen anti-aliasing (FSA) (introduced in Chapter 9). Normally, you use oversampling anti-aliasing (OSA) to get rid of render-aliasing (stair-stepping), and everything is fine. However, when using Z Combine to combine objects, normal OSA might not be enough to get rid of the aliasing that results. To solve this and other problems, Blender offers FSA. To enable FSA, first enable Save Buffers and enable Full Sample in the Output panel, as shown in Figure 11-17. The normal OSA button then changes to FSA. A comparison of the OSA image is shown in Figure 11-17. Note the black pixels around the cage where it is overlaid when using just OSA.

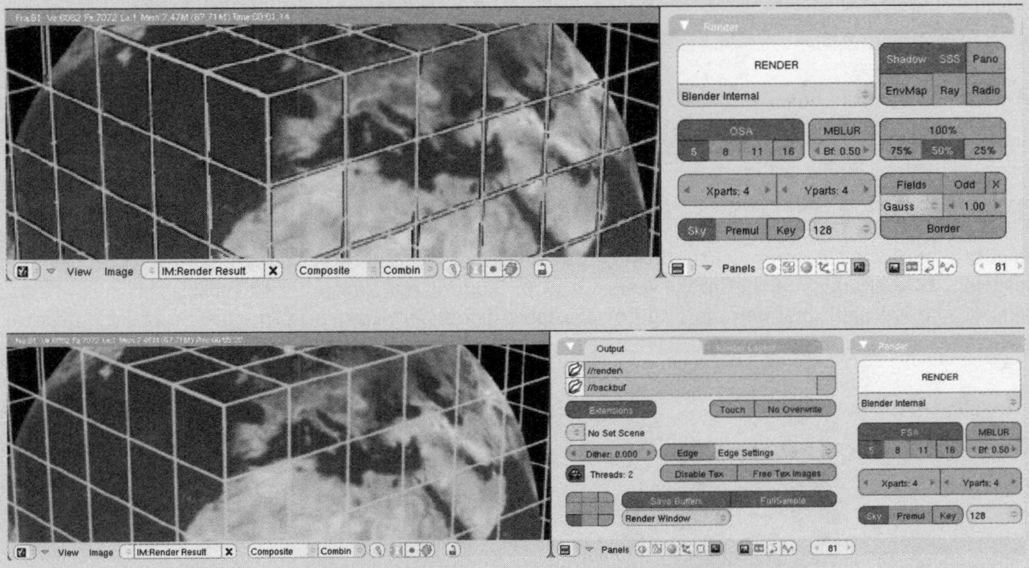

Figure 11-17. OSA is insufficient (above) and with FSA is fine (below).

Tonemap node

The OpenEXR high-quality image format provides a huge range of colors using 32-bit numbers for each pixel. Because there is such precision, there are many different colors, and an image can contain pure black to pure white—the whole range of colors with a high degree of fidelity, capturing very subtle differences in color. Therefore, these images are called high-dynamic range (HDR) images. Digital cameras that can take (and Blender can render) these HDR images are on the market now. Images with a lot of contrast can look great on high-contrast devices such as motion picture screens, but look overblown when played on monitors and other normal viewing devices. To convert these HDR images for normal viewing, use the Tonemap node shown in Figure 11-18. This node is programmed to process images captured the R/D photoreceptors and also provides a Ph Simple tonemapping algorithm. (Refer to Chapter 6 for more information.)

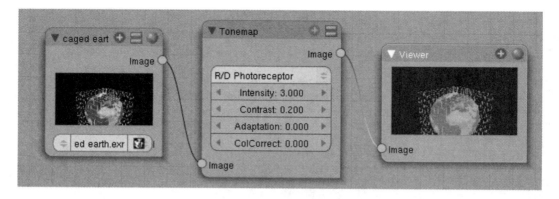

Figure 11-18. Tonemap node

Conversion nodes

Very often, you will see an image that is nice but not great. Sometimes making a subtle (or dramatic) adjustment to a channel of the image makes it pop. Blender has a number of nodes that convert an image into constituent channels, and add or change channels, so that you can work on them individually. These nodes are lumped into the Convertor group, shown in Figure 11-19.

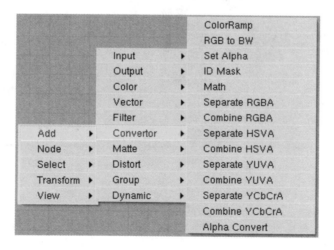

Figure 11-19. Convertor node menu

RGB to BW node

This simple node converts a color image to its black-and-white counterpart, with shades of gray between. I used this node back in Figure 11-14 to convert the color image to a grayscale prior to colorizing it. Blender can do this conversion automatically in some cases; for example, piping an RGB image out through an output socket of one node into an input socket that is expecting to receive grayscale (for example, the factor socket) will automatically convert the incoming image based on the red channel values. However, that can be risky, and it's always best to thread in this node to perform the conversion.

Set Alpha node

This node sets the alpha channel value of the image. Use this node to override (or create, in the case of .jpg images) an alpha channel. By default, the alpha value is 1.0. In Figure 11-20, I use the alpha channel of a mask (which we created in an exercise in Chapter 5, pulled in from the 3D View through the Render Layer node in the figure) to be the alpha channel of the base .jpg image. The output then is shown in the Composite node, which shows the checkered (alpha 0) background.

> Be sure to enable RGBA and choose a format that supports the alpha channel (refer to Chapter 4) when saving your composite!

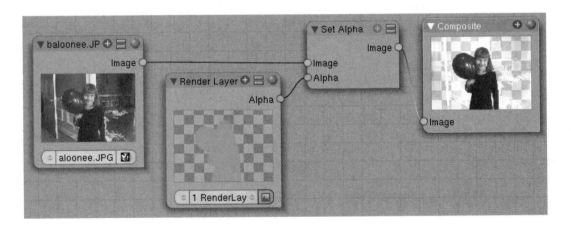

Figure 11-20. Setting Alpha node

Math node

When working with image channels, especially the alpha and Z channels, you may need to cut them in half, scale (multiply) them up, or add an offset to move them in virtual space. To do this, use the Math node. The node has two inputs and an operation selector (see in Figure 11-21). This example shows how you can multiply two masks together, thus taking away the grass in front of the tree.

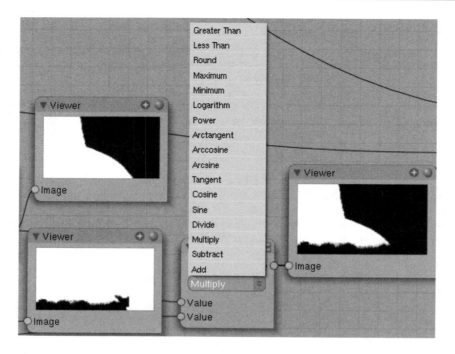

Figure 11-21. Math node can combine masks in creative ways.

All the popular math functions are supported, and I know you are just itching to dig out your calculus textbook and look up that arctangent function. The Math node is very useful when working with, say, the Z-buffer. I have used the Round function to give a retro look.

Minimum mode passes out the minimum value for a pixel between the two sockets. Looked at another way, it sets an upper bound and only passes values no higher than the minimum. If a pixel has a value higher than the value set in the second socket, the second socket value is passed on. Maximum does the opposite: the socket that has a higher value gets passed on (for that pixel).

Using Math to use watermarks

The term *watermark* goes back to the days of making paper. Manufacturers marked paper with a subtle yet identifiable logo and/or name to denote that the paper came from them—sort of like built-in advertising and a "quality-so-good-I-sign-my-name-to-it" thing. In today's competitive world, with piracy issues abounding, artists might want to watermark their images in case they have to prove ownership. So, the goal is to embed some distinguishing mark without degrading the image. You can accomplish this by using the nodes you have learned thus far. The first step is to encode the water-mark in the image. The second is to decode the watermark from (what we think is) our image.

Encoding a watermark

To encode a watermark, first you need the mark itself. In Figure 11-22, I am pulling in a subtle word from the render layer, but this could be your logo or a copyright notice. I am embedding the word over a building, so I rotate and translate it to be over a background skyscraper. The mark is a pure black-and-white image, so the Divide node scales it down to .05. That image is then added to the original image using another Math node that is shown collapsed in the figure.

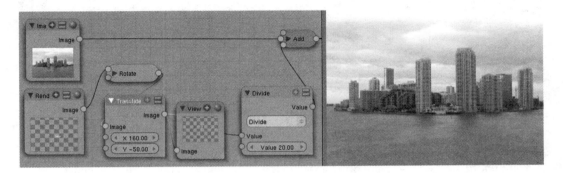

Figure 11-22. Encoding a mark in an Image

Your mark must not be a reflection or naturally occurring feature or texture of the building, and cannot be construed as a naturally occurring artifact. You need to ensure that the only conclusion a judge or jury could come to is that it must be man-made and added by the artist during post-pro. You want to add your mark to an area of the image where it is less likely to be noticed.

Second, you should use something that uniquely identifies you (or your company) as the copyright holder. Of course, you must be the copyright holder and you must be prepared to defend your rights (it gets expensive, believe me). Next, the image must have no other conflicting marks. So if you mark an image of a guy in a Nike baseball cap, and you don't have the right to publish its mark, and so you have introduced a conflict that clouds your ownership. Assuming that you have not made any mistakes, the image must be yours because it has your mark. You have the right to license that art as you see fit.

You could encode the mark in the alpha channel, but if the culprit simply resaves the image as a .jpg, the alpha channel is lost. It is best to encode the mark directly into the image itself to avoid the counter-argument that you added that channel to *his* image.

Decoding a watermark

So you've stumbled across an image that you think is yours. What to do? Well, in this example, someone might have been standing right next to me when I took the picture and happened to take the same photo. To see whether this is my image, you have to find the un-watermarked (original) image in your library and take the difference, after accounting for any image manipulation (translating, contrasting, and coloring) that might have been done. Figure 11-23 shows the noodle you need to construct that uses the Mix node in difference mode to show you the differences between the two images that when multiplied clearly reveal the mark. Notice that the difference initially is all black to the naked eye; only when those differences are magnified can you see that the image had been adjusted, but not enough to remove the mark.

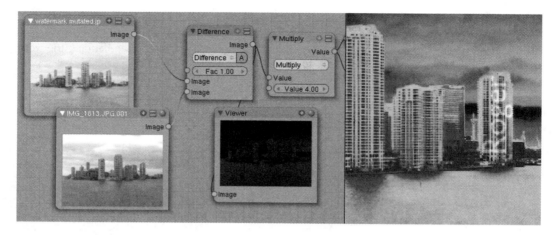

Figure 11-23. Decoding an image to find a mark

It might not be necessary to mark every image in the video; you could mark the beginning, middle, and end. Your case is stronger if you mark certain images from a keyframe because you can then show prior evidence of such a registration, policy, and practice. Disclaimer: I'm not a lawyer; I'm just a technician, so seek legal advice on protecting your intellectual property from a competent authority. However, if you want to mark your video and images as yours, Blender is certainly capable of helping you do that.

Alpha Convert node

This node converts premultiplied images to keyed, and vice versa, restoring proper color values or premultiplying them. Certain other photo-processing packages expect images premultiplied; others expect keyed. Use this node to convert your image to the desired format.

ColorRamp node

Ramps are available all over in Blender, and the compositor is no exception. Recall from Chapter 7 that you can assign a material to an element, which consists of a primary diffuse and specular color (and a whole bunch of other stuff). Well, that diffuse and specular color does not have to be a single color; it might be a range of colors. The same holds true for textures. Although we usually tend to think of procedural textures as a black-and-white pattern of some sort, you can use color ramps to make them a range of colors. Within the compositor, the ColorRamp node allows you to convert any number or image pixel value from one value to another. I talked about the ramp control in Chapter 7 when I discussed the blend texture, and this node is the same control, just in node form. I use this node and provide examples in the next section.

Separate/Combine channel nodes

When dealing with live action film, each shot may be filmed under different light conditions. So in post-pro two shots that are supposed to go back to back (or even edited to be interspersed) might have a different coloration that needs to be corrected. Previously, I talked about the Bright/Contrast node, which takes care of different light levels, but there also might be a shot where the quality and coloration of the light is different.

At the other extreme end from "correcting" color is "pushing" the color from live action. The most extreme example I can think of is *Sin City* (Frank Miller, Robert Rodriguez, 2005) starring Bruce Willis and Jessica Alba. The film pushed the limits in many areas, including color adjustment of the live action film. Actually, for that film, *adjustment* is not the right word; *dramatic redux* might be a better term. When working in CG with either abstract or artistic intentions, you also open up a whole range of possibilities. Some crazy music videos that feature massive eye candy, interspersed with highly stylized and pushed images of the band come to mind, such as "Tripeace," featured on MTV; "Je suis venu te dire que je m'en vais," by Liqueur Brune/Gainsbourg from the album *Liqueur Brune*; and "Arms of Marianne," by Pete Teo.

To support correction and artistic pushing, Blender has a family of nodes that support individual channel separation and manipulation for every colorspace, either directly or indirectly:

- RGB: red, green, and blue—the three guns used now in CRTs
- HSV: hue, saturation, and value
- YUV: luminance, with U and V as values between -.5 and +.5 (the EU broadcast standard)
- YCbCr: the new HD image transmission format that better supports how LEDs show color (Cb is chrominance in the blue direction; Cr in the red direction)

The YCbCr space is shown in Figure 11-24, and any UV coordinate can be seen as a color, with a Y value supplying the strength (value) of that color. I used a vertical blend to stimulate the Cb (blue chrominance) and a horizontal blend to stimulate the Cr (red chrominance) channels, thus providing all possibilities for a fixed luminance value.

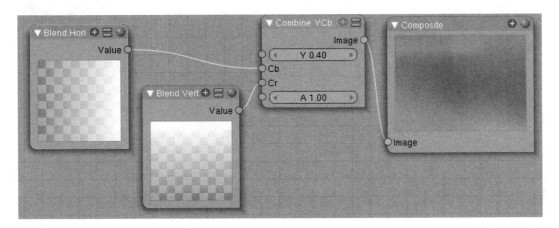

Figure 11-24. Visualizing the YCbCr space

All the Y-series formats support a separate channel that addresses how bright the pixel is. Studies have shown that the eye is most sensitive to changes in luminance, so you can often make an image better just by tweaking this channel. Figure 11-25 shows a common rig I use to work on each channel, just by changing the interpolation modes or adding additional color steps in the color ramp.

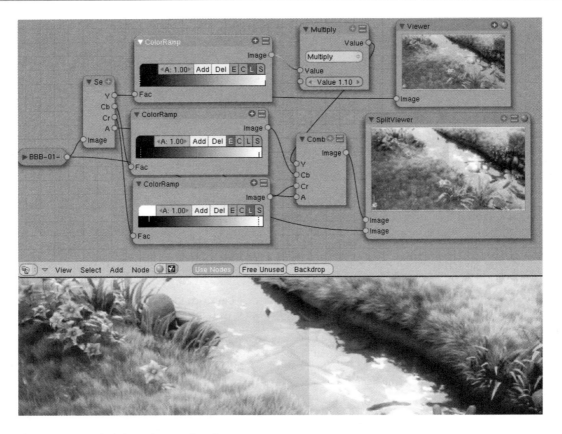

Figure 11-25. Typical channel separation rig

In this example, I examined the dynamic range of the image by threading the luminance (Y) channel to a viewer node, and dragged my mouse over areas of the UV/image editor. I saw dark blacks, but the highest white I saw was .85. So, I threaded in the Multiply node, entered 1/.85, and Blender then told me that multiplying the luminance by 1.15 would make that channel full range. Then I changed the blue chrominance (Cb) channels to be an exponential transition from the normal linear. This has the effect of increasing color contrast and dynamic range. I also compressed the CbCr channels slightly by grabbing and pulling the end value markers toward the middle of the ramp. In Figure 11-25, the original image is on the left; the right side shows the result of the fiddling.

Of course, these changes are just slight adjustments. Try shifting down the Cb and pushing the Cr to give it the blues. Remember the Mr. Freeze scenes from *Batman and Robin* (Joel Schumacher, 1997)? With these shifts, everything looks frozen and surrealistic, as shown in Figure 11-26.

Figure 11-26. Really pushing the channels

An even more flexible approach is to use a curve node to control the translation from input to output, shown in Figure 11-27. In this example, I wanted the sky to be bluer. So, I did two things; first a horizontal blend texture feeds the factor input, so any curve adjustment has more effect toward the top of the image. Then I connected the blue channel and curved that up, so that any blue that was in the sky would be enhanced. In the split viewer, I split the clouds. The original orange cloud is on the left, and the revised pink cotton candy cloud is on the right. Notice that I fed the horizontal blend texture to the factor socket. Without the texture, the whole image would be bluer, which would look colder and would not be the desired effect.

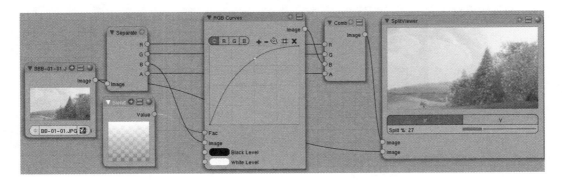

Figure 11-27. Curving the channels

Pulling an object's mask using the ID Mask node

Many times, instead of working with the whole image, you want to work on only one character or one specific object. Maybe it came out too red, or too dark, and although everything else in the scene is fine and well lit, that one object needs adjustment. Blender provides a way to pull a mask of just that object in post-pro, allowing you to isolate that element from the overall scene and adjust it.

The process for doing this actually begins during modeling, when each object that might need some post-pro is assigned a unique PassIndex number. This number is entered in the Object and Links panel prior to rendering. Figure 11-28 shows the selected object getting a PassIndex number of 315. While the initial thought for the aquarium to have a flat black finish, it was subject to change. So, when the model file was handed off to the compositor for rendering, I assigned it an index number just in case.

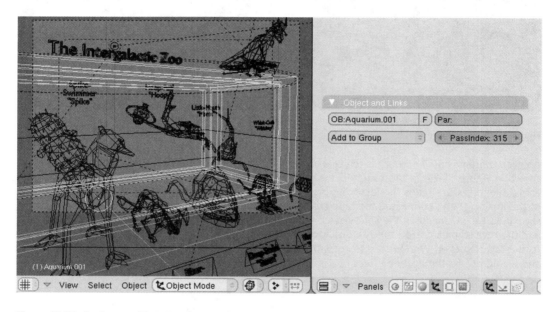

Figure 11-28. Setting up object IDs via PassIndex

It isn't strictly necessary that each object get a unique identifier; just those that might want to be worked on together in post-pro. For example, if you think you might want to recolor all text in a composite, you can assign the same PassIndex number to all text objects. Next, when getting ready to render the image, you have to do two things (see Figure 11-29).

- Enable the object ID pass for all render layers (pass button section, far right, top row)
- Render to a multilayer format to store the object ID pass

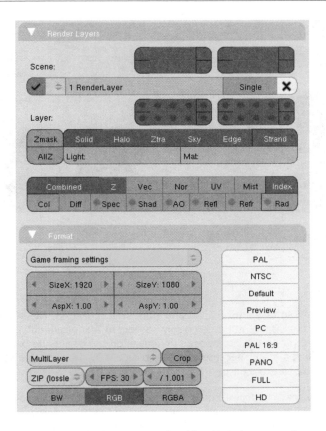

Figure 11-29. Setting up to render object ID: index pass and multilayer format

Now your render will be saved as a sequence of `.exr` files. In post-pro, you can pull the mask of just that object in the compositing noodle (see Figure 11-30). If the object is behind another object, the mask shows you only the pixels for that object visible in the image. The mask changes for every frame in the sequence. Because the ID Mask node produces an alpha channel, you can feed that to the factor input on an AlphaOver node to merge it back into the image or to the factor input on a Mix node, or feed it to the alpha channel of the composite output, and you will have extracted that object as an element to be used in future composites. Sure enough, black just wasn't dramatic enough. "What does red look like?" was the question. Without having to rerender the whole scene (and each frame), I was able to pull out just that element for recoloring.

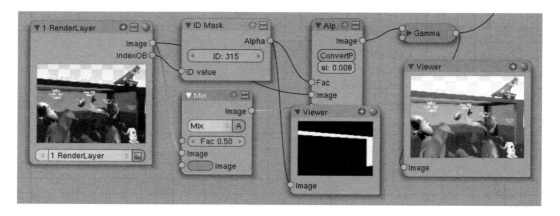

Figure 11-30. Using an object ID to pull a mask

Matte nodes

So far, we have seen how to take a pixel apart and work on its channels. The Matte nodes allow us to turn a pixel of the image transparent, based on some aspect of that pixel's color. Once transparent, we can then use the AlphaOver node to composite the image on top of a matte painting, or background. I call this process "pulling a mask" because I have to direct Blender to reach into the image and pull out a mask that I can use to extract a portion of the image.

Recall that with the ID Mask node we pulled a mask based on Blender's knowledge of that object. Here, we have to infer what an object is and what the rest of the background is, so it gets a little trickier. A little planning ahead of time goes a long way. As you will see, you can (and probably will have to) combine other techniques (such as masking) to eliminate other artifacts from the resulting element.

The most common use of Matte nodes is for green-screen or blue-screen conversion of an image into a foreground element that can be layered over a background matte. Blender provides four different nodes, each specialized to pull a mask from different kinds of matte images:

- Luminance Key node is based on the Y channel, or luminance of the image
- Channel Key node pulls a mask based on a range of values within the matte's channels
- Chroma Key node pulls a mask based on the image's chrominance values
- Difference Key node is based on a difference from the image and some reference color

The first three node titles should use terms and concepts familiar to you. You used the difference mode of the Mix node to examine the differences between two images. You played with the luminance (Y) channel of YUV and YCbCr images to make them more brilliant and have a wider dynamic range. Finally, you mapped the chrominance values of the new HD transmission standard. These nodes extend your understanding of ways to manipulate the pixels of an image and build on what you already know. A fifth node, Color Spill, gets rid of any green or blue that might radiate onto the actor's clothes or props from the background screen.

You can string these nodes together to progressively build up a good mask; possibly using different nodes to pull different parts of the image and then build the masks back up together, as with the Math node in multiply mode. So if you use one node but aren't getting good results from just that one, consider using a few. The goal is to avoid having to keyframe and match move each frame; instead program Blender to figure it out for you.

Luminance Key node

Let's start with the simplest Matte node, the Luminance Key node, which chooses foreground/background based on a simple range of brightness values. Many stock photos have a white or black background, and you can pull a great mask in about two seconds using this node for those kinds of images.

Start with a new compositing desktop, and add an Image input node, a Luminance Key node, and a Viewer node. Click Load New in the Image node, and load lib/images/NASA/STS030-77-059.JPG from the DVD, which was taken by NASA as yet another spectacular sunrise occurs in space, and is included on your DVD for educational purposes (as are all NASA images). Because we are keying the black out, set the High luminance very low by barely nudging the slider, or clicking on the value and entering 0.1 and pressing Enter. The result is shown in Figure 11-31.

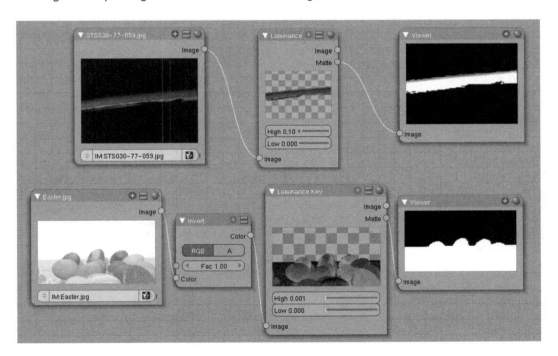

Figure 11-31. Pulling a matte by keying on Luminance. NASA photo courtesy of NASA.

I also included another example in that figure, keying an image with a white background. You key on a white background by inverting the image before keying, as shown. This is an image (on your DVD under lib\images\Things) as Easter.jpg and is from an HD video that I license through http://www.iStockPhoto.com. Many stock photos on that site and elsewhere use this white background. Please notice that the High setting is 0.001 and this pulls a good matte. Too high of a high, and you will start losing pixels that you should keep. This image is now ready to be saved as an element for use in a springtime ad over a garden or blue sky background matte.

Channel Key node

The Channel Key node has two parts: channel set selection and channel value settings. First, you have to look at the image and figure out which set of channels provides the best differentiation between background (to be turned alpha 0) and foreground (kept):

- RGB
- HSV
- YUV
- YCbCr

When you select a channel set, you then pick one of those channels to be the one that discriminates the mask. Then you set the range of values to be keyed. At this point I usually hook up a viewer to the Image node so that I can drag round in the UV/image editor to see the RGB values. Any value for a color in this channel higher than the value you set will be keyed 100 percent opaque (white in the matte). With the Low slider, any color pixel that has a color channel value lower (beneath) that value will be keyed transparent (black). The resulting matte is, depending on your settings, a pure black-and-white mask or a gradient.

Let's try an example—you can paint my car! First, select a well-ventilated area to work in—your office should do nicely. Next, start a new Blender session, switch to the compositing screen, and add an Image input node to the compositor node editor window. Load a picture of my Viper from lib\images\things\Viper.jpg. Thread in a Channel Key node, and thread a viewer out from the matte socket (it will want to connect to the image, but we are more interested in the matte). Duplicate the viewer node (Shift-D), move it over, and connect it to the image output socket. Your UV/image editor should now display the Viper picture, assuming that it is set to display the results from the active Viewer node.

If you drag around inside the UV/image editor, you will see that my baby is *red*; no matter where you drag over her body, the red stays at 255 (1.0) on the top of her hood, and gets down to about 0.4 near her front wheel. So, select the red channel of the Channel Key node and then set High to 0.90 and low to 0. You should be pulling a beautiful gradient mask of just the car body, not the red-bricked house behind it, as shown in Figure 11-32. Now we want to use this mask to take out the red and put in whatever color we want. Therefore, we need to invert it. When we do, we now have a "positive" image with a black background and white (gray) reflecting the intensity of the red. If you drag over this positive, you will see values in the range of 0 to 0.7. Therefore, if we divide this image by 0.7, the result will be a matte with values between 0 and 1 (a full range). Your math teacher just thanked me for reminding you that any number divided by itself is 1.

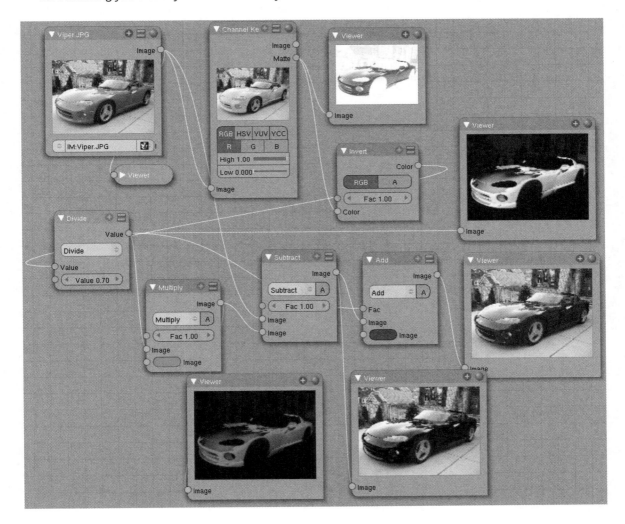

Figure 11-32. Pulling and using a mask by keying on the red channel

Now let's use this full-range mask to repaint the car, first by taking out the red and then adding whatever color we want—I'm considering midnight blue. Take the red out, as the Visine commercial says, add a Multiply node, and use the dropper on the bottom socket to sample a bright red color from the image, threading the gradient to the top socket. Thread the output to another Subtract node bottom socket and thread the original image to the top socket. This node then subtracts the result from the original image. Because the matte output is black where there is no car, the original image is unaffected where there is no car. If you thread another viewer to the output of the Subtract node, you should be left with a black Viper. If you drag your mouse over the sleek black body (careful—don't scratch her!) in the UV/image editor, you will see that there's plenty of red, green, and blue color there, but because it is evenly balanced our brains tell us it is black (or some shade of gray). Thread this to an Add Mix node to mix in whatever color you like, using the gradient mask as a guide to the factor of the node.

Difference Key node

The Difference Key node is just like the Channel Key node, but it allows you to set a tolerance around the three channels, and the three channel values that you are trying to mask out is set by a Key Color swatch. As with the Channel Key node, you pick your channel set and then set tolerances for each of the channels. Falloff is the gradient range for the mask; use it to get partial alpha values, especially when keying hair.

As an example, let's choose a real challenge: lib\images\People\Rebe\20060826-01-SHD.jpg, which features a white sheet wrinkled with sidelight shaded blue. As you can see in Figure 11-33, you can daisy chain two Difference Key nodes, with the output from one Difference Key node feeding into the next one, each with slightly different shades of the background (pick one sample from the left; the other from the right using the eyedropper when you click on the Key Color swatch). This technique progressively builds up the matte.

Now you have an issue, however. Because the swimsuit was a shade of blue, the Difference Key is also pulling it as a matte. To get the swimsuit back, make a quick Bezier circle and add the Render Layer alpha channel with the matte (using the maximum mode on the Mix node), further building up the matte. It then pulls a perfectly clean mask.

This exercise shows how you can combine multiple nodes, together with a mask from 3D View, to provide an excellent solution using Blender.

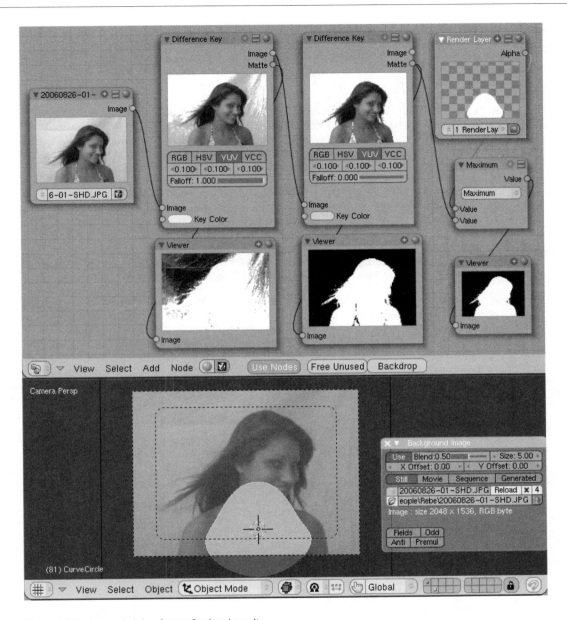

Figure 11-33. Daisy chaining for professional results

Chroma Key node

Ah yes, the green screen. In most green screen situations, the screen does not cover the whole lot or back stage, and just a portion. You can either create a quick mask, like I did in the previous node, or use the crop function to crop out the rigging.

Use an Image node to load lib\images\robcollins\green.mov, which is a green screen shot for a TV commercial. Thread it into the Chroma Key node and matte it out to a viewer. As with all the other Matte nodes, it has an image area to show you the keyed image with alpha. Click the Key Color swatch and then click the Sample eyedropper in the popup color picker. Select a color of the green screen, close to his body.

To check the keying, thread the image output to the *bottom* socket of an AlphaOver node, leaving the top swatch/socket white. Threading the output to a viewer, you should have a good key with just the default settings!

Acceptance sets the deviation from the color swatch that is keyed, cutoff sets a minimum, and you can lift (brighten) the background and gain (multiply, enhance) the background. If you are shooting green screen outside, shadows may fall on the green screen itself; use Shadow Adjust to compensate.

Finally, you can see that the shot was wider than the green screen itself, so you have to crop the image. If you drag over the upper-right corner of the video, you will see from the displayed XY coordinates that it is a full HD 1920×1080p movie. The screen covers the entire vertical dimension of the screen, so Y2 should be 1080. You have to eyeball X1 and X2; 300 and 1600 work well for me. The finished result is shown in Figure 11-34.

As with all these results, thread the final result to the Composite node and render at your desired resolution. If keeping the alpha channel, be sure to enable RGBA in the Format panel and use an image format with the alpha channel.

Figure 11-34. Chroma Key and crop for a one-stop shop

Deinterlacing with Blender

Recall from Chapter 4 that broadcast TV transmits frames of video in either interlaced or progressive scans. Modern cameras that film in "progressive" mode do not interlace the video, but older cameras do interlace the video. With interlaced video, each frame is either an odd or an even set of scan lines. When the two are combined into an image, you see the whole image. However, where there is motion, one set of lines will be 1/30th of a second later than the other, as shown in Figure 11-35.

Figure 11-35. Interlaced footage showing horizontal scan line differences

When you film in a TV studio in front of the green screen, you get footage like that shown here. While interlacing provides a natural motion blur for the eye, it wreaks havoc on digital processing filters (such as Matte nodes) when trying to figure out where the "edge" is.

Before processing interlaced video, you should convert it to a deinterlaced frame sequence first. Then pull in that sequence using the Image input node, pull the matte, and save it as a post-processed deinterlaced frame sequence.

To reinterlace the video, select Field/Image of 1 in the Image input node, load the sequence, and deselect Fields in the Scene Render panel. Blender will read in two images files for every frame, but write one image for every two frames, combining them per the even/odd setting. We discussed fielded (interlaced) images in Chapters 4 and 9, so consult those chapters for more info.

Summary

This chapter covered three sets of very useful nodes for adjusting an image's color; converting and combining images; and pulling mattes from green screen, blue screen, white screen, and any old screen in between. I hope I've given you some interesting examples, hints, tips, and techniques along the way to effectively use these basic nodes in your workflow. Now let's move on to the next chapter, in which we get fancy with even more nodes for image processing.

Chapter 12

ADVANCED NODES

Now that we have covered the basic effects that can be accomplished using the compositor and nodes, let's take a look at some advanced postprocessing techniques. In this chapter, you will learn about the vector and filter sets of nodes, explore some techniques using these nodes, and learn how to hide complexity (and allow reuse of noodles) through node groups. At the conclusion of this chapter, I am very pleased to highlight and explore the work of a very talented artist, Robert J. Tiess, and dive into the techniques he used to create a stunning image using nodes.

Vector nodes

When something moves in the 3D view, it has a speed and a direction. The combination of the two is called a *vector*. A vector can be visualized as an arrow sticking out of the ground at an angle (as shown in Figure 12-1), where the speed is represented by the length of the arrow (called the *magnitude*), and the direction as the angle of the vector. This angle is defined within a coordinate system, which defines which way each of the three axes (X, Y, and Z) is oriented. You can describe the vector by measuring where the tip is in terms of its east/west direction as X, up/down direction (height above or below ground) as Y, and north/south direction as Z. If the sun were directly overhead and shining down on the ground, the shadow would be called its *normal.* With regard to images, in addition to computing the color of a pixel, Blender also calculates the vector of the object it represents, and thus also the vector of that pixel. We can use that information in the compositor. This vector information is sent through the Vec render pass.

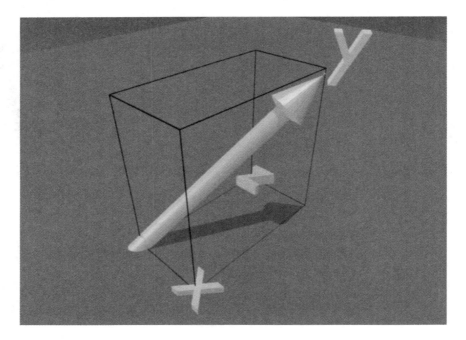

Figure 12-1. A vector and its normal shadow

Normalize node

Normalize is an engineering term that means to transform one set of values into another set of values that is easier to understand. The Normalize node does this for any range of values and greatly simplifies the problem of visualizing information that is out of the range of 0 to 1, such as the Z-depth buffer, or the speed of something. Figure 12-2 shows two very common uses for this new node in compositing.

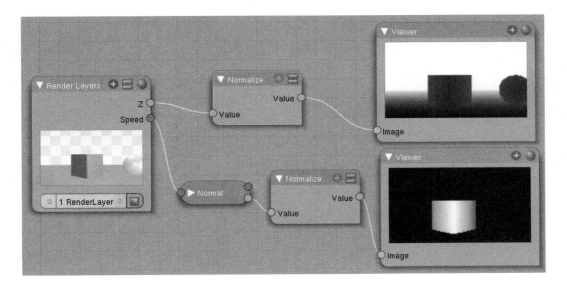

Figure 12-2. Normalize node in action

Using this node greatly simplifies the process of examining Z values because it intelligently scales "real" values (noninfinity) to a range of 0 to 1. In Figure 12-2, the alpha-zero horizon has an infinite range, whereas the ground plane extends back about 20 units from the camera. The node scales the range of 0 to 40 to 0 to 1, providing a nice gray-scaled image representing the distance of the objects from the camera.

In the second thread, the Speed vector is processed. This vector tells how fast, and in what direction, the pixels in the image are moving, which is essential to making motion blur and other very cool effects. Because Speed is a vector, you have to take the dot product using the Normal node (described in the following section). This node produces a modified vector and the dot product. When it is normalized, the cube is moving and/or spinning. You know it is moving because its pixels have a nonzero value. It is spinning because its pixels do not all have the same shade of gray; some are moving faster than others, which means it has to be spinning.

Normal node

The Normal node creates a vector (you saw a brief example in the Texture node discussion in Chapter 10). The easiest way to control the texture is to use a Normal node, as shown in Figure 12-3.

As shown in Figure 12-3, dragging the ball up "twists" the texture clockwise, and dragging it down or left twists it in the other direction. A slight change scales the texture to cover a broad area, whereas a large amount scales it to cover a small space. Try it in Blender by creating a wood texture for any material; then load the texture and normal node in the compositor, as shown.

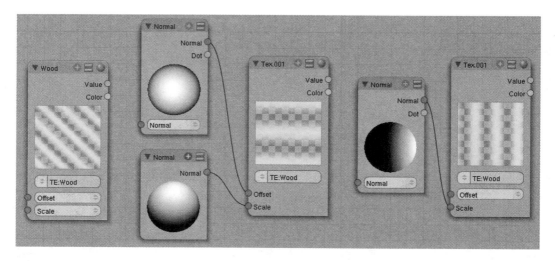

Figure 12-3. Normal node twists a texture.

Changing apparent light direction

Let's look at another neat use of the Normal node. If applied to an existing normal, using the ball control changes the vector direction of the surface normals, enhancing those that face in the direction of the ball. If the vector represents speed, the apparent direction of the object will change (although not the location from frame to frame, which would be an interesting special effect). If the vector represents the surface direction, those that face the same direction as the ball will be filtered higher (whiter) than the others. Consider the example shown in Figure 12-4, which can be found in the Normal.Lamp scene in the tut\nodes.blend file on your DVD.

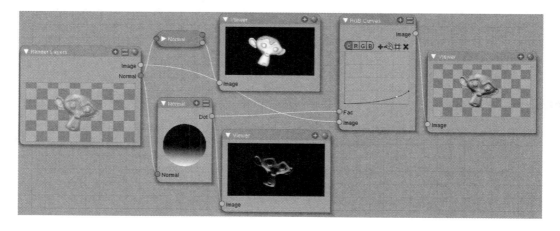

Figure 12-4. Normal node applied to surface normal

In this example, the Render Layers' normal pass was enabled, which provides the normal socket in the Render Layers node. Without modification, shown on the top branch of the noodle, the surface is evenly "lit" because most normals face the camera. In the bottom thread, however, the ball is dragged down, thus emphasizing those normals that face down. When we use that as a factor to the Curves node, the Curves node then affects those pixels that are bright. What does the Curves node do to those pixels? With the curve shown in the figure, the node darkens them. Thus, the pixels that are facing down (relative to the camera) are darkened. We perceive them as shadows (or uneven lighting) from an overhead lamp.

To make the effect extreme, we could have used another Normal, but this one emphasized the "up" normals and used nodes to brighten them. By brightening certain channels, we can recolor the image to look as if it were lit above by a red lamp, as shown in Figure 12-5.

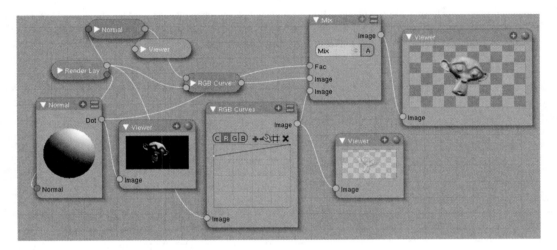

Figure 12-5. Dueling normals light above and below

In this noodle, I minimized the "shadow" normal branch discussed previously, and added another "highlight" normal branch that really cranks up the red. The Dot product (shown in the viewer node as a grayscale image) controls the Mix node by feeding its factor socket, taking from the shadowed image where the dot product is black, and mixing in the red image where the dot product is lighter (on "top"). The result preserves the shadows and adds a red tint on top of the monkey's head and eyebrows, making it look like she was lit from above her with a red light.

This is an example of tweaking the material or render in postprocessing to enhance the look of the image. Clients often want an image to be more dramatic, or even over the top, to see how "wow" they can make it. Blender's compositor allows you to make these kinds of changes here instead of fiddling with the lights in the 3D view and then rerendering.

Map Value node

Very often you will want to do something to a range of values: scale them, offset them by a distance, and/or clamp them to a certain range. The Map Value node is your true friend in these cases because it can perform all these functions in a single node. The node takes a vector or value range set, and then does the following:

1. Adds an offset (positive or negative)
2. Scales (multiplies) the result by a size
3. If Min is enabled, clamps the value to the minimum value entered
4. If Max is clicked, clamps the value to the maximum value shown

Clamp means to squeeze the value into the range. For the minimum clamp, if the value is below the minimum, the value is changed to the minimum value. A maximum clamp works the other way, preventing any values greater than the maximum from being passed on.

> *The Map Value node is also known as a band pass filter because it allows values to pass through that are only within a certain band, or range, of values.*

In the example shown in Figure 12-6, the Z-depth channel is processed. First, all the Z values are reduced by 5 (the offset is -5). The result is divided in half (multiplied by size 0.5), and any values outside of 0 to 1 are clamped to 0 or 1, respectively. So, let's say a pixel was only 3 units from the camera. (3-5)*0.5 is -1, which is less than the minimum of 0, so the value for that pixel would be 0. If the Z were 7: (7-5)*0.5=1, which is right at the maximum. Working through this math you can see that Z values between 5 and 7 are normalized to 1 (by being scaled by 0.5, or one-half, after the offset). Any values greater than 7 are clamped to 1. That result is passed on to the ColorRamp node, which then translates that 0 to 1 value range into a color. The resulting image helps you visualize the depth geometry of the object for those pixels that are between 5 and 7 units from the camera.

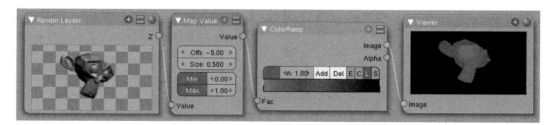

Figure 12-6. Map Value nodes selecting the Z range for false coloring

> *False coloring is often used in topography and geospatial applications. Generic or expected values, such as snow-capped white peaks to green valleys, are assigned based on elevation values, which is the Z-depth from a camera looking downward from a bird's-eye view.*

Filter nodes

There are many effective uses of blurred textures and images, and all the variations provide a powerful arsenal in the compositor's war chest. This section explores these different nodes, each of which provides some kind of blur or image enhancement. In addition, some of the nodes provide different modes or algorithms, thus providing a net of more than 20 different ways to enhance an image.

> *A word of caution in using filters is in order. Because these filters work on an image and really do not know anything about the underlying geometry of the things in the image, their results are determined by (and can vary based on changes in) color, lighting, and contrast. When working with a static image, a filter node that feeds a contrast node, for example, may produce a different net result than a contrast node feeding a filter node because the contrast node may bring out edges and changes that are then detected by the filter. Similarly, the edges detected in one frame of an animation may be vastly different from those in the next frame if the lighting or orientation of the objects changes between frames.*

Blur node

The main use of basic blur in compositing is to take your eye *off* the object being blurred. That way, the nonblurred objects are sharply in focus—easier for the eye to see and the brain to discern—and become the focal point of attention. Figure 12-7 shows the Blur node in action in Peach/simple blends/compositing.comp.blend, blurring a perfectly pretty matte painting used as the backdrop for a scene.

There's an old saying about matte painters being underappreciated; that their job is to paint a beautiful painting so that it can be all covered up (or blurred, in this case). I cringe when I look at this example because I know that each blade of grass (visible on the left) was individually computer-generated, only to be all blurred together. However, blurring the background matte image is a traditional way to achieve a basic depth of field (DOF) effect.

There are several algorithms for how the Blur node should combine the current pixel with the ones around it:

- **Flat**: even weight of all pixels in range
- **Tent**: linear falloff
- **Quad**: quadratic attenuation as the square of the distance; favors nearer pixels
- **Cubic**: weight falls off as the cube of the distance; sharper falloff than Quad
- **Gauss and Flat Gauss**: Gaussian tone matching helps blend values
- **Catrom and Mitch**: help preserve clarity and avoid aliasing patterns from emerging in tiled or lined images.

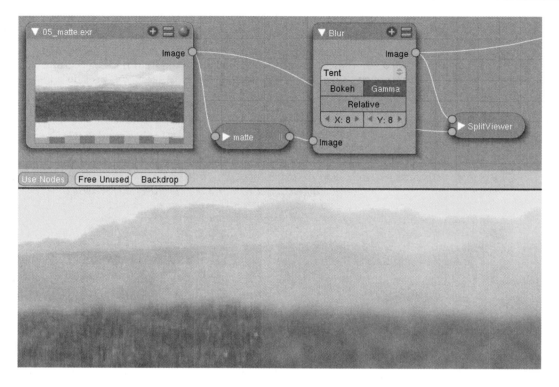

Figure 12-7. Blur node applied (right) to matte painting (left)

> It is said that Monet, who was very short-sighted, simply painted what he saw without his glasses, giving the impression of the scene. Having seen his painting Lilies at Giverny, I can attest to the beauty of huge mattes. Perhaps today he would be a matte painter.

Two features beneath the algorithm selection include Bokeh, which uses a circular type of inclusion/weighting that selects pixels in a circle around the selected pixels (not the square); and Gamma (shown enabled), which Gamma-corrects brightness as pixels are combined.

The area around each pixel to be blurred is set by Absolute or Relative terms. Relative is not enabled by default, and the X and Y values specify the actual number of pixels to be included in each direction in a grid-like fashion (unless Bokeh is enabled). If you enable Relative, X and Y specify a percentage of the image's dimensions.

Faking a focusing act

If you hook up a Time node to the size socket and invert the time curve, as shown in Figure 12-8, you see video that looks like the cameraman was using the focusing ring. This effect is handy for drawing attention to the object you want the audience to focus on, specifically because it literally is "coming into focus." In this case, I used the Relative mode to specify the blur radius. The Time node starts with a size value of 1 and reduces it over time to 0, eventually removing the blur completely, which looks as if the image has been brought into focus.

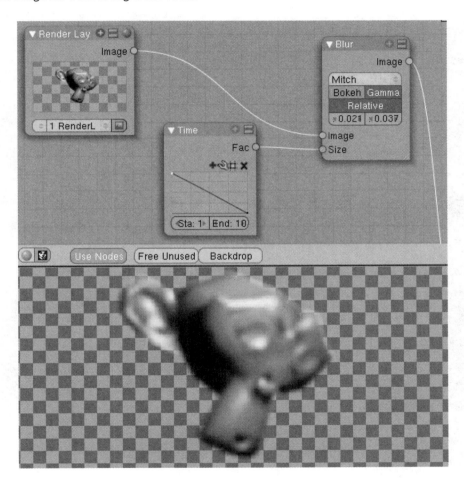

Figure 12-8. Blurring over time

Soften filter

If rendered with a high grain (or with each hair individually rendered), a fur coat may appear prickly in harsh light. The Soften filter softens the image, literally making the fur look soft and silky, as shown in Figure 12-9. The factor socket can be a universal number or a mask if you want to soften certain areas of the coat (or whatever object you are processing). Models' faces, especially baby faces, often get the Soften filter to blend out all those minor imperfections.

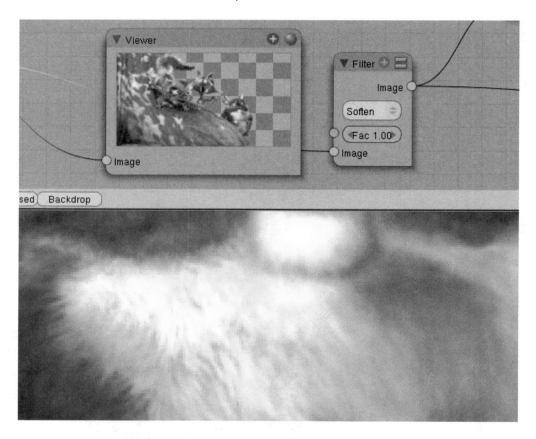

Figure 12-9. Soften hair (right side) to avoid a bristly look (left)

Sharpen filter

The opposite of the Soften filter is the Sharpen filter. Use this filter on anything you want to give a hard edge to, as shown in Figure 12-10. A little goes a long way—the sharpened portion on the right is overdone, but I want to clearly show the drama. This filter effectively increases the contrast between pixels.

Figure 12-10. Sharpen (right side, overdone for illustration) to enhance intraimage contrast

Laplace filter

When used with a low factor, this filter enhances the contrast over an area. Figure 12-11 shows the intelligent contrast enhancement feature, with a factor setting of 0.40 of a brightened elevator shaft image from *Elephants Dream* (Orange\production\lib\machine\elevator\elevatorshaft RdW. blend; the original is too dark for example purposes). Less lighting and using this filter with a distance blur gives a foreboding effect. If you reengage the composite noodle, you will see how to use the Laplace filter to enhance the contrast and give the idea that the light fades off as you recede into the shaft. Then use a Blur to blur those objects far away to give a depth of field.

The Laplace transform algorithm is named in honor of the mathematician and astronomer Pierre-Simon Laplace, who used the transform in his work on probability theory.

Figure 12-11. *Laplace with a 0.4 factor (right) intelligently enhances contrast.*

The other mode for Laplace is on a high setting against a fairly smooth surface with edges. In this mode, the Laplace transform is particularly adept at detecting edges. When properly applied and visualized, it produces a thin, pixel-wide border in which there is a high contrast. To get the effect of red at the edges, I used a Render Layer and overrode all the material with a flat gray color. The render, as shown, allowed the filter to clearly detect the edges. I then boosted it by a factor of 10, clamped, and cut it in half to use to feed the Mix node, which mixed in red where the edges were detected. This file is on your DVD as Orange\production\lib\machine\elevator\snarldoor RdW.blend. In the file, the door is animated to open and close like an iris; this shot is frame 281. So, in this example, you can use this filter to give a dangerous red tint to edges.

With all compositor files, once you open them, you have to press E to execute the noodle so it refreshes.

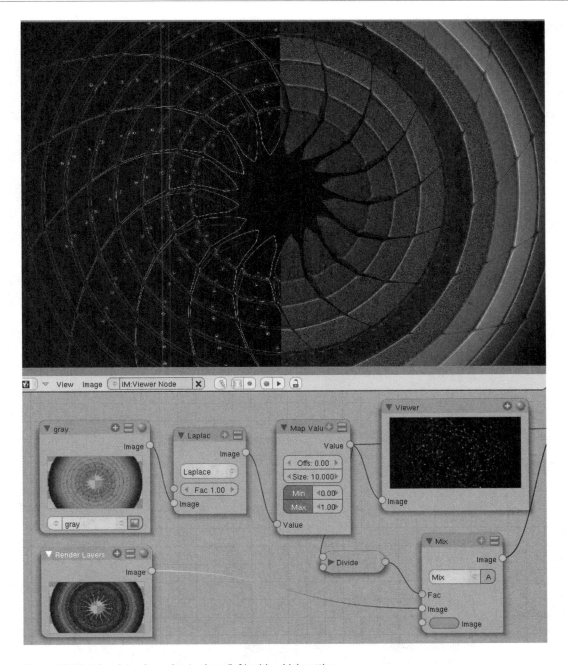

Figure 12-12. Edge detection using Laplace (left) with a high setting

Sobel filter

Continuing on the journey into edge detection, you'll now discover Irwin Sobel, a mathematician who formulated a wonderful equation that detects edges. In looking at the capsule in which Proog and Emo from the movie *Elephants Dream* are hurled into Proog's mindspace (available on your DVD in Orange\production\lib\machine\elevator\capsule RdW.blend), I imagined Proog's mind to be portrayed as a cold dark vacuum, so the capsule should look cold, as if it were frozen. But how? I knew that ice and coldness are conveyed through the color blue, but how could I portray the idea that the capsule was cold, very cold—maybe with bits of ice accumulating on the outer shell of the capsule in the nooks and crannies? Well, Sobel to the rescue (as shown in Figure 12-13), which takes the top normal image, applies the Sobel filter as shown, and adds in the blue where the Sobel tells it to, resulting in the bottom image in the figure.

Figure 12-13. Sobel edge detection above and applied using a Mix below

Prewitt filter

Edge detection in image processing is important to enable machine vision. Humans are excellent at detecting edges of things and recognizing shapes based on outlines. We think it is a key to perception and understanding. For a robot to pick out bad bolts from a jumbled bin, it first has to be able to detect edges. Figure 12-14 shows the Prewitt filter in use, enhanced through the Bright/Contrast node so you can clearly see the edges that it detects. In this example, I might use this pass, multiplied by a yellow color, to give an edge glow to the wires.

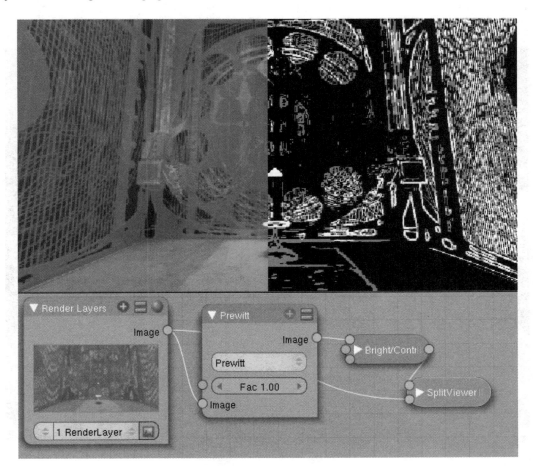

Figure 12-14. Edge detection (right) using the Prewitt filter

Your eyes immediately detect the table, lamp, and wires behind. With the Prewitt filter, Blender does the same. Practical applications for using this filter include adding a glint to the wires so they stand out more, instead of melding gloomily into the background. It sharpens the image for you, but just at the edges. You can render this image by pressing F12 after opening Orange\production\lib\machine\ telephoneroom\telephoneroom RdW.blend. Be patient, however, because it contains more than 5 million faces (it takes my poor little 2GB machine about 9 minutes to render).

Kirsch filter

Throwing caution to the wind, you now arrive at Dr. Kirsch's filter, which I think provides superior edge detection. As you will see at the end of the chapter, in an F1 image, this filter allows you to outline the edges of models, as used in cell shading. Another common use is to add a glint, or sharpness, to the edges of any image to make it pop out. Although Blender does have edge settings that draw an edge line based on geometry, it is good only for objects from the 3D view, and if you are working only with images, you don't have that information (the geometry). So using the Kirsch filter (as shown in Figure 12-15) gives an effect similar to enabling Edge when rendering, but in a postproduction environment. To reproduce this image, open `Orange\production\lib\machine\mach01\mach01 RdW.blend`.

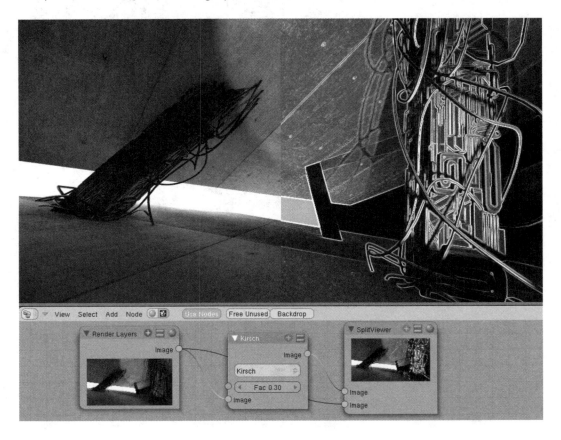

Figure 12-15. Super edge detection with Kirsch

Shadow filter

Last in the list of edge detectors is the Shadow filter. This puppy attempts to determine where shadows are in your image, allowing you to recolor or otherwise enhance them for more drama. Figure 12-16 shows the mach04 RdW render from the Orange files. On the right, white has replaced the shadows from the wires on the floor of the tunnel.

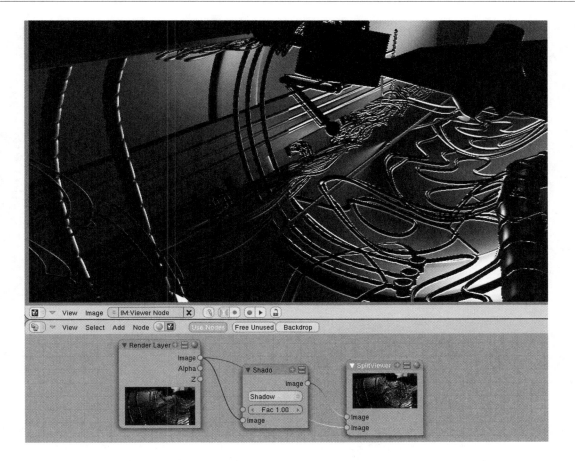

Figure 12-16. Shadow detection

Dilate/Erode node

Now that I have covered edge detection, let's talk about things you can do with that edge. As you saw in previous examples, you can use the edge to give a glint or coloration. The Dilate/Erode node is two nodes in one: it allows you to actually shrink or expand the edge. When you make a mask of an object in an image, you cannot match your mask exactly with the outline of the real object. When you are doing green screen, you might get some rim lighting around the edge where the object is colored a little green. Depending on your situation, you may need to shrink your mask by a pixel or two to get rid of any green haze. This is where you want to use the Dilate/Erode node, as shown in Figure 12-17. The left side of the figure shows the after-erosion, and the right side shows what it looks like without the erode.

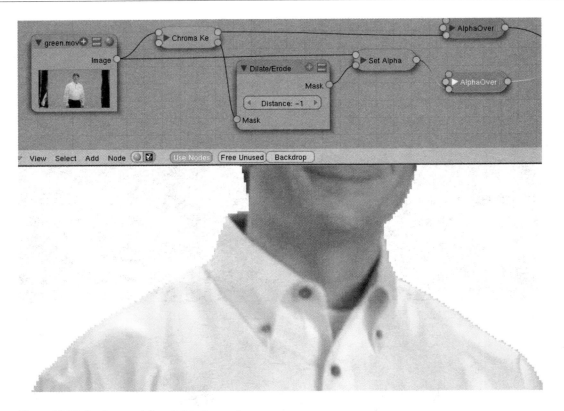

Figure 12-17. Erode a mask to get rid of green haze

In Figure 12-17, I used the Chroma Key node to pull a matte, but around his cheek and his shoulder, there is still one pixel at the border that has some green spill. So, I can use a Distance of -1 (see the Dilate/Erode node setting) on the matte output to shrink that mask. We use that mask output of the erode (I call it *erode* because the distance is negative) to set the alpha channel of the image, which means the AlphaOver node can be used to swap in another (in this case, solid white) background.

Glowing magic aura with Dilate

You can dilate a mask or just a channel to spread that object's/channel's influence onto neighboring pixels. This process creates a sort of glowing or pseudoradiosity effect, as shown in Figure 12-18. In this noodle, I dilated the green channel and then subtracted from the original to get just the edge border. The divide node is there just in case I want to tone down the effect, and it feeds a blur to give that glow. The glow is then added back to the original green, and now I have gamma-radiated eggs all aglow. Be sure to wear stretchy pants if you eat these for breakfast!

> *Use Erode to shrink the object's mask, blur it, and add it back to the object to make the glow look as if it is coming from within the magic orb, or crystal skull.*

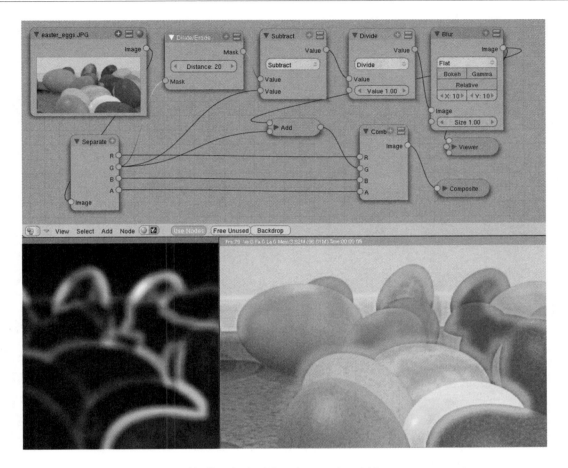

Figure 12-18. Hulking Easter eggs with dilated edge left and green glow right

A perfectly simple fake glow is shown in Figure 12-19. This technique adds a glow to any masked area of an image, so you can use it with any mask to add a glow to live action footage as well, just by match-moving the mask to the object you wish to glow.

This example shows a yellow Suzanne that is glowing red hot as a result of a mystical spell. This noodle brings together several concepts, so let's walk through it. First, the mask is identified with a PassIndex, as discussed in Chapter 11. In the Object buttons of the Object and Links panel, shown in Figure 12-19, I set the PassIndex to 1 for Suzanne. In the compositor, using the Object ID Mask node to process this pass, I get a simple black-and-white mask of where Suzanne is in the shot. A volumetric glow extends outward into the environment, so I use the Dilate/Erode node set on a fairly hefty 20-pixel positive dilation (this is a 640x480 shot). This node then expands that mask by 20 pixels. I find that a blur in the X and Y direction of twice the dilation gives a good smoothing. You can use more or less to indicate more or less dispersion. In this example, I wanted it to appear as if the surface were giving off the haze, not that the haze was emitting from the center. If I wanted that, I would use a higher blurring radius.

369

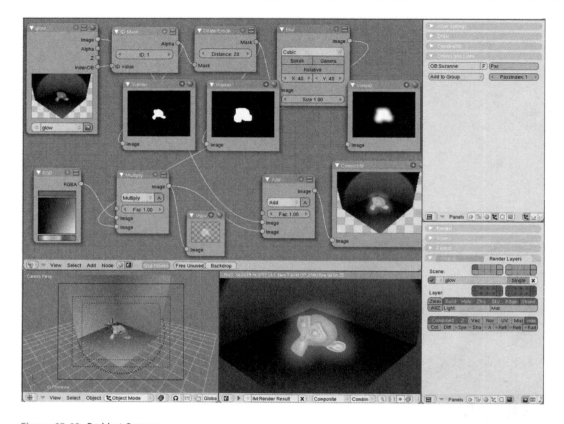

Figure 12-19. Red hot Suzanne

Depth of field with the Defocus node

When a real camera takes a photo, the light passes through a lens that has an iris to admit a certain amount of light. The lens causes some rays to be in focus at the backplane but rays for a different distance to be smeared. There is an imaginary plane that hangs out there in front of the camera that defines what is in perfect focus. Anything within a certain range or depth from the camera is in the field of focus, a.k.a. depth of field. As an object is closer or farther out of that field, its image gets smeared, or blurred. Photographers use DOF subtly (or extravagantly) to draw your attention to those objects in focus. In CG, there is no iris, so everything is always in focus. To simulate a real camera lens, we have to defocus the scene based on an actual or supplied Z-depth buffer, as shown in Figure 12-20.

Defocus node is a blur node in which the blur factor is based on distance from the camera. The iris on a real camera is formed by a number of overlapping plates, which form an *n*-gon shape, such as a hexagon or octagon; or for a perfect quality lens, a disk. Once you select an *n*-gon shape in the node, you can rotate that shape as well for ultra-subtle differences. Gamma Correct allows the blur to be corrected for differences in brightness.

Figure 12-20. Defocus node (right) using Z of actual 3D view (left)

The node can work with an actual Z-buffer from the CG scene or not, but it can also work if given a Z-depth map of some sort (see the following sections for ideas on making a Z-buffer). If you're defocusing a scene that is being rendered in Blender (or some other program that exports Z information), you will have a depth map to work with. Otherwise, you have to make one.

371

The next control on this node is an fStop. The fStop on a real camera sets the size of the iris and thus the DOF. 128 is a very small hole (pupil), so your DOF is practically infinite (like a pinhole camera). In contrast, an fStop of 2.8 is a very big opening and thus provides a narrow DOF.

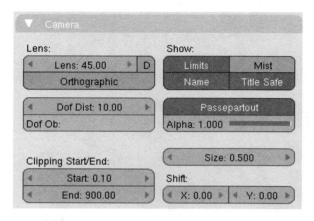

Figure 12-21. Camera panel

In the simple scene of tut\nodes-dof.blend, we have a camera with a DOF distance of 10. Keep in mind that the focal plane is the Z-depth that is in focus and is taken from the camera settings—either a manually entered distance (such as using a manual focusing ring) or an object named in the camera's properties (such as an autotracking-focus, if there is such a thing), even if the camera isn't directly looking at it. The Camera panel is shown in Figure 12-21, and the Dof Dist is the focal plane distance in Blender units. Alternatively, you can enter the name of an object (such as Frankie) in the Dof Ob field, and the camera will use the distance to that object as the focal plane.

The DOF depends on the fStop, and the blurring is exacerbated as the object gets farther out of that field. You can limit the size of the blur by setting Maxblur. Maxblur, if something other than zero, specifies maximum number of pixels to blur.

Technically, light coming from behind an object cannot blur the edge of a foreground object because light does not blend. However, with multielement lenses, some funky bending and blending of light can occur. In your CG scene, you might see this as well, and BThreshold gives you some control over that bleeding/blending.

> When activated, especially in HD, the node can take some time. It reports its progress in the Console window, reporting each time it goes through each set of horizontal scan lines.

Preview is a mode that gives you a low quality but fast previsualization of the defocus. When enabled, the Samples setting specifies how fine a grain to make the blur, with higher settings taking more time but giving a closer approximation to what the final result will be.

Making or faking a Z-buffer

You can insert or create your own Z-buffer, as shown in Figure 12-22. In this image, I created a mask of Becca. The alpha channel of this 3D view is 1 where the mask is and 0 elsewhere. The Map Value node multiplies those values by 10, but puts out a floor of 2, so that the Defocus node thinks (because the camera's Dof Dist is 10) that the pixels covered by the mask are 10 units away and in focus, whereas all other pixels are 2 units away. (It is totally fake because they were actually behind her in real life.) Because defocus blur occurs to objects both behind and in front of the focal plane, they are blurred.

Figure 12-22. Using fake Z-buffer to introduce DOF

> *Try not to feed a zero value to the Z socket of the Defocus node by using this technique because artifacts and errors may result.*

The No zbuffer option ignores the camera's Dof Dist and allows you to use a grayscale image to control the defocus/blur effect. An example is shown in Figure 12-23, in which I am using an inverted alpha mask (the nonmasked area is white, which equals 1), and the masked area is 0. Using a Zscale of 10, I am effectively telling the defocus node to uniformly blur everything except where the mask is, thus blurring the background. The blur is scaled from zero, with black portions of the image not getting any blur, to white portions getting full blur.

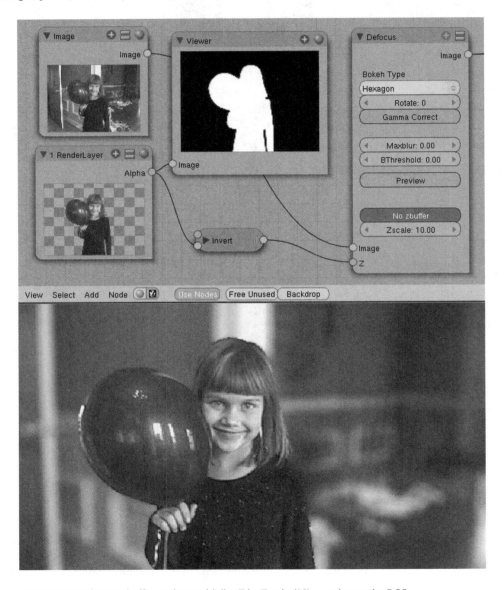

Figure 12-23. The No zbuffer option multiplies Z by Zscale (10) to enhance the DOF.

> *Using either of these techniques, you can create DOF from any image format, even if it does not have an alpha or Z value.*

Both of these examples are supplied on the DVD in tut\nodes-dof_nozbuffer.blend, in the FakeZ and No zbuffer scenes, respectively.

Rack focus

Rack focus changes the focal plane during filming. You can easily change the focal plane by animating the location of an Empty object, and entering its name in the Dof Ob field in the camera properties. When the Dof Ob field is filled in, the Z location of that object overrides any value in the Dof Dist field. (We discussed animating the location of an object in Chapter 8.)

If you are faking your Z-buffer, of course, any manipulation of that mask (altering its brightness) will cause Blender to think that the Z is changing. You can use the Math node to alter any mask in a uniform manner.

Directional Blur node

So far, our blurs have been omnidirectional in that they blur the pixels all around a target pixel or based on the distance from the camera. The Directional Blur node enables very fine control over what direction to blur something. We can vary the magnitude and angle of the blur. If the object or mask is moving, this vector can be pointed in any direction, such as rotating by 90 degrees, spiraling, and even zooming in toward the camera to make it larger than the original. In the noodle shown in Figure 12-24, you see the screenshot from tut\flying_squirrel_RW.blend, in which there are two render layers. In the top Render Layers node is Frankie, which is only Frankie, but he is dropping very fast. Below that it is another Render Layers node that feeds in the 1-RenderLayer, which is everything. We blur Frankie, and then AlphaOver the full image over the blur. Feel the power of Frankie!

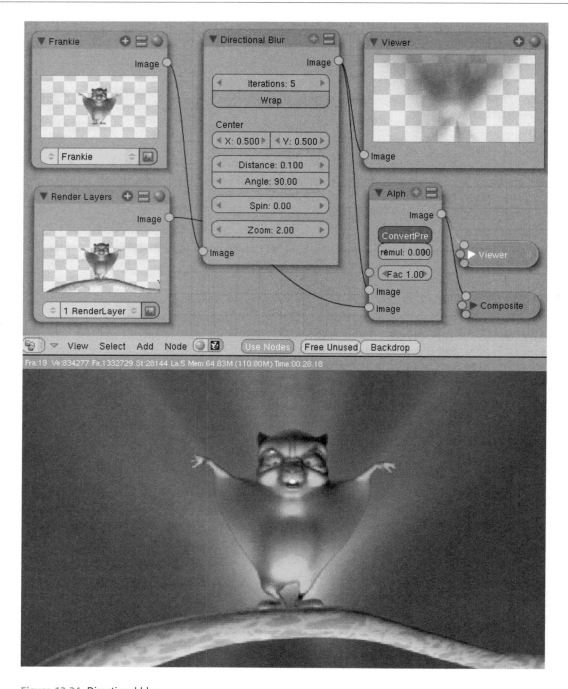

Figure 12-24. Directional blur

Bilateral Blur node

One of the biggest complaints about sampled functions, such as ambient occlusion (AO), is that they can look speckled because they are sampled, and you have to quit sometime or else you will be waiting (for what seems like) forever for the render to finish. The issue (up until this node popped on the scene) has been in applying the pass to the image without it looking "noisy." Based on edge detection, this node blurs out the speckles but only in the middle. Iterations increase the quality, and feeding the Determinator socket with a guiding image can help the node with edge detection. In Figure 12-25, you see the AO pass on the left and after processing by the Bilateral node on the right. As you can see, the AO matte is very smooth and continuous, which would make a great matte and can be applied in many ways.

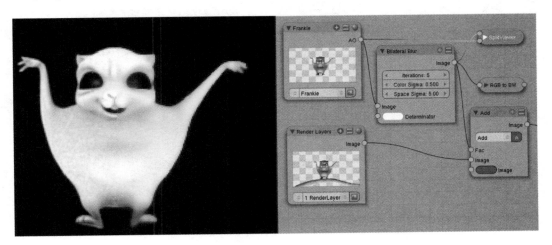

Figure 12-25. Bilateral node smears inside edges.

Motion blur via the Vector Blur node

Traditional motion blur is enabled in the Buttons window, Scene-Render panel; and the button is called MBlur. When enabled, it causes Blender to compute the current frame. Then, based on the blur factor (set under the MBlur button), it computes frame(s) a fraction of a frame before and then melds those frames together. Any apparent movement (caused by camera movement) or actual movement (animation of an object's location, rotation, and so on) causes a blur. Figure 12-26 shows a motion blur image, which took 8:40 to render.

Figure 12-26. Motion blur—render time 8:40

The same scene and render result is shown in Figure 12-27, but it uses the Vector Blur node. In this image, I did use a higher blur factor for an augmented effect, but I could afford to do many iterations because each render takes only 1:14, more than 7 times faster. For a 30-second commercial (900-frame) render, Vector Blur changes a total render time from 130 hours (more than 5 days) to about 18 hours. Although the speed increase is significant, there are some things to watch out for: neither item can be seen through Z-transparency, and any cast shadows will be blurred with the Vector Blur node.

In old-school photography, to convey speed and motion through a still image, you would select a slower shutter speed and pan the camera while the shutter was open, keeping the athlete in the center of the viewfinder. In this way, the background is blurred while the athlete's nonmoving parts (the head, for example) stay sharp. You can introduce this effect by playing both sides of the house, as they say. In the 3D side of Blender, parent the camera to the moving object so that the camera moves along with it. Add a Track To constraint to the camera to always look at the object. Then make your render using either Motion Blur or Vector Blur. Because everything except the object moves relative to the camera, it will be blurred; because the object remains stationary relative to the camera, it will not blur.

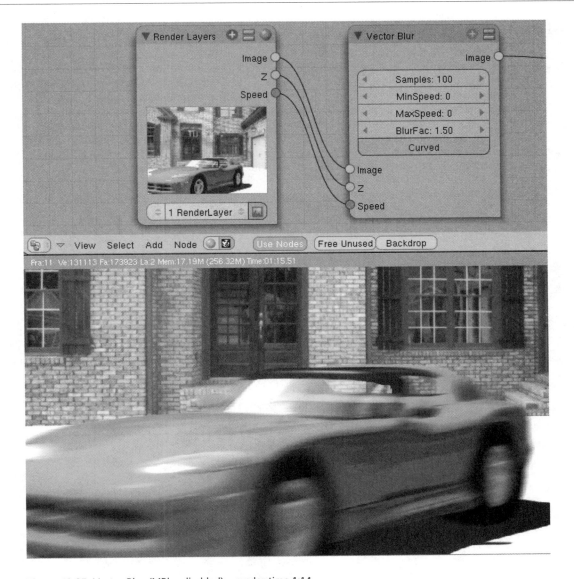

Figure 12-27. Vector Blur (MBlur disabled)—render time 1:14

You can also animate a mask of a still image or video, and then use the mask's speed vector as input to the Vector Blur node. Blender will then be faked out to think that the pixels identified by the mask are the ones moving and then blur them accordingly.

Glare node

One of the most frequently used effects is to give a glow, or glare, to an image. Blender provides a very simple, easy-to-use node: Glare (shown in Figure 12-28). Here I used the streaking mode to really make the image (unprocessed on the left) of this underwater scene pop out and look like intense sunlight is at the water surface. We have quite a few modes to choose from: Ghosts, Streaks, Fog, and Star. Underneath that, you have a quality selector; choose from low quality but fast results (use this when adjusting settings) to high quality but slow render. Iterations (1 to 5) control the smoothing/blending effect of the glow. Depending on the glare mode, there are a few different controls. Common controls are Mix, ranging from -1 (original image only) to 1 (glow only), and a brightness threshold. If a pixel is below the threshold, it isn't considered "glaring," so it does not participate in emitting a glare.

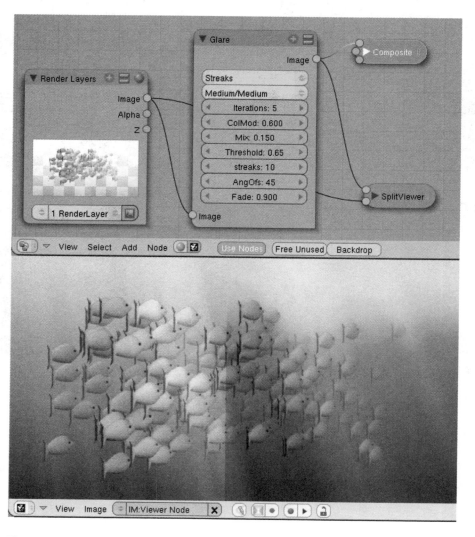

Figure 12-28. Glare node (right)

Node groups

Render nodes eventually can become challenging to manage as the render network grows more complex and lengthy. For this reason, we have the ability to lump them together into a group, which allows us to "black box" their functionality. When named well, we can readily grasp their overall purpose and not be bogged down in the details. To create a node group, simply select the nodes you want to be grouped together and select Node ➤ Make Group.

A node group, which is shown with a green header, does complex or multistep functions. Groups are created by you and "collapse" into a green node, with input sockets reflecting the net inputs into the group and output sockets reflecting the net outputs. You should make a node group if you have a specific series of nodes that you create and use over and over again to achieve a certain effect. Making a node group of that functionality allows you to easily reuse it in all your future noodles. When you append or link into a blend file, you will see NodeTree as an item in the list of object types. Simply drill down into that to see the node groups.

Group nodes have a special "expand" icon on the far right side of their header that enables you to see inside the group and look/modify the nodes and connections inside the group. Clicking anywhere outside the group collapses the group down to look like a single node. When collapsed, the group appears to be a single node, with whatever inputs and outputs existed in the group's components. In this way, you can make your own nodes by assembling a bunch of more primitive nodes into a reusable noodle. To ungroup a group, select the group and press Alt-G or select Node ➤ Ungroup from the menu. Blender might not immediately recognize the group as a group; try a few times to convince it to destroy the group. When destroyed, the contents of the group are placed onto your editor window workspace.

> When defining a group, do not thread a viewer node on the end of your output, or Blender will think that is the end of the noodle and will not give you an output socket. Do not include a Composite Output node in a group.

Sample node groups (shown in Figure 12-9) are taken from peach\simple scenes\compositing\compo. blend. The group frank is collapsed, forest (left middle) is minimized, and Mist is expanded.

Inside the Mist group, all the nodes that are not meant to be adjusted are collapsed (for example, the constant Gamma and Alpha correction), but the RGB Curves node is expanded, allowing you to quickly adjust the blue color of the forest. These are all node groups from the Peach\production\ scenes\ 12_peach\14.blend file. Note that the input socket into the group aligns with the Gamma input node, and the numeric input socket lines up with and splices into the ColorRamp node. On the output side, the only unconnected socket is from the Mix node, so it lines up on the border of the group node, allowing you to connect it further down the chain.

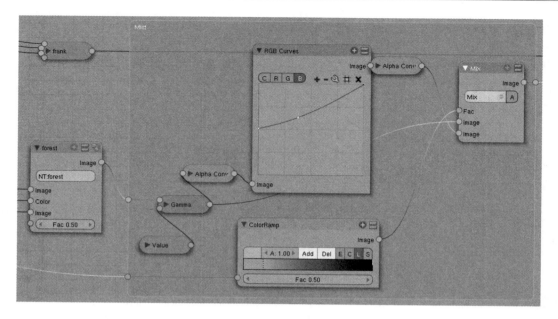

Figure 12-29. Node group in green outlined box area (right)

Posterizing and retro

Believe it or not, now that millions of colors are available, there's a retro movement back to 8-bit (256 possible colors). In this practice, which is called *quantization* or *posterizing*, a range of colors is restricted to a single color. As discussed in Chapter 4, this is essentially what .jpg compression does. Figure 12-30 contains a noodle that takes any image back to 256 possible colors.

In the early days of digital imaging, a byte was allocated to store the color of each pixel or index into a table that defined the color of that pixel. A byte is 8 bits, and each bit can store a 0 or 1. By stringing bits together, you count in base 2 and get possible quantities of colors of 2, 4, 8, 16, 32, and so on. The noodle shown in Figure 12-30 splits up an image into the YCbCr set of three channels. Then the task is to decide how to allocate those 8 bits to the 3 channels. Because the eye is most sensitive to luminosity, we want to restrict that to the fewest values. When we do, the colors will be very distinctly different from one another. Therefore, for the top channel, we use a value of 4, which is 2 bits. The Cb and Cr channels get a maximum value of 8 (shown in the next 2 multiply nodes down), which is 3 bits each, bringing the total to 8 bits. Of course, your choice of how many bits and how to allocate them is totally up to you, so I have given you this scene in tut\node-posterize.blend.

I used a node group to save display space, with the one *Y channel expanded to show the contents. The general idea of the group is to take a value, multiply it by the number supplied, round that result to a whole number, and then divide it back into the range of 0 to 1. So for an example with 4, the group takes in the value 4 and subtracts 1 to set a maximum value of 3 because you want (before the divide) possible values of 0, 1, 2, and 3 (4 possible values). The way math works, only perfectly white values will translate to 3, so we need a ColorRamp node to shift a small range of bright values all the way to 1.

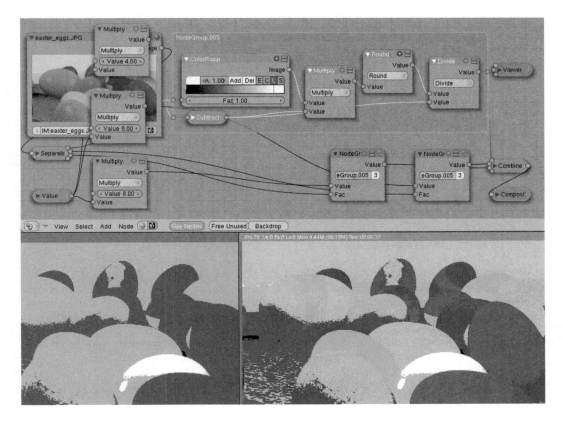

Figure 12-30. Posterizing to restrict the number of colors

Grease Pencil tool

When reviewing your composite output over time, you might want to mark it up for changes. Alternatively, the customer (director, producer, boss) or peer reviewer (often a coworker or even a review team) might want to suggest changes at some point in the video. A very nifty markup feature in Blender is the Grease Pencil tool, which has been recently introduced (as discussed online at http://www.blender.org/development/release-logs/blender-248/grease-pencil/). Like a real grease pencil, you can annotate video or images anywhere they are shown inside of these Blender window types:

- UV/image editor
- 3D view (each view has its own layer)
- Node editor
- Sequence editor (image preview modes)

Start Blender and examine the View menu of any window type. You will see a Grease Pencil option with an icon indicating that it makes a panel. Click it, and the Grease Pencil panel appears in your window. Enable Use Grease Pencil and then click Add Layer, as shown in Figure 12-31.

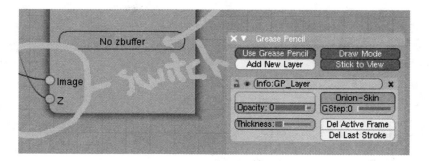

Figure 12-31. Grease Pencil in use

Each window uses its own Grease Pencil layer, so for a given frame you can make one set of notes in the node editor (to correct those switched threads, for example), another on the sequenced composite (such as to suggest a transition change), a third in the 3D view (to suggest an model or camera movement change, for example), and a fourth in the UV/image editor (to suggest an animation change).

By using each window type to make different kinds of changes, all kinds of comments can be communicated once, reducing the cycles of rework and review, and thus speeding workflow.

> *Grease Pencil preferences are set up in the* User Preferences ➤ Edit Methods ➤ Grease Pencil *panel, and include sensitivity and radius settings.*

First, choose Add New Layer and pick a color (black is the default). As with all color swatches, click to see the color picker and set a color. I like cyan-ish colors, although others like yellow. You might want to use different colored grease pencils for different purposes, such as red for mesh or texture errors, yellow for direction or animation cleanup, cyan for compliments, and so on. Each time you click Add New Layer, you can make a new layer of markings (and I suggest using a different pencil color). You can lock a layer so that it always shows or mute it by clicking the eyeball. When you want to use your mouse to draw (or a pen if using a tablet), enable Draw Mode.

Normally, clicking and dragging in the UV/image editor gives you pixel coordinate, color, alpha, and distance information. To draw, click Draw Mode; now your strokes will add a markup to the frame.

> *Pen/tablet users have finer control and make better edits than mouse users, and line thickness is controlled by pen pressure.*

Grease pencil markups can be like videos in the blend file, showing up only for a range of frames (for example, annotating only a portion of an animation). Change the time-location of a markup in the action editor. To see the action editor window, change a window pane in your screen layout to an Action Editor window. In the Action Editor header, change the display mode to Grease Pencil and you will see a channel for each grease pencil layer, and a keyframe diamond to indicate when the layer becomes active and is shown. So, if the timing changes, simply grab the keyframe. If a layer is no longer needed, delete the keyframe and you delete the layer. You can also lock and mute layers in the action editor channel.

Visualizing the win

So let's see what we can come up with if we creatively string these nodes together. One Blender artist whose work I admire (and there are many of you!) is RobertT, whose F1 entry is shown here. Each year, Blender sponsors an F1 Challenge, which uses Blender to design a race car, factual or fantasy. His entry is shown in Figure 12-32.

Figure 12-32. "Visualizing the Win," by Robert J Tiess. All rights reserved.

This op-art piece starts as a 3D view model of a car, animated as an object to be moving, and is then transformed by the nodes to arrive at the final composition shown. Robert says, "I wanted to take more of an artistic and expressive approach to my F1 entry (this year). The major goals in doing so were to portray the intensity of high-speed, futuristic racing while offering a sense of the driver's own emotions and thoughts of winning as another corner is turned."

The technical goal was to transform an ordinary-looking racing vehicle (as if any F1 is ordinary-looking!) into something extraordinarily expressive and visually stunning. I think he succeeded!

According to Robert, "Early on, I decided the final image needed to remain quite crisp and energetic; a moment frozen in time yet somehow still flowing. There still was the desire (and challenge) to convey a sense of motion without animation or the static semblance of a vehicle photographed as it whipped around a corner of a race track toward the finish line."

Although exactly how Robert did it is his intellectual property, let's walk through the major transformations he used to achieve this brilliant artistic effect using the noodle shown in Figure 12-33. First up, his Render Layers transmits only three passes: Combined Image, Z, and Speed. In 3D view, the car is animated to move. The image is fed to four different places in the noodle.

The first part goes to two daisy-chain vector blurs for double the effect (recall that I daisy-chained two matte nodes in Chapter 11). The image is lightened and then fed to the top row, in which a directional blur branches to a burn and to another directional blur. He then uses a Kirsch filter on a combination of the original and the mix in progress to give a staggered edge rendering.

After that powerful Kirsch filter, which is softened a bit, the two images are divided by one another, while the result spawns off a side branch where more direction blur is added at an angle (to make the car look like it is sliding around the corner), which is mixed back together with the work in progress.

Robert then glares to give some highlights to the image and uses the defocus node with the Z channel to give the image depth, which I think helps to make the car look like it is leaping out of the page. (Although, as he explains later, he mainly used it to give a little randomness to the colorations.) The bottom row of nodes puts the finishing touches on the image, making it high contrast (note the S curve in the RGB Curves node, which was discussed in Chapter 11).

Robert comments that the Sobel and Kirsch filter nodes were used at various intervals in the render network to augment line accentuation. Because each of these nodes can "sharpen" the render considerably, the results were tempered through Soften filters and Blur nodes along the way. Difference and Divide Mix nodes can alter colors dramatically, if not drastically, so they must be used with care. Because this project intentionally steers its render toward the "daring side" of Blender's capabilities, this was the perfect opportunity to use nodes in ways that would be excessive for other more conventional projects.

The Defocus node was used in an unconventional way. It was not included for the purposes of creating DOF; it instead inserted introduced controlled noise into the render, intended to help the image feel more alive—not to mention less of an obvious CG project. In being set to Preview mode (normally used to give you a quick and low-resolution indication of DOF) and using a low sample rate, the Defocus node generates a fuzzy image. This image, when fed into the last of the Sobel filter nodes, helps to create intense results.

With that, Robert's project crosses the finish line in first place! I wanted to show you this noodle to make you aware that although I have presented the nodes in fairly simple arrangement because I have had to teach each one individually or in small groups, using them all together creates a synergy in which the total end product is much better than simply the sum of its parts (see Figure 12-33).

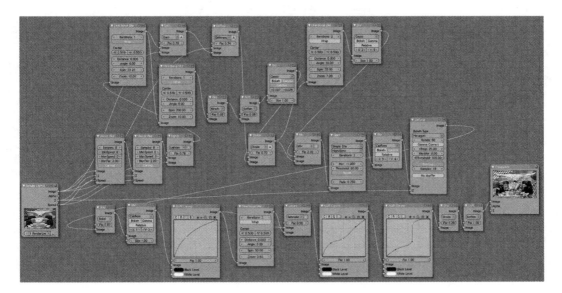

Figure 12-33. F1 noodle

Nodes are incredibly versatile and powerful, allowing you to take total control over nearly every aspect of your composite's final appearance. As deceptively simple as individual composite nodes might appear, they become increasingly capable and flexible when used with other nodes. Just as the lowly individual transistor is just a simple switch, millions of them make the brain of a computer. Although each node has a range of functions and intended purposes, you can use them in imaginative ways to produce new and thrilling results.

Because nodes are nondestructive (they do not permanently alter your project and its ultimately rendered image), you can experiment with different values interactively, checking the results in a quick render, and adjust values until the render reaches the desired outcome. You can also branch off and process the same image differently in parallel and then combine the results using the Mix or AlphaOver node.

Robert gives the following advice to other artists: "There comes a point in a project where your work might seem to be heading in the wrong direction, but perhaps it is simply that you have not gone far enough in that direction to reach what you really wanted (or needed); the best result could be just a few more steps away! Persistence and patience are among your strongest allies at this point."

As an artist, you have to make choices about the postprocessing nodes you put in place and use your judgment in determining whether each choice adds value to your art. I often make subbranches of the noodle, using the viewer node to evaluate what it looks like and then combine it back in to see whether it helps the overall composition. The possibilities are limitless and open up a whole new world of expression.

Summary

In this and the preceding chapters on the compositor and nodes, you have learned about the individual nodes and how to combine them. In addition, you have seen how to use the 3D view with the compositor to feed in masks and other CG elements to be used in conjunction with the nodes to achieve artistic effects. Any complex effect that you see in film (or even on some TV commercials) involves many layers and elements creatively combined and built upon one another to enhance the story or message that is being communicated.

Generally, the more complicated the special effect, the more complex and integrated the techniques used by the artist. There is no magic SFX node or single technique. I've discussed here and elsewhere how the various compositing elements of Blender come together to produce footage. Achieving professional results means understanding the capability of the tools in your toolbox, and I hope you enjoyed learning about all these great image-processing nodes.

Chapter 13

NONLINEAR VIDEO EDITOR

Blender's Video Sequence Editor (VSE) window type is a major functional component of Blender that allows nonlinear editing (NLE) of video strips into a finished product. *Nonlinear editing* is a fancy way of saying that you can jump around and don't have to jog forward and backward through the film clip. In the old days of videotape and film editing, you spliced strips of media (film using a cutter, and videotape using a magnetized razor blade) together with tape. Blender transforms that workflow into the digital age but still uses "strips" as a metaphor for shots of video.

The VSE can be used stand-alone just to mix or edit video, or it can be used in conjunction with the 3D view and/or compositor as I discussed in Chapter 2. Using the VSE, you import and arrange shots (video strips) and effect strips into channels, sequencing one after the other, and transitioning from one shot to another through some sort of blend or splice. You can layer alpha-channel shots over backgrounds, adjust the exposure and tone of previously shot video, add special effects, and render the finished product to one seamless and continuous video file. A few years ago, I tackled the job of writing the online user manual for this section of the software, which was then followed by Peter Schlaile, a volunteer programmer, devoting a lot of time to make major upgrades, which in turn was followed by another program-mer (Rob, a.k.a. paprmh) to develop a green-screen matte plug-in effect. It seems that each time someone works on this functionality, it just keeps getting better and better. Thanks, guys.

Combined with the other areas of Blender, this integrated workbench is a very powerful video editor. You can select a predefined desktop that incorporates the VSE from the SR drop-down menu in the user preferences header, as shown in Figure 13-1.

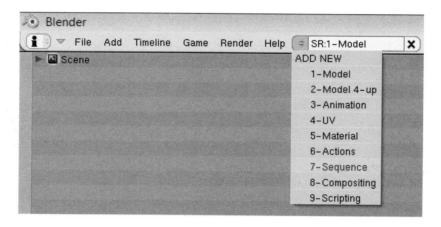

Figure 13-1. Selecting the NLE desktop

Another important note is that the VSE is the only place where you mix and layer an audio track to embed into a movie or to use as a reference. For example, when I am doing lip-syncing (recall the earlier examples where I made a dog talk by match-moving and using shape keys), I load the audio track in the VSE, and use the video as a background image.

To export a movie with an audio track, you use the FFmpeg library format (see Chapter 4), which can create a wide variety of audio-video formats and containers. The VSE puts together the audio and the video for professional output, and can mix down and layer many audio tracks together. Blender's VSE has functionality similar to Apple's Final Cut Pro, Sony's Vegas Pro, Windows Movie Maker, and probably a dozen others in that space.

The VSE window display modes

The VSE window type is actually a few different windows in one, in that it has a few (but very different) display modes, selected in the header shown in Figure 13-2:

- Sequence: Sequence of strips; your main working mode, allowing you to sequence shots in order
- Image Preview: Net result of a current frame, allowing you to see the final result
- Luma Waveform: Shows the brightness of the image (luminosity), allowing you to evaluate the overall brightness and focus of the image
- Chroma Vectorscope: Color-balance information about the image, allowing you to match color spaces from shot to shot
- Histogram: A graph of the color values distributed throughout the image, allowing you to balance the color

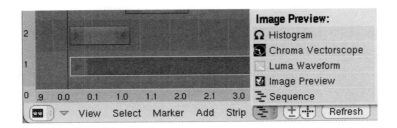

Figure 13-2. VSE window display modes

Just like other Blender windows, the VSE window has an adjustable frame and a header that can be at the top or bottom of the window pane. Also like other Blender windows, the header menu and options change based on the mode of the window, and each is described in this chapter.

Sequence display mode

In this mode, whose icon is a little film strip, you work with strips stacked in channels. These strips layer up to produce the resultant composited image. This is the "normal" working mode for the VSE. Strips are placed in channels, an example of which is shown in Figure 13-3.

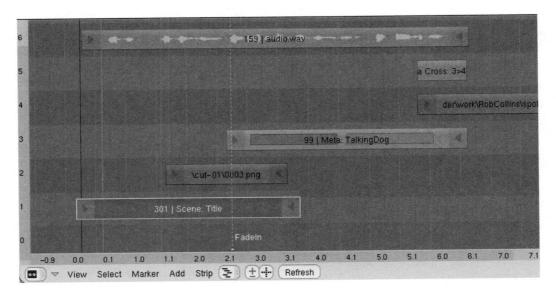

Figure 13-3. VSE sequence window type with some strips loaded

The x-axis is the frame number or time within the video, and the y-axis is a channel. Strips layer in these channels on top of one another, building up. For example, in Figure 13-3 the purple PNG image strip in channel 2 layers on top of the green scene strip in channel 1. In the default color theme, strips are color-coded based on what they contain:

- Audio strips are in cyan.
- Image strips are in purple.
- Video strips are in blue.
- Metastrips are shown as a strip-within-a-strip (audio-video strips are shown as two strips, or can be combined into a metastrip as shown).
- Effects strips in brown.
- 3D view (Scene) strips are green
- Color strips are drawn in the color they generate.

Markers are shown in the VSE and timeline windows as yellow triangles, and may be named as shown in Figure 13-3 (FadeIn is the first marker at 2.1 seconds). These are the same markers that can be found in the general Timeline window, and windows like the Action Editor.

The channels are arranged and numbered vertically upward, and you can layer hundreds of them. As you finalize parts of your sequence, say two video clips and four audio clips that all work together, you can combine for convenience into a single metastrip, like the one shown in Channel 3 in Figure 13-3. Channel 0 is the output channel, but you cannot put a strip there directly. The strips occur at some point in the timeline, horizontally, and the timeline is shown at the bottom of the pane. Press T to change the time code from frames to seconds. The real-time duration of a strip is computed based on the frames-per-second setting in the Scene Render Format panel (see Chapter 9). The current frame is drawn as a green vertical line and is enumerated in the Timeline window header.

Strips are named based on where they come from. If you zoom in on a Movie strip, the ending frame number is shown, followed by its file name, or, if you have given it your own name in the Edit panel, the word *Movie* and then the name you gave it. This is all designed for you to be able to recognize and comprehend the strip.

What is a video strip?

In the VSE, you work with strips that represent a series of frames of video or duration of audio, and place them in channels to assemble your final product. A strip can be any of the following:

- A rendering of the current scene
- A postprocessed image stream from Blender's compositor
- A single image from disk repeated many times as frames
- A numbered sequence of images frames
- A random collection of images from a folder
- A compressed or uncompressed video file
- A metastrip, which is a combination of other strips
- An audio file containing a mono or stereo track read from hard disk
- An audio stream loaded into memory (RAM)

A strip in the VSE is analogous to a segment of film or a strip of audio tape, if you're old enough to remember reel-to-reels and cassettes. Since any strip can come from any source, the VSE is the place where you can use a blend in a CG lightsaber into a live-action shot, add the whoozing sound effect, and splice in a title sequence. The VSE provides many easy- and quick-to-access effects strips and features for common tasks you face. A special kind of effects strip is called a plug-in, and I discuss all of the effects strips in the next chapter.

There's a ton of things you can do with a strip, as shown in Figure 13-4. Most of the options are self-evident from their name. Muting is very neat, in that you can "hide" a strip from the rendering engine. I use this a lot on audio strips, when layering background music and Foleys that I know are properly placed (they get annoying when you have to scrub over them a dozen times). To cut a strip (using that digital razor blade), simply position your time cursor to the frame where you want to cut, select the strip(s), and press K for the knife (which is very similar to the action in editing a mesh). To prevent a strip from moving, lock it in place. If the source video is moved, you will need to remap its path. To delete the selected strip, press X.

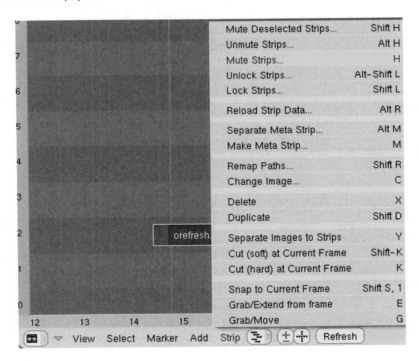

Figure 13-4. Strip menu

When cutting a video, be very aware that many codecs cannot properly and accurately cut an encoded stream. In other words, if you are going to be cutting video, like a MOV or AVI file, first convert the video to an image sequence, such as to PNG, and load the PNG image sequence as a strip instead of the video strip. Then cut to your heart's content. The actual image sequence files will not be affected or deleted when you cut them from the VSE. The image sequence strip is only a reference to those files, and the files are actually read in during image processing.

Do sequence

To tell Blender to use the image composited in the video sequencer as the output, you must click Do Sequence in the Buttons Window, Scene Render context, Anim panel as shown in Figure 13-5.

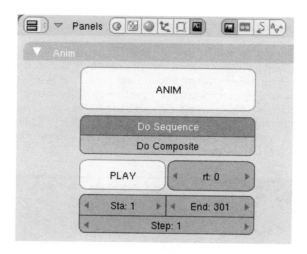

Figure 13-5. Do Sequence Enabled

If Do Composite is also enabled, then any green scene strip in the VSE takes in the image from the compositor's Composite Output node, as opposed to the objects rendered directly from the 3D view camera.

Image preview display mode

This mode shows you the composite output of all the strips combined. You can click-drag your left mouse button in this window, and the display will show you the pixel location and the RGBA values for that pixel under the mouse. This is handy for tracking down mixing or cropping issues. This is the mode used by the top VSE window in the desktop. It simply shows the image, as in the top window of the next figures in this chapter.

The composite image is shown in a VSE window in output mode immediately upon frame change. For example, if you click somewhere in a VSE window in sequence mode or click in a timeline window, you will jump to that frame, and a VSE window in Image preview mode will instantly show you the composite result. When you click Render or press F12, the images will be regenerated based on what strips you have loaded and are active (not muted) for the current frame in the VSE window, and show the render in either a pop-up window or Image Editor window in render result mode (depending on what you have configured).

Depending on the power of your computer, the number of effects you are processing, and the size (resolution) of the images you are working with, you can scrub back and forth in real time; that is, as you click and drag your mouse through the timeline window, the VSE output window will show you the image that is the corresponding composite of that frame.

The timeline window type was presented in Chapter 8. Previous and future versions may support dragging in the image preview window to scrub.

Luma waveform display mode

The eye is most sensitive to luminance, or the brightness of an image, especially if it contrasts sharply from the surrounding area. If you want the viewer to look somewhere on the screen, you vary the luminance. If you want them to look in the center of the screen, the center should be the brightest. The luma waveform plots the luminance of the pixels in an image, left to right, using the luminance value as the y-axis. In Figure 13-6, we have a big dip right in the center, where the black rabbit hole is located. The rest of the image is uniformly lit, which thus draws our eye to that black hole. Luminance is another way of looking at your image to see if it does what you want it to do, by directing the viewer's attention and ensuring that something in each scene draws the viewer's eye to the key feature. Use the luma mode to determine this using the graph shown in Figure 13-6.

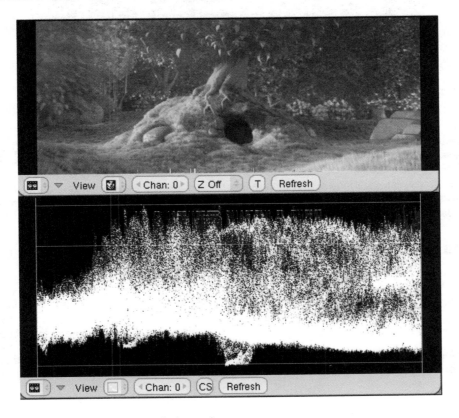

Figure 13-6. Luma waveform display mode

If you had an actress center field, but a bright car or something off to the left, the luma waveform would show you that the bright car, even though you don't notice it, will compete with the actress for the viewer's attention.

You can separate the color channels and display the luminosity of each channel as shown in Figure 13-7 by enabling the CS button in the header, which separates the color spaces in the window.

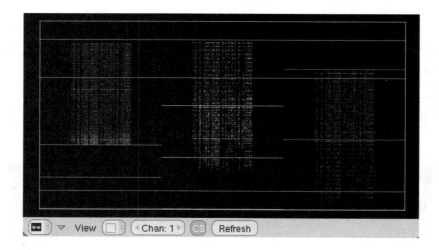

Figure 13-7. Luma channel display mode

In this mode, the luminosity of each channel is displayed separately, in the color it represents. We can see there is a lot of yellow (red and green) in this shot, tending more toward deep greens. Use this display to compare the current frame with the luma channel display from the previous shot in your sequence so you can determine if they are the same, thus providing a smooth transition. Or if you are, say, building up to a dangerous scene, then you might want to see the reds come up over time to give that visual hint of danger, and you can use this display to graph that.

Chroma vectorscope display mode

The vectorscope is a hexagon, with points of the hexagon representing the color channel red, blue, and green, with then magenta, cyan, and yellow in between them, respectively. (Magenta is a combination of red and blue.) For each pixel in the image, regardless of location, its color is plotted inside the hexagon. The chroma vectorscope shows you the color distribution of the pixels in the image. Consider Figure 13-8, which shows two sequential shots from *Big Buck Bunny* (BBB), with their vectroscopes.

By looking at the vectorscopes, we can see that these two images use basically the same color space—yellow-brown-green—and thus will not contrast from one another, and will flow nicely together in a smooth transition.

In CG you want scenes that logically follow one another to also follow one another in terms of the coloring they use. If you want two scenes to contrast each another, you want one to be bright and the other dark (which you can assess using the luma waveform), or you want the two scenes to use a different color palette, such as one with red tones and the other with blue tones.

Figure 13-8. Two sequential shots that we want to visually flow together

On a similar note, when shooting live action video, *white* is not pure white, because it is affected by ambient light and off-color lighting, the sun, radiant light, lens coatings, and so on. This makes it really difficult to merge in CG characters, because, if you render using pure white light, it "just won't look quite right" and the colors will be off. So, you should hold up a white piece of cardboard or acrylic in front of the camera/subject before you start filming. You can then use the color histogram of that frame, cropped to be only the white board, to see the color spectra that existed during filming. You can then use that spectra info to color-correct the rest of the video. When you do, flesh tones will look like real flesh tones.

Histogram display mode

Color balance is very important in presenting a pleasing video. If the film is tinted blue, it will look cold. If it is tinted red, it will look alarming at best, or hot, devilish, or just . . . crappy. A green tint looks sick, although in a forest scene it makes it look lush and tropical. Sometimes color is thrown off by the film stock, other times it is the camera or the lights, or maybe the way it was developed. Video can suffer from oversaturation of a particular color as well. Also, from shot to shot the light can change (if filming during the day) and when you are doing the compositing, the audience will notice if the color, such as the background color, changes from shot to shot, especially if you are interleaving many shots in rapid succession. For this reason alone, many shots are filmed at night or in a studio under controlled lighting conditions.

The other way of looking at the color space of an image is by counting up the number of pixels that have a certain color, and plotting that as a curve. You use this information to assess whether an image is correctly exposed, and whether it has an even color saturation. You wouldn't want to count up pixels, but a computer can do it quite quickly.

In Blender 2.48, the histogram works only on a single image in replace mode; any other mode disables the histogram display.

Later on we will look at a practical way of using the histogram mode to assess and correct color by adjusting lift and gain.

An NLE screen layout

As I just hinted, a few windows can work together to make an efficient NLE workbench. Editing and final assembly of your images and shots into a final cut is a distinct step in the overall workflow. As a compositor, you'll find that the VSE window will become your "very best friend." Thus, out of the box, a generic screen layout is provided with the distribution. This screen desktop is designed for smaller displays, and has the standard user preferences window at the top, an Ipo window, a headerless VSE window in composite display mode, and another VSE window in strip display mode. I prefer a slightly different arrangement, as shown in Figure 13-9. This arrangement is for larger displays and incorporates some additional window types: an image/asset outliner and timeline window.

Figure 13-9. Suggested NLE desktop

Because a window header can take up valuable screen real estate, you can hide any header and make that screen area available to the work area. To do this, hover your mouse cursor over any area of the window border and right-click. The pop-up menu will have an option to move or hide the header. If the header is already hidden, the menu will enable you to reshow the header.

Since Blender is an integrated tool, various window types work together, as shown in Figure 13-9, into an efficient desktop screen layout. For example, if you change the frame number by clicking in the timeline window, the VSE windows update to show you the image for that frame. In the context of this desktop, the layout provides these windows:

- **User Preferences**: By convention, this window at the very top provides that "main menu" and access to important system properties. It's important for the VSE that you set the MEM Cache Limit as big as possible (1024 if you have a lot of RAM on your PC), and that you prefetch a few frames (I like a second's worth, or 24 when working in film), as shown in Figure 13-10. Higher settings use more PC resources but give you smoother responsiveness.

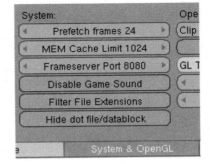

Figure 13-10. VSE preferences

- **Outliner**: A special mode of the outliner window on the left is the sequence mode, which displays the assets used in the VSE window type. Each type of asset has a little icon indicating what type it is, such as a waveform to represent an audio track.

- **VSE window in image preview mode**: This headerless window shows the net resultant image for the current frame. In addition, like with the UV/image editor or render window, left-click-dragging in this window shows you pixel information.

- **VSE window in sequence mode**: This window shows you the strip arrangement and allows you to position and work with the strips.

- **Timeline window**: A visual scale of your project, which allows you to scrub through the project and change the duration, set markers, and play back your project using VCR-type controls, and to mute audio. Refer to Chapter 8, where I introduced the timeline window.

- **Properties window**: Panels of information about the selected strip are shown here and allow you to quickly change any modifiable property. In addition, you can change context to Render to inspect and change any output options.

- **IPO window**: The influence of special effects is animated in this window, set to sequence type. Just Ctrl-click in this window to set animation handles and the curve.

Scene sequencer buttons

Under the Scene context in the buttons window, there is a separate subcontext for the sequencer, where panels appear for all the different settings that are in effect for the selected strip. Each kind of strip, and indeed each different effect, has a configuration panel in this context that allows you to control it. Most of the strips have a common set of configuration options, discussed in this section based on the panel where they appear.

Sequencer Input panel

As its name implies, this panel tells you where the strip is coming from, and allows you to preprocess it. If the strip source has been updated during your working session, click Reload to reload a fresh copy.

This panel gives you basic information about the active strip (the last strip selected). Depending on the type of strip, slightly different info is given. For images and video, the Dir field provides the location of the strip, broken out into the folder and the file name. If the video source is updated after you begin your session, click Reload to make sure Blender has the latest copy. Selected strips are shown with a white outline. For Scenes, it allows you to switch scenes that the strip represents.

A quick note on relative paths. The Dir field contains the path to the source file. You will either see a string that begins with a drive letter, like C:, or one that begins with //. If it begins with a drive letter (a hard drive, a system file folder on your PC (Linux), or a mapped drive through your operating system), the path is called an *absolute path specification*. This path must match exactly. If you move the file, you must change this string to match. If you lose a file, you can use the Find File feature to try to find it (discussed in Chapter 1). In Blender, the // means the folder where your blend file is saved. This is called a *relative path specification*. If you collect all your files in subfolders under your project, you should use relative path specifications. If you move the blend file and its subfolders, such as by zipping them up and mailing them to your friend, your friend can unpack the ZIP file and the project will maintain integrity.

Preprocessing strips using crop and translate

To demonstrate cropping and translating, let's add a subtitle to the BBB movie. To keep things simple, I've taken a snapshot of keyframes from each of the four opening shots in Scene 1, and put them in your lib/images/Peach folder, and loaded them in tut/13-subtitle.blend. Each of the four images should be loaded using a relative file path as shown in the Input panel. I've made a rather complicated screen for subtitling (as you will see if you open the file) that includes the original text and a 3D view as shown in Figure 13-11. It shows the screen that combines the 3D view that is brought in through the scene strip, and the camera animation IPO window. The LocZ curve is the only curve (I deleted the x and y curves), and it is set into Curve ➤ Interpolation ➤ Constant so that we get that "instant change" stair-step effect, for the camera to hop from line to line. What's left is to crop out the portion of the image we don't want; namely, the lines that have already been shown.

> In this subtitle example, the images have been set to an auto-blending mode of Alpha Under so that they slip under the subtitle in the composite image.

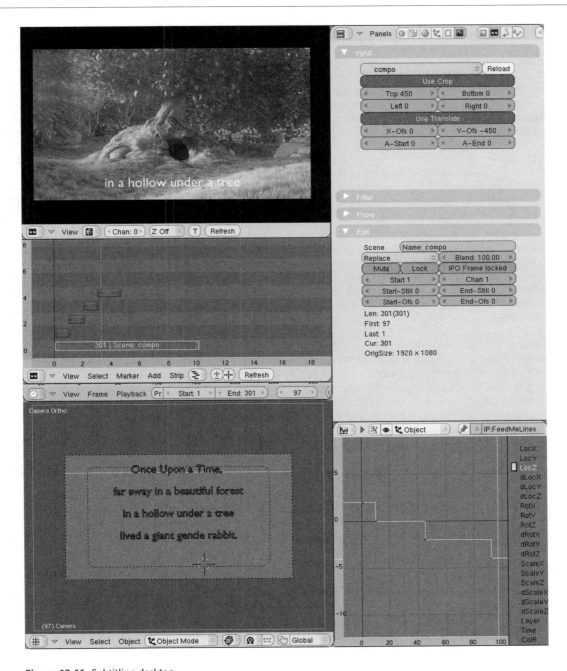

Figure 13-11. Subtitling desktop

Crop

Cropping is removing a portion of an image by cutting out what you don't want. When shooting video, sometimes a curtain or tripod leg will find its way into the frame. An inattentive grip may let the microphone dip into the scene. In these cases, you need to crop the offending element out of the image. When Use Crop is enabled, several more controls appear, allowing you to specify the area you want to be seen. By default, a strip is automatically resized to match the output resolution. Cropping allows you to take off pixels from the top left and bottom right, and any combination in between. Using these controls, you can select any rectangular portion of an image.

> *To select multiple portions of the same image, just duplicate the strip (Shift+D) and set the second crop, and change the blending mode (you will have to use the* Translate *setting to offset the portions).*

In our example, shown in Figure 13-11, we crop the top 450 pixels of the 3D view (the subtitles), which cuts off the top half of the Scene image. With our subtitles, the text object is set to double-spaced (line spacing of 2.0), so we don't have to be exact and worry about overhanging descenders from letters like *y* and *j*. Whenever we want to show the next line of text, we just drop the camera down another two units, and the crop will cut out the lines that have already been shown, leaving only one line of text.

Suppose you are preparing some video for NTSC broadcast, and need the result to be 720×480 resolution. If you are working with input video that is also 480 pixels high, and have to crop the top 50 pixels from a 480-pixel-high video, you are left with 430 pixels, which obviously won't fit into your output. You have a few choices. You can letterbox it, where you center the video and let the top and bottom be black bars of 25 pixels each. You can stretch it, but that may cause unacceptable distortion. You can crop a little off the sides, and then when the sequencer expands it, it will not distort. Or, if you don't like your job, you can suggest to the director that they should reshoot the video, which will make you very popular (not!).

Translate

When enabled, the translate function shifts an image in any direction in the specified number of pixels. Enter a positive number to pan (shift) the image right or up, and a negative number to pan left or down (the origin is the lower-left corner). The unused pixels (where the image does not appear) are black but alpha 0 so you can easily layer something underneath.

In our subtitle example, I shift the scene down by 450 pixels, by setting Y-Ofs to –450, which shoves lines that are to follow off-screen, and therefore, only the current line is left (since previous lines were cropped earlier. When you enable Use Translate, you control it through the following fields:

> *I used the trick of left-click dragging on the render output window (or UV/image editor showing the render result) to get the coordinates of the crop edge. That always helps me figure out the pixel numbers.*

- A-Start: The starting frame of the animation (as an addition to the Start-Ofs offset in the Edit panel.

- A-End: The ending frame of the animation (as an additional rolldown from the offset in the End-Ofs setting). The A-Start and A-End allow you to crop (or some would say *translate*) the start and end of the animation. If the strip is a movie, sequence, or scene, you can offset the start of the strip's animation by entering a frame count here. For example, entering 100 in A-Start means that if the strip starts on frame 1, frame 101 will be culled out from the strip for our animation frame 1.

- MPEG-Preseek (shown if the strip is a video): To improve performance and image quality, this setting preloads images the specified number of frames so that the image can be accurately and quickly shown.

Sequencer Filter panel

This panel allows you to preprocess the strip in a few different ways. I introduced how to use the color-balance aspect of this panel previously in conjunction with the histogram display mode.

- Premul: Different programs handle transparency differently, especially when it has been processed by Photoshop or other graphics programs. If a white pixel is half-transparent, then the RGBA values might be (1,1,1,.5). If the program premultiplies those values, then the RGBA values would be (.5, .5, .5, .5). Within the program, the color would be shown as white, but in Blender an RGB values of .5 would show as gray. Enabling PreMul tells Blender to treat the image as premultiplied (see Chapter 4). An incorrect setting here results in an image that has a strange halo around the edge where the transparent image is alpha-layered on top of another.

- Float: OpenEXR uses a floating-point number to represent a color, either 16 or 32 bits. Enable this to convert the pixel color values to a floating-point number for more accuracy.

- De-Interlace: TV broadcast and DV video use fields rendering (see Chapter 4). Enable this, and Blender will combine two frames into one.

- FlipX and FlipY: Use these to "reverse" an image left-to-right or up-to-down, respectively.

- Flip Time: Use this to reverse a video clip and make it play "backwards."

- Mul: Multiply the image by a color. In addition to brightening or darkening, if you use a color, it will tint the image that color or bring out a certain color.

- Strobe: Select every *n*th frame.

- Use Color Balance: Enable this to adjust the video brightness, Gamma correction, and contrast (gain). You can lift, correct, or gain the entire image or a color value.

Sequencer Proxy panel

A proxy is a stand-in for the real thing. It acts like the real thing, but is usually smaller and thus more easily processed and quicker to practice on. When the real render is made, the real image is processed. Using a proxy while working and scrubbing back and forth saves processing power and makes the system much more responsive. Use proxies especially when working in HD to enable real-time scrubbing through the video.

When you want to work with proxies instead of the real 100% image, you choose whether to use a proxy image that is sized 25%, 50%, or 75% of the final size, by clicking the 25, 50, or 75 button in the Scene Render context, Render panel. In the sequencer context, when you enable Use Proxy, Blender will create thumbnails of the input image into the directory you specify, into a folder named 25, 50, or 75, and create small JPG images in there for each frame. It will then use these frames as a sort of proxy cache so that it can load them very fast and still give you real-time response, even if your full images are huge.

Making a proxy

In the lib/images/NASA folder, open STS120.blend. This is a video of the liftoff of the 120th mission of the space shuttle. The file should open to the Make Proxy scene, in the 7-Sequence desktop shown in Figure 13-12.

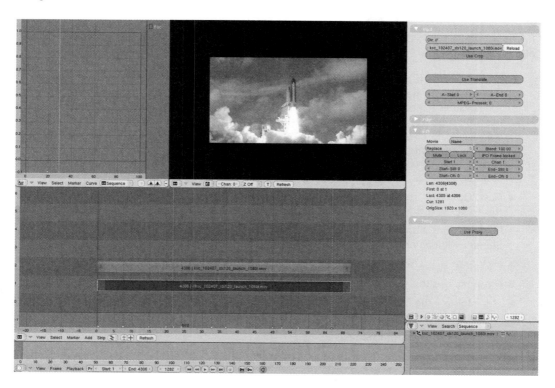

Figure 13-12. You need a proxy when working with huge HD files.

Unless you specify a Custom Dir, Blender will put the proxy images in a folder under the source footage. If the footage is local to your machine, that's fine. However, if the footage is somewhere over the network, you may want the proxies to be stored on your hard disk, so that they are loaded faster and avoid network traffic. In this case, you want to proxies saved in a custom directory.

Here are notable settings in the Scene Render properties:

- Output **panel**: Output is set to a subfolder named HD. Frames per second is set to 60 divided by 1.001, since the video was shot using 1080i. This means HD gives you jitter-free video in spectacular resolution.
- Save Buffers is enabled, which saves each rendered tile as an OpenEXR image as it is rendered, saving memory.
- Render **panel**: OSA and all other rendering options are off. **The size is set to 25%.**

> *I have set Xparts to 16, and Yparts to 9 to match the aspect ratio of the image being processed. While not technically required, it makes all tiles square and divides the image into a reasonable number that each CPU on my PC can handle. See Chapter 10 for more info. On normal machines, though, more parts slows down rendering of simple scenes, but enables rendering of complex ones.*

- Anim **panel**: Do Sequence is enabled so that output from the VSE will be saved into the output folder specified (HD). The end frame is set to 4307, which is the last frame in the video.
- Format: I clicked the HD preset, which filled in SizeX:1920 and SizeY:1080 with square pixels. I selected PNG format since I like to work with frames rather than mess with codec compression while I am working on a video sequence. Only on final composite output do I switch over to FFmpeg encoding. The FPS is set to 60 on this panel, and the divider is set to 1.001. The quality setting I leave at 50 for when I am using JPGs.

  You can click and drag your middle mouse button (MMB) up and down to see the other panels.

Switch now to the Scene Sequencer context, and let me point out how to enable automatic proxies:

- Proxy **panel**: Use Proxy is enabled, along with the Custom Dir. As mentioned, this puts the proxies in the folder that you specify in the Dir field. If you click ReBuild Proxies to refresh (like if the source video has changed) the JPGs will be recomputed and used, so long as you stay in 25% resolution in the Scene-Render context Render panel.

  If you are starting with a fresh project, click Enable Proxies, and the proxies will be built. Rebuilding these 4300 images takes about 5 minutes on my machine, and this is where high-speed (10K RPM, 16M buffer, SATA) hard drives become very important, as disk I/O is often the bottleneck in video.

  - Edit **panel**: This panel shows the frame range covered by the strip, and tells us there are 4306 frames, which run from 1 to 4307.

Making a proxy image sequence can take quite a bit of time and result in in a lot of files. If you don't use a custom directory, the proxy will wind up in a folder under the source video, in a BL_proxy folder. The name of the folder under BL_proxy is the name of the video clip. By using a common folder as the base for all proxies, a team or multiple projects using the same video can use the same proxy, reducing overall disk space and allowing them to be reused.

The proxy sequence for this NASA footage uses 285MB. The compressed MOV video itself uses 78MB. So why use proxies, you may ask, when they take up so much more disk space? The answer is processing speed. To reconstruct an image for you to see, Blender can either simply pull a small 70K JPG file, or it has to call upon the codec to reconstruct the image based on the last keyframe and all changes since. This codec-reconstruction approach takes more real time and lags when working in HD.

An automatic proxy is a frame sequence that is automatically generated for each of the three "less than full" settings: 25%, 50%, and 75%. In Figure 13-12 notice that the blend file has 25% specified in the Render panel. Figure 13-13 shows that Blender creates a folder with the name of the video strip, and under that, a 25 folder. In that folder is a JPG image for each frame, as shown in Figure 13-13. The source video was filmed at 1080i and has a resolution of 60 frames per second. Evidently, this footage was shot at double speed, in HD! I love NASA! If you wanted to extract only 30 FPS, set the step size to 2 in the Anim panel.

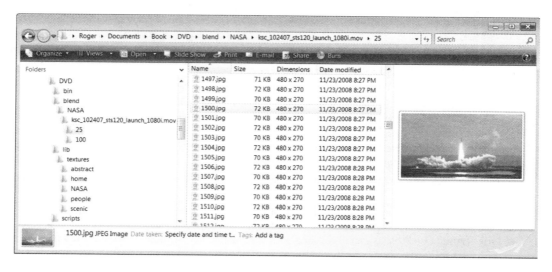

Figure 13-13. Proxy sequence

Real-time scrubbing

With a proxy enabled and now used, you can real-time-scrub back and forth in the timeline window. Simply click and drag left or right. The display will keep up with you, even on a modest PC.

Sequencer Edit panel

This is a very useful panel that, among other things, allows you to quickly position a strip precisely where you want it to occur in your movie. Here are its settings:

- Name: Enter a logical or meaningful the name of the strip here. If blank, the file name is shown in the strip, which may or may not be very helpful in telling what the strip actually shows you.
- Blend Mode: By default, this strip will replace the image of any other strip. Other options include Cross, Add, Sub, Alpha Over, Alpha Under, Gamma Cross, Multiply, and Alpha Over Drop. Each of these modes uses the same formula as those used in texture channels and nodes

- Blend %: The amount of the blend mode to apply. This value has a similar effect as the Col slider when a texture is mapped to color, or the Fac number in a node.

- Mute: When enabled, this strip does not participate in the composite. A great example is shown in the next chapter.

- Lock: Freezes this strip in place—for example, when it is matched up to an audio track—to prevent accidental movement or changes.

- Ipo Frame locked: Enable or disable this to specify whether the blend effect should take place relative to the strip, or relative to the duration of the overall video. When disabled (by default), the Ipo curve runs from 0 to 100, where the "frame" is the percentage along the strip, and the curve denotes the factor to be applied. For example, consider the example in Figure 13-9 where we have a curve that run from 0.0 to 1.0 in the y-axis, and 0 to 100 in the x-axis. This curve means that the blend effect will be 0 at the beginning of the strip, and 1.0 (or 100%) at the very end of the strip. This relative kind of curve will produce the blend effect no matter where this strip is located in the video.

  When Ipo Frame Locked is enabled, then the x-axis of the Ipo curve is an absolute frame number..

- Start: Specifies the starting frame number of the strip. Changing the number here is the same as grabbing and moving the strip left or right with the mouse. I find it much easier, when importing a strip, to just drop it into the channel with the mouse and then change the number here to align the strip horizontally.

- Chan: Specifies the vertical channel number of the strip. Changing the number here is the same as grabbing and moving the strip up and down with the mouse. If any effects are tied to the strip, they also move with the strip. Note that strips cannot lay on top of one another in the same channel. So, if any part of a strip, with the change, would overlay another, Blender keeps going in the direction you indicated to find a clear channel where it can lay alone and not overlay other strips.

- Start-Still: Has the same effect as right-clicking and dragging the left (starting) handle to the left, thus extending the start of the strip. The first image of the video is shown for the specified number of strips before the video starts rolling.

- Start-Ofs: When you bring in a video strip, very often there will be *roll-up*, or frames at the start of camera roll, through the clapper and up to the start of action. All of that video will not make it into the cut, so you can specify here the frame number where you actually want to start using frames. For example, to avoid 10 seconds of roll-up at 24 FPS, set this number to 240. You can also right-click and drag on the left strip handle to change the start offset.

- End-Still: Extends the ending frame of a video strip by the number of frames. This is the same as dragging a strip's right handle to the right.

- End-Ofs: In live-action footage, there is always roll-down, where the action stops, the director yells "cut," and the camera stops rolling. The number here is the offset from the end of the strip where you want to stop using the video. Like Start Ofs, this number is in frames and is relative to the length of the strip. You can also right-click and drag on the right strip handle to change the start offset.

Other information about the strip is displayed for you, such as the number of frames in the strip, the first and last frames that are being used (Start and End Offset), the current frame number being pulled from the video, and the resolution (size in pixels) of each frame.

Practical examples

As I promised earlier in the chapter, we'll now put the histogram view mode and some practical advice together and run through some real-world examples. A digital camera takes an image using a chip that is sensitive to light. However, it is not perfect and may favor certain hues over others, so a bright-red sweater may look like a medium-red sweater. If the picture were taken at night using room light, and the lamp had a blue lampshade, it would look even darker, since the light reaching the sweater was "weak" in the reds, or out of balance. The shadow of the person, cast onto the wall, would be tinted blue as well. To correct for these conditions and make your image look right, you can *lift* some or all colors, and minimize others. While I work through some examples using the whole image, you can apply masks and thus lift a shadow in one area of the image while deepening the shadow in another. *Gain* is brightening an image, or some colors in an image, to "bring them out" and make them more prominent in the picture. Finally, gamma correction can be applied to a CG scene to bring it in line with the background image taken with a camera.

Adjusting lift and gain

Some cameras have a White Balance button and a setting procedure to adjust lift and gain before filming, thus color-correcting during filming. You are able to do the same in postproduction using Blender. If your strip is too dark or light, you can increase the lift to make the overall image brighter, or enter a negative number to make it darker. If you shot at night or under funky lighting conditions, you can adjust the relative strengths of other colors to bring everything into balance.

To make a proper color correction, we will start with some really off-color video that was shot in a brown room at night under horrible lighting (I love a challenge). In the Filter panel, click Use Color Balance, as shown in Figure 13-14.

Without any lift, gain, or gamma correction, the histogram is lumped at the low end. The first step is to lift it all up a little by using an inverse gain of a slight shade of gray, as shown in Figure 13-15.

A normal lift enhances only the colors in the swatch, so we could color-correct for filtered colors using lift. An example is to lift red in underwater pictures, since red is readily filtered out by the water.

We can now see that the Star Destroyer looks brown, not gray as it is in real life in normal light. But if we take out the brown, it will be gray. We do that by clicking on the Gain swatch, and use the eyedropper to sample the Star Destroyer. Clicking Inverse takes out the brown color, resulting in Figure 13-16.

I've given you the Star Destroyer video in the Images/Things folder. As a final adjustment, I also looked at the high end of the spectrum to see that a little red was creeping in at the top end. So, by reclicking on the Gain swatch and sliding the red up a little, I took out the red and balanced the colors nicely.

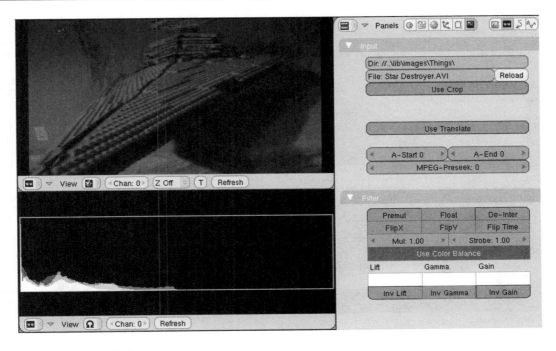

Figure 13-14. Really bad exposure

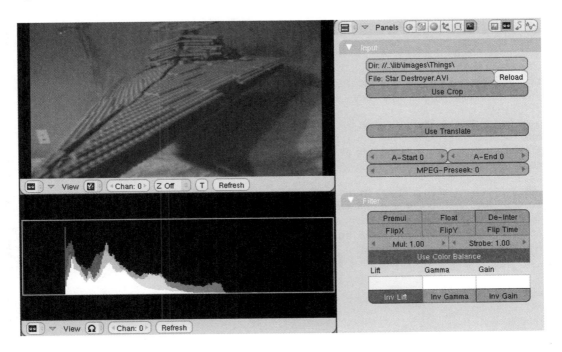

Figure 13-15. Inverse lift to uniformly reduce a color

411

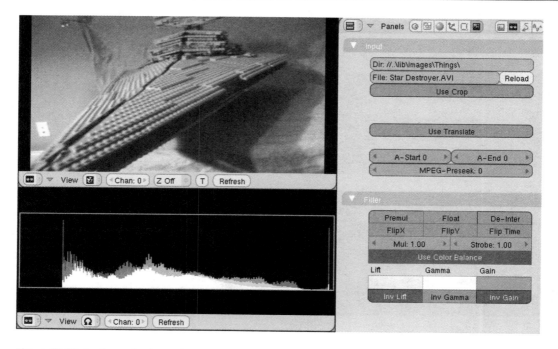

Figure 13-16. Really good color and exposure

Making a slide show

Your poor friend in Jersey is really envious of your vacation, so now let's send her a video slide show of your vacation photos. I'll walk you through composing the first two slides, and then you can decide how badly to rub it in. We will add on to what we have started and make some refinements, just so you can see how things can be done.

Start by opening up 13-SlideShow.blend in the tut folder. It has the first image loaded at 5 seconds into the video, and is set to put out an AVI JPG at 10 frames per second (which should keep down the file size so we can easily e-mail it to all our friends). The buttons window is in the Sequencer buttons context, so you'll have to switch to Render subcontext to see the Render settings.

First let's add a title strip. If you switch to the 3D view layout (1-Model), you will see a text object in 3D space that I have added as a title (we went over title text objects in Chapter 5). Add that as a scene strip into the VSE window—with your cursor in the sequencer window, press the spacebar, click Scene, and then select Scene from the list (the list has only one item, since there is only one scene in this file). Drop the strip around frame 1.

We want this scene to cross over to the first image in a smooth transition, so right-click on the scene strip's rightmost handle and drag it out to frame 70, which is 7 seconds into the video. Your VSE window should now look like Figure 13-17.

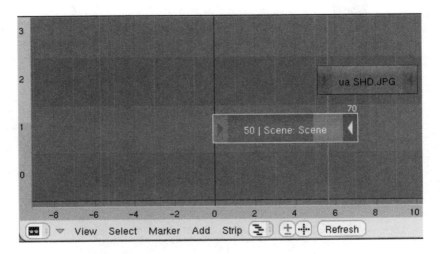

Figure 13-17. Adding a scene strip

Cross and fade transitions

A *cross* is when you blend from one image to another. It sets up a smooth transition from one thought to another or one part of the storyline, to another.

A *fade in* is a transition from a color (typically black) to an image, and a *fade out* is a transition from the image to a color. How long a fade lasts is up to you, but is typically a few seconds. The duration sets the beat, or timing, and partially the mood for the rest of the movie.

To add a cross from the title to our first image, select (right-click) the scene strip, then Shift-select (hold the Shift key down while right-clicking) the image strip, press the spacebar, select Gamma Cross from the menu, and click to drop it into channel 3. Your display, especially your VSE image preview, should now look like Figure 13-18 if you left-click to set the current frame during the cross.

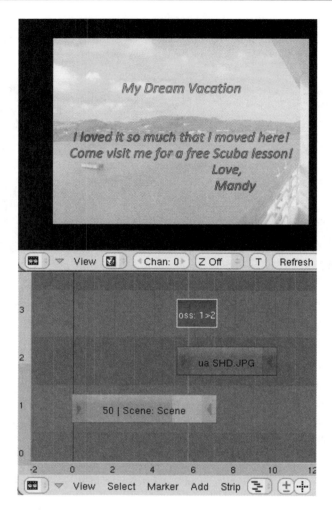

Figure 13-18. Crossing two strips

I want each image to be fully visible for three seconds. If the crosses on the front end and on the back end take 2 seconds each, then each image strip should be 7 seconds long. Select that first image strip, right-click on the right handle, and extend it out to 12 seconds (frame 120). Now just repeat the strip-adding process with beach.jpg in that same directory. Shift-select the two image strips and add another cross, building up your slide show as shown in Figure 13-19.

Figure 13-19. Building your slide show

Cut splice transitions

A splice is any junction between two strips. If the strips are end-to-end, it is called a *cut splice* because the video makes a hard cut from one strip to the next. A cut splice keeps the video lively and interesting. Using cut splice every second or so is great for dialogue, and splices every even given of time, say every two seconds, establish a kind of heartbeat to the video. Once you've set up a "beat," you can then alter that to create a mood, such as by increasing the rate of cuts to build a climax. As a compositor, you have to think in the time dimension as well as the color and image spectra. For example, cuts are important when there's a heated dialogue going on between two people, especially when shots are being fired back and forth, or when a battle is raging. Cuts are disconcerting, sudden, and abrupt.

Let's build a cut splice into our slide show to shock our friend into action by cutting to our contact information. Add a new scene (click on the SCE: selector and select Add New), choose Full Copy and name the scene something like Contact (click into the SCE: name field and edit it). Switch to 1-Model view and edit the text object with something like "Call Me at xxx-xxx-xxxx." Go back to your original scene and add the new scene strip. This time the scene-selection pop-up menu will have Contact in the list.

Drag and drop the Contact scene strip so that it butts right up against the last image (you can put it in the same channel if you wish), so that you have a VSE display as shown in Figure 13-20.

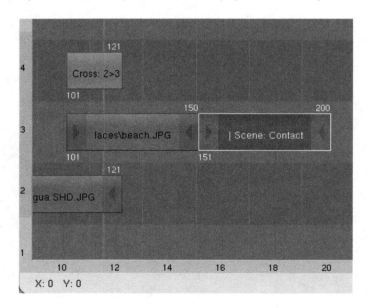

Figure 13-20. Cut splice

> *If a strip has a red outline while you are dragging it around, that means it cannot be dropped there, usually because it would cover up another strip. If you try to click to drop it, Blender will move it up to the next open channel where it will fit.*

Finally, set Animation End to 200 frames, and click the Anim button to render out the video. Your console window will report when it creates the empty video file (along with where it put it), and then report how much time each frame takes to render, as shown in Figure 13-21, if you are using the console window.

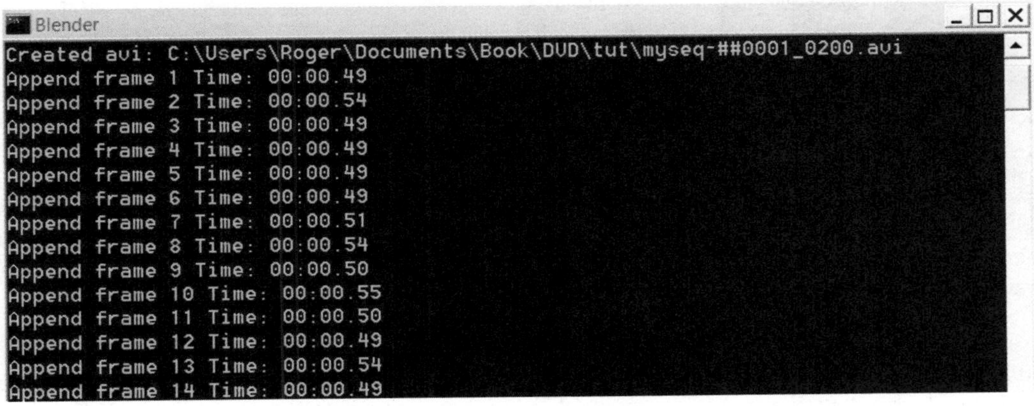

```
Blender                                                          _ □ ×
Created avi: C:\Users\Roger\Documents\Book\DVD\tut\myseq-##0001_0200.avi
Append frame 1 Time: 00:00.49
Append frame 2 Time: 00:00.54
Append frame 3 Time: 00:00.49
Append frame 4 Time: 00:00.49
Append frame 5 Time: 00:00.49
Append frame 6 Time: 00:00.49
Append frame 7 Time: 00:00.51
Append frame 8 Time: 00:00.54
Append frame 9 Time: 00:00.50
Append frame 10 Time: 00:00.55
Append frame 11 Time: 00:00.50
Append frame 12 Time: 00:00.49
Append frame 13 Time: 00:00.54
Append frame 14 Time: 00:00.49
```

Figure 13-21. Console output

When finished, the video, in the format specified in the Format panel, is put in the directory specified in the Output panel, ready to be e-mailed to your jealous friend in Jersey.

Image-format conversion

To solidify your understanding of the VSE, let's examine a simple use of the VSE: resizing/reformatting an image. Assume we want to e-mail a vacation photo, but it is very high resolution and is a large file size. In the VSE window header, click Add ➤ Images, and a window pane will switch to a file browser. Locate the image lib\images\places\Antigua SHD.JPG on the DVD. In the file browser, select the image by right-clicking on the file name, and click Select Images. Immediately, the strip will appear in the VSE window, and be "rubber-banded" to your mouse cursor. Click to drop the strip about at the start of frame 10 in channel 1, as shown in Figure 13-22. Don't worry too much if you can't get it exactly, because now I want you to switch to the buttons window to the Scene Sequencer set of panels. In the Edit panel, locate the Starting Frame and Channel fields, and change them both to 1. Your image strip should now look like the figure.

> You can also hover your mouse in the VSE window and press the spacebar, which (just like in 3D view) brings up a list of what you can add. Blender assumes you probably want to add some sort of sequence strip, and shows you what you can add or do in a rather long list. This list basically breaks down into images, video, audio, a scene, and effects.

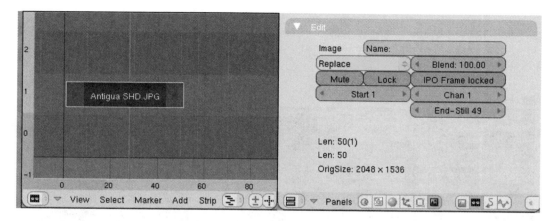

Figure 13-22. Image strip

In the buttons window, switch to the Render context, and click the PC preset on the Format panel, and of course the Do Sequence button on the Anim panel. If you press F12 now (with your timeline on frame 1), the source image is shown in 640×480, even though the source image is 2048×1536. Blender automatically stretches or reduces the image to fit the whole render size. If you select, say, 25% HD and click Render, you still get the image filling the whole frame, distorted slightly to fit the different image aspect ratio.

To e-mail this image, we want to not only reduce the image in resolution, but also in file size. Therefore, in the Format panel, set the image format to JPG, and use a 60% quality compression (the Q: field), as shown in Figure 13-23.

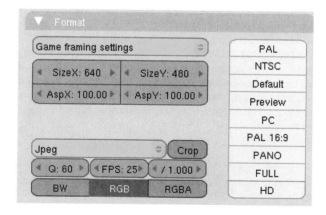

Figure 13-23. JPEG image compression

Now press F12 and voilà! The image pops up in a render window, formatted and compressed. We can now press F3 to save the image in a new file, and e-mail it to our friend who is freezing in New Jersey in the middle of winter, and gloat.

Compositor and sequencer scale and use images differently

Notice that when we added the image, the VSE created an image strip 50 frames long and resized the large image to fit the smaller output. 50 frames is 2 seconds of video at 25 FPS. This behavior is unlike the compositor in two aspects. First, a compositor image-input node will put out the image for every frame through its image socket, forever and not just 50 frames. Second, the compositor takes the middle set of pixels and goes outward in a cropping type of behavior (unless you scale it with a scale node), whereas the sequencer automatically scales to the output. If the input image is smaller than you desired, the VSE will stretch the image to fit the larger canvas. Conversely, the compositor will simply make a border around the image (unless you scale it with a scale node).

Automatic video/image conversion

If the input image to the strip is any other still image format, such as a PNG, Blender automatically converts the image format to JPG (or whatever output format you choose) when you save it. **Blender can mix and match any combination of any supported image or video format**. If the input strip were a video, such as an AVI, and you set a still image format (JPG in this example) to save in, then Blender would decode and save just that single frame as a JPG image when you press F3 or select File ➤ Save Rendered Image. In other words, if you have set your output format to a still image, such as JPG, then you will save either one JPG image or a sequence of JPG images, depending on whether you render and save one *image* (by clicking the Render button followed by F3, or by pressing F12 and then saving the image via F3), or whether you click the Anim button or press Ctrl+F12.

The output image/sequence always goes to the folder specified in the Output panel. The file name of the files in the image sequence is also what you enter in the Output panel. For example, clicking Anim (with a Start of 1, an End of 50, and an output of "myseq-##" as shown in Figure 13-24) will result in 50 files named myseq-01.jpg, myseq-02.jpg, and so on through myseq-50.jpg. This is great for splitting a video file into individual frames, possibly for hand-painting or other custom processing.

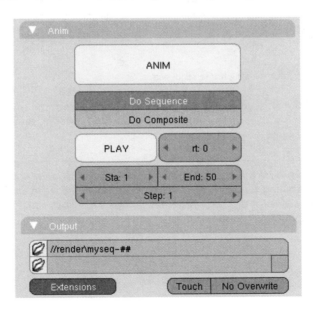

Figure 13-24. Fifty-frame-sequence output

If you click Anim to produce an animation, but you have a still image format as your output format, Blender creates a *frame sequence*. A frame sequence is a series of files, each on an image, with one file per frame. By convention, the frames are named and numbered by using the output folder/filespec name, and then appending a four-digit frame number. If you want fewer or more digits in the file name, use a pound sign (#) for each digit. Figure 13-25 shows both the console output and render settings when you click Anim using a still image format.

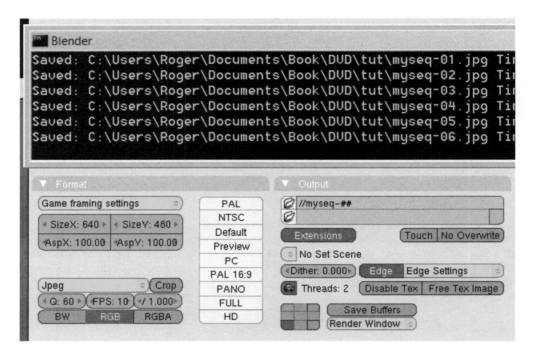

Figure 13-25. Console output showing frame sequence

If you specify a video format, such as AVI, Blender makes a video from the strips based on the frame range set up in the Anim panel. If there aren't any strip portions covering some frames, then Blender just makes those frames black.

> If you are going to be doing a lot of cutting and editing of an AVI or MOV strip, I **strongly recommend** that you convert it first to a frame sequence, and do the work with the frame sequence strip, not the original movie. I have had issues with the codec splitting the video incorrectly or inconsistently.

To use a frame sequence as an input, select Add ➤ Images as before, since the individual files are images. Then, in the file browser, navigate to the parent directory containing the image sequence. You now have three choices:

- To use all the image files in the folder, just right-click on the folder name and click Select Images. Each of the images will be brought in, one image per frame.

- If you left-click on a folder name, you drill into that folder. If you want to use all of the files in that folder, just press A to select all (just like selecting all in 3D view or in the compositor) and then click Select Images. Each image will be brought in as one frame per image, even if the image files are not named sequentially.

- To use some of the image files in the folder, left-click on the folder name to drill into the folder. You will see the names of all the images files there. Otherwise, select the files you wish by right-clicking and dragging, in a box type of selection, over the files you want. To make the selection cumulative so you can Shift-right-click and drag, right-click and drag some more to add to the selected list. Right-click on a selected file to deselect it. Selected files are highlighted in yellow, and indicated as image files with a blue box icon next to their name. Click Select Images to bring those images in, one image per frame.

> *Press X to delete the selected strips, just like X deletes objects in 3D view.*

Summary

In this chapter you learned how to make the most basic use of Blender's sequencer to arrange and combine video strips. The functionality discussed integrates any kind of image, video, and CG elements from the 3D view. While a few standard screens have been defined for you, you can create new screens that better suit the task at hand. The VSE can create one file that contains your movie, or a series of files that are each a frame. You use a frame sequence if you are going to be doing later compositing and/or using various codecs to compress the final video, balancing file size and image quality. Finally, the VSE has several display modes that help you produce good-looking video that is exposed and colored correctly. Let's move on and examine some advanced uses of the VSE, including audio integration into your final video output.

Chapter 14

SEQUENCER EFFECTS

So far, we've been working with only video images in the sequencer, but audio also conveys information and a lot of excitement, so let's dive into that in this chapter. We'll discuss editing strips, bringing in two shots from a movie, editing them, and then adding a title through splices and transitions. I'll then present some special effects and good old masking, and go into detail on how to animate those built-in effects. I will then discuss the sequencer plug-in system, and highlight a particularly useful plug-in that I have used for green-screen processing. You will then learn about processing audio, and we'll conclude with a short discussion on a very interesting new form of media: user-generated content called *mashups*.

Loading combined audio/video

There are two ways to handle film and an audio track. Most movies that you load will have the video and audio already integrated, and when you load that strip, two strips appear in the VSE; one for the audio (green) and another for the video (blue). As long as you have the FPS set correctly, they both will be of exactly the same length and be synchronized. However, you may get them as separate files, and thus you need to synchronize them. A common method to synchronize them is to clap at the beginning of the video using either your hands or a slate that has a hinged top part that you slap together to make an audio spike. To start, you load the film track (Images or Movie), and the audio tracks separately and align them so that the claps synchronize—the audio spike on the soundtrack, and the video image of the clapper (slate) coming together.

> *Be sure to set the matching FPS in the* Format *panel before loading a video strip, or else the audio length won't match the video.*

Let's work through an example and produce a final product of a title sequence and two clips that transition from one to another. Start a new Blender session and switch to the 8-Sequence screen. Enable the speaker in your timeline window header so that audio strips added to the sequencer will be heard during scrubbing and playback.

To set up your output, you have to know a little about your input. The clips we will be using were shot in HD at 29.97 FPS (NTSC speed). The quick way to replicate this is as follows:

1. Click the NTSC preset (sets your FPS to 30 and divider to 1.001 to give 29.97 FPS exactly).

2. Click the HD preset (sets the proper aspect/resolution to match the input).

While you're at it, go ahead and set up your output as well, with all of the settings shown in Figure 14-1:

1. To save space and time, click 50% proxy size in the Render panel.

2. Enable Do Sequence and set your end frame to 1500.

3. Set where you want your output to go, i.e., //render\ in the output path.

4. Change the format to FFmpeg (allows us to save an audio-video (AV) movie).

5. In the Video panel (revealed when you change the format to FFmpeg), select QuickTime as the format, and H.264 as the codec.

6. In the Audio panel (revealed when you change format to FFMPEG), enable multiplex audio and choose MP3 as the audio format.

> *The default FFmpeg video preset is using the MPEG-2 codec, which is very popular. You can leave it as is, but it produces a file that ends in .dvd. While the VLC player plays that fine, QuickTime cannot. Windows Media Player does not recognize .dvd as a valid media extension, but it can play it—just change the extension to mpg.*

That completes the setup steps, so save your file now. If you will be working a lot in HD for NTSC broadcast, you might want to save an extra copy in your library as a template. Now we are going to load in the first clip and render a quick test.

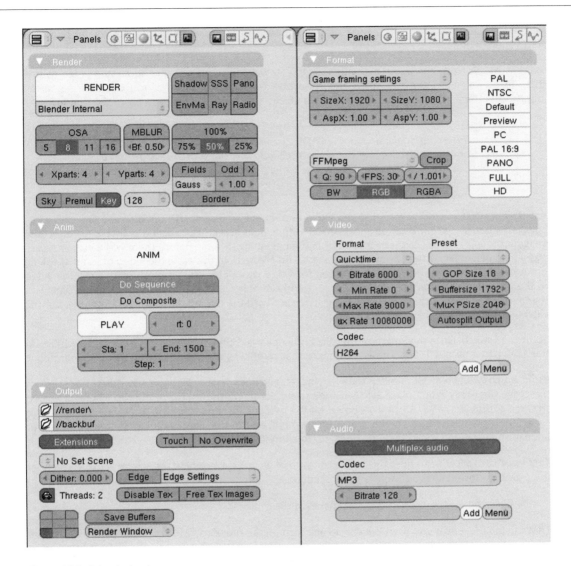

Figure 14-1. Setup to load

Load the movie clip: From the sequence window header menu, select Add ➤ Movie+Audio(HD). Select lib/images/RobCollins/48-01.mov, which is a 53-second clip from Rob Collins' latest 48-hour project, a Gatsby-era retrospective. Drop the 1,599-frame clip into channel 1, frame 1. Note that when you drop it, the video (blue) and audio (green) strips occupy channels 1 and 2, respectively. Be sure to enable the speaker icon on the timeline if you want to hear the audio. The audio and video strips should be the same length; if they aren't then you do not have the FPS set correctly. There are only so many frames in a video file, but the audio length is computed based on a duration (seconds) when it is loaded. Using these two different measurement units gives you a visual confirmation that you have set the FPS correctly. Changing the FPS *after* you load will not resize the strips; you have to reload or adjust them manually.

Make a meta: Since the audio and video align, you want to work with the audio and video as one strip. To do so, select the two strips and choose Strip ➤ Make Meta Strip. You can then name the metastrip in the Edit panel and it will be shown on the strip in the Video Sequence Editor window.

> Some video containers, such as WMV files, can be processed if you load just the Movie strip from the WMV file, and then separately add the Audio (HD) strip, rather than all at once using Movie+Audio. Then make a meta strip from those two separate strips.

You do not want to work with audio and video as a meta if you want the audio to overlap, or bridge, between video shots. For example, a voiceover with a black screen can make a dramatic introduction. Imagine *the voice* (James Earl Jones) saying, "In the beginning of time, before there was a heaven, there was a man unlike any other" as the video fades in on *the hero*. In this case, the video of Jones speaking is not needed; we want only the audio track; for video we will be using a black screen and the video of the actor. Making a music video is another good example: you need to keep the band in sync with the music as you interleave other shots and special effects; the audio track plays continuously, but the video is chopped up.

Span the length: Note the length of the clip, and copy that number into your animation end frame in the Anim panel (about 1500). This is set now so that scrubbing and playback won't end prematurely.

Build a proxy: Enable Use Proxy in the Proxy panel, and click Rebuild Proxy. If you don't use a custom directory, the proxy is put in a specially named subfolder under the source of the clip. There can be up to three subfolders: a 25, 50, and 75 based on the percentage resolution you are rendering at (in our case, 50). A proxy operation builds a proxy for every frame in the video, not just the ones inside your animation range, and it can take a bit of time to complete.

Test your setup: Let's rerender this movie to test that we have everything set up correctly. To rerender the movie, follow this very complicated procedure:

- Click the Anim button in the Anim panel in the Buttons Scene Render context.

That's it! Simple, eh? If you used the QuickTime format, the file 0001-1500.mov will be in your output folder, which you should be able to play using QuickTime or VLC. If you used the default MPEG2 format and haven't specified any file-name prefix, the file 0001_1500.dvd will be created in your output folder, which you can play in the VLC player (rename to .mpg to play it in WMP).

We have just converted one HD audio/video movie to another that is 50% smaller in resolution. Personally, I like the H.264 codec in any video, as it gives an overall balance between quality (a minimum of compression artifacts) and file size. Rendering our first example creates a file that is only 5MB, compared to the original 166MB. Confirm that it plays well outside of Blender in the popular and free QuickTime Player (Windows/Mac) or the VLC player (Windows/Mac/Linux).

Editing strips

Within a movie strip there is some usable footage, and when dealing with footage there are some important considerations. When you film, the director calls for quiet on the set, and the cameraman starts filming. There may be a clapper snapped in camera view to document the scene and to provide a nice sync point for audio to the film. The director then calls for "action" and the actors start acting. The action ends, and the director yells "cut" and the camera rolls to a stop.

> *The word "footage" comes from the fact that a reel of real film stock was once sold in feet. At 24 FPS, you shot 2 feet of film per second.*

The shot that you are working with contains footage at the beginning that needs to be cut out (called *roll-up*), and footage at the end (called *roll-down*).

Open the file tut/14-takes.blend, and all of this should be set up for you. Take a moment to review all the settings that we have discussed. Our first clip is 1599 frames long. Go ahead and scrub the footage and figure out when you would want to cut the roll-up and roll-down. Since the audio-video was recorded in-camera, there's no need for a clapper—Rob just started filming and you can hear him announce, "We're rolling!" and do a countdown. Around frame 250 is a good place to start, with frames 1 through 249 being the roll-up. After the actors deliver their lines, when the psychiatrist says, "Or maybe it's you're crazy; I don't know" (around frame 1,370) would be a good place to cut. Use your PR preview (in the timeline window header) to test.

There are several ways to deal with roll-up/roll-down:

- If the strip is the first in the set you are working on, simply drag its "start" into negative frame territory, as shown in Figure 14-2. Since Blender can start rendering only at frame 1 or greater, it will pick up and start midstrip.

- If the strip is the first one in the overall movie, change your animation start as shown in Figure 14-3. Blender now starts rendering at that frame (251 in the example), not frame 1.

- Either set the Start-Ofs field manually, or right-click and drag the left end of the strip to the right (click when you have the desired offset) to offset or redefine what frame to use as the first frame of the strip. An underline shows what has been "cut," as shown in Figure 14-4. I prefer this method to cut roll-up when dealing with an encoded video. The net length of the strip is shown as Len:, with the original length in parentheses.

- Physically cut the strip by positioning in time where you want the cut, and press K. This cuts the strip into two strips, and the left-hand strip will be selected as shown in Figure 14-5. You can press X to delete the left strip since it is roll-up (or to cut the right one when cutting roll-down). I prefer this method when working with image sequences. I have had issues with the codec not properly decoding a strip segment using this method. However, this method works flawlessly when working with frame sequences, discussed in the previous chapter.

Figure 14-2. Drag the first clip of a movie into negative territory to cut roll-up. Image courtesy of Rob Collins Productions.

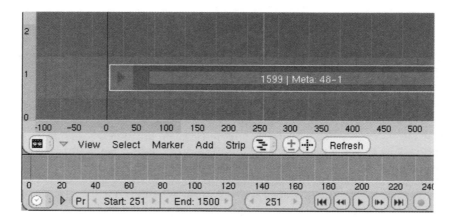

Figure 14-3. Change the animation-range start.

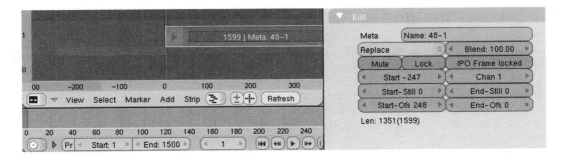

Figure 14-4. Change the start offset (recommended for encoded video).

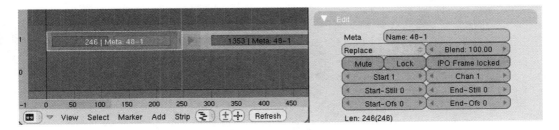

Figure 14-5. Cut a strip at the current frame by pressing K. Recommended for image sequence strips.

Since we are dealing with an encoded video, let's use the offset method. Enter 250 in Start-Ofs, and, since we want it to end at original frame 1370, enter 1599–1370 in End-Ofs (which should give 229 when you press Enter). Drag the strip so that the first usable frame of the strip is at frame 91 in the main timeline (as you drag, Blender shows you the starting frame number).

Editing multiple takes

You can use the VSE to evaluate multiple takes to see which shot you want as the final. Once you find the take you like, simply edit it using one of the techniques described previously.

> The Stamp panel allows you to overlay the movie with critical information about the shot, such as the time code, that allows easy reference to the movie in making criticisms or suggesting changes.

Interleaving multiple cameras

Many times a scene will be shot from multiple camera angles, either with the actors repeating the scene with the camera in two different locations, or with two cameras rolling simultaneously. An example is filming two people talking about something and sharing *opposing* viewpoints. Rather than present them together in the same frame (which visually implies a link, or togetherness), the director chooses to present them in their own independent frame. That way, they do not appear together, and are thus visually apart (reinforcing that notion that they don't get along). Even though they are looking directly at each other, they don't share screen space.

A practical example is simply filming each actor face-on to the camera as they recite their lines. There will be two video strips to load; cut each one to extract a good take of a delivery, ignoring any flubs, trimming any roll-down, and interleave the two with cut splices as shown in Figure 14-6.

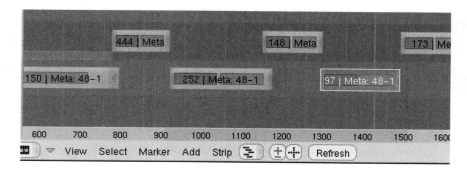

Figure 14-6. Interleave cut strips for dialogue. Actor A is on the top channel, Actor B is beneath.

Interleaving might be another situation in which you don't want the audio and video together as a metastrip. For example, if you want to show Actor A's reaction to what Actor B is saying, then you would have the audio track for Actor B play while the video for Actor A is showing, and you'd "mute" the video for Actor B.

Splice and transition effects

Now let's load and work with the second shot and talk about splices and transitions. To mute the first strip so that it doesn't get in your way, press H (analogous to Hide in 3D view). Load the second clip, 48-2.mov, from that same directory, dropping it in channel 2, starting around frame 900. Review the footage and repeat the editing process (cutting roll-up and roll-down). You should make a proxy and determine the usable footage; I suggest that frames 301–816 of the strip are usable since that span starts with her turning and looking just off camera, and just catches the main actor calling out her name. A great ending to the shot is when the main actor gets punched out, around frame 816, and of course before everyone on-set starts laughing (which is good stuff for the bloopers roll). Use these numbers to enter your starting and ending offsets. If you are following my suggestions, the action for the second strip starts at frame 1213. As you drag the second strip, Blender cues you to the fact that strip 1 ends at frame 1212. So, if you drop the second strip right at 1213, strip one will end and cut right over to strip two. This is a cut splice, as the video from channel 1 is cut off from and goes to the next shot at the next frame because the strip in channel 2 is in replace mode.

Normally the video from one strip will replace the video from a strip in a lower-numbered channel. Simply putting a video in channel 3 will cause that image to be displayed instead of the video from a strip in channel 2, because the default blend mode, shown in Figure 14-7, is Replace. Thus, if we put shot 48-2 in channel 2, and shot 48-1 in channel 1, we really don't need to worry about "ending" strip 48-1, since 48-2 will replace it when it starts. Use this tip to speed your workflow; you don't really need to worry about roll-down when using cut splices, since the end of the strip is cut off anyway.

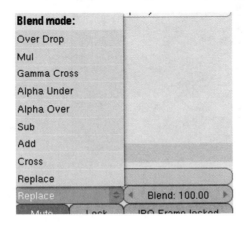

Figure 14-7. Strip blending modes

Let's explore the other blending modes and add a title sequence to our two shots. Switch to 3D view and make a title using text objects—use your imagination. Set the render alpha type to Key so that the sky color does not affect your text.

Back on the sequence screen screen, add the scene strip to channel 3, enable Premultiply, and extend it from frames 1 to 121 by right-clicking on the end of the strip, dragging to the left, and left-clicking to drop the ending in place. Change its blend mode to Alpha Over. Select the first strip and unmute it, and should have something like Figure 14-8.

If you set your end to about 1725, you should now have a title sequence and two shots in the can!

"In the can" is yet another saying from film antiquity, when exposed film was put back into the canister it came in and sent out for developing. Since filming was complete, the shot was said to be "in the can," meaning principal photography was done, a major milestone in the project.

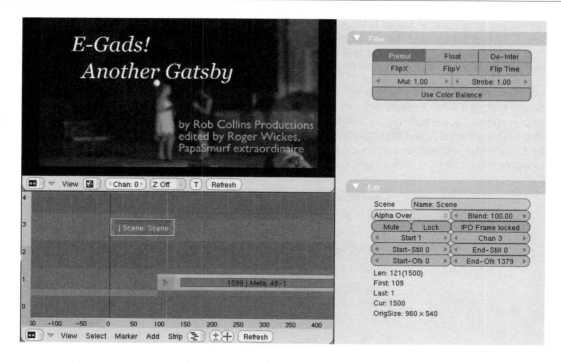

Figure 14-8. Blending a scene strip. Image courtesy of Rob Collins Productions.

Gamma cross-fade

We talked about cross and fade in the previous chapter, but specifically the Gamma Cross effect makes a smooth transition from one strip to another since it introduces gamma correction during the transition. To try this, you can overlap shot 48-1 and shot 48-2 by a few frames, select strip 1, Shift-select strip 2, and then choose Add ➤ Effect ➤ Gamma Cross as shown in Figure 14-9.

When you select Gamma Cross, a new effects strip will be rubber-banded to your cursor; simply click to drop it in place, and it will seek out the highest channel, thus overriding any strips below it. It generates its image based on what you have told it to do—namely, to make a gamma-corrected image by fading from one image to the other, as shown in Figure 14-10.

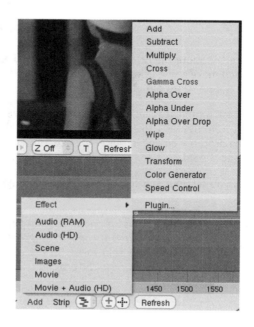

Figure 14-9. Fading between two strips

Figure 14-10. Gamma Cross fade. Image courtesy of Rob Collins Productions.

In this case, to use this fade effectively, we need to reduce the starting offset of the first strip so that the "maybe you're crazy" audio from the psychiatrist ends as the main actor calls out, "Ruby." Blending these two images, thus putting the psychiatrist and Ruby in the same image, visually conveys the notion that the main actor is crazy about Ruby, thus reinforcing the dialogue and making it stronger.

Wipe effect and other effects in general

Different effects strips have different controls, and those controls will be located on their Effect panel, an example of which is shown in Figure 14-11. The Wipe effect is actually four wipe effects in one, selected via the top selector: single, double, iris, and clock. Experiment with each of these to see how they work.

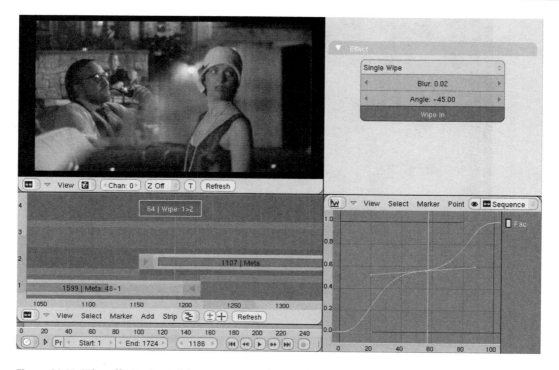

Figure 14-11. Wipe effect animated. Image courtesy of Rob Collins Productions.

Since each effect is different, there are different controls for each. Thankfully, most of the controls are self-evident. Notice that I have animated the effect to hang slightly in the middle. You will notice this wipe in action in the *Star Wars* films (and in many TV commercials).

Juxtapose

TV news shows often have an announcer and a remote commenter or subject-matter expert onscreen, side by side. To achieve this look, load the two video streams, one above the other. Translate the top strip (as described in Chapter 13) by half the resolution width, and set the blending mode to AlphaOver. In Figure 14-12, the left image of the urban cowboy is selected and translated left, the balloon girl is translated right, and the sequencer takes the result and scales it automatically to fit within the final output window resolution. When juxtaposing, try to keep both actors' eyelines even with each other.

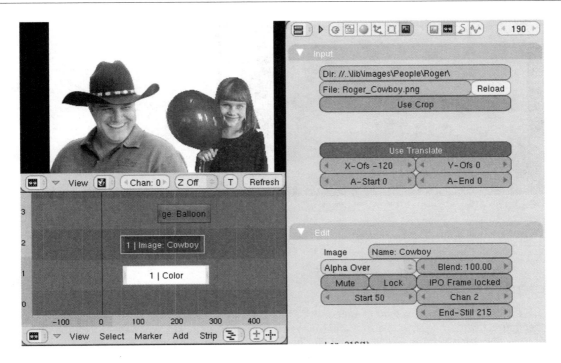

Figure 14-12. Juxtaposing two images/videos in the same frame

Glow effect

A very cool effect is a luminous, volumetric kind of glowing that can be added to any image. In Figure 14-13, we've applied the glow to a scene where the young lovers are, well, glowing with love. This effect also blurs the background with light, and blurs a particularly annoying lamp that was, unfortunately, right between them and very distracting to the image. Use this effect on lightsabers, fire, mystical magical orbs, and the like. I think that glowing gives a warm, beautiful effect when used subtly. When used to the extreme, of course (and animated as I discuss later), it can be used to simulate begin phasered out of existence or being heated (especially when a little red is added from a color effects strip).

Figure 14-13. Glow effect. Image courtesy of Rob Collins Productions.

Speed Control effect

Use the Speed Control strip type to speed up (Global Speed >1) or slow down (<1.0) a film clip. The speed effect works on the whole strip and throws off the audio track, so if you want to vary the speed of the video, such as normal-slow-normal, (for instance, as the lovers embrace, slow it down just a lit-tle), you will need to cut the audio separately and readjust the position of the remaining audio so that it resynchronizes with the resumed action. With the video strip selected, create a Sequence Ipo curve.. If the Ipo value runs from [0..1] are enabled, Y values in the Ipo curve correspond to frames within the strip that should be rendered. A Y value of 0 (zero) tells Blender to pull and render frames from the beginning frame of the strip, 1 means the end frame of the strip, and values in between mean that percentage along the middle of the strip. In Figure 14-14, the actors were a little stiff in their embrace, and slowing it down just a touch made it smoother and more loving. In this figure I enabled IPO is Velocity, which changes the meaning of the Sequence curve. When enabled, the Y value is a velocity multiplier; 1 means normal speed, 0 means stop action, 2 means twice as fast, and so on.

The speed effect remaps the frames but does not change the strip length, so you have to extend the strip out so that you can use all the frames (in the case of a slowdown), or shrink it if you speed it up, as the strip will run out of frames to show. I've seen this effect used very effectively when the boy sees the girl of his dreams, and time seems to slow as she smiles at him. Ah, love. A touch of glow helps convey this emotion as well. If you are slowing down a lot, click Enable Frame Blending, or the video may look choppy because Blender does not have the in-between frames to supply at the correct frame rate. When frame blending is enabled, Blender will attempt to intelligently create them for you by merging the boundary frames.

Figure 14-14. Speed control (animated)

Offset blending effect

This is a very neat, slinky kind of effect, shown in Figure 14-15, which is very simple to do. Simply start with a base color or image. Add your CG scene strip and set its blending mode to Alpha Over. Then press Shift+D to duplicate the strip, and move it one channel up and one frame over. Set the Blend factor to 10% less, and repeat this ten times or so. Add motion blur, and any action in your CG scene will be hyper-blurred, leaving a long trail that fades out over time. This example is in the HyperBlur scene of the tut\14-plugins file. Please note that motion blur (MBlur on the Render panel) is on for effectively ten frames for every frame, so rendering takes awhile.

I would be remiss if I did not mention the original sequencer tutorial, created about ten years ago but still fantastic (it instilled the love of the sequencer in me). It's available at http://wiki.blender. org/index.php/Doc:Tutorials/Sequencer/Learning_the_sequencer_(old). In that tutorial, this offset blending is done very well with a cube and a wireframe of the cube to make a very neat following effect.

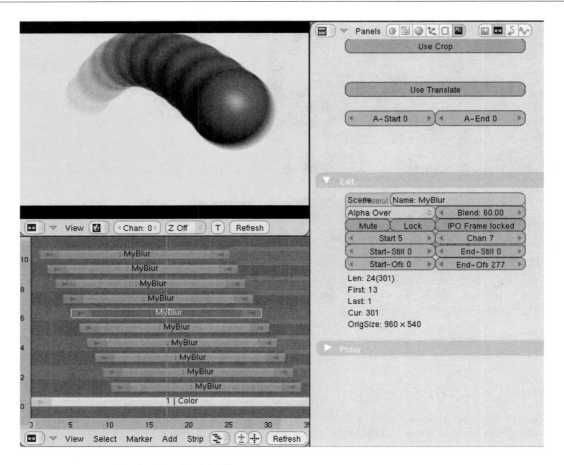

Figure 14-15. Hyper-blurring via offset blending

Masking in the sequencer

In your 3D view, you create an object that will function as a mask. You have two choices. First, you can assign a shadeless material so that the mask is white. Then, the image for the scene will be black-and-white, which will make a great mask. You then add the scene strip. Alternatively, you can add the scene strip and use the Alphamatte plug-in effect on the scene strip, which will convert the alpha channel to a black-and-white mask.

Add the image you wish to mask, and set its blending mode to Mul to multiply it times the mask below it. The result will be the masked result that you can then save as an RGBA image to be used as an element later on, as shown in Figure 14-16.

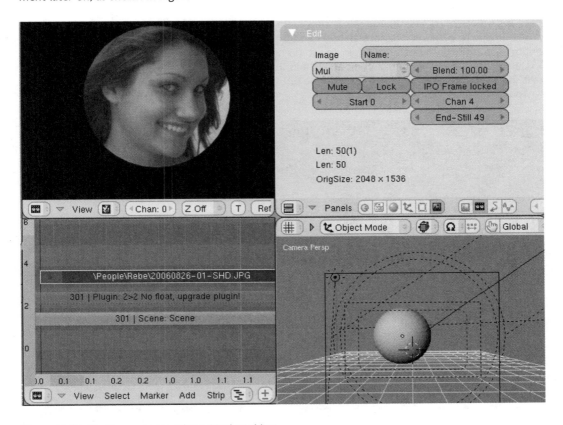

Figure 14-16. Masking an image using a 3D view object

This effect was also used as a sort of spotlight effect in the James Bond movies' opening sequences, where the spotlight was supposed to be the vision through the barrel of a gun, and the image masked was just a video strip of James walking (and firing the deadly shot).

Animate the mask as an object (in the James Bond case, a simple sphere or circle), moving it closer to the camera to enlarge, or farther away to shrink. Alternatively, animate the scale of the mask object to make it change size.

Animating VSE effects

Animation is done through the sequence mode of the Ipo, shown in the header of the Ipo window type. The counter at the bottom of the Ipo window (the x-axis) is the percentage complete of the strip, regardless of its length. The y-axis runs from 0 to 1.0 and reflects the percentage application of the effect. To demonstrate, let's animate a title to fade out as the first shot starts, so that it has a smoother transition. In the Ipo window, select Ipo type Sequence and select the scene strip. At around 75%, Ctrl-click to place a control point at 1.0, and then at 100%, Ctrl-click at 0, giving an Ipo curve like that shown in Figure 14-17, which should fade out the title as the first clip starts. In this case, the Ipo curve is animating the general opacity.

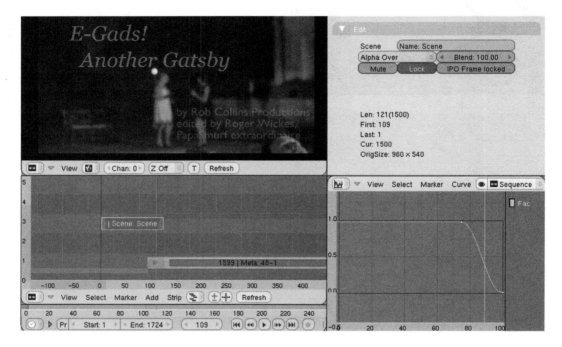

Figure 14-17. Animating the blending mode effect. Image courtesy of Rob Collins Productions.

Any effect is animated this way, with one exception: the Translate Input effect, which is animated by specifying the frame offset in the A-Start and A-End fields (at A-End the translate is in full effect).

To animate any of the blending effects, you need to use an effects strip, not simply the strip-blending mode. For example, to change the precise timing or speed of a cross using an Ipo curve, Shift-select both strips (both of which are in the replace blending mode) and choose Add ➤ Effect ➤ Cross. Then with the cross strip selected, create the Ipo curve. This animates the cross effect from a linear type of cross-blending to an accelerated or spline blend. You can warble an effect by making a sinusoidal curve.

VSE plug-in effects

There are over 20 neat and useful effects that have been coded and can be downloaded for free and plugged in when needed. These take the form of a dynamic load library (DLL). You download these DLLs and put them in a folder, the path and name of which is specified in the user preferences window, File Paths context, Seq Plugins field. I keep all of mine on my Windows machine in the c:\ blender\lib\bin\seq-plugin folder. There is no "installation" procedure; simply put the file there. The semiofficial repository of plug-ins is hosted by the University of Minnesota at their web site: http://www-users.cs.umn.edu/~mein/blender/plugins/sequence.html, and many thanks to Blender programmer paprmh for recompiling and organizing them.

When you wish to use a plug-in effect, simply choose Add ➤ Effect ➤ Plugin, and a file browser window will open, positioned to your Sequence Plug-in folder. You just choose the plug-in and click Select Plug-in. For Windows machines, plug-ins have a .dll extension and their Linux and OS X cousins have a .so extension. They both do the same thing, but are compiled to run on the different operating systems. Please note that a plug-in compiled for Linux will have a .so extension, but will not run on a Mac, and vice versa. The file name must indicate which operating system the plug-in is for, such as greenscreen-OSX.so.

Example plug-in: green screen

I'd like to highlight one plug-in in particular, the green-screen plug-in by Rob (aka paprmh). To demonstrate, load the green-screen footage from your DVD in lib/images/RobCollins/green.mov.

With the video strip selected, choose Add ➤ Effect ➤ Plugin, navigate to the bin\seq-plugins\ folder on your DVD, and select greenscreen1.3.dll (or whichever .so variety is appropriate for your operating system), click Select Plug-in, and then click to drop the clip.

Activate the plug-in by enabling the greenscreen1.3 button in the upper-left-hand corner of the Effect panel. Enable edge blur, and you have pulled a great matte! The plug-in works pretty much automagically, as shown in Figure 14-18. If you need to tune the settings, just go to http://paprmh. googlepages.com/greenscreen for a full discussion of each one.

Now, because the green screen did not cover the complete camera view, you have to crop out the left and right sides by 350 pixels, and then translate X-Ofs by 350 to recenter the actor. Load your background image or B-roll into the sequencer (or you can use the plug-in to directly substitute a pleasing solid color), set it to Alpha under the plug-in strip, and away you go!

The only issue with green screen, in general, is matching the lighting in the studio with that of the real background. In Figure 14-18, you can see the stack of effect strips that layer up to make the final composition. I added a slight glow to the actor because the background image was obviously shot in bright sunshine. The other issue is matching camera angles between elements. You can open tut\14-plugins.blend to play with the live example. There you will see that I had to shift both the background image and the green-screen footage to get what I thought was a realistic camera angle (and to center the actor's face at the upper-third line, which follows the compositing rule of thirds).

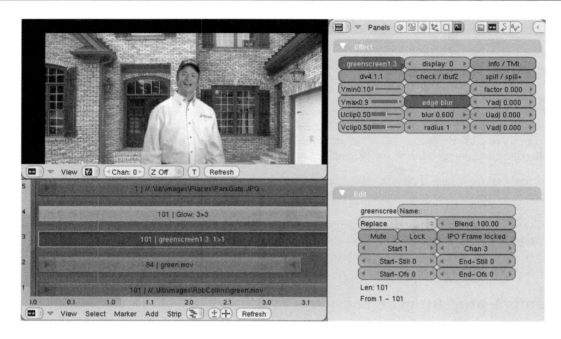

Figure 14-18. Green-screen plug-in at work. Foreground image courtesy of Rob Collins Productions.

Other plug-ins

I've written the online wiki book on all of the Blender plug-ins, with examples, at http://wiki.blender.org/index.php/Doc:Manual/Sequencer/Effects/Plugins, so I won't repeat that here. In summary, plug-ins that I know work and that are pretty cool include the following:

- **Alpha Matte**: Turns an alpha channel into a black-and-white matte image, allowing you to use Multiply and/or additional masking operations.
- **Blur**: Blurs an image.
- **Cartoon**: Outlines/edges an image.
- **Chromakey RGB**: Pulls a matte of any color.
- **Chromakey YUV**: Pulls a matte based on a YUV color range.
- **Clockwipe**: Transitions using a clockwise wipe, but may now be redundant with the wipe effect discussed previously.
- **Desaturate**: Makes colors enhanced or flatter.
- **Dice**: Dissolves the image into tiny squares.
- **Diff**: Subtracts one image from another.
- **Invert**: Flips an image; useful for mattes.

- **Iris**: Transitions between two clips in a circular manner, like the iris of a lens.
- **Jitter**: Jiggles the image; simulates high-velocity turbulence and shake, or footsteps from a T. rex on the prowl.
- **Lightsaber**: Much like the glow effect, but adds color all in one step.
- **LSD**: Warbles the color in a far-out way, dude.
- **OldMovie**: Adds spots and streaks to an image, and turns it black-and-white like, well, an old movie.
- **Pixelize**: Reduces the resolution of an image.
- **Red-Green Stereo Plugin Effect**: For making stereograms with those funky red-green glasses. Use two video strips, each shot from different angles. For live motion, you can duct-tape two cameras side by side while filming, and use this plug-in to make a 3-D movie.
- **Scatter Plugin Effect**: Simulates a poor video signal.
- **Splitnslide**: Splits the video and slides it over for juxtaposing two video clips.
- **Sweep**: Fourteen different kinds of transitions (more than Wipe has).
- **Warp**: Similar to displace node; warps an image.

Some plug-ins don't play well with threaded rendering, so you might have to turn that off if you notice compositing artifacts. Also, some plug-ins were compiled with a 32-bit setting (one byte per channel), and floating-point support of each channel's value was added some versions back. Therefore, you may see a warning about "No float, upgrade plug-in." You may safely ignore this warning. If a plug-in will not work at all, it just will fail to load (or in some extreme cases, crash Blender, so save your work before loading).

Audio sequences

Audio is just as important as video, and Blender enables you to work with it in two ways: streaming from your hard drive (Audio HD), or loaded in to memory (Audio RAM). A wide variety of audio formats can be streamed in via Audio HD, including MP3. The audio file format for Audio RAM is limited to the .wav format, 16-bit, sampled at either 44.1 or 48.0 kHz (a.k.a. CD quality).

The two ways appear very similar in the VSE as strips, since they are both audio, but there are a few important distinctions. Streaming from the hard drive gives you the best quality, and should be used for your final output. However, when audio is loaded into memory (RAM), Blender can compute the waveform of the audio and show the waveform to you as a background to the strip, as shown in Figure 14-19. You layer and mix an infinite number of sound files of any format for whatever reason: as a voiceover overlaid with a Foley sound effect superimposed over some background music. You simply add the audio and position it in a channel, using gain and animation (the animation curve affects the loudness of the strip) to vary its relative contribution to the overall sound. You move, extend, contract, and cut audio strips the exact same way as video. Audio strips are automixing in that if you layer one strip on channel 3 and another above in on channel 4, the resulting mix will be a composite of the two sounds.

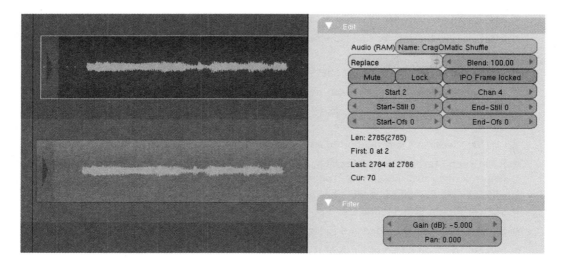

Figure 14-19. Audio strips and adding reverb

Here, the same audio file (from your library, lib\wav\CraigoMatic\church shuffle.wav, is loaded. This audio and the other clips in that folder were given to me by CraigoMatic, a good friend and talented guitarist in Texas and are released to you under the Creative Commons with Attribution license.

There are only three panels in the Sequence context for audio: Input, Edit, and Filter. Filter gives you gain (volume) and pan (left/right) control. In the image, the offset strip has a -5 gain, so it is lower in volume than the original. By offsetting it in time and volume, the strip in channel 4 shown in the figure adds an echo effect, a.k.a. reverb.

All audio strips are mixed (added) to produce the final audio. Use the animation Ipo curve on a strip to dynamically adjust the gain, such as to fade out an audio strip. You can cross-fade audio by making a descending Ipo curve for the strip fading out, and an ascending curve for the one fading in. If not Ipo-locked, the Ipo curve is a percentage relative to the length of the strip, same as video strips. The Edit panel works the same for audio as it does for video.

Audio has another context shown in Figure 14-20, which has two relevant panels: Sequencer and Sound. Use the Sound panel to load audio WAV files into memory. Click Play to play it, and press Escape to stopand to play/review any loaded files. The Sequencer panel has some very important features:

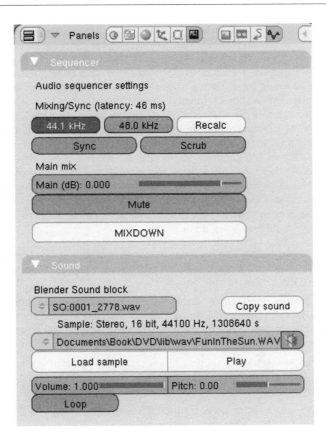

Figure 14-20. Scene sound block buttons

- **Scrub**: Plays the tiny portion of audio as you scrub between frames in the sequencer. This is vital for lip-syncing (making your CG character's facial expressions and mouth shapes match the words that are being spoken), as it allows you to identify the individual sound that is being made at that frame.

- **Mixdown**: Takes any loaded audio strips, mixes them, and saves the results (for the animation frame range) to a WAV file in the Output Render directory, using the same file-name conventions (and frame numbering) as video. You can also use this feature to create a separate audio track from a movie. For instance, if you want to use the Audio RAM feature to see a movie's waveform, load the Movie+Audio (HD), then mix down, delete the audio HD strip from the movie, and load the mixed audio file as Audio RAM.

- **Format and conversion**: The format of audio clips is important. Some compressed audio will be loadable and playable as Audio HD, but not as Audio RAM. For example, Blender and my system do not like the PCM audio codec used in an Audio RAM file, but Blender loads an audio .wav file saved with no compression as Audio RAM. You can always load a compressed audio file as Audio HD and convert it to a RAM-loadable file via the mixdown described earlier.

Mashups

A new art form, in the realm of user-generated content (which was discussed in Chapter 1) is evolving. Using clips from Internet video sources (such as YouTube) and editing them heavily to make new video, users are mixing in sound bites (such as musical tones or snippets from presidential utterances) and combining those elements with other diverse imagery and sounds to make a new video. Blender is perfectly adaptable to this task. Be warned though, that mashups require a *lot* of editing, down to the frame level. In general, of course, you should use only material with the author's permission, or at the very least give the author credit and make fair use of others' content. For simple video-editing examples, search "The Day in 100 seconds" on YouTube. This is a series where the author collects various clips and then cuts them into a finished (100-second) sequence. For the ultimate example of a mashup, search for "Kutiman Mashup" on YouTube; Kutiman's mashup "Thru-You" is excellent and he has even posted an "about" video; additionally, he has a website at http://www.thru-you.com. I cannot publish any examples or anything specific in this book for legal reasons, but I can tell you in basic terms how to make a mashup using Blender.

1. First select your source clips. This is harder than it sounds, because you are building up a library of sound and imagery, and a short little file name may be inadequate to really describe what the sound is. Use file folders to stay organized.

2. Select a good melody line (someone singing), a motif (a short sequence of notes that make a catchy tune), or even just a chord progression that sets a good theme for the rest of the mashup. Music has rhythm, a motif, and a key. The rhythm you will create through editing, but the sounds have to work in harmony and share the same key.

3. Make a good percussive (drum) rhythm. Using clips, find some with a good timbre (a pleasing sound quality). Then cut each individual sound, like a drum hit, and squeeze them together to create a new rhythm. Combine the slices into meta strips for easy duplication.

4. Select a bass line, which is the lower-frequency sounds like those of a double bass or bass guitar, and cut notes that harmonize with the motif.

The clips will be very short, less than a second. Use Shift+D to duplicate these sound and video bites. I suggest you keep one library element on a channel, and duplicate it in the X (left/right) direction. The repetition of video creates a hypnotic, trancelike effect. Use the audio gain to balance the sound level (gain) so that the audio blends together.

Mashups are neat because they combine musical elements from instruments around the world, originating from diverse cultures and traditions, played by artists who have never and probably will never see each other, and who never intended to "play together," all synthesized by you to create a synergistic result.

Summary

Blender's Video Sequence Editor provides a full workbench for compositing video clips into a completed movie. With either node-based or sequencer-based Gamma correction, Blender adapts to a linear workflow to seamlessly overlay and integrate CG scene strips with real-world video from any source. An unlimited number of audio channels allow you to mix and match a wide variety of sound-file formats, mixing them down to provide a composite audio track. The VSE serves as the final point where 3D view scenes, library elements, and/or compositor results are combined with audio into your final movie.

As you have seen in this book, Blender provides a very capable and robust yet versatile digital-compositing workbench. It can integrate into your pipeline and adapt to your workflow. Since it is open source, you can "own" your own copy and change it to suit your needs. The three main components, the 3D view, the compositor, and the sequencer, all work together to enable you to achieve professional results. The worldwide community that supports Blender is continually making improvements in the software, always aimed at making artists more productive and supporting their creativity. The next release of Blender, 2.5, will enable the user interface to be completely customizable, and I look forward to a bright future for Blender. Thank you again for buying this book, and for supporting the Blender community around the world.

Apress License Agreement (Single-User Products)

THIS IS A LEGAL AGREEMENT BETWEEN YOU, THE END USER, AND APRESS. BY OPENING THE SEALED DVD PACKAGE, YOU ARE AGREEING TO BE BOUND BY THE TERMS OF THIS AGREEMENT. IF YOU DO NOT AGREE TO THE TERMS OF THIS AGREEMENT, PROMPTLY RETURN THE UNOPENED DISK PACKAGE AND THE ACCOMPANYING ITEMS (INCLUDING WRITTEN MATERIALS AND BINDERS AND OTHER CONTAINERS) TO THE PLACE YOU OBTAINED THEM FOR A FULL REFUND.

APRESS SOFTWARE LICENSE

1. GRANT OF LICENSE. Apress grants you the right to use one copy of the enclosed Blender software program collectively (the "SOFTWARE") on a single terminal connected to a single computer (e.g., with a single CPU). You may not network the SOFTWARE or otherwise use it on more than one computer or computer terminal at the same time.

2. COPYRIGHT. The SOFTWARE copyright is owned by Blender and is protected by United States copyright laws and international treaty provisions. The SOFTWARE contains licensed software programs, the use of which are governed by English language end user license agreements inside the licensed software programs. Therefore, you must treat each of the SOFTWARE programs like any other copyrighted material (e.g., a book or musical recording) except that you may either (a) make one copy of the SOFTWARE solely for backup or archival purposes, or (b) transfer the SOFTWARE to a single hard disk, provided you keep the original solely for backup or archival purposes. You may not copy the written material accompanying the SOFTWARE.

3. OTHER RESTRICTIONS. You may not rent or lease the SOFTWARE, but you may transfer the SOFTWARE and accompanying written materials on a permanent basis provided you retain no copies and the recipient agrees to the terms of this Agreement. You may not reverse engineer, decompile, or disassemble the SOFTWARE. If SOFTWARE is an update, any transfer must include the update and all prior versions. Distributors, dealers, and other resellers are prohibited from altering or opening the licensed SOFTWARE package.

4. By breaking the seal on the disc package, you agree to the terms and conditions printed in the Apress License Agreement. If you do not agree with the terms, simply return this book with the still-sealed DVD package to the place of purchase for a refund.

DISCLAIMER OF WARRANTY

The program included in this book was supplied under a special license arrangement with Blender. For this reason Apress is responsible for the product warranty. If the media is defective, please return it to Apress which will arrange for its replacement. PLEASE DO NOT REUTRN IT TO OR CONTACT Blender FOR SOFTWARE SUPPORT. This product is provided for free, and no support is provided for by Apress or Blender. To the extent of any inconsistencies between this statement and the End User License Agreement which accompanies the program, this statement shall govern.

NO WARRANTIES. Apress disclaims all warranties, either express or implied, including, but not limited to, implied warranties of merchantability and fitness for a particular purpose, with respect to the SOFTWARE and the accompanying written materials. The software and any related documentation is provided "as is." You may have other rights, which vary from state to state.

NO LIABILITIES FOR CONSEQUENTIAL DAMAGES. In no event shall Apress be liable for any damages whatsoever (including, without limitation, damages from loss of business profits, business interruption, loss of business information, or other pecuniary loss) arising out of the use or inability to use this product, even if Apress has been advised of the possibility of such damages. Because some states do not allow the exclusion or limitation of liability for consequential or incidental damages, the above limitation may not apply to you.

U.S. GOVERNMENT RESTRICTED RIGHTS

The SOFTWARE and documentation are provided with RESTRICTED RIGHTS. Use, duplication, or disclosure by the Government is subject to restriction as set forth in subparagraph (c) (1) (ii) of The Rights in Technical Data and Computer Software clause at 52.227-7013. Contractor/manufacturer is Apress, 2855 Telegraph Avenue, Suite 600, Berkeley, California, 94705.

This Agreement is governed by the laws of the State of California.

Should you have any questions concerning this Agreement, or if you wish to contact Apress for any reason, please write to Apress, Apress, 2855Telegraph Avenue, Suite 600, Berkeley, California, 94705.

INDEX

symbols

(pound sign), 420
+ control, 280
+ icon, 210
= control, 280

numerics

0-Isometric scene, 153
0-Ortho scene, 153
2D animation, 41
2D still, 41
2-point scene, 151
3D elements
    empty targets, 134–136
    images
        changing shapes (morphing), 121–122
        overview, 116–117
        rotoscoping with shape keys, 123
        UV mapping, 117–120
    layering in 3D space, 123–125
    masking
        with Bezier curves, 127–130
        creating elements from masked images, 131
        with meshes, 132
        overview, 125
        setting up 3D view and camera for, 125–126
    objects
        adding, 114
        editing, 115–116
        hotkey commands, 112–113
        modes, 112
        overview, 111–112
        setting Edit Methods preferences, 115
    overview, 111
    rotoscoping with shape keys, 123
    text, 137–140
3D transform widget, 61
3D view
    alpha channel socket, 286–287
    Background Image panel, 65–67
    for masking, 125–126

    orientation and perspectives, 62–63
    overview, 61, 284
    Render background buffer, 68
    Render Layer node, 284–286
    Render Layers panel, 289–291
    render passes, 287–288
    Transform Properties panel, 64–65
    View Properties panel, 64
4-Sequence.blend file, 103
6DOF (six degrees of freedom), 61
8-Sequence screen, 424

A

A channel. *See* alpha channel
absolute path specification, 402
AccZ file, 237
actions, 21–22
Active filter, 79
Add new objects section, 115
Add option, header menu, 277
Advanced Raster Graphics Adapter format, 99
A-End field, 405
algorithms, shading, 178
aliases, 253
Align handle, 127
Aligned to View mode, 115
All Scenes filter, 79
alpha (A) channel
    Portable Network Graphics (PNG) and, 96–99
    rendering, 251–252
alpha channel socket, 286–287
Alpha Convert node, 334
Alpha Matte plug-in, 438, 442
Alpha option, 187
Alpha slider, 222
AlphaOver node, 96, 242, 320–321, 339–340, 346
Amb option, 187
ambient light (Am), 156, 166
ambient occlusion (AO) pass, 288
AngMap image, 165
angular maps, 164–166
ANIM button, 105, 266, 268

Anim folder, 46
Anim panel, 105, 268, 271, 407
animated effects
    camera animation, 219–222
    coordinating, 244–245
    lighting animation, 227–230
    mask animation, 231–233
    object animation
        adding finishing touches to, 218
        animating layers, 213–215
        moving elements into range, 215–216
        moving elements into view, 204–213
        navigating in time, 204
        overview, 203–204
    overview, 201–203
    particle effects
        Bake panel, 244
        boids physics engine, 239–242
        colliders, 238
        combining, 243
        creating particle systems, 234–235
        emitter particle system, 235–238
        force fields, 238
        overview, 234
    shader animation, 222–226
animatic video, 33
animating
    text, 140
    VSE effects, 440
anti-aliasing, 253–254
AO (ambient occlusion) pass, 288
Apert, 219
apparent sun, 166
appending assets, 70, 72–73
Append/Link function, 72
Apple iPhone, 15
Apple Shake, 13
Art folder, 46
aspect ratio, 248, 308–309
AspX field, 249
AspY field, 249
asset file formats, 90
assets
    linking to, 43–44
    reusable, 70–73
A-Start field, 405
Atmosphere setting, 156
Audacity, 29
Audio folder, 46
Audio panel, 107, 270
audio sequences, 443–445
Auto handle, 127
Auto icon, 293

Auto Refresh control, 67, 189
Auto Save tab, 60
Autodesk Mudbox, 35
Autosplit Output panel, 270
AVI Codec format, 269
AVI container format, 269
AVI Jpeg format, 269
AVI Raw format, 269

B

B button, 316
B slider, 177
Backdrop control, 277
Background Image panel, 65–67, 125, 189
Badlands scene, 159
Bake panel, 244
base subfolder, 68
Basic section, emitter system, 235
batch mode, 53
.B.blend file, 61
Bezier curves, 115, 127–130, 203
Bf (Blur Factor) setting, 255
Big Buck Bunny world compositing example, 166–171
Big Ugly Rendering Project (BURP), 40, 271
bitmap (BMP) file, 93
Bitrate setting, 270
BL_proxy folder, 407
Black Level swatch, 317
Blank Render of Darkness (BROD), 290
Blend % setting, 409
.blend file, 16, 33, 39, 43
blend files
    appending or linking from another, 80–82
    importing from current, 80
    saving, 86–87
Blend Mode setting, Sequencer Edit panel, 408
Blend option, Background Image panel, 66
Blend texture, 169, 196–198
Blender
    compositing pipeline, 38–43
    creativity and, 12–13
    at different production process stages, 10–12
    digital compositing, 14–16
    production capability, 13–14
    properties, actions, and tools, 21–22
    setup, 16–17
    window types, 23
Blender Logo object, 80
Blender Model Repositories, 32
Blender MultiChannel file option, 92
Blender/Lib folder, 47
.blendx files, 86

blue chrominance (Cb), 335–336
Blue control, 281
Blur Factor (Bf) setting, 255
Blur node, 281, 357–359
Blur plug-in, 442
BMP (bitmap) file, 93
Boids option, 237
boids physics engine, 239–242
Boinc protocol, 40
Bokeh, 358
border rendering, 251
bottom socket, 346
bounding box, 148
Bright/Contrast node, 315, 335
Bright.Down swatch, 318
BROD (Blank Render of Darkness), 290
built-in text editor, 12
burning, 324–325
BURP (Big Ugly Rendering Project), 40, 271
buttons window, 23, 69–70, 377

C

C button, 316
C: drive, 46
CalcAlpha setting, 253
calloc( ) returns nil message, 261
camera animation, 219–222
camera clipping range, 215–216
Camera object, 114
Camera panel, 144, 149, 153, 219
camera shake, 219–220
cameras
    overview, 143–144
    perspectives
        matching vanishing points, 148–150
        one-point, 153
        overview, 147–148
        two-point, 151–153
        zero-point, 153
    properties of, 144–145
    rule of thirds, 155
    tracking to objects, 145–147
Capability Maturity Model Integrated (CMMI) framework, 28
Cartoon plug-in, 442
CASE (computer-aided software engineering) tools, 279
Cb (blue chrominance), 335–336
CbCr channels, 336
cellular phones, 16
Celtx, 29
CG modeling, 29
CGSociety, 41
Chan setting, 409

Channel Key node, 340, 342–344
Channel Properties panel, 209
Chroma Key node, 340, 346
chroma vectorscope display mode, 392, 398–399
Chromakey RGB plug-in, 442
Chromakey YUV plug-in, 442
circle of influence, 122
Clamp, 356
Clipping Start/End control, 145, 219
Clockwipe plug-in, 442
cloning assets, 70–72
Clouds texture, 168–169, 196
CMMI (Capability Maturity Model Integrated) framework, 28
CMS (content management system), 48–49
CMYK (cyan, magenta, yellow, and black), 327
codec (compression-decompression), 13, 106
Codec selector field, 269
Col pass, 177, 187, 288
Collapse/expand arrow control, 280
colliders, 238
Collision control, 238
color (RGB) node, 297
color balance, 399
color channels support, 93
color math, 323
color nodes
    AlphaOver node, 320–321
    Bright/Contrast node, 315
    CMYK, 327
    fades, 326
    Gamma node, 315
    Invert node, 314
    Mix node, 321–325
    overview, 313–314
    RGB Curves node, 316–318
    sepia tones, 326
    Tonemap node, 329
    transitions, 326
    Value node, 295
    Z Combine node, 328–329
Color Spill node, 340
Colorband option, 198
ColorRamp node, 334, 381
colors. See also color nodes
    shading, 177–178
    world, 156–157
Colors panel, 227
Combined pass, 287, 291
commercial off-the-shelf (COTS), 28
Composite node, 298, 331, 346
compositing
    complexity, 261
    digital, 8–16

Compositing.Blend file, 76
compositor
    compositing screen layout, 275
    controls, 279–283
    node editor, 276–279
    overview, 274
compression-decompression (codec), 13, 106
computer graphics, 12
computer-aided software engineering (CASE) tools, 279
console window, 54
Constraints panel, 134, 146
container formats
    overview, 107–108
    rendering, 268–270
    selecting, 265–266
content management system (CMS), 48–49
contexts, buttons window, 69
Contrast Up swatch, 318
control window, 23
controls, node, 279–283
conversion nodes
    Alpha Convert node, 334
    ColorRamp node, 334
    ID Mask node, 338–339
    Math node, 331–334
    overview, 330
    RGB to BW node, 331
    Separate/Combine channel nodes, 334–337
    Set Alpha node, 331
ConvertPremul, 320
COTS (commercial off-the-shelf), 28
Cr (red chrominance), 335
Creative Commons Attribution-Noncommercial-No-
        Derivative-Works license, 36
Creative Commons license, 15, 36
creativity, Blender, 12–13
Crop node, 300
cropping, 309–310, 402–405
cross transitions, 413–414
Current Scene filter, 79
Curve and Surface panel, 221–222, 259
Curve object, 114, 210
CurveCircle object, 80
CurveFollow object, 222
CurveFollow relationship, 220
curves, rendering, 259–260
curves widget, 297
cut splice transitions, 416–417
cyan, magenta, yellow, and black (CMYK), 327
cyclic dependencies, 281
Cyclic option, 67, 293

D

D control, 144
DAM, see digital asset management
DARPANet, 15
deceleration, 218
decoding watermarks, 333–334
Defocus node
    overview, 370–372
    rack focus, 375
    unconventional use of, 386
    Z-buffer, 372–375
DefResolU control, 259
De-Interlace option, 405
deinterlacing, 347–348
depth of field (DOF), 287, 357, 370–375
Depth of Field node, 219
Desaturate plug-in, 442
Dice plug-in, 442
Diff (Diffuse) pass, 288
Diff plug-in, 442
Difference Key node, 340, 344
Diffuse (Diff) pass, 288
Diffuse setting, 227
digital asset management (DAM)
    content and digital asset management systems, 48–49
    disk space, 50
    image sources, 49–50
    library folders, 47–48
    links to assets, 43–44
    overview, 43
    project folder organization, 45–46
digital compositing
    compositing elements, 8
    music videos and movies, 14–15
    sequencing video, 9–10
    user-generated content, 15–16
digital rights management, 36–38
Dilate/Erode node, 367–369
Dir field, 402
Disable Tex button, 262
disk space, 50
Dispersion control, 303
Displace node, 301
Display, View & Controls tab, 60
Dist setting, 160
Distort control, 303
distort processing nodes
    Crop node, 300
    Displace node, 301
    Lens Distortion node, 301–303
    Map UV node, 303

overview, 300
   Rotate node, 304
   Scale node, 304
   Translate node, 305
Divide node, 333
DivX codec, 106
DivX Media Player, 108
DLL (dynamic load library), 441
Do Composite option, 396
Do Sequence option, 256, 396
dodging, 324–325
DOF (depth of field), 287, 357, 370–375
Dof Dis control, 145
Dof Ob control, 145
Dof Ob field, 146
dots per inch (dpi), 248
downscaling, 310
Draw Mode, 384
Draw Stamp button, 256
DSpace, 49
duration, video rendering, 263
dX setting, 169
dY setting, 169
dynamic load library (DLL), 441

E

Easter.jpg file, 342
Eclipse, 55
Edge component, 291
Edge detection, 365
edge rendering, 255
Edit Methods preferences, 115
Edit Mode, 112
Edit panel, 80, 407
Editing Modifiers panel, 260
Editing properties, 125
Eint settings, wire, 184
Emit option, 187
emitter particle system, 235–238
Empty object, 114
empty targets, 134–136
Enable part, 290
Enable Stamp button, 256
encoding watermarks, 333
End field, 263
End-Ofs setting, 409
End-Still setting, 409
EnvMap panel, 251
Expand control, 280
exposure (Exp), 157–158
.exr files, 339

Extensions panel, 257
Extrapolated option, 297
Extras panel, 236
Extrude value, 139

F

F control, World panel, 156
F icon, Ipo selector, 210
Fact\ value, 316
FadeIn marker, 394
fading, 298, 326, 413–414
fairy light, 230
fake light, 227
falloff, 121
False coloring, 356
FDist, 219
Fedora, 29
FFmpeg container, 106–108, 269–270, 424
Fie/Img option, 67
field of focus, 370
Field/Image panel, 348
Fields panel, 265, 348
fields rendering, 264–265
file browser window, 23, 68–69
File name field, 67
File Output node, 300
File Paths tab, 60
filter nodes
   Blur node, 357–359, 375, 377
   Defocus node, 370–375
   Dilate/Erode node, 367–369
   Glare node, 380
   Kirsch filter, 366
   Laplace filter, 361–362
   overview, 357
   Prewitt filter, 365
   Shadow filter, 366
   Sharpen filter, 361
   Sobel filter, 364
   Soften filter, 360
   Vector Blur node, 377–379
Filter value blurs, 192
Fit control, 303
Flare controls, 183
Flat mapping, 187
Flip Time option, 405
FlipX option, 405
FlipY option, 405
Float option, 405
floating point, 92
Flock object, 241

flying cameras, 219
Focus object, 146
focusing ring effect, 359
FollowPath constraint, 222
Font panel, 139
footage, 427
force fields, 238
format conversion, 307–310
Format panel
    alpha channel rendering, 251
    file format selector, 256
    NTSC output, 102–103
    QuickTime movie, 108
formats
    asset file, 90
    audio file, 106–107
    container, 107–108
    image file
        BMP and color channels support, 93
        JPEG, 93–95
        OpenEXR, Z-buffer, and multilayer, 99–101
        overview, 93
        PNG and alpha channel, 96–99
        Targa and TIFF, 99
    interchange, 91–93
    overview, 89–90
    players, 108
    video
        codecs, 106
        frame sequences, 103–106
        high-definition (HD) formats, 103
        NTSC and PAL formats, 101–102
        overview, 101
FPS field, 208
Frame menu, 208
frame sequences, 420
frames, defined, 101
Frames option, 67
frames per second, 263
Free Cache panel, 244
Free Tex Images field, 262
Free Unused control, 277
FreeMind, 29
Friction control, 238
Frs option, 293
fStop, 372
full-screen anti-aliasing (FSA), 254, 328, 329
Fun! text element, 212

G

G button, 316
G slider, 177

gain, adjusting, 410
Game context, 69
gamma cross-fade, 432–433
Gamma node, 315
Generated option, 67
ghost effect, 321
GIMP (Gnu Image Manipulation Program), 29, 50
Glare node, 380
glow effect, 435
glowing orbs, 230
Gnu Image Manipulation Program (GIMP), 29, 50
Google, 11
Gray control, 281
Grease Pencil tool, 17, 383–385
Green Button, 271
green-screen integration, 14
Grid object, 114
Ground plane, 166
Group asset class, 73
groups, 70, 76
Groups filter, 79

H

H.264 codec, 108
Hair system, 235
Halo material, 175, 180–183, 230, 255, 291
hand-painting, 50
Hard option, 187
HD (high-definition), 50, 103, 340
HDR (high-dynamic range), 50, 99, 329
header, node, 208, 276–277, 280
headless mode, 53
heat lightning, 230
Height setting, 160
helloworld.jpg file, 257
Hierarchical Input Process Output (HIPO) chart, 279
high-definition (HD), 50, 103, 340
high-dynamic range (HDR), 50, 99, 329
HIPO (Hierarchical Input Process Output) chart, 279
histogram display mode, 392, 399–400
home media recording, 16
home video cameras, 16
horizon (Hori), 156, 165
Horizontal option, 297
hotkey commands, 112–113
house left, 214
hue, saturation, and value (HSV) button, 177
hue, saturation, and value (HSV) channel, 93, 323
hue, saturation, and value (HSV) colorspace, 335
hydra network, 44

I

ID Mask node, 338–339
IM: field, 293
IM option, 67
Image browser, 23
image file formats
    BMP and color channels support, 93
    conversion, 307–308, 417–421
    JPEG, 93–95
    OpenEXR, Z-buffer, and multilayer, 99–101
    overview, 93
    PNG and alpha channel, 96–99
    Targa and TIFF, 99
Image input node, 342
image manipulation, 333
Image node, 292–294
Image option, 67
Image panel, 120
image preview display mode, 392, 396
image socket, 298
image sources, 49–50
image standards, 256–257
image textures
    blending computer-generated elements into photos,
        195
    interpolating, 192–193
    overview, 188–191
    recoloring image elements, 191–192
    stretching, 193
image-editing programs, 73
images
    3D elements, 116–123
    color nodes
        AlphaOver node, 320–321
        Bright/Contrast node, 315
        CMYK, 327
        fades, 326
        Gamma node, 315
        Invert node, 314
        Mix node, 321–325
        overview, 313–314
        RGB Curves node, 316–318
        sepia tones, 326
        Tonemap node, 329
        transitions, 326
        Z Combine node, 328–329
    conversion nodes
        Alpha Convert node, 334
        ColorRamp node, 334
        ID Mask node, 338–339
        Math node, 331–334
        overview, 330
        RGB to BW node, 331

Separate/Combine channel nodes, 334–337
        Set Alpha node, 331
    defined, 274
    importing as elements, 82
    Matte nodes
        Channel Key node, 342–344
        Chroma Key node, 346
        deinterlacing, 347–348
        Difference Key node, 344
        Luminance Key node, 341–342
        overview, 340–341
    morphing, 121–122
    rendering
        anti-aliasing, 253–254
        aspect ratio, 248
        curves, 259–260
        edge rendering, 255
        image standards, 256–257
        information stamping, 255–256
        motion blur, 254–255
        multithreaded rendering, 258–259
        output, 257–258
        overview, 248
        resolution, 248–252
        test render, 253
        troubleshooting, 260–262
    resolution, 294
    retouching, 14
\images folder, 48
importing elements, 80–82
index of refraction (IOR) settings, 224, 287
Index pass, 288
Inf (influence) channel, 146, 222
information stamping, 255–256
Information Technology Infrastructure Library (ITIL), 28
Inkscape SVG format, 82
input devices, 58
input nodes
    3D view
        alpha channel socket, 286–287
        overview, 284
        Render Layer node, 284–286
        Render Layers panel, 289–291
        render passes, 287–288
        visualizing render passes, 288
    Image node, 292–294
    overview, 284
    RGB (color) node, 297
    Texture node, 294–295
    Time node for animation, 296–297
    Value node, 295
Insert Key menu, 214
interchange file formats, 91–93

interface window, 55–58
interlacing, 264–265
International Standards Organization (ISO), 28
interoperability, media pipeline, 35–36
interpolating image textures, 192–193
Invert node, 314
Invert plug-in, 442
IOR (index of refraction) settings, 224, 287
iPhone, Apple, 15
Ipo curves, 203, 444
Ipo Frame locked setting, 409
Ipo selector, 211
Ipo value, 436
Ipo window, 201, 209–210, 401
IpoRocket object, 244–245
Iris plug-in, 443
ISO (International Standards Organization), 28
ITIL (Information Technology Infrastructure Library), 28

J

Jitter control, 303
Jitter plug-in, 443
Joint Photographic Experts Group (JPEG) images, 22,
        93–95, 331
juxtaposing, 434

K

Key channel, 252
Key Color swatch, 344, 346
Key object, 210
Keyed option, 237
keyframe mode, 202
Kill control, 238
Kirsch filter, 366

L

Lambert diffuse algorithm, 178
LAMP architecture, 49
lamps, 173
Language & Font tab, 60
Laplace filter, 361–362
late binding, 12
layer 2 button, 215
Layer channel, 214
Layer Manager script UI, 75
layers, 70, 73–75, 123–125, 213–215
Lens channel, 219
Lens control, 144
Lens Distortion node, 301–303
letterboxing, 309–310

libmgr.py script, 75
library folders, 47–48
license, image, 37
Life field, 236
lift, adjusting, 410
Light component, 291
lighting and color specialist, 11
lighting animation, 203, 227–230
lightning, 230
Lights object, 114
Lightsaber plug-in, 443
Limits control, 145
Lin setting, 160
Linear Workflow, 315
Link and Materials panel, 70, 137
linking assets, 43–44, 72–73
Links and Materials panel, 71
Links and Pipeline panel, 174–176, 180, 184
Linux, 16
live-action plates, 228–230
Load New setting, 341
Load UI button, 72
loading, 423–426
Loc properties, 21
lock icon, Ipo window, 210
Lock setting, 409
LocX control, 63
LocX field, 65, 203, 209, 212, 244
LocY control, 63
LocY field, 65, 203, 209, 244
LocZ control, 63
LocZ field, 65, 203, 209
logo.blend file, 80
Lorem button, 139, 155
lossy compression format, 93
Low slider, 342
LSD plug-in, 443
luma waveform display mode, 392, 397–398
luminance, defined, 397
luminance channel, 340
Luminance Key node, 341–342
Lush Tropical swatch, 318

M

MA: field, 175
Mac OS X Console application, 16, 54
Magnetic field, 238
magnitude, 351
Make Proxy scene, 406–408
malloc( ) returns nil message, 261
manipulator widget, 116
Map Image panel, 192, 252
Map Input control, 185

Map Input panel, 186, 189, 221
Map To control, 185
Map To panel, 164, 187, 189, 193
Map UV node, 303
Map Value node, 100, 356
mapping textures, 186–187
Marker menu, 209
markers, 394
mashups, 423, 446
mask animation, 231–233
Mask object, 22
masking
    with Bezier curves, 127–130
    creating elements from masked images, 131
    with meshes, 132
    overview, 125
    in sequencer, 438–439
    setting up 3D view and camera for, 125–126
mastering, 13
match moving, 231–232
Material Ball control, 280
Material component, 291
Material Ipo, 211, 245
Material Ipos, 211
Material panel, 84, 222
Material Texture context, 161
Material type Ipo, 223
Material World subcontext, 161, 167
materials
    shading
        adding, 174–176
        defining, 176–178
        Halo material, 180–183
        OnlyCast material, 184
        OnlyShad material, 179
        overview, 174
        shadeless materials, 179
        Wire material, 184
    window type, 23
Materials context, 185
\materials folder, 48
Math node, 331–334
matte, defined, 68
Matte nodes
    Channel Key node, 342–344
    Chroma Key node, 346
    deinterlacing, 347–348
    Difference Key node, 344
    Luminance Key node, 341–342
    overview, 340–341
matte paintings, 170–171
Maxblur, 372
Maximum mode, 332

MBLUR button, 255
MBlur button, 377
ME: field, 71, 175
media pipeline
    interoperability, 35–36
    open source products in pipeline, 28–32
    overview, 26–28
    work products, 32–33
medium format conversion, 308–309
menus, 60
Mesh object, 114
meshes, masking with, 132
metastrip, 430
methodology, 27
Middle mouse button, 61
Minimum mode, 332
Mir control, 177
mist, 159–160
Mist control, 145
Mist group, 381
Mist pass, 287
Mist setting, 160
Mist-Linear scene, 160
Mist/Stars/Physics panel, 160
Mix node, 294, 321–325, 339
Mixdown button, 445
mixing textures, 187–188
Model screen, 70
modelers, 10
morph targets, 203
morphing, 121–122
motion blur, 254–255, 377–379
Motion Picture Association of America (MPAA), 10
mouse, 58
mouse wheel, 61
Movie option, 67
movies
    music videos and, 14–15
    sequences and, 293
moving elements
    into range, 215–216
    into view
        animating object, 212–213
        making things change, 210–212
        overview, 204–207
        using Ipo window, 209–210
        using timeline window, 208–209
moving subtitles, 226
MPAA (Motion Picture Association of America), 10
MPEG-4 video codec, 269
MPEG-Preseek field, 405
Mul blending mode, 439
Mul option, 405

multilayer format, 101
Multiply node, 295, 344
multithreaded rendering, 258–259
music videos, 14–15
Mute setting, 409
muting, 79
my-anim-0031.exr frame, 266
MySQL, 49

N

Name control, Camera panel, 145
Name part, 290
Name setting, Sequencer Edit panel, 408
NASA scene, 191
NegAlpha setting, 253
network, 274
Newtonian option, 237
NLE. See nonlinear video editor
No Overwrite option, 258, 266–267
No Specular setting, 191
No zbuffer option, 374
Node compositor, 23
node editor, 276–279
Node family selector control, 277
node groups, 381
Node menu, 282–283
Node name control, 280
Node option, header menu, 277
node tree, 274
node-based compositing
    combining nodes, 305–307
    compositor
        compositing screen layout, 275
        controls, 279–283
        node editor, 276–279
        overview, 274
    distort processing nodes
        Crop node, 300
        Displace node, 301
        Lens Distortion node, 301–303
        Map UV node, 303
        overview, 300
        Rotate node, 304
        Scale node, 304
        Translate node, 305
    format conversion, 307–310
    input nodes
        3D view, 284–291
        Image node, 292–294
        overview, 284
        RGB (color), 297
        RGB node, 297

        Texture, 294–295
        Texture node, 294–295
        Time node for animation, 296–297
        Value node, 295
    output nodes, 298–300
    overview, 273–274
nodes
    filter
        Blur node, 357–359, 375–377
        Defocus node, 370–375
        Dilate/Erode node, 367–369
        Glare node, 380
        Kirsch filter, 366
        Laplace filter, 361–362
        overview, 357
        Prewitt filter, 365
        Shadow filter, 366
        Sharpen filter, 361
        Sobel filter, 364
        Soften filter, 360
        Vector Blur node, 377–379
    Grease Pencil tool, 383–385
    groups, 381
    overview, 351
    posterizing, 382
    vector
        Map Value node, 356
        Normal node, 353–355
        Normalize node, 352–353
        overview, 351–352
Noise Basis selector, 168
None option, 237
nonlinear editing (NLE). See nonlinear video editor
nonlinear video editor
    gain, adjusting, 410
    image-format conversion, 417–421
    lift, adjusting, 410
    NLE screen layout, 400–401
    overview, 391–392, 410
    scene sequencer buttons
        overview, 402
        Sequencer Edit panel, 408–409
        Sequencer Filter panel, 405
        Sequencer Input panel, 402–405
        Sequencer Proxy panel, 405–408
    slide shows, 412–417
    VSE window display modes
        chroma vectorscope display, 398–399
        histogram display, 399–400
        image preview display, 396
        luma waveform display, 397–398
        overview, 392–393
        sequence display, 393–396

Nor (Normal) pass, 287
Nor option, 187
Normal material, 175
Normal node, 353–355
Normalize node, 352–353

O

OB setting, 187
Object and Links panel, 338
object animation
    adding finishing touches to, 218
    animating layers, 213–215
    defined, 202
    moving elements into range, 215–216
    moving elements into view
        animating object, 212–213
        making things change, 210–212
        overview, 204–207
        using Ipo window, 209–210
        using timeline window, 208–209
    navigating in time, 204
    overview, 203–204
Object context, 69, 234
\object folder, 48
Object Ipo, 211, 213, 244
Object Ipo curve, 203, 219, 245
Object Mode object, 76, 112
Object panel, 80
objects
    adding, 114
    complexity, 261
    editing, 115–116
    hotkey commands, 112–113
    modes, 112
    overview, 111–112
    setting Edit Methods preferences, 115
    visibility, 70, 78–79
Odd option, 67
Odd switches, 265
Offs option, 67, 293
offset blending effect, 437
offsetX property, 224
ofsX field, 187
ofsZ field, 187
ofY field, 187
OldMovie plug-in, 443
Olympic flag file, 82
one-point perspective, 153
OnlyCast material, 184
OnlyShad material, 175, 179
open source products, 28–32
OpenEXR format, 99–101, 256–257, 329

OpenGL rendering, 250
Orange project, 32
Orco setting, 187
orienting textures, 186–187
Orthographic button, 153
Orthographic control, 144
orthographic rendering, 153
OSA (oversampling anti-aliasing), 329
Outliner window, 23, 58, 401
output
    image rendering, 257–258
    video rendering, 266
output nodes, 298–300
Output panel, 78, 184, 257–259, 266–267, 407
override shading, 264
oversampling, 253
oversampling anti-aliasing (OSA), 329

P

paintbrush tool, 22
Pano panel, 251
parent object, 213
parent-child relationship, 146, 213
parenting, 70, 76–77, 145–146, 213
Particle Definition, emitter system, 235
particle effects
    Bake panel, 244
    boids physics engine, 239–242
    colliders, 238
    combining, 243
    emitter system, 235–238
    force fields, 238
    generating, 234–235
    overview, 234
Particle subcontext, 234
Particle System properties panel, 234
Passepartout control, 145
passes
    Col, 177, 187, 288
    Combined, 287, 291
    defined, 284
    Diff (Diffuse), 288
    Index, 288
    Mist, 287
    Nor (Normal), 287
    Rad (Radiosity), 288
    Refl (Reflection), 288
    Refr (Refraction), 288
    render, 287–288
    Shad (Shadows), 288
    Spe (Specularity), 288
    UV, 287

Vec (Vector), 287, 291
Z, 287, 291
Path follow command, 221
Path Ipo type, 222
PathLen object, 222
paths, following, 220–222
Peach project, 32
Peach simple_blends\compositing\comp.blend Frankie
    group, 314
Peach/production/chars/rabbit.blend file, 73
Peach\production\scenes\01_intro\04 works.blend file,
    166
Permeability control, 238
perspectives
    matching vanishing points, 148–150
    one-point, 153
    overview, 147–148
    two-point, 151–153
    zero-point, 153
Physics panel, 242
pipeline
    Blender compositing pipeline, 38–43
    components, 251
    digital asset management
        content and, 48–49
        disk space, 50
        image sources, 49–50
        library folders, 47–48
        linking to assets, 43–44
        overview, 43
        project folder organization, 45–46
    digital rights management, 36–38
    media
        interoperability, 35–36
        open source products in pipeline, 28–32
        overview, 26–28
        work products, 32–33
    overview, 26
    render, 247
Pixelize plug-in, 443
plain old telephone system (POTS), 15
plane object, 114, 140
PLAY button, 268
playback control, 208
players, 108
plug-ins, defined, 395
Portable Network Graphics (PNG), 96–99, 125
\pose folder, 48
Positive-Z field, 239
posterizing, 382
POTS (plain old telephone system), 15
pound sign (#), 420
power points, 155
Pr (preview) button, 208

Premul channel, 252
Premul option, 405
Preprod folder, 46
preview (Pr) button, 208
Preview panel, 163, 167, 179, 252, 261
Prewitt filter, 365
procedural (computed) textures, 196–198
Prod folder, 46
production capability, Blender, 13–14
project folder organization, 45–46
Project Peach, 15
Projector control, 303
proof sheet, 46
properties, Blender, 21–22
proxy, defined, 405
Proxy panel, 407
proxy rendering, 250
Public folder, 271
Python, 54
PythonPath argument, 54

Q
Quad setting, 160
quantization, 382
QuickTime container, 269
QuickTime panel, 269
QuickTime Player, 108

R
R button, 316
R slider, 177
rack focus, 375
Rad (Radiosity) pass, 174, 288
Radio panel, 251
RAM, 17
Ray object, 251
Ray panel, 251
ray transparency, 286
RayMir option, 187
Reactor system, 235
ReallyBigRender script, 41
rebe subfolder, 44
red, green, and blue (RGB), 93, 342
red chrominance (Cr) channels, 335
Red-Green Stereo Plugin Effect, 443
Ref folder, 46
Ref option, 187
Refl (Reflection) pass, 288
Refr (Refraction) pass, 288
relative path specification, 402
Relative Paths button, 65
Render background buffer, 68

RENDER button, 253, 266
Render context, 125
render farms, 40, 270–271
Render Format panel, 284
Render Layer alpha channel, 344
Render Layer node, 284–286, 331
render layers, 50, 284
Render Layers panel, 214, 289–291
Render panel, 96, 143, 223, 253–254, 407
render passes, 287–288
render pipeline, 175–176, 247
render subfolder, 104, 266
Render This Window button, 250
rendering
    containers, 268–270
    images
        anti-aliasing, 253–254
        aspect ratio, 248
        curves, 259–260
        edge rendering, 255
        image standards, 256–257
        information stamping, 255–256
        motion blur, 254–255
        multithreaded rendering, 258–259
        output, 257–258
        overview, 248
        resolution, 248–252
        test render, 253
        troubleshooting, 260–262
    overview, 247
    render farms, 270–271
    video
        containers, 265–266
        duration, 263
        frames per second, 263
        interlacing, 264–265
        output, 266
        override shading, 264
        overview, 262
        packaging, 268
        playing back, 268
        step rendering, 264
        storyboard, 262–263
Rendering context, 69
RenderMan Interface Bytestream (RIB) protocol file, 35
resolution, image rendering, 248–252
ResourceSpace, 49
reusable assets, 70–73
RGB (red, green, and blue), 93, 342
RGB Curves node, 281, 297, 316–318
RGB node, 297, 335
RGB to BW node, 331
RGBA control, 346
RIB (RenderMan Interface Bytestream) protocol file, 35

Rigger, 10
\rigs folder, 48
Roadsign.blend file, 85–86
Roadsign.blend1 file, 86
Roadsign.blend2 file, 86
roll-down, 427
roll-up, 427
Rotate node, 304
rotoscoping, 123, 231–232
RotY field, 212
RotZ arrow, 83
Round function, 332
route, 26
rule of thirds, 155

S

Sales folder, 46
Same Type filter, 79
Sample eyedropper, 346
saturation, 323, 327
Save Buffers setting, 254, 262, 329, 407
scale, 218
Scale control, 144, 153
Scale node, 304
Scale.Black swatch, 318
ScaleX field, 82
ScaleY field, 82
ScaleZ field, 212
Scanned images, 50
Scatter Plugin Effect, 443
SCE: selector, 80
Scene context, 125
Scene Render Animation panel field, 204
scene selector, 77
scene sequencer buttons
    overview, 402
    Sequencer Edit panel, 408–409
    Sequencer Filter panel, 405
    Sequencer Input panel, 402–405
    Sequencer Proxy panel, 405–408
Scene-Render panel, 208, 377
scenes, 23, 70, 77–78
Sched folder, 46
screen layout, 56, 58
Screen Size scaling option, 307
screens, 56, 275
Screens control, 275
Script folder, 46
Scripting screen layout, 75
Scriptlinks context, 69
scripts folder, 75
Scripts window, 23
Scrub button, 445

scrubbing, 396, 408
Sculpt Mode, 112
Seamless integration, 26
SEI (Software Engineering Institute), 28
SELECT IMAGE setting, 163
Select menu, 209
Select option, header menu, 277
Select with category, 61
Selected filter, 79
Selector part, 290
Separate/Combine channel nodes, 334–337
sepia tones, 326
Sequence curve, 436
sequence display mode, 393–396
Sequence filter, 79
Sequence option, 67
Sequence Strip stamps, 256
Sequencer Edit panel, 408–409
sequencer effects
    audio sequences, 443–445
    editing strips, 427–430
    glow effect, 435
    loading combined audio/video, 423–426
    mashups, 446
    masking in sequencer, 438–439
    offset blending effect, 437
    overview, 423
    speed control effect, 436
    splice and transition effects, 430–434
    VSE effects, 440–443
Sequencer Filter panel, 405
Sequencer Input panel, 402–405
Sequencer Proxy panel, 405–408
sequences and movies, 293
sequencing video, 9–10
Set Alpha node, 331
setup, Blender, 16–17
SFra option, 293
Shad (Shadows) pass, 288
ShadBuf control, 184
shadeless material, 179, 191, 195, 438
Shadeless panel, 189
Shadeless setting, 227
Shader animation, 203
shader animation, 222–226
Shaders panel, 157, 176, 180, 191, 222
shading
    categories of, 173–174
    materials
        adding, 174–176
        defining, 176–178
        Halo material, 180–183
        OnlyCast material, 184

OnlyShad material, 179
        overview, 174
        shadeless materials, 179
        Wire material, 184
    overview, 173
    textures
        adding, 185–186
        image, 188–195
        mapping, 186–187
        mixing, 187–188
        overview, 184
        procedural, 196–198
Shading buttons, 173
Shading context, 69, 156, 188, 221
Shading Material context, 84
Shading panel, 80
Shading properties, 84
Shading World subcontext, 161
Shadow Adjust, 346
Shadow filter, 366
Shadow object, 251
Shadow panel, 251
Shadows (Shad) pass, 288
Shake, Apple, 13
shape keys, 121, 123, 232
Shape panel, 233
Sharpen filter, 361
Shift control, 145
Shift X, 219
Shift Y, 219
Single part, 290
six degrees of freedom (6DOF), 61
six mesh planes, 72
Size option, 66, 261
SizeX field, 103, 187, 248–249
SizeY field, 103, 187, 248–249
SizeZ field, 187
sketch artist, 10
Sky channel, 252
Sky component, 291
Sky setting, 156
slide shows, 412–417
Snap to grid, 60
Sobel, Irwin, 364
Sobel filter, 364
sockets, 278, 281
SodaCan.blend file, 90
Soften filter, 360
Software Engineering Institute (SEI), 28
Solaris, 16
Solid component, 291
Spe (Specularity) pass, 288
Spe control, 177

Spec option, 187
Special-purpose talent, 11
Specials menu, 121
Specular setting, 227
Specularity (Spe) pass, 288
speed control effect, 436
Speed vector, 353
sphere maps, 161–164
Sphere texture, 169
splice effects, 430–434
Split Viewer node, 299
Splitnslide plug-in, 443
spot1a 001.png file, 68
Spring Stimulus Special text element, 212
Sqr setting, 160
SR: selector, 56
SR:2-Model 4-up screen layout, 62
SSS (subsurface scattering), 251, 261
Sta field, 263
stage left, 214
stage right, 214
Stamp panel, 256, 429
stars, 160
Start setting, 160, 409
Start/End field, 208
StartFr option, 67
Start-Ofs setting, 409
Start-Still setting, 409
Status folder, 46
step rendering, 264
still images, 13
Still option, 67
Stock photos, 49
storyboard, 262–263
storyboarder, 10
Strand component, 291
stretching, images, 193
strips, editing
    editing multiple takes, 429
    interleaving multiple cameras, 430
    overview, 427–429
Strobe option, 405
sts123.jpg file, 104
subcontexts, 69
Subsurf modifier, 260
subsurface scattering (SSS), 251, 261
subtitles, moving, 226
Subtract node, 344
Summer of Code, 11
Sun grid, 271
Sweep plug-in, 443
Switch to Edit Mode, 115
System & OpenGL tab, 60

T

Targa format, 99
Target field, 222
TCO (total cost of ownership), 30
Technical director, 10
test renders, 253
Tex folder, 262
Tex texture, 188
Tex1K folder, 262
Tex4K folder, 262
text, 137–140
Text editor, 23
Texture and Input panel, 161, 164–165, 167
Texture context, 131
Texture Face panel, 118
Texture Image panel, 252
Texture Ipo, 211
Texture node, 294–295
Texture Paint, 10, 112
Texture panel, 162, 186–187, 189
texture shading, 173
Texture subcontext, 168, 188
Texture Type selector, 186
textures
    adding, 185–186
    image
        blending computer-generated elements into photos, 195
        interpolating, 192–193
        overview, 188–191
        recoloring image elements, 191–192
        stretching, 193
    mapping, 186–187
    mixing, 187–188
    overview, 184
    procedural, 196–198
    shader animation, 223–226
    world
        angular maps, 164–166
        overview, 161
        sphere maps, 161–164
\textures folder, 48
Textures Preview panel, 174
textures/world/roadsign.jpg file, 83
.tga extension, 99
Themes tab, 60
thirds scene, 155
threads, 281
threads, defined, 278
Threads indicator, 258
three-point perspective, 147
three-quarters perspective, 153
Tiess, Robert J., 351

.tif format, 99
TIFF format, 99
Time node, 203, 318, 326
Time node for animation, 296–297
timeline window, 208–209, 401
Title Safe control, 145
Tonemap node, 329
Toolbox click, 60
tools, 21–22
Toon shader, 178–179
total cost of ownership (TCO), 30
Totem, 108
Touch option, 258, 267
Traceability, 255
Track To constraint, 146–147
tracking cameras to objects, 145–147
Transform Properties floating panel, 63, 233
Transform Properties panel, 64–65, 149, 189, 222
Transform Properties properties, 124
transitions
    cross, 413–414
    cut splice, 416–417
    effects, 430–434
    fades and, 326, 413–414
Translate node, 305
translating, video strips, 402–405
troubleshooting, image rendering, 260–262
tweens, 201
two-point perspective, 151–153

U

upscaling, 310
Use Background Image button, 65
Use Color Balance option, 405
Use Crop option, 404
Use Nodes control, 277
Use option, 66
Use Proxy option, 406
Use Translate option, 404
UseAlpha class, 193
user preferences window, 23, 59–61, 401
user-generated content, 15–16
UV mapping, 117–120
UV pass, 287
UV setting, 187
UV/image editor, 23
UV/image editor window, 299
UVTex slot, 117

V

value, 323
Value node, 295

vanishing points, 148–150
Vec (Vector) pass, 287, 291
vector, defined, 351
Vector Blur node, 377–379
vector nodes
    Map Value node, 356
    Normal node, 353–355
    Normalize node, 352–353
    overview, 351–352
Verse, 29
vertex, 115
Vertex Paint, 112
Vertex X panel, 233
Vertex Y panel, 233
video
    formats, 13
    rendering
        containers, 265–266
        duration, 263
        frames per second, 263
        interlacing, 264–265
        output, 266
        override shading, 264
        overview, 262
        packaging, 268
        playing back, 268
        step rendering, 264
        storyboard, 262–263
Video panel, 269
Video Sequence Editor (VSE) window display modes
    chroma vectorscope display mode, 398–399
    effects, 440
    histogram display mode, 399–400
    image preview display mode, 396
    image preview mode, 401
    luma waveform display mode, 397–398
    overview, 392–393
    sequence display mode, 393–396
    sequence mode, 401
video strips, 394–395, 402–405
VideoLan Compressor (VLC), 108
View ➤ Render Preview panel, 174
View menu, 208–209
View option, header menu, 277
View Properties panel, 64, 118, 125
View rotation category, 60
View zoom category, 60
Viewer node, 288, 298, 342
Views & Controls tab, 60
Visible Layers filter, 79
Visualization panel, 238
visualizing render passes, 288
VLC (VideoLan Compressor), 108
Voronoi Crackle formula, 196

vortex force, 234
VSE window display modes. *See* Video Sequence Editor window display modes

W

Wacom, 58
Warp plug-in, 443
watermarks, 332–334
.wav files, 107
\wav folder, 48
.wav format, 106
widescreen, 102
Win setting, 187
window panes, 56–58
window types
 3D view window
  Background Image panel, 65–67
  orientation and perspectives, 62–63
  overview, 61
  Render background buffer, 68
  Transform Properties panel, 64–65
  View Properties panel, 64
 Blender, 23
 buttons window, 23, 69–70, 377
 file browser window, 68–69
 overview, 58
 user preferences window, 59–61
Windows Media Player, 108
wipe effect, 433–434
Wire material, 175, 184
work product, 89
work products
 Blender compositing pipeline, 43
 media pipeline and, 32–33
workflow, 26–27
workspace
 distort processing nodes
  Crop node, 300
  Displace node, 301
  Lens Distortion node, 301–303
  Map UV node, 303
  overview, 300
  Rotate node, 304
  Scale node, 304
  Translate node, 305
 format conversion, 307–310
 input nodes
  3D view, 284–291
  Image node, 291–294
  RGB (color) node, 297–298
  Texture node, 294–295
  Time node for animation, 296–297
  Value node, 295–296

node editor, 277–279
timeline window, 208
world
 Big Buck Bunny compositing example, 166–171
 colors, 156–157
 dynamic range, 157–158
 exposure, 157–158
 mist, 159–160
 overview, 156
 range of visibility, 216
 stars, 159–160
 textures
  angular maps, 164–166
  overview, 161
  sphere maps, 161–164
World Ipo, 211
World subcontext, 156

X

X icon, 210
X Offset option, 66
X part, 290
X switch, 265
X tool, 297
Xparts field, 258, 262
XPlanner, 29
Xtra folder, 46
Xvid codec, 106
Xvid player, 108

Y

Y direction, 224
Y Offset option, 66
YCbCr colorspace, 335
Yellow control, 281, 323
Yparts field, 258, 262
Y-series formats, 335
YUV colorspace, 335

Z

Z channels, 331
Z Combine node, 328–329
Z pass, 287, 291
Z values, 356
Zbuf control, 257
Z-buffer, 99–101, 372–375
zenith (Ze), 156
zero-point perspective, 153
Z-mask, 290
Ztra component, 291
ZTransp option, 177, 179, 286

Foundation
XML for Flash

1-59059-543-2 $39.99 [US]

Foundation
Actionscript Animation
Making Things Move!

1-59059-518-1 $39.99 [US]

Foundation
Flash 8

1-59059-542-4 $36.99 [US]

Foundation
ASP.NET 2.0 for Flash

1-59059-517-3 $39.99 [US]

Foundation
Flash 8 Video

1-59059-651-X $44.99 [US]

Foundation
Flash Applications for Mobile Devices

1-59059-558-0 $49.99 [US]

New Masters of Flash

1-59059-314-6 $59.99 [US]

New Masters of Photoshop

1-59059-315-4 $59.99 [US]

Object-Oriented ActionScript for Flash 8

1-59059-619-6 $44.99 [US]

Extending Flash MX 2004
Complete Guide and Reference to JavaScript Flash

1-59059-304-9 $49.99 [US]

Apache Essentials
Install, Configure, Maintain

1-59059-355-3 $24.99 [US]

Dreamweaver MX 2004 Design, Projects

1-59059-409-6 $39.99 [US]

From After Effects to Flash

1-59059-748-6 $49.99 [US]

AdvancED ActionScript Components
Mastering the Flash Component Architecture

1-59059-593-9 $49.99 [US]

AdvancED Flash Interface Design

1-59059-555-6 $44.99 [US]

DOM Scripting
Web Design with JavaScript and the Document Object Model

1-59059-533-5 $34.99 [US]

Web Accessibility
Web Standards and Regulatory Compliance

1-59059-638-2 $49.99 [US]

HTML Mastery
Semantics, Standards, and Styling

Paul Haine

1-59059-765-6 $34.99 [US]

Blog Design Solutions

1-59059-581-5 $39.99 [US]

CSS Mastery
Advanced Web Standards Solutions

ANDY BUDD

1-59059-614-5 $34.99 [US]

Flash Application Design Solutions
The Flash Usability Handbook

KA WAI CHEUNG and CRAIG BRYANT

1-59059-594-7 $39.99 [US]

WEB STANDARDS SOLUTIONS
The Markup and Style Handbook

1-59059-381-2 $34.99 [US]

PODCAST SOLUTIONS
The Complete Guide to Podcasting

BY MICHAEL W. GEOGHEGAN and DAN KLASS

1-59059-554-8 $24.99 [US]